CW00765639

THE ESSENCE OF NIHILISM

THE ESSENCE OF NIHILISM

EMANUELE SEVERINO

TRANSLATED BY GIACOMO DONIS

EDITED BY INES TESTONI AND ALESSANDRO CARRERA

VERSO

London • New York

This translation was supported by the University of Padua, with thanks to the master's program in Death Studies & the End of Life, directed by Ines Testoni, and special thanks to rector emeritus Vincenzo Milanesi and rector emeritus Giuseppe Zaccaria.

Verso Books acknowledges the support of the Ugo Di Portanova Fund for Italian Studies at the University of Houston, directed by Alessandro Carrera, for editing this book.

This English-language edition published by Verso 2016
Originally published in Italian by Paideia as *Essenza del nichilismo*
© Adelphi Edizioni 1982
Translation © Giacomo Donis 2016

All rights reserved

The moral rights of the authors have been asserted

1 3 5 7 9 10 8 6 4 2

Verso
UK: 6 Meard Street, London W1F 0EG
US: 20 Jay Street, Suite 1010, Brooklyn, NY 11201
versobooks.com

Verso is the imprint of New Left Books

ISBN-13: 978-1-78478-611-3
ISBN-13: 978-1-78478-610-6 (HBK)
ISBN-13: 978-1-78478-612-0 (UK EBK)
ISBN-13: 978-1-78478-613-7 (US EBK)

British Library Cataloguing in Publication Data
A catalogue record for this book is available from the British Library

Library of Congress Cataloging-in-Publication Data
A catalog record for this book is available from the Library of Congress

Typeset in Minion by Hewer Text UK, Ltd, Edinburgh
Printed and bound by CPI Group (UK) Ltd, Croydon, CR0 4YY

Contents

Foreword

SEVERINO'S MAGICAL CASTLE
BY ALESSANDRO CARRERA

Emanuele Severino has fashioned a philosophical system that works like a magical castle. *The Essence of Nihilism* is the key to the main entrance, but the reader must be warned: it will take quite some time to explore the whole building. You get in, lose yourself in its hallways and rooms, and even if you do not agree with the architecture, which is perhaps too solid for your postmodern sensibility, you do not want to get out. The next turn will open up an unexpected view on the interior; the sudden shift of a window curtain will allow you to glimpse outside. From those impregnable walls, you will be able to look from a distance at what the modern world has become. See over there the sad fate of religion dissecting God to bits and pieces for ungodly purposes; witness from a balcony the inevitable decline of all totalitarian systems, including planetary capitalism; get a chill from the next window down the corridor while you watch the military parade of technology passing by. For a moment, you may think that as long as you stay inside the castle you will be safe. Outside, everything is transient and destined to decay. Inside, everything is incontrovertible, eternal, joyous, and glorious.

Then Severino himself, like the gentle host he is, will come to tell you that you are mistaken. There is no safe haven from the pervasive nihilism of a civilization embracing the unquestioned belief that "all things must pass." You should welcome the opposite notion instead, that *nothing passes* and everything is eternal *inside and outside* the castle. To be more accurate: everything *goes beyond*, everything *crosses the threshold* of what appears, fading away into the invisible land of what does not appear. What no longer appears, however, *stays*; and stays forever, because there is no place where what has been, is, or will be can cease to exist. You object that the wisdom of the world says the opposite. It says that there is no place where that which does not appear could reside. But Severino will give you no quarter. Can Being turn into nothingness? Can nothingness really turn into Being? Do you really believe *that*?

Nietzsche was elated and terrified at the intimation of the Eternal Return. Heidegger despaired over the inadequacy of language to conceptualize the Event that changes the history of Being. For his part, Severino will suggest that the terror at the idea that nothing goes away, or the cry over the impossibility of rationalizing the logic of Becoming, must be superseded by the realization that our transience and our pains, as great as they are, are already comprehended in the glory of All-Being, whose fundamental emotion is Joy.

Firmly anti-Nietzschean and anti-Heideggerian, Severino has always opposed Being's submission to the tyranny of time. In his vision, the ultimate nihilism of our civilization has been (and is) to reduce Being to a product of time. Aiming to counter such "Western folly," Severino argues for a triple eternity: eternity of the entity, eternity of the horizon where the entity appears, and eternity of the Order where entities hide or show themselves against the horizon of appearing. The anti-Platonic edifice that Severino has built is *not* meant to demonstrate that the everyday world is just an appearance and that we live in the Matrix. On the contrary, Severino's point is that every appearance *is*, no matter how deceiving, since it could not reside outside of Being. That everything exists forever and everything is eternal does not mean that the empirical you and I are immortal *in time* (eternity is not immortality), but that each moment, every slice of reality *is*, and therefore is forever, since whatever is cannot come into being or cease to be.

Initially billed as "Neoparmenidism," Severino's philosophy is an all-encompassing critique of the "wrong path" taken by post-Parmenidean metaphysics, namely, the assumption that time and becoming are self-evident, need no demonstration, and consequently, in violation of Parmenides' sharp distinction between Being and non-being, it is acceptable to think that beings come into being or emerge from nothing only to disappear into nothingness after their time has run its course. Paraphrasing *King Lear*, Severino wants you to understand that "nothing will come of nothing." Beings cannot "come into being"; either they are or they are not. Not only that: beings cannot be *created*. The very act of creation implies that things can emerge from nothing by virtue of an external agency and, as long as they have been brought into the world, can be annihilated too. In the 1960s, Severino's criticism of the nihilistic core of creation led him to a long and painful dispute with the Vatican hierarchy and the Catholic University in Milan, where he was an associate professor. The controversy culminated in 1970 with a verdict of heresy from the Supreme Sacred Congregation of the Holy Office (now the Congregation for the Doctrine of the Faith) and the termination of his appointment.

The assumption that beings come into being and return to nothingness, either by creation or by production, gives rise to the notion that the world can be produced or destroyed as it pleases God or man. Yet, if all beings exist eternally (in a sense that has nothing to do with the religious notion of eternal life or eternity imagined as time stretching into infinity), they cannot be annihilated. Equally critical of Catholic creationism and Heidegger's emphasis on time and ontological difference at the expense of Being; equally critical of communism and capitalism (both based on a nihilistic faith in the infinity of production), Severino's philosophical enterprise has commanded respect, not to mention fascination, even among thinkers who could not disagree more with him.

The greatest challenge in *The Essence of Nihilism* is the problematic connection between destiny and agency, i.e., between the implied absence of possibilities on the part of human agents and the chance of overcoming a destiny that is stronger than any personal or historical chance. We will not deny that Severino's positions may encounter resistance and refutations. Coming from a phenomenological-hermeneutic background, we too feel challenged by Severino's criticism of interpretation, possibility, and decision. Yet Severino asks questions that cannot be easily dismissed, and he does so with an extraordinary logical and stylistic consistency.

His account of Plato's creation of "the world" bears a striking resemblance to the emergence of the primal signifier in Lacan's

Seminar, Book VII. Plato's parricide of Parmenides did not open up "a" world but "the" world—the world of appearances and ideas, the world where we constantly negotiate between the imaginary and the symbolic. Plato's world is the signified of the signifier that summons the fullness of Being into the light of Appearing—the light of the phenomena. The price Plato paid, however, was the nullification of Being's Oneness. Plato reduced the absolute Real of Parmenides' Being, where there was no place for the nuances of possibility and impossibility, to the disposable remainder of pre-dialectic times.

Severino has taken upon himself the Herculean task of bringing back the Real of Being, knowing very well that his "discourse in the Real of Being" cannot but look paradoxical and untenable to the "discourse of philosophy," which has established itself precisely on the dismissal of that Real. When Severino says that every totality of appearing is eternal (every moment, every segment of each thing that is happening in any moment in time), what exactly is he saying? Let's put it this way: if we could take a picture of the whole universe in a specific moment, and if we could discern in that picture each thing that is actually happening (not unlike the vision haunting the narrator in Borges's "The Aleph"), what we would see would not be "the world," because the world is made of visible and invisible things, of beings and ideas, of the past that is no more and the future that is not yet.

What would we see instead? We would see a piece of *the Real,* of "the" Being without the reassuring barriers of the symbolic order. A synchronic picture of every totality of appearances that has disappeared from the horizon of appearing, and of every totality of appearances that will appear within the horizon of appearing, including the totality of appearing that appears in the moment the picture is taken, would be perhaps a not inadequate approximation of Severino's Being. Possibly, it would be something akin to the synchronic vision of Rome that appeared to Freud at the beginning of *Civilization and Its Discontents.*

Severino's salvific message, beginning with *Destino della necessità: Katà tò chreón* (1980/1999) and continuing today, does not rely on an easy ecumenism. It is a salvation without God, but not without Gnosis, and Gnosis requires initiation. We sense Gnostic overtones in Severino's use of theologically charged terms such as "Joy" and

"Glory." His assertion that becoming is a state in the horizon of appearing that is always-already overcome by eternity, and that all the evil in the world is always-already overcome in the eternal Joy, is akin to a Gnostic claim. To be sure, Severino's Gnosis includes neither a clumsy Demiurge (unless, in an ironic reversal of Plato's *Timaeus*, the Demiurge is Plato himself) nor a renunciation of the world of the flesh. Yet there are many paths to Gnosis, and one of them is the exaltation of the "divine spark" preceding or replacing creation, present in every soul, and exempt from annihilation because it coexists with God. It is the "dew of light" of Isaiah 26:19 that becomes the eternal shine in the *Corpus Hermeticum* and among the Valentinians. God, as Severino has often pointed out, is not the same as Being. Very much like God, however, Severino's Being is *causa sui*. Was it the old specter of Gnosis that in 1970 scared the Holy Office into declaring him a heretic?

FEAR OF DEATH? WHAT ABOUT ETERNITY . . .
BY INES TESTONI

Emanuele Severino's journey starts at only eighteen years of age, in 1947, when in his thesis *Heidegger and Metaphysics*, against the dominant interpretations, he defends the idea that Heidegger can be viewed as a metaphysician. And although this is one of his first significant contributions, his perspective does not yield to the phenomenological fashion of the day, from which he distances himself immediately. In those years, after the predominance of Benedetto Croce's and Giovanni Gentile's neo-idealism, Italian intellectuals were developing a strong interest in other European philosophies like phenomenology, existentialism, logical empiricism, pragmatism, and Marxism. However, none of these philosophies was compelling enough to influence the trajectory of Severino's thought.

Severino's academic and intellectual career was very precocious as well as brilliant. When he was only twenty-two, he obtained a lecturer position in theoretical philosophy. Later, after serving as full professor in moral philosophy at the Catholic University in Milan, he became full professor of theoretical philosophy at the University of Venice, where he is now emeritus. Drawing the attention of the Holy Office, he became one of the last thinkers to undergo an inquisition process and to be convicted for his ideas. Later in life, he became a member of the prestigious Accademia dei Lincei,[1] and he was nominated Cavaliere di Gran Croce by the president of the Italian Republic. He still teaches courses in Fundamental Ontology at the University San Raffaele in Milan and in the master's program in Death Studies & the End of Life at the University of Padua.

These biographical aspects, however, contribute less to his exceptional value than his work, which is an organic, unitary, and structurally coherent system of thought—as is rarely the case in contemporary philosophy. This intrinsic cogency derives from the essential dimension on which Severino's research focuses, namely, the redefinition of the notion of "truth."

Precisely because of this foundation, his discourse developed by deeply questioning the entire meaning of knowledge and action, of being and death. At the beginning of this journey, in the middle of the past century, the Italian philosophical scene, consistent with the European cultural climate, displayed an urge to tear down the key principles upon which the philosophical tradition had been building the forms of certainty concerning the meaning of truth for more than two millennia. This movement produced significant analyses, but these were obscured by the success of other European thinkers. In those years, the hypothetical and post-structuralist philosophies of the Anglophone, French, and German schools were already dominating, and later became even more popular, even beyond European borders.

Despite the growing success of the epistemologies of suspicion, of the thought of disenchantment, and of the perspectives of uncertainty, Severino's reflections consciously developed in the opposite direction. His analysis proceeds through a vigorous critique of the *weakness* characterizing the form which contemporary thought regards as the

---

1 The Accademia dei Lincei (Lincean Academy) is one of the most important academies in the world. Founded in 1603, Galileo Galilei was once among its members. The academy closed in 1651 and reopened in the 1870s to become the national academy of Italy, encompassing both literature and science among its concerns.

means for overcoming the traditional idea of truth. At the same time, he has never underestimated the significance of such contributions, which he investigates starting from their conceptual foundation. Severino's goal is to identify the dynamics that necessarily produce the death of truth as understood by traditional thought, and above all, to show that they are at the same time the expression of the extreme alienation reached by Western civilization.

Since the beginning, Severino's thought has irrevocably distanced itself from the entire history of philosophy, as it has aimed to show that—once philosophy got on the path that led from Greek metaphysics to Hegel—this framework could not but engender the destruction of the whole philosophical tradition and especially of the attempt to know the ultimate truth about the meaning of reality. And this path, which questions the way in which the meaning of truth has been understood by the tradition, is not only inevitable, but is also an expression of the greatest rigor achieved by the Western tradition. The rigor of Severino's thought, however, goes past this level, showing that it is necessary to overcome this very critique. He reaches this conclusion after identifying the most ancient origin of the process, which started with the "path of night"—the supreme alienation of thought. This has always been opposed by a different path, the "path of Day."

The West achieves its full coherence by denying the truth, but in this way it expresses its most profound alienation. The path of Day shows the authentic meaning of truth, which is crucially different from the one proposed by traditional thought. And if rigorous thinking may sometimes appear less than fascinating, Severino's texts are an exception: the more rigorous they are, the more interesting they become. This is not so much a psychological outcome as it is a philosophical one, because it is determined by the overcoming of what human beings, in their lives, believe to be most interesting. The interest concerns the meaning to be attributed to the life in which human beings are immersed. The term itself, "interest," comes from the Latin *inter-esse*, i.e., "to be in between," which ultimately amounts to the desire to know where human beings come from and what their destination is; which events belong to the past and which ones are awaiting them in the future.

Published in 1972, *The Essence of Nihilism* displays precisely this kind of interesting rigor.

The essays included in this volume, which has already been translated into several European languages,[2] are crucial texts constituting the core of Severino's work from the end of the 1940s to the present. For the last fifty years they have been at the center of Italy's philosophical debate, and the Church declared them to be irreconcilable with the Catholic religion. These essays strengthen the effort to reclaim the absolute primacy of philosophy, which cannot be made subordinate to any religion; they also go in the opposite direction with respect to the nineteenth century's tendency to assign philosophy a role secondary to science. Before *The Essence of Nihilism*, some of Severino's works laid the foundation of this primacy. These works include: *The Original Structure*, which I discuss below; *Toward a Renewed Interpretation of Fichte's Philosophy*, which develops the discussion of Hegel's dialectic, considered as the culmination of the epistemic-metaphysical tradition, by revisiting the philosophies of Fichte and Schelling; and *Studies in the Philosophy of Praxis*, which examines the deeply problematic relation between truth and faith and emphasizes the incompatibility between truth and religious faith. The translation and discussion of Carnap's *Der Logische Aufbau der Welt* is also a significant task, which Severino undertakes precisely in order to analyze one of the most coherent manifestations of philosophy's subordination to science.[3]

---

2   In chronological order: *Vom Wesen des Nihilismus*, Stuttgart: Klett-Cotta, 1983; *Esencia del nihilismo*, Madrid: Taurus Humanidades, 1991; *Eternité et violence*, Paris: Mimesis-France, 2010. The following pieces have not been included in this translation: "Risposta ai critici" (Reply to the Critics), the ample "Risposta alla Chiesa" (Reply to the Church), and "La parola di Anassimandro" (Anaximander's Word); the editors decided to include, instead, the essays "Senso e destino dell'Europa" (Europe's Sense and Destiny) and "Tempo e alienazione" (Time and Alienation), from the work *Gli abitatori del tempo* (*The Inhabitants of Time*, 1978).

3   E. Severino, *La Struttura Originaria*, Brescia: La Scuola, 1958; revised edition, with new introduction (1979), in *Scritti di Emanuele Severino*, Milan: Adelphi, 1981. E. Severino, *Per un rinnovamento nella interpretazione della filosofia fichtiana*, Brescia: La Scuola, 1960. E. Severino, *Studi di filosofia della prassi*, Milan: Vita e pensiero, 1963; expanded edition Milan: Adelphi, 1984. Rudolf Carnap (1961), *La costruzione logica del mondo. Pseudoproblemi nella filosofia*, ed. and trans. E. Severino, Torino: Utet, 1997.

1. The extreme and most rigorous alternative—the eternity of Being

The scholar approaching Severino's work should expect to be presented with something strikingly different from everything she knows. Severino's philosophy does not simply differentiate itself from other philosophical perspectives; rather, it posits itself in absolute opposition to the whole of Western culture and civilization and to any history of culture and civilization.

The exposition of the essential content of this alternative could appear as a mere myth, perhaps even a fascinating one, but still a myth. Unfortunately, however, a short introduction to this thought must face the risk of producing such a distortion.

The essence of such an alternative is the claim that *every being is eternal*.

This means that every "being"—every thing, relation, instant, experience, state of consciousness and nature, every event, from the most irrelevant to the most significant, everything appearing in any way and also everything that does not appear and cannot be experienced, is eternal. "Eternal" means: it is necessary that each being be and be as it is. And it is impossible for any being not to be. Everything that is not a nothing is a *being*. Every being is eternal.

The rigor with which Severino shows the necessity of the eternity of beings cannot be that of scientific knowledge, as the latter defines itself as hypothetical and falsifiable. But it is not the rigor introduced by Greek philosophy either, i.e., the "*epistéme* of truth," which culminates in Hegel's thought and in Husserl's "philosophy as rigorous science" (*Philosophie als strenge Wissenschaft*). Severino shows that it is precisely Greek philosophy which brings to light the error that will not only dominate the entire path of Western philosophy, but will also invest the entire history of Western civilization. The error lies in the claim that the appearance of "becoming" in the world amounts to the appearance of the annihilation of that which becomes, and that the death of human beings and things amounts to their annihilation.

Severino shows that, contrary to what Western philosophy assumes, no becoming appears in the sense of the appearance of the annihilation or of the becoming *ex nihilo* of beings. It is thus incorrect to say that this perspective denies experience and that claiming the eternity of every being amounts to denying the manifold display of what appears. On the contrary, Severino contends that the content which actually appears does not testify to the annihilation and creation of beings in any way. The afterword to *The Essence of Nihilism* expounds the foundation of this argument. Briefly, the core of the argument is as follows: *what is erased cannot be erased and still continue to appear* (that is, it cannot continue to belong to "experience") *in the same way as it appeared before.* In this sense, appearance—experience—cannot attest to the fact that what no longer belongs, or what does not yet belong to experience, has become nothing or is still a nothing.

To consider the "becoming" testified to by experience as the coming from or returning to nothingness is thus only the content of a *theory* which prevailed over others, also because it was favored by the realization—achieved by the ancients—that the dead do not return. When philosophy addresses the meaning of being and nothingness, it believes itself able to conclude that the dead—and dead things—do not return because they became nothing. The cyclical character of time does not concern *every* being, but the general forms of life, which belong to the divine, the dimension in which being is eternal (that is, it does not come from nothing and does not return to it)—not because it is a being, but because it is a privileged being. Already for this reason Severino views the eternity of the divine, asserted throughout the history of Western culture, as one of the most radical forms of the denial of the true meaning of eternity—which is the eternity of being as being. "God" (a concept that is still present in *The Essence of Nihilism*) is the totality of beings, albeit not in a pantheistic sense, because as the totality of beings, "God" is the totality of eternal things which does not have the corruptible, becoming, contingent world below itself. It is important to emphasize here that the term "God" as well as the term "*epistéme*" are presented in this work with an entirely new meaning, that is, with the meaning of the "destiny of truth," as I explain below.

The extreme error coincides with the extreme violence of believing that becoming testifies to the creation and annihilation of beings. Since the fundamental categories of Western philosophy became the fundamental categories of the entire culture, it is culture itself that produces the extreme *violence* of imposing on the world an essence it doesn't have. Greek philosophy is the origin of this extreme error and of this extreme violence, which in turn engenders the most dreadful and terrifying meaning of death, that of going into nothingness. This meaning gives shape to the whole formation of the meaning of life and action, at both the individual and the social level. Everything which has been thought from this origin on, which is the "faith in becoming," is intimately corrupted by this error.

2. The destiny of truth

While pointing at the extreme error, Severino also shows its recognizability through its relation with the "non-error," namely, what he calls the "original structure" and later the "original structure of the destiny of truth." He still considers his work *The Original Structure* as the foundation from which all of his writings "receive their proper sense."[4] Severino will later call the opposite of the extreme error "destiny," thereby taking into account the Indo-European root *stha*, which is preserved in the English word and which names the *staying*. The original structure of destiny is the appearing of what is not other than itself, that is, of the being itself of every being and above all of the beings which appear. A thing's being itself is the dimension whose negation is self-negation.

In this respect, in *The Essence of Nihilism*, section 6 of "Returning to Parmenides"—entitled "The 'Value' of the Opposition of the Positive and the Negative"—is particularly illuminating. There, Severino discusses and at the same time approaches in a new way Aristotle's "refutation" (*élenchos*) of those who deny the "principle of noncontradiction." (The "positive" is every being; the "negative" is what is other than any one being.) In turn, the "existence" (being, i.e., not being a nothing) of the beings which appear cannot be negated, because such negation is a self-negation. Since, thus, the negation of the content of the original structure is a self-negation, such content is "absolutely and originally incontrovertible," that is, what neither human beings nor gods—as Severino writes at times—nor changes in epoch and cultural customs can overturn or negate. In the original structure each form of incontrovertible knowledge has its own foundation.

---

4   E. Severino, "Introduzione," *La struttura originaria.*

The thesis concerning the authentic meaning of what appears is one of the extreme features of the alternative Severino has been proposing since the 1950s, as it is indissolubly tied to the necessity of the eternity of every being, that is, to the impossibility that being be not. The impossibility of creation and annihilation consists in the impossibility of the existence of a time in which being is "not yet" or "no longer." And "it is impossible" means: the claim that "a being is not" is the negation of the original structure, and more specifically it is the negation of the opposition of the positive and the negative, it is the claim that being is other than itself. And this claim is indeed the negation of that whose negation is self-negation.

In this sense, if one claims of any being (or thing) that it is not, that is, that at a certain time it is not yet and at another time it no longer is, one is indeed claiming that "the thing is nothing." And nothingness is what is absolutely other than being. Here the extreme character of the alternative presented by Severino's thought becomes fully clear. *The Essence of Nihilism* shows this in the most rigorous way. If one negates that every being is eternal, one negates the absolutely incontrovertible.

By placing beings in time, and thereby claiming that, in time, they are not, violence is brought to its culmination, because it is joined to the violence that, as I said above, attributes to what appears a mask that hides and alters its true essence, namely, eternity. By pushing beings into time they become identified with nothingness, they are thought and experienced as nothingness, they are given a death from which there is no return.

The authentic meaning of nihilism, the "essence of nihilism," resides in this way of thinking and experiencing beings. Every other critique of nihilism (for example Jacobi's, or Nietzsche's and Heidegger's) is thus in itself a form of the very essence of nihilism. These critiques are presented by still accepting the premise that, in time, beings come from and return to nothingness, and that their coming from it and returning to it is something that appears.

Severino can then conclude that, throughout the history of Western culture, the very "principle of noncontradiction" (like the "principle of identity") is contradictory. This principle assumes that, *only when and as long as being is*, being is itself and not other than itself; and it also assumes that, when it is nothing, its being itself and not other than itself is also nothing. But in this way the "principle of noncontradiction" unwittingly asserts the nothingness of being and thus identifies being with nothingness, thereby negating precisely what it means to affirm.

As the negation of the authentic meaning of nihilism, the destiny of truth posits itself beyond both the philosophical tradition and the destruction of this tradition.

3. Nihilism between tradition and contemporary thought

Destiny is the dimension where the contrast between tradition and contemporary thought manifests itself, but it is also where nihilism comes to light in its true essence. Philosophy inherits the pre-philosophical faith in the existence of the becoming-other of things, and in this way evokes the extreme form of becoming other: becoming nothingness. In other words, it evokes the extreme form of death and therefore the most profound anguish. In order to render life bearable and therefore possible, the thought evoking the most profound anguish must also be the one shaping the remedy to horror. Severino sees in the early history of Greek thought, in particular in the thought of Aeschylus, the will to posit God as "the" remedy for the pain and the terror of death: the God that starting with Anaximander safeguards everything that comes from him and that returns to him. Nihilism, i.e., the alienation of truth, views the immutable and eternal God as the salvation subtracting what is most important to human beings from nothingness. However, as Severino shows by analyzing the ground on which contemporary thought is built, this remedy is founded upon the faith in becoming, thus it turns out to be impossible. The existence of every "immutable" being negates becoming, and the rejection of traditional thought—that is, of the epistemic-metaphysical remedy—is based on the awareness that every eternal being imposes itself on the totality of being and therefore demands that everything be subjected to it. The submission to eternal beings cancels the contingent character of events, that is, the possibility of understanding them as being nothing before they happen and after they have happened. Every immutable being, as an absolute that the epistemic-metaphysical tradition evoked first through the concepts of God and salvation, cancels the coming from and returning to nothingness.

The very ground where every remedy aiming to resort to the absolute is obliterated, according to Severino, is inhabited by the great masters of nihilism. Among these, Nietzsche and two Italian philosophers emerge: Giovanni Gentile, who for Severino has unjustly received little attention, and Giacomo Leopardi, whose philosophical work has become available in English only recently. These great masters of nihilism are those who showed the impossibility of any remedy for death based on the idea of God, as epistemic metaphysics wanted to demonstrate with "truth."[5]

But nihilism, as the alienation of the authentic truth, is self-negation, and thus, starting from the destiny of truth, both epistemic metaphysics and contemporary thought are forms of the alienation of truth.

This is a complex theme, discussed in *The Essence of Nihilism* in the context of the "self-negation of the negation of the original structure," in section 6 of "Returning to Parmenides." More specifically, this section examines the following objection against the original structure of truth: if it is in virtue of the self-negation of the negation of the content of the original structure that such content is the *absolutely incontrovertible*, then this structure cannot be original, but must be a dimension founded upon the manifestation of that self-negation, and therefore it cannot be the foundation of every incontrovertible knowledge. Here I will only recall the main points of the answer resolving the objection in that section. The fact that *being* is not other than itself (that is, the opposition of the positive and the negative) is the "universal" of which *a certain being's* not being other than itself is an "individuation." For example, this book's or this room's or this memory's not being other than themselves are "individuations" of the universal quality of "not being other than itself" (that is, of the universal opposition of the positive and the negative). Section 6 of "Returning to Parmenides" shows that the *élenchos* of the negation of being itself, that is, the self-negation of the negation of the original structure, is a set of connections which are *individuations of the universal* quality of

---

5   E. Severino, *L'anello del ritorno*, Milan: Adelphi, 1999. E. Severino, *Il nulla e la poesia. Alla fine dell'età della tecnica: Leopardi*, Milan: Rizzoli, 1990; new edition 2005. E. Severino, *Cosa arcana e stupenda. L'Occidente e Leopardi*, Milan: Rizzoli, 1998; new edition 2006.

"not being other than itself" (that is, of the universal quality of a thing's "being itself"). This structure is original only insofar as it is the appearing of the synthesis of this universal and of this set of individuations of this universal. Precisely for this reason, the *élenchos* is not something external to the original structure, which would thus remain founded by it and could no longer be the originally incontrovertible.

4. After *The Essence of Nihilism*

After *The Essence of Nihilism*, Severino's thought develops and expands on two main themes: on the one hand, the issues addressed in the essay "The Earth and the Essence of Human," included in this volume; and on the other hand, the analysis of the fundamental structure of Western history, from Greek thought to its culmination in the civilization of technology—an analysis that is also outlined in *The Essence of Nihilism*, in the essay "The Path of Day."

I will only observe a couple of things on the first theme. The coming from and the return to nothingness cannot appear, and every being is eternal. On the other hand, *variation* in the world—that is, the appearing and disappearing of beings—appears incontrovertibly. Thus, it must be the case (as it is said in the afterword) that every *variation* in the world is the beginning of the appearing of an "eternal" being which did not appear before, or the no-longer-appearing of an eternal being which appeared before. In other words, variation in the world cannot be the becoming-other of beings, and therefore this variation cannot be the extreme form of becoming other which is becoming nothing (or coming from nothing). The meaning of death needs to be completely reconsidered. Every state of human life, from birth to death, is eternal. Later, Severino will show that everything which disappears must eventually reappear and stay in the appearing permanently. And the coming into appearing of eternal beings, as well as their abandoning it, is the coming and abandoning of that eternal being which is appearing itself, in which also time appears, as well as everything that (culture) ineffectively tries to think as "absolutely other" than thought. The destiny of truth is the appearing of eternal beings.

At the same time, nihilism itself is eternal. Nihilism is not a nothing; it is persuasion, faith, will; it is a being. Therefore, it is eternal. To believe and to will that beings be nothing is not itself a nothing. The

West is grounded upon this believing and willing, but the appearing of the West is only possible insofar as everything that appears, which Severino calls "earth," becomes isolated from the destiny of truth and presents itself as the framework to which human beings surely relate. The "isolation of the earth from destiny" is the world in whose existence, in most cases, human beings believe. Such isolation is the original belief-will in which the variation of the earth cannot but be understood—at first—as the becoming other and becoming nothing of things. The deepest conviction of the alienated human being is the belief that the isolated earth is the terrain to which he certainly relates, because it is of the isolated earth that *language* (which is an aspect of the isolated earth itself) mostly speaks, thereby leaving the destiny of truth unnamed. In "The Earth and the Essence of Human," Severino argues that the essence of human being is the contrast between the appearing of the destiny of truth and the appearing of the isolated earth. In addition, the appearing of the destiny of truth is not only eternal, but it is the destiny of every being, the predicate of every being. Therefore, as we can see in "The Earth and the Essence of Human," no being can appear if the destiny of truth doesn't appear—in other words, if the original structure of destiny doesn't appear first. The destiny of truth is the background of everything that appears. Destiny appears eternally and receives the earth. In this sense, human being is the eternal appearing of the destiny of truth.

Among Severino's most recent works, these themes are developed in the books *The Destiny of Necessity*, *Glory*, *Crossing*, and *Death and the Earth*.[6] These works achieve quite significant results, which were in various ways implied in the previous works but were not yet fully articulated. For example, *The Essence of Nihilism* excludes that the contingency of beings and the freedom of decisions can be understood, respectively, as the possibility that what is could have not been as opposed to being, and as the situation in which the decisions that have been made could have not been made. But in this work Severino still

---

6   E. Severino, *Destino della necessità: Katà tò chreón*, Milan: Adelphi, 1980; new edition 1999. E. Severino, *La Gloria*, Milan: Adelphi, 2001. E. Severino, *Oltrepassare*, Milan: Adelphi, 2007. E. Severino, *La morte e la terra*, Milan: Adelphi, 2011.

claims that the determinations of the earth which come into the appearing—events and decisions—could have not appeared, that is, that the beings which start to appear could have not appeared. *The Destiny of Necessity* leaves this thesis from *The Essence of Nihilism* behind because it regards it as a residue of nihilism, which this work clearly rejects. But the necessity of the appearing of every determination of the earth is not a destiny that oppresses the beings' coming out of nothingness and their return into it, precisely because this form of the beings' relation with nothingness is impossible. Therefore, the necessity that the earth happen and happen exactly the way it does belongs to the essence itself, to the very heart of what happens.

One further, crucial example: the argument presented in *Glory* is developed from the impossibility that a connection between beings might start to become necessary. A connection is authentically necessary precisely because it does not *start* to be necessary, since it is necessary all the time. It follows with necessity—but it is a consequence that also stimulates human interest to a maximum—that everything which appears (every being on the earth) is necessarily surpassed by other determinations of the earth. It is surpassed, *not* annihilated, that is, surpassed and at the same time preserved. In fact—but again, in this context I can only hint at the reason—if what appears were not surpassed, thus arresting the course and variation of the earth, a necessary connection would start to subsist between it and the background, which would mean that the impossible would exist.

All of this means that not only all beings and all human beings are eternal, but also that what appears in human experiences is an endless display of plains of eternal beings. And since also the isolation of the earth is something that has appeared, it is necessary that it too be surpassed by an earth which saves the destiny of truth from its contrast with the isolated earth. *Glory*, then, is precisely this infinite journey of the earth.

Regarding, on the other hand, the analysis of Western history—from Greek thought to the civilization of technology—outlined, among other themes, in the already mentioned essays on Leopardi and Nietzsche but also in "The Path of Day," it is worth remembering, among others works by Severino, *The Inhabitants of Time, Techne, The Fundamental Trend of Our Time, Future Philosophy, War, The Scale,*

The Decline of Capitalism, The Destiny of Technology, Lectures on Politics, From Islam to Prometheus, and *Capitalism without Future.*[7] At the basis of these writings is the awareness that the decline of the Western tradition (especially the philosophical tradition) is necessary. In its essence, the philosophy of our time realizes that the ultimate and incontrovertible truth is the creation and annihilation of every truth. In this situation, what persists is the struggle between the world powers and the capacity of one to prevail over the others for the control of the movement leading things out of nothingness and back into it. The strongest power today is technology, guided by modern science. The great powers that want to dominate the world avail themselves of it: capitalism, communism, democracy, the state, Christianity, Islam. The fundamental thesis Severino holds, which has been long debated not only in the philosophical, but also in the economic, political, and legal spheres, is that in order to prevail on the other powers and to achieve its goal, every power must strengthen the portion of the technological-scientific apparatus it controls, up to the point where this strengthening ends up itself becoming, for the winning power, the actual goal. And since every action is defined by its purpose, the so-called winning power is winning because it has renounced itself.

Severino illustrates this process especially in relation to the power dominating today, namely, capitalism. Capitalism, however, is only dominant in virtue of the technological-scientific dimension it assumes to be able to exploit indefinitely. The planet is destined for the civilization of technology (which, however, is in turn destined for a time where the technological heaven will decline). This is the thesis Severino firmly articulates and argues for in these works. It is worth noticing, however, that in these works human history (*res gestae*) is not the

---

7   E. Severino, *Gli abitatori del tempo. Cristianesimo, marxismo, tecnica*, Roma: Armando, 1978; new expanded edition 1981. E. Severino, *Téchne. Le radici della violenza*, Milan: Rusconi, 1979; second edition 1988; new expanded edition Milan: Rizzoli, 2002. E. Severino, *La filosofia futura*, Milan: Rizzoli, 1989; new expanded edition 2005. E. Severino, *La guerra*, Milan: Rizzoli, 1992. E. Severino, *La bilancia. Pensieri sul nostro tempo*, Milan: Rizzoli, 1992. E. Severino, *Il declino del capitalismo*, Milan: Rizzoli, 1993; new edition 2007. E. Severino, *Il destino della tecnica*, Milan: Rizzoli, 1998; new edition 2009. E. Severino, *Lezioni sulla politica*, Milan: Marinotti, 2002. E. Severino, *Dall'Islam a Prometeo*, Milan: Rizzoli, 2003. E. Severino, *Capitalismo senza futuro*, Milan: Rizzoli, 2012.

content of an incontrovertible knowledge. History appears within the original belief-will in which the isolation of the earth consists: it appears within the originally *interpreting* belief-will. Within the destiny of truth, the existence of the isolated earth, that is, of the belief in the becoming-other, appears incontrovertibly; but it appears in it as the interpreting which isolates the earth from destiny, as the extreme error which interpreting is.

As a concluding note, I wish to state that the development of the two main themes I just recalled (i.e., the development of the issues addressed in "The Earth and the Essence of Human" and the development of the fundamental structure of Western history, that is, of the analysis outlined in "The Path of Day") is accompanied by writings that, in turn, develop and expand on the meaning of "staying" in the truth and the relation between language, this staying, and the eternity of beings. Regarding this issue, the reader can refer to Severino's *Law and Chance*, *The Missed Patricide*, *Beyond Language*, *Tautotes*, *The Foundation of Contradiction*, and *On the Meaning of Nothingness*.[8]

Lastly, after *The Essence of Nihilism*, in the works where Severino develops most fully the themes from "The Earth and the Essence of Human," the will presents a meaning that is further and further removed from the one assigned to it by the alienation of truth. Here, too, I will limit myself to a hint (which still refers to *The Destiny of Necessity*), after what I said regarding the radical negation of contingency and of free will. The isolation of the earth is the original will upon which the will of the individual human being is founded. As isolated from the earth, the will wants becoming other to be an observable "fact"; as the will of the individual human being, the will wants to make things become other than themselves. Precisely for this reason, the will wants the impossible. Thus, when it claims to *achieve*, it is deceiving itself. It is impossible for it to be a power capable of transforming beings: it is the persuasion, the belief of transforming them. At bottom, when the will decides, it believes—thereby deceiving

---

8   E. Severino, *Legge e caso*, Milan: Adelphi, 1979. E. Severino, *Il parricidio mancato*, Milan: Adelphi, 1985. E. Severino, *Oltre il linguaggio*, Milan: Adelphi, 1992. E. Severino, *Tautótēs*, Milan: Adelphi, 1995. E. Severino, *Fondamento della contraddizione*, Milan: Adelphi, 2005. E. Severino, *Intorno al senso del nulla*, Milan: Adelphi, 2013.

itself—that what it wants is incontrovertibly achieved. But the destiny of truth is actually what the will wishes to be. Since destiny is the appearing of necessity, it is the eternally and incontrovertibly "achieving" of what it is "persuaded" of. In other words, the authentic form of the will is the incontrovertible appearance of necessity.

In *Death and the Earth*, Severino will then show that the death of the individual human being, that is, the death of her will, is the appearing, *within the essence of the human being* (within the appearing of the contrast between the destiny and the isolation of the earth), of the *instant* preceding the advent of the earth that saves. The "empirical" human being dies *within* the essence of the human being. It is within this essence that the earth which saves comes into appearing. The latter brings the isolated earth to its decline while at the same time preserving it. It does not forget error and death, and precisely for this reason it is their most radical overcoming.

The Structure of Western History and the Supersession of the Alienated Critique of Alienation

The *structure* of Western civilization envelops every element of our history and is therefore ever present. Yet to grasp its authentic meaning one must descend into a substratum essentially deeper than that explored by Hegel, Marxism, psychoanalysis, the hermeneutical current of Nietzsche-Heidegger, or structuralism. This substratum can be reached only if one does not set out in the company of any of the various historical reconstructions formulated by Western culture; indeed, only if one does not "set out" at all. Rather, it can be reached only if the *locus of Necessity* (i.e., the original structure of Necessity, always already open *outside* the structure of the West) permits language to testify to it, and to testify to its being abysmally alien to the structure of Western history. The structure of the West continues to be the essential *unconscious* of our civilization; yet that other structure—the locus of Necessity—is the unconscious of this unconscious, the substratum of the substratum, that which envelops the enveloping. It is to this *ultimate* substratum that the present work is addressed.

---

1 The introduction is composed of two chapters extracted from the opera *Gli abitatori del tempo* (The Inhabitants of Time), published in 1978 (Rome: Armando). The reader should keep in mind the epoch in which the text was written, for example, the fact that in this period the Soviet Union was still in existence. Furthermore, as indicated before, in footnote 2 of the foreword, this translation of *The Essence of Nihilism* does not include the chapters "Risposta ai critici" (Reply to the Critics), the ample "Risposta alla Chiesa" (Reply to the Church), and "La parola di Anassimandro" (Anaximander's Word), which appear in the original Italian edition [*Editor's note*].

The structure of the West—the *intermediate* substratum—is the will that things be time. The original structure of Necessity—i.e., the ultimate substratum—shows that the will that things be time (and therefore history, Becoming) implies with Necessity the will that things *be nothing*, or that *the not-Nothing be nothing*. This will is *nihilism*. Nihilism, in its authentic essence, is the structure of the West. But the authentic essence of nihilism can manifest itself in language only if language succeeds in testifying to that ultimate and unexplored substratum in which the structure of Necessity always already opens.

Time is not the novelty introduced by Christian thought or by modern culture, but is what was first thought—and thought decisively—by the Greeks, and which, as technology, today rules the earth unchallenged. It is all the more unchallenged the more it remains unexplored in its authentic meaning; and it is all the more unexplored the more one thinks one grasps (as is the case with Heidegger) the meaning of the identity of Being and time in Greek thought. The inhabitants of time are the forms of culture, the social institutions, the individuals, the masses, and the peoples that have progressively been subjected to this dominant structure—Europe, first of all.

1. THE MEANING AND THE DESTINY OF EUROPE

What is Europe? The solution of this problem is by no means an abstract cultural exercise. For there are, today, substantial forces working to complete the process of European unification—forces whose aim is to transform the reality of Europe. But to transform an object (even the simplest one) in a certain way, one must first know what the object is. Even the communist revolution is based upon knowledge of what that revolution intends to transform, i.e., on the analysis of capitalist society. The revolution's success depends upon the soundness of this analysis. Similarly, the success of any political action that intends to consider Europe as an object to be transformed inevitably depends upon the validity of its knowledge of European reality.

Yet difficulties arise as soon as the problem is formulated; indeed, they concern the formulation of the problem itself. In the first place: which branch of knowledge shall deal with the problem of the meaning of Europe? Within what type of knowledge is its solution to be found?

Europe is a problem for the historical, social, and natural sciences, for ethnology and anthropology, for political geography and economy, and for the philosophy of history. Each of these disciplines claims to have established what Europe is, and the result that stands before us is not Europe, but many Europes: as many Europes as there are scientific specializations that study the object "Europe."

The unification of scientific knowledge today is considered a necessity, and yet we are a very long way from its realization. In fact, modern sciences have arisen precisely insofar as they have methodically restricted research to particular and distinct fields of study; precisely, that is, insofar as they have hindered in principle the gaze that seeks to grasp that unity which gathers the particular fields together. Today, scientific activity entails the delimitation of a particular field of objects by means of a strictly formulated method. Everything that manifests itself independently of scientific method is held to be either nonexistent or valueless. The successes of modern science are due to its specialization; but in these conditions the unification of scientific knowledge can only be the juxtaposition of many separate worlds—a juxtaposition giving rise to a fortuitous unity, inevitably of that very nonspecialistic and ingenuous stamp which science wishes to avoid. Consequently, either one lets each of the individual sciences carry on in its own way—but then their unity, as the unification of various specializations, is a fortuitous and arbitrary juxtaposition—or else one resolves to establish a true unity, which does not simply set disciplines side-by-side while they continue to be practiced separately. This, however, would call for a transformation of the method and meaning of science—and who today can embark upon such an undertaking? And so the unification of scientific knowledge remains, in fact, a dream. Europe remains hidden and we are left to deal with the many Europes of scientific specializations.

The state of the modern sciences inevitably affects political action. In addition to the aspects of European reality that come to light within the various scientific specializations, the political forces that are now working towards the unity of Europe do, admittedly, intend to consider historical and spiritual traditions as well, and in particular the ethical, religious, and aesthetic traditions of the European peoples. These traditions, however, are no longer presented to the contemporary statesman in their peculiar nonscientific aspect—rather, they too appear under the guise of what has become an object of the methodology of the socio-historical sciences. The forces working for the political unification of Europe are faced with many Europes, which they attempt to organize politically. They attempt to assign a unitary goal to an object—Europe—which is unitary in name only. This object in effect comprises many objects, each of which goes its own way and for which, therefore, no common goal can be set. Just as the unification of scientific knowledge is a juxtaposition of worlds, so the political unification of Europe and political action in general must also be a juxtaposition of goals. Even in the case of individual nations, one cannot fail to notice the fortuitous and arbitrary character of political action, which is incapable of giving a single direction to the separate and contrasting needs of national life. What we have here is not simply a subjective incapacity of the political class—or at least this incapacity is not the decisive factor—but rather a structural defect, due to the fact that what one wishes to organize and unify simply does not lend itself to organization and unification.

In this situation the many Europes inevitably clash, with the result that the stronger Europe prevails—namely, "economic" Europe, or what Europe is from the standpoint of political economy. The conviction thus takes hold that the most valid reason for bringing about the political unification of Europe is provided by the capitalistic organization of European industrial production, which to compete with international big business must be freed from the fetters of the traditional organization of the European states themselves. For these fetters impede the infinite increase of production and consequent unlimited expansion of the market that the logic of capitalism demands. The juxtaposition of political goals produces a unilaterality of political action in which the weaker goals become mere satellites of the economic goal, which prevails. This situation gives rise to that type of political eclecticism, so widespread in the Western world, which resolves to uphold the so-called "values" of European civilization—but only as peripheral to the nucleus of the economy.

But does Europe crumble into an infinity of Europes simply because modern science is incapable of grasping the unity of this multiplicity, or rather because the selfsame object we call "Europe" is divided within itself into a multiplicity of separate and contrasting parts?

There can be little doubt that the spectacle of struggles, contradictions, conflicts, and subtle and radical distinctions that even a summary glance at the history of European civilization reveals, is not to be found in any other civilization. The intensity of the economic, political, religious, and ideological conflicts that have shaped European civilization is indeed unique. If Europe itself is essentially struggle and opposition, to what possible organic unity can political action assign a common goal?

And yet, in the conflict between the forces into which the whole that we call "Europe" has been broken up, some forces do gain the upper hand. The supreme force that today rules unchallenged over all the others is techno-scientific action organized according to a politico-economic plan. The United States and the Soviet Union control the decisive sources of worldwide technological force, but technology, as the application of modern science to industry and thus as the factor that determines every aspect of the existence of entire masses of humanity, is essentially a European phenomenon—technological civilization was born in Europe at the beginning of the nineteenth century. Techno-scientific force, while today dominating all other forces, also constitutes the deepest break in the continuity of European history—deeper than that produced by any ideological conflict, since it is itself the decisive factor in the crisis of every ideology. Today, the universal crisis of traditional civilization (both inside and outside Europe) is not simply accompanied, but is produced by the project that underlines techno-scientific force. This force not only dominates every other force on earth, but is based upon the project of unlimited dominion over all things; i.e., upon the project of the controlled and unlimited production and destruction of the universe. For this project, nothing in principle exists that cannot be dominated (i.e., produced and destroyed). And indeed, all limits to human action, once laid down as absolute laws—God's law, natural law, moral law—are now falling before the onslaught of technology's productive-destructive capabilities. Technology surmounts all limits as it progressively invents a new world that is freeing itself from the old; no longer limited to the production of consumer goods and the hold on human labor, it has now undertaken to produce man himself—his life, feelings, thought processes, and his idea of ultimate happiness. Technology, in setting out to liberate man from pain and death, undertakes to effectively produce that which traditional culture was unable to render credible— namely God, understood as the sure possession of happiness. The meaning of reality is no longer a mere object of contemplation but is something produced by scientific action, itself far more effective than any ideological revolution. Within the horizon of techno-scientific action, a "thing" is nothing other than an absolute availability to be produced and destroyed; a thing not available in this way is unreal.

At the outset of the modern era the project of an unlimited dominion over all things was only expressly formulated by a few individuals—Bacon, Galileo, Descartes—and even they were not free from all reservations due to the persistence of traditional culture. But with the advent of the machine age, capitalism presented this project as the ultimate horizon within which the labor of the masses becomes meaningful and of which ever greater masses of workers are gaining consciousness. The world as it is *within* the technological project—the world as a place where all things can be dominated, produced, and destroyed— is the fundamental spectacle set before the working masses. The masses know that they do not rule the world, but they also know that by means of their labor all things are about to be opened up to unlimited production and destruction. The technological meaning of the "thing" is rapidly becoming the meaning the "thing" assumes for the European masses. The capitalistic organization of industrial production measures every other "world" of European man against the world of technology, and technology's ever greater productive-destructive capabilities give rise to the crisis of those traditional worlds, and so to the triumph of the meaning that reality assumes within the world of technology. This supreme spectacle, which in European man from the nineteenth century onward has overshadowed every other spectacle— this technological meaning of Being—is in no way questioned by communism. Marxism and neo-Marxism do not reject industry and technology, but only their capitalistic organization. The communist revolution simply replaces the capitalistic with a socialistic organization of technology, while both forms of organization share that meaning which reality—which the "thing"—assumes within technology itself. And today it is *within* this meaning—*within* the project of the production and destruction of all things—that any attempt to render technological civilization less inhuman must be made. Socialist humanism and ecology do not advocate the abolition of this project— they simply affirm that, if rendered more rational, it would become more efficient and more in keeping with the essential values of the day. And while Christianity and its churches do not believe (and certainly do not hope) that technology will be capable of destroying the kingdom of God, they cannot fail to realize that Christian love between peoples is impossible today outside of the techno-scientific elaboration of existence. Ideological conflict is heightened when there is great technological disparity between opposing forces (as between international guerrilla movements and the established order), but it is milder in cases where the technological potential of the antagonists tends to be balanced. Thus we are approaching a historical situation in which the capitalistic and socialistic character of the organization of technology will be superseded by the purely technological character of this organization. And if one should object that the tools of technology ultimately draw their force from the moral force of the men who use them, then it must be pointed out that technology today has undertaken to reshape the individual's mental structure, in order to give it just those psychological qualities (or "moral forces") which are required for these tools to function efficiently.

Where do these considerations lead us? We remarked at the outset that scientific specialization makes it impossible to speak of Europe as a single object. Furthermore, European history appears in itself as a struggle between opposing forces, where the most radical break with the past is constituted by that destruction of traditional European civilization which technological civilization is now bringing to completion. But in this selfsame act, technological civilization also produces the profoundest unification of Europe's, and the world's, present. For a *single* meaning of the world has become worldwide: that meaning which the world assumes within the project of an unlimited domination of all things. The "world" is the scene of this domination. At the root of scientific specialization lies that very orientation towards domination that has in specialization itself the indispensable condition for its own realization. Dominating means marking out a particular dimension and positing it as independent of the whole. Undertaking to dominate all things demands a vision of the whole as broken up into a multiplicity of isolated worlds. To dominate, a unitary vision of the world has to be abandoned. The world lets itself be dominated precisely insofar as it is broken up into many, infinite worlds controlled by individual scientific specializations—and yet this dealing with many worlds is an inevitable consequence of the essentially unitary meaning the world assumes within the attitude and civilization of science and technology. This unitary meaning—which constitutes the *essence* of present-day Europe (an essence that now advances far beyond the geographic borders of Europe and dominates the world)—is nothing else than the availability of every thing to unlimited production and destruction.

Europe today is unified by technological domination. As the matrix of technological civilization, it is the destruction of its own past. *And yet this past is the secret of the present.* We have to prepare ourselves to understand that this "technological" meaning of the world is by no means a deviation from the spirit of traditional European culture. On the contrary—its origin lies in the remotest past of this very tradition and the historical course of this meaning is its progressive branching out into the great forms of traditional European civilization. This course is, in fact, the unitary meaning of European history. Technological civilization brings the great forms of European tradition to their setting[2] not because the meaning of the world that dominates them differs from the meaning that dominates technological civilization, but rather because such forms are in contradiction with their own essence. For indeed, this essence is nothing but the meaning of the world that rules unchallenged in technological civilization, where its form has now become adequate to its essence. The essence of traditional European civilization and culture finds in technological

---

2 "Setting" (*tramontare*), here *et passim*, is one of the fundamental notions of Severino's philosophy. It indicates the transcendental law of motion by which things, rather than ceasing to *be*, leave the horizon of what *appears*: like the sun or the stars, which "set" but do not perish or pass away [*Translator's note*].

civilization its most complete and rigorous realization. The old European world can be itself only in the new European world that is destroying it. How can this be so?

It should be observed, first, that "the meaning of the world" of which we are speaking has nothing to do with a *Weltanschauung*, an "intuition of the world." A *Weltanschauung* is an ideology, a specific mode of understanding the origin, value, destination, and purpose of human life in the world. Indeed, there has been a succession of differing and contrasting *Weltanschauungen* in the course of European history. But when we speak here of the "meaning of the world" that dominates the entire history of Europe, we are referring to the deep substratum that persists identically beneath such *Weltanschauungen* and guides this variation. This substratum is essentially deeper than any structure upon which structuralism may be based; but, at the same time, it distinguishes European history and is not to be found elsewhere. For Marxism, European history remains a mystery as long as one insists upon understanding it as a development of ideologies. All ideologies (economics, law, philosophy, art, politics) mirror on the theoretical plane the mode in which man, through his labor, produces. Ideologies are functions of production, whose constitution and variation derive from economic conditions. The earth, says Marx, is the common object of human labor; it is transformed according to man's purposes. In fact Marx agrees that labor is purposive activity (*zweckmässige Tätigkeit*). But this means that man can set to work only insofar as he sees the difference between the earth still untouched by his labor and the ideal project he intends to realize. To act purposively means to see the difference between things as they are and as one wishes them to be, and so it means that labor—all labor—is based upon the manifestation, the presence, the *appearing* of things. If for Marxism the ground of every ideology lies in the mode of human labor, it is also essential to note that the ground of all labor entails the manifestation of things and hence the manifestation of the meaning that the "thing" has for man. When the lumberjack carries out his work, the fir tree he is cutting down stands before him not simply as a fir tree but as a *thing*, and the way in which he wields his ax is not determined simply by the meaning that the fir tree has for him but, fundamentally, by the meaning that the *thing* has for him. This meaning envelops and guides the lumberjack's whole life and work, for everything with which he deals is, indeed, a thing. For Marx as for a European lumberjack of, say, the nineteenth century, the meaning of the word "thing" is beyond dispute (as, moreover, it is for *every* Western philosopher who nonetheless explicitly undertakes to grasp the meaning of the "thing"); and yet this meaning is not constant throughout man's history. Rather, it is itself historical and its varying constitutes the ultimate ground of the variation of historical epochs.

So, in saying that a single meaning of the world pervades Europe and renders it an organic whole, we mean that a single mode of understanding what the thing is—a single meaning of the "thing"—guides, establishes, and unifies the immense variety of events and works of European history. At a certain moment in man's history, a meaning of the *thing* came to light in Europe that was progressively to impose itself on all other meanings and that today dominates unchallenged every aspect of Western civilization. What exactly are we referring to?

In the techno-scientific project of a controlled and unlimited production-destruction of all things, the *thing* is understood as absolute availability to be produced and destroyed. A thing is that which may be produced and destroyed without limit. And we all know what it means to produce and to destroy a thing. To produce it means to bring it into being, to make it issue forth from nothingness; to destroy it means to takes its being away, to make it return to nothingness. Physics tells us that, after the atom bomb destroyed Hiroshima, the total amount of energy in the universe remained the same. But Hiroshima was not simply a quantity of energy. This quantity existed as a specific unity of shapes, colors, sounds, states of mind; and it is *of this unity* that we say that it has become nothing. If it had not become nothing (or if no aspect of Hiroshima had become a Nothing), we would not say that Hiroshima has been destroyed.

But do we really believe that this discourse on Being and Nothing has no surprise in store? Do we believe that it is perfectly "natural"? Or did it rather begin at a specific moment in human history—at the moment when the history of European civilization began?

It must be understood that the thing is an *absolute* availability to production and destruction by virtue of the fact that it is available to

Being and to *nothingness*, i.e., to the *absolutely* opposed. Technology can undertake to produce and destroy things without limit only insofar as the thing is first thought as that which issues from and returns to nothingness; i.e., as that which issues from the extreme, unlimited remoteness of nothingness and returns there. Here, the thing is not simply available to new forms, states, and encounters—it is available to the two ways that grow so distant from one another that they reach the infinite distance that is the distance from Being to nothingness. As available to both these ways, the thing is an infinite oscillation that bridges the infinite distance separating Being from nothingness.

For the first time in the history of man, several centuries before Christ, Greek philosophy brought to light the meaning of this absolute availability of the thing: in the moment, that is, when it understood the thing as that which oscillates between Being and Nothing. The thing, as such, is "what is": what *is*, but what was not (did not exist), will not be, and might not have been. "What is" the Greeks called *to on*, "being" [*ente*]. For the Greeks, God is immutable and eternal (i.e., neither issues from nor returns to nothingness) not insofar as he is a being, but insofar as he is *a certain* being, a privileged being, enjoying a nature not possessed by other beings. *Qua* being—considered purely and simply as being—even God would be an oscillation between Being and nothingness. Being *as* being *is* this oscillation. The testimony to the meaning of Being and of Nothing, and thus the meaning of the thing for Greek thought, has no precedent in the history of man. Greek philosophy *thought* for the first time the infinite distance that opposes being to nothingness and the infinite agility that allows being to bridge it, thus becoming nothing, and that allows Nothing to bridge it, thus becoming being.

From this moment onward the totality of things appears as the totality of beings and the Greek meaning of being sets out on the course that will lead it to progressively envelop, dominate, and unify all the great forms of European culture. Little by little, in each of these forms, the things with which man deals manifest themselves as *beings*. If the lumberjack cuts down his fir tree, if the religious man works for the salvation of his soul, if technology constructs an artificial satellite or paradise on earth, if the politician works for the construction of European unity—then the fir tree, the soul's salvation, artificial

satellites, heaven on earth, and the political unity of Europe are manifest first of all as *beings*, and their being *beings* establishes the meaning,
the tone, the intensity—the being *so* and not otherwise—of all the
human activities that refer to them.

Technological civilization and scientific specialization are essentially grounded in Greek metaphysics, as openness of the meaning of
being. Only if being as such is that which is available to Being and to
nothingness can one then devise the project of unlimited production
and destruction of all things. In the beginning, the task of producing
and destroying things was entrusted, fundamentally, to a divine art, or
techne (Plato's term is *theía techne*). Subsequently, modern Europe
realized that, if God existed, the creative activity of man would be
impossible: God would have already done everything. Man, accordingly, supplants the old God but maintains his fundamental trait: that
of being the force which dominates the creation and destruction of
things. Science and modern technology have heightened this force to
unprecedented intensity. Yet theology is but the earliest form of technology, and technology but the latest form of theology. The thing, in its
availability to Being and to nothingness, is prey to divine and human
forces that tear it away from Being and from nothingness. The original
expression of the will to power lies in the very way that Greek metaphysics opened up the meaning of the thing: the will to power means,
originally, the will that things be *being*—be, that is, an issuing from
and returning to nothingness. (And any rejection of the will to power
by modern philosophy—by Marx, Heidegger, or others—is merely
apparent, since the entire history of philosophic thought moves wholly
within the Greek meaning of the thing.) The forms of domination and
exploitation of man and of nature, which have characterized European
history, have been possible only insofar as Greek metaphysics opened
up the original horizon of the will to power. And indeed, the practical
spirit of modern European man is grounded upon that contemplative
spirit which finds in metaphysics its most rigorously consistent
realization.

At an early date, the metaphysical meaning of the thing passed
beyond the boundaries of philosophic thought. While the historical
sciences are well aware of the ubiquity of the categories of Greek
thought even in the most disparate regions of European civilization,

they fail to recognize the essential dominance established with the diffusion of these categories. The vehicle of this diffusion is *language*, and the education of whole generations of Europeans has been based upon a grammar of Greek and Latin that draws directly upon Greek logic and its meaning of the "thing." This meaning was then transmitted to the grammatical elaborations that govern the formation of national European languages as they shed their initially popular character and become an expression of cultural values. The various sectors of the modern sciences constitute the linguistic field where the European national languages most clearly show their common Greek root. After penetrating the nonphilosophic forms of Greek culture, the Greek meaning of the thing enveloped Roman civilization, the Christian message, the history of Western philosophy, Justinian's codification of Roman law, and later the entire history of European law, the fundamental categories of the European economic and political orders, the new science of nature and its application to industry, the world of European poetry, architecture, and music, operations upon mathematical entities, and, finally, the common way of thinking and the public opinion of the European peoples, and now—through technology's worldwide dominance—of all the peoples on earth. The history of Europe is the progressive appropriation of things, i.e., the progressive exploitation of their absolute availability, their infinite oscillation between Being and nothingness. The technological project of domination puts aside all reservations regarding this availability. It abolishes all limits to domination—and in so doing celebrates the triumph of metaphysics. Modern science, in transforming reality, thinks it has destroyed sterile metaphysical contemplation. The European bourgeoisie saw in natural science the true form of knowledge, useful for production and exchange, and on the basis of the democratic character of intersubjective scientific knowledge rejected metaphysics as useless and aristocratic. Christianity made itself master of the European masses, denying metaphysics' claim to be the supreme form of human knowledge. All contemporary philosophy is a rejection of metaphysics. Indeed, the failure of metaphysics is an expression of the success of European science, economics, politics, and religion; i.e., of the dominant forces of modern Europe. And yet—the *essence* of these forces is the very meaning of being that makes possible the scientific domination of nature, industrial production and commercial exchange, and the Christian conception of a divine creation of the world. It is that meaning of being which the Greeks opened up once and for all. And thus the destruction of metaphysics is at the same time its triumph—the triumph, that is, of the original form of the will to power.

If the European vocation for technological domination of the universe goes back to Greek metaphysics, and if this is what the unitary meaning of Europe essentially is, then the goal that must be assigned to Europe, when undertaking its political unification, has to consist in freeing this vocation from any form of traditional civilization that still obstructs, hinders, and delays the dominance of the technological essence of things. European history itself is the progressive liberation of this essence from all the forms of traditional European culture (i.e., the political, ethical, religious, and philosophical ideologies) that, while themselves forms of this essence, are nonetheless in contradiction with it, since they attempt to limit the absolute and infinite dominability of things. *All* contemporary criticism raised on the basis of Western culture against technological civilization nonetheless moves within that essential horizon—the Greek meaning of the thing—whose most rigorous and coherent testimony and realization is technological civilization itself. This fact has been overlooked by those who wish to pit the United States and the Soviet Union against a Europe that, while by no means economically underdeveloped, is above all the bearer of values allegedly on a level different from and superior to the will to power as it is now expressed in the technological domination of all things. The "spiritual values" of traditional European civilization are in fact inadequate forms of the will to power, from which technological civilization, as the adequate form of the will to power, is radically freeing itself. If the unitary meaning of European civilization is the will to power, as openness of the technological meaning of the thing, then the political effort to make Europe the scene of an extreme intensification of technological development is definitely on the right track.

Although we may seem to be nearing the end of our discourse, in fact we have not yet touched upon the decisive aspect of the problem. We have glimpsed how it is possible to trace the events of European history back to their unitary meaning: to a *structure* that, while dominating the entire history of the West, consistently eludes our historical consciousness. *But what would occur if this meaning, i.e., the European meaning of the thing—the essence of our civilization (and thus that of which we are most deeply convinced)—were to appear as the deepest alienation of man, essentially deeper than any original sin, than any economic or psychological alienation, than any error?* What would occur if the affirmation of the essential alienation of European civilization were to appear not simply as the opinion of one of us, or of a prophet, not as a faith or a hypothesis but as the *truth* that no time, no omnipotent God, and no other power on earth can destroy or deny? To know what man's true alienation is, is it not in fact necessary to know what *truth* is? And will true alienation not be, then, the alienation of truth?

For European civilization, the *thing* is that which issues from and returns to nothingness. Being and Nothing establish the meaning of the birth and death, the production and destruction of things. For this civilization, the supreme evidence is that there is a time, the past, when things became nothing, and a time, the future, when things will be nothing once more. Being is in time, by which it is devoured. The essential alienation of the West stands right before our eyes—but presents itself as supreme and indisputable evidence. If essential alienation irretrievably eludes our consciousness, this is not because it is hidden in some remote and unexplored region, but rather because it has long stood before us as so utterly indisputable that no one even deigns to pay it any heed.

We say, "things past and things future are nothing." What could be more indisputable? But in this indisputable conviction we by no means intend to affirm that "*Nothing* is nothing"; that is, it is not *of Nothing* that we intend to say that it is a Nothing, but rather *of things past* or *of things future*, i.e., of that whose meaning is not identical with the meaning "nothing." But that whose meaning is not identical with the meaning "nothing" is not a Nothing. We say of the city Hiroshima that it became nothing. But Hiroshima does not mean "nothing," and thus is not a Nothing. Hiroshima, of which we say that now it is a Nothing, is not a Nothing. And so we think that that which is *not* a Nothing is a Nothing. The past and the future are the time when things—i.e., that which is not a Nothing—are nothing. If they were to tell us that the past and the future are the time when the circle is squared, we would be quick to rejoin that there can be no such time—that any such identification of circle and square would be absurd. But this sense of the absurd—which makes us reject a time when the circle is squared—does not prevent us from thinking of a time when the thing, i.e., that which is not a Nothing, is nothing, nor does it prevent us from living and acting according to this thought. We *think* and we *live* things as if they were Nothing. For European civilization things are nothing: the meaning of the thing, which guides Western history, is the nothingness of things. *Nihilism* is the essence of European civilization, since the fundamental meaning of nihilism is the nihilation of things, i.e., the belief that being is a Nothing: nihilism is the action guided and shaped by this conviction. Greek metaphysics is the original and decisive expression of nihilism. The will that the thing be "being" is the will that the thing be *nothing*. And it is *within* nihilism that the most irremediable conflicts of Western civilization have developed: Christianity and anti-Christianity, theism and atheism, lordship and bondage, spiritualism and materialism, philosophic realism and philosophic idealism, metaphysics and antimetaphysics, contemplatism and pragmatism, philosophy and antiphilosophy, faith and reason, bourgeois economics and socialistic economics, democracy and absolutism, traditionalism and the global challenge to society. All these inexorable antagonists clash *within* a substantial agreement, they express antithetically the same dominant thought. They share the decisive and fundamental trait that guides the West. Nihilism is the *ethos*, the dwelling-place of the West. It is the West's structure.

The history of the West is a history of nihilism in an abysmally different sense from that denounced by Nietzsche and Heidegger. The genuine meaning of European nihilism, in which even the masses, public opinion, and the most ordinary people are now living, is something essentially different from, and infinitely more radical than, the human situation as depicted by existentialism. For existentialism, human life issues from and returns to nothingness and is not guaranteed by a transcendent God. But existentialism does not claim that when man lives, his life is nothing. For existentialism, existing means having to do with nothingness, but this having to do with nothingness is not itself a Nothing; existence is a flash in the night of nothingness, but this flash is not a Nothing. *Nihilism*, by contrast, as the authentic and deeply hidden essence of European civilization—as the essence that guides not only the entire development of Western philosophy, but even the everyday behavior of the man in the street and the superficial conviction of public opinion—is something essentially more radical than existentialism, or than the world as it appears in the consciousness of an existentialist philosopher. The nihilism of European civilization lies in a substratum essentially deeper and more unexplored than the terrain that European philosophical consciousness is able to chart. Europe may come to express its own essence as a flash in the night of nothingness. But Europe's underlying thought, consistently *unexpressed* in European consciousness, is that the flash of existence is, *itself*, the night of nothingness—is that things, as such, are Nothing.

The essential alienation of European civilization can be indicated, then, in a few words. But the *comprehension* of these words is decisive for Europe's and the world's destiny. The words are these: thinking that things are not (when they were not yet born or not yet produced, or when they perish or are destroyed) means thinking that things—i.e., that which is not a Nothing—are Nothing. *This* is the thought that originated with Greek metaphysics and that guides and unifies the entire history of the West.

Indeed, this thought is the basis of every historical interpretation, from Hegel to Nietzsche, from Weber and Husserl to Heidegger and the Frankfurt School, that discerns in Greek thought the secret of European civilization. Nihilism, in its authentic and unexplored meaning, envelops even those philosophies that proclaim the nihilistic character of European history (and the very notion of "history" and "historical Becoming" is a reflection of nihilism). For Nietzsche and Heidegger too, nihilism is the essence of Europe. But even they fail to recognize the authentic meaning of nihilism, and indeed their very philosophies represent one of the most typical forms of what nihilism really is. To this day, philosophic thought has failed to recognize the genuine meaning of European nihilism—and thus it is incapable of saying *what* Europe is. Even when contemporary philosophy is critical of technology it is still dominated by that essence whose most radical realization is technology itself. For European technology is nihilism not insofar as technology is used "badly," but insofar as it is *technology*. The ideologies that cause it to be used "badly" or "well" share with the so-called "neutral nature" of technology the decisive trait of nihilism: the belief that things (men, the sky, stars, planets, history) are Nothing.

But European civilization can appear as the locus of essential alienation only insofar as the *truth* of things appears. In truth, things are not separated from Being to be entrusted to Nothing—rather, all things share the nature of the incorruptible gods. Parmenides said: "You shall not sunder Being from its connection with Being" (Fr. 4). In the truth of Being, first testified to by Parmenides, this is to say that *everything is eternal* and that history is the process of the rising and setting of the whole (which includes the very night of nihilism). Contrary to what we have firmly believed for more than two thousand years, the gods of the West *are* jealous:[3] they attempt to keep the nature of the incorruptible for themselves, while leaving birth and death, the issuing from and returning to nothingness, to things. Technological civilization is the offspring of this jealousy of the gods. The gods deceived Prometheus when they let him steal divine fire: what they left him was the technological capacity to produce and destroy that presupposes the birth and death of things, while they themselves had long attempted to oppose that birth and death with their own eternity. European civilization was later to destroy the gods, but it has continued to live as the offspring of their jealousy. The setting of the West's gods still belongs to the inner history of nihilism, but the setting of their jealousy is the supersession of nihilism and the testimony to the eternity of every thing. The truth of Being states that everything is eternal. In undertaking to dominate the creation and annihilation of things, the West attempts the impossible—it attempts to make being nothing. But the impossible does become possible simply because one attempts it. Alienation means attempting the impossible, and the history of the West is the concrete aspect of this attempt.

Attempting the impossible, the West is inevitably destined to experience the most radical anxiety. In fact, technological civilization is grounded on the modern science of nature, which originated as a

---

3   Cf. *Metaphysics*, 983 a, where Aristotle denies—once and for all—that the gods are jealous of the "divine knowledge" man can attain through philosophy.

rejection of Greek *episteme*. *Episteme* is the thought that intends to constitute itself as "science," in the sense of incontrovertible and necessary truth, and that as metaphysical-theoretical knowledge guides the entire course of pre-Renaissance civilization. The rejection of *episteme* later entered the domain of philosophic knowledge, with the result that philosophy today sees itself as hypothetical, provisional, open to revision. This means that the technological project to dominate all things no longer finds any theoretical obstacle in its path. Truth today means power, and technology is the supreme power. But precisely because technology is the negation of any definitive truth—and to dominate the transformation of things it must be this negation—the destiny of the West is radical anxiety. Indeed, any happiness—any paradise—that may be constructed by techno-scientific praxis will be insecure. Technological civilization can produce all things and eliminate the regret for any happiness that religion once gave, yet it cannot produce the incontrovertible and definitive security of its own dominion. Any logic that undertakes to ground this security is inevitably insecure, precisely because it is hypothetical. If the whole is to be dominated it can have no definitive truth. Yet technological civilization wishes its domination of the whole to be definitive truth—but no hypothetical logic can ground the definitive truth of its dominion. The ultimate power destined to be realized by the West is essentially insecure. It is threatened by the possibility of utter ruin, because there does not (and in technological civilization *cannot*) exist an incontrovertible and definitive truth that can ground the impossibility of losing the happiness attained. But the fact that radical anxiety is the destiny of the West cannot be avoided by reinstating *episteme* and its world, since modern science and technological civilization are the inevitable consequence of the way in which Greek *episteme*—the original locus of nihilism—first thought the meaning of Being.

The forces that are working today for the political unification of Europe assign Europe a goal. But to assign Europe a goal, one needs to know *what* Europe is. Nihilism is the essence of Europe—yet the *supersession* of nihilism is the hidden goal that guides this alienated essence. *Here* lies the salvation of Europe and, today, of the world. If nihilism is to set, its essential meaning must first of all come out of the darkness that envelopes it. But nihilism is no longer a mere mode of thought—it has become the concrete life of peoples, their institutions, and their values. If nihilism is to set it is not sufficient that thought, denouncing the essential alienation of Western civilization, testify to the truth of Being—even if this testimony is indeed the first fundamental step toward the salvation of the West. If nihilism is to set the *works* of nihilism must set. This setting is a revolution which, recognizing the nihilistic character of all the revolutions in Western history, opens up the dimension of a new, and essentially different, meaning of action—a dimension in which a history of peoples can begin that is not a history of nihilism. Every attempt to resolve the problems of contemporary civilization treats the symptoms of a mortal sickness the essence of which is ignored, and every such attempt is therefore destined to fail— if failure means remaining within the most abysmal alienation of the essence of man. On a sinking ship one may no doubt be concerned that provisions be evenly distributed, that the crew does not riot, and that life on board be bearable for all. But the essential concern is to find the leak. If the leak is not found it cannot be repaired, and the shipwreck that follows not only renders the solution of the problems of life on board altogether superfluous, but shows how no solutions have been provided at all, or that the solutions provided were merely illusory. And today this illusion has convinced us all. We are willing to consider only particular and immediate problems that can be faced one at a time—problems whose solutions are already in sight. As regards the unification of Europe, the problems of the day concern the augmentation of production and technological development, under-developed areas, the relation of parliamentary democracy with communism and fascism, extra-European relations. And everything we have said here in no way helps to resolve them. Yet this pragmatic attitude that, exclusively concerned with the problems of life on board, will not even hear of a leak in the hull is itself—like the specialization of scientific knowledge—an inevitable consequence of what the Greeks understood by the word "being." If things issue from nothingness and are therefore altogether unpredictable, it is impossible to diagnose a sickness and a fundamental alienation of existence. Rather, one is obliged to take things as they come, facing the problems they bring with specific techniques. The pragmatic attitude is an inevitable consequence of metaphysical speculation, i.e., of the belief that things are nothing. And Europe will have to assume this attitude to an even greater degree if it is to remain faithful to its own metaphysical essence. But if truth brings the conviction of the nothingness of things to their setting, then the solutions, past and projected, to the problems of European civilization will be revealed for what they are: illusions.

And yet—it is through European civilization that man's salvation must pass, for *Europe* is the locus of the mortal sickness of man. The great Oriental civilizations developed outside of European nihilism not because the Orient is the dominion of truth, but because it did not reach the fork where the "path of Night" (*nuktos keleuthos*, as Parmenides called it), travelled by European civilization, branches off from the "path of Day" (*ematos keleuthos*), where history grows in the light of truth and which has not yet been travelled by men. The Orient was not saved: it had not yet reached the place where salvation or perdition is decided. The Orient is not health; it is the state that precedes sickness. Europe has sunk into the deepest alienation precisely because Europe alone, in the history of man, attempted to testify to the truth of Being. Europe is blind because Europe alone attempted to look at the sun. Man must pass through this blindness, he must travel to the end of the path of Night, for truth at last to illuminate his gaze. We do not know if this be man's portion, but if travelling the path of Day is in fact part of his destiny then this road is open to him only because Europe, turning toward the truth of Being, was blinded by this truth and took up the burden of essential alienation. Europe alone thought the meaning of the "thing" in relation to the meaning of Being and Nothing. But Europe did not lose its way because it established this relation, but rather because it separated things from Being, entrusting them to Nothing (thus initiating a development that has led to the very refusal, so widespread in contemporary philosophical culture, to recognize as meaningful the words "Being" and "Nothing"). The setting of nihilism is the setting of the European meaning of the "thing," but it is the *repetition* of the attempt (which is what Europe essentially is) to testify to the meaning of Being. Europe must set, for the voice that called it to be heard. Will Europe be able to hearken to this voice?

2. TIME AND ALIENATION

"Happy the man who can say 'when,' 'before,' and 'after'!" So writes Robert Musil in *The Man Without Qualities*. In *De Interpretatione* Aristotle conveys his own conception of bliss: "When what is, is, it necessarily is; and when what is not, is not, it necessarily is not. But it is not of necessity that everything that is, is; nor that everything that is not, is not. That everything that is necessarily is, when it is, is not the same thing as being purely and simply of necessity. The same must be said as regards what is not" (19 a, 23–27).

"What-is" is *to on*, being [*ente*]. The participle *on* indicates not simply "is" (*estin*), but, precisely, *what-is*, the synthesis of a certain determination (e.g., house, star, man) and its Being [*essere*]. Accordingly, Aristotle's text states first of all that *when* (*otan*) *what-is*—say, a house—is, *then* indeed the house necessarily is; but not that it necessarily is *aplos*, *tout court*; i.e., the house does not exist of necessity. In fact, just as we say, "when a house is," so we also say, "when a house is not." A house "is not" when it has not yet been built, and when it has been destroyed. The phrase "when a house is not" means either "before it was" or "after it has been." Thus all the occasions of Musil's "bliss" are accounted for.

But this bliss now dominates the earth. Greek thought established once and for all the meaning of "when," of "before," and of "after," relating them to *Being* and to *not-Being* (to *estin* and to *me estin*). The whole of Western civilization grows within this rigorously consistent "bliss" (even when we think Greek ontology no longer concerns us). And yet it is the very symptom of alienation. In spite of everything, Western civilization still remains within the meaning that the Greeks gave to time. Indeed, time itself coincides with this meaning. But the aim of these pages is to recall, once again, the fact that *time* is the very essence of *alienation*. And the essence of alienation is *essential* alienation, infinitely more radical and infinitely deeper than any religious, economic, psychological, or existential alienation.

When a house is not, Aristotle says, it is *me on*, non-being. Western man is concerned with establishing that when what-is-not is not, it necessarily is not. But he leaves in the deepest and most unexplored darkness the meaning of the expression "when a house is not" (or "when a man, trees, stars, the earth, love, peace, war are not"). That which, when it is not, is not, is—for example—a house. When a house has been destroyed and has become something past, it is not. Normally one adds the word "longer," and says it "is no longer": but, indeed, that which is no longer is not (and that which is not yet is not). Thus it is *of a house and of men, of stars, of the earth, of love, of peace, of war*, that Western man says that they are past and therefore are not. But a house (and the other things said to "pass") is not a Nothing. A house is a place that shelters mortals from the harshness of the seasons—it is the openness of a determinate meaning: "house" does not signify "nothing" (the meaning in which a house consists does not signify "nothing"), and for this very reason a house is not a Nothing. In fact, Western man's very language draws a distinction between the phrases "when *a house* is not" and "when *a Nothing* (or Nothing) is not." Such language does not believe that it can replace the phrase "when a house is not" with the phrase "when a Nothing is not," precisely because it does not take to be a Nothing that which it affirms is not. And this means that Western thought affirms *of a not-Nothing* that when it is not, it is not: for this is affirmed *of* a house, *of* a man, *of* the earth, *of* what is past, *of* what is future. "When a house is not" means therefore "when a not-Nothing is not," which is to say, "when a being is not." In stating that it is not of necessity that everything that is—*to on apan*—is, Aristotle is in fact stating that some being can not-be. And it is *of this being* that, when it is not, one must say "when a being is not." To be a being means in fact to be a not-Nothing. Accordingly, in the Aristotelian affirmation "when what is not (*to me on*) is not, it necessarily is not," the term *me on* does not indicate Nothing and thus the affirmation does *not* mean "when Nothing is not it necessarily is not." In this affirmation the term *to me on* does not indicate Nothing—on the contrary, it indicates *not*-Nothing or *being* (in its happening to not-be), and therefore the phrase "when what is not is not" signifies "when a not-Nothing, i.e., a being (e.g., a house) that happens to not-be is not." Or: "when *being* that is not is not."

When a house, once destroyed, becomes something past (or when it is still something future), it is not. For Western man, what "passes" does not pass completely: something remains of what is past. Memories, traces, regrets, hates, consequences, effects—these remain. But not *all* of what is past remains. If everything should remain, then *nothing* would be past. What remains, we say, "is"; what does not remain "is no longer." When a house is no longer, something of it does not remain. Ruins and memories remain, but something does not remain, something "is no longer." For Greek thought and for the whole of Western civilization, saying that something "does not remain" and "is no longer" means saying that it has become a Nothing. It is true that from Aristotle to Marx the destruction of a house is not its total annihilation (precisely because something remains even after its destruction)—yet it is also true that, for Western thought, with the destruction of a house at least *something* of the house has to become a Nothing. At least the unity and form that the materials of the house possessed, when the house was, become a Nothing, as does the unique atmosphere created by this unity and form. When a house is not, something of the house (at least the specific unity of the materials of which it was made) has become a Nothing. And it is of this very *something* become a Nothing that we are thinking when we say, "when the house is not." Thus for a house to be destroyed and become something past and be no longer, at least something of the house must become a Nothing. If *nothing* of the house became a Nothing, Western man would not even say that the house has been destroyed, that it is past, that it is no longer. And this something that belongs to the house, once again, is not a Nothing, but is *being*—it is the specific unity of the atmosphere and materials of the house that was destroyed. It is this *being* that, when a house becomes something past, becomes a Nothing. In saying "when a house is not," by the word "house" language does not refer to that which remains of the house (ruins, memories), but rather to that very *something*, to that *being* which becomes nothing and which is less a something that belongs *to* the house, that is part of the house, than it is the *house itself* as a specific and irreplaceable mode and atmosphere of dwelling.

"When a house is not" means therefore, "when a being is nothing." The phrase "when the sky is blue" contains the affirmation "the sky is blue." And thus the phrase "when being is nothing" contains the affirmation "being is nothing." If one asks a Western man if being (a house, a man, a star, a tree, love, peace, war) is nothing, his answer will most certainly be *no*, being is not a Nothing. Yet for more than two thousand years he has continued to say of being, "when being is not," and he goes on thinking that being is nothing. And he continues to experience being as if it were a Nothing. If someone were to say, "when the sun is the moon" or "when the circle is square," "when stones are birds" or "when even is odd," anyone in the West would immediately respond that this "when," a time in which the sun is the moon and the circle is squared, stones are birds and even is odd, is not possible. But this sense of the absurd does not prevent him from thinking, "when being is nothing"; it does not prevent him from thinking *that* being is nothing. That bliss which Musil praised (but the whole Western world is of one mind in praising it) rests on the conviction that being is nothing. "Before" means "before being is," and one can say "before being is" when being is not (yet), or when it is nothing; and "after" means "after being is," and one can say "after being is" when being is no longer, or when, once again, it is a Nothing. The belief that *time is*, postulates the faith that *being is nothing*. Time can exist, in fact, only if a "when being is not"—a "when being is nothing"—exists; therefore time can exist only if being is nothing. The nothingness of being is *nihilism*, and nihilism is essential alienation. Western civilization grows within the belief that being is *in time* and thus is *nothing*.

All this seems, to the eyes of Western man, to be based upon pseudo-intellectual subtleties. He objects, "When being, by becoming something past, has become a Nothing, it is a Nothing. When it is nothing, it is nothing. Hence it is not true that, in positing a time when being is not, one thinks that being is nothing." When being is nothing, it is nothing, he says. But essential alienation consists in the very faith that there exists a "when" it—namely, being (!)—is nothing. Western man establishes an identity between the Nothing and the "when" (that is, the time in which) being is a Nothing. But this apparent identity between Nothing and Nothing conceals the identity between *being* and Nothing—the identity that constitutes itself when one accepts *time*, the "when being is nothing."

It is believed that *tempus* and the *templum* alike are a *temnein*—a *separating* of the sacred from the profane. But *tempus* is a separation abysmally more radical than the separation of the sacred from the profane. *Tempus* separates beings from their Being, it separates the "what" from its "is." Only on the ground of this original separation can one conceive that a "when" being (the "what") is united *to* Being, and a "when" being is separated *from* Being (i.e., a "when being is" and a "when being is not"). Original separation of being from Being, as the essence of time, shows that being, as such, is a Nothing: to not-be a Nothing it must be united to that Being from which it was originally separated. In testifying to this fundamental meaning of *tempus* (the Greek *chronos* still echoes the word *krinein*, i.e., to separate), Greek thought brings to light the hidden, implicit ground upon which the separation of the sacred and the profane rests in archaic pre-ontological (i.e., pre-Western) civilizations; while in Christianity the fundamental meaning of *tempus*—the Greek meaning of time—becomes the explicit ground of the separation of the sacred from the profane. It is because being—a stone, a tree, a star, a man's life, the earth—is originally separated from Being and is lived out in this separation, it is because being is lived out in *time* that it finds itself abandoned to nothingness and goes in search of a source, an *axis mundi*, a god, something sacred, or a *kerygma* that guarantees its anion with Being. It is because man lives in time—which is to say, in essential alienation—that he builds *templa* and evokes the sacred, be it the cosmic sacred or the historical sacred of the Christian *kerygma*. But it is also because man lives in time that he entrusts his salvation to modern science and the technology to which it gave rise, when he realizes that the sacred cannot save him from nothingness. The sacred and technology are the two fundamental ways in which the inhabitant of time, i.e., of essential alienation, seeks his own salvation, or seeks to save that being, which is his world and his life, anchoring it to Being. But such salvation is impossible—for it does not transcend alienation, but rather attempts to survive within it. Since inhabiting time means separating being from Being, to will this separation is to will the impossible (because *that being is not*—i.e., that being is nothing—is the epitome of impossibility, and salvation is impossible precisely because it is the will to survive within impossibility). And yet it is this "will to the impossible" that, as techno-scientific will, now dominates the earth.

Paul Ricoeur, among others, has attempted a "mediation" between the cosmic sacred and the Christian *kerygma*, in contrast with the program of demythologization and desacralization of the Christian message and the separation of religion and faith. This program is based on a recognition of the fact that science has destroyed the universe of myth. But, for Ricoeur, if science has eliminated the sacred from the modern world, the ideology of science and technology has now itself become a problem. And he finds allies for his thesis in Heidegger, Marcuse, Habermas, and Ellul. Referring to Habermas—for whom "the interest of empirical knowledge and the exploitation of nature is limited to that of practically and theoretically controlling the world of man," so that "modernity takes the form of the boundless extension of a single interest at the expense of all others, and above all at the expense of an interest in communication and liberation"—Ricoeur affirms that "modernity—i.e., techno-scientific ideology—is neither a fact nor a destiny: it has become an open question."[4]

But if time is the essential alienation in which the existence of mortals grows, then the techno-scientific domination of being and the consequent destruction of every mythical universe and of every *kerygma* is not only a fact, but is the *destiny* demanded by the essence of time. For the inhabitants of time, "modernity" is objectively a *closed* question, even if some among them cling to the illusion of being able to open it.

For the Time-dwellers, time is "original evidence." It is "evident" that the beings of the world are that of which it must be said "when it is" and "when it is not," or "when it is not a Nothing" and "when it is a Nothing." Being is that which issues from and returns to nothingness. When being had not yet issued from nothingness, it was a Nothing; when it returns there, it is a Nothing once more. But only because being is in *time*—only because being is thought and lived out as a Nothing—can the project of guiding its oscillation between Being and nothingness arise. Only on the basis of *time* is *domination* of being possible. And, in the openness of time, the birth of the project of dominating and exploiting being is not only possible, but is inevitable. Inhabiting time is the very essence of this project. Time is in fact that separation (*temnein*) of being from Being, which takes possession of being as that which can be assigned to Being (from which it was originally separated) and to Nothing, confronting it in its availability to the decision that so assigns it. With this separation being becomes an absolute availability to the forces that tear it away from and thrust it back into nothingness. The will that being be time—the will that wills that the meaning of being be time—is the original form of the *will to power*. The original will to power, which takes possession of being, separating it from Being and making it available to domination, is the very will to guide and control being's oscillation between Being and nothingness. The will that drives its domination of being to the point of identifying it with Nothing—driving it to the remotest distance from itself—is the original project *destined* to be realized as techno-scientific domination of being—the domination that destroys the domination of being attempted through sacralization of being, religious invocation, and Christian faith. In fact, the will to power first dominates being by conjoining it with the sacred and the archetype, i.e., with the source of Being. Eliade, who is a point of reference for Ricoeur, recognizes the fact that if archaic languages lack such terms as "Being," "non-Being," and "Becoming," the *thing* [the fact] of "Being," "non-Being," and "Becoming" is nevertheless present. And the "thing" is that beings (both human and nonhuman) become sacred only insofar as they participate in the Being of an archetypal world that transcends them. Removed from this participation, beings become "the profane world" that, as Eliade says at the beginning of *The Myth of the Eternal Return*, "is the unreal par excellence, the non-created, the nonexistent: the Nothing." The will to power dominates being by immersing it in the sacred, i.e., in Being. But Eliade maintains that for archaic man the immersion of being in the sacred is cyclical and that this cyclical return of being to the sacred "betrays an ontology uncontaminated by time and Becoming." Nevertheless, the return to the sacred—the will to be as the archetypes are—is, for Eliade, the way in which archaic man "opposes," "endures," and "defends himself" against *history*. It is, in short, his way of dominating "history." But "history" is time. Precisely because Eliade's archaic man accepts time—and so lives in essential alienation—he attempts to defend himself against time and to master it through identification with the archetype. It is because he is an inhabitant of time that he attempts to master time both by fashioning an ontology not dominated by time and Becoming, and by restoring being to the original world of the sacred. The same thing occurs in Christianity and in all the formulations of Greco-Christian theology. The opposition affirmed by Eliade between archaic man's anti-historicism and Christian man's historicism remains within the acceptance of time. It is because mortals have separated, implicitly or explicitly, being from Being that man has need of God (or of revolutionary praxis, or of technology)—that is, of a *ground* of being. Jesus wishes to save man and give him eternal life because Jesus too is an inhabitant of time and sees around him only beings abandoned to nothingness and thus in need of salvation. The search for salvation (which is one and the same with the project of dominating being) is an expression of the essential alienation of man. When men such as Bultmann or Bonhoeffer demythologize the Christian message and separate faith from religion, they too inevitably remain within this alienation. Their endeavor is based on the consciousness that the sacred is powerless to dominate being, and that salvation (domination of being) must be pursued in some other way.

For success, power, and the domination and exploitation of being is the destiny of whoever dwells in time. To dwell in time is to dominate, and domination demands the destruction of every form of domination that proves to be powerless. Science and modern technology have shown the impotence of the domination of being through union with the sacred and with God. The power of technology has shown the impotence of the sacred and of God, just as it has shown the impotence of every ideology that, like Marxism, purports to dominate the earth. For the Time-dwellers, "modernity"—techno-scientific power—is the destiny of the West. The openness of time is the original power, and the logic of power requires that every power fall before a power more powerful. That the interest constituted by theoretically and practically controlling man's environment should expand at the expense of all less powerful interests, such as those of communication and liberation (this is Habermas's critique, taken up by Ricoeur)—this *de facto* encroachment of the will to mastery is itself the irrefutable *reason* why the interest constituted by techno-scientific will to mastery is destined to destroy all other interests. To inhabit time is to inhabit the logic of power, and this logic decrees that the force which is *in fact* more powerful is destined to dominate every other force and alternative interest. Spirit, human dignity, values, brotherhood, love, liberation, morals, politics, the sacred, God, Christ—all the forms of Western civilization matured within the acceptance of time—have progressively proved to be powerless when confronted by the power of technology. They have proved to be impotent forms of the will to power. Their destruction is therefore not only a fact to be recorded, but is the destiny that can no longer be avoided since mortals dwell in time.

The triumph of technology is the triumph of nihilism. Much of contemporary culture recognizes this fact. But Western culture has not recognized the essential *meaning* of nihilism. Ricoeur affirms that "both the scientistic illusion and the retreat of the sacred ... derive from the same forgetfulness of our roots. In two different but converging ways, *the desert grows.* What we are on the point of discovering, in spite of techno-scientific ideology, which is also military-industrial ideology, is that man is absolutely not possible without the sacred ... man must not die."[5] But why must man be possible? Why must man not die? It is clear that Ricoeur is speaking of man in terms of value; but why must this value not die? Since time is the meaning of being, the essence of being is its potentiality for being destroyed and constructed, created and annihilated. Since being is availability to Being and nothingness, being (and thus also man) is destined to be manipulated, violated, and exploited by gods, masters, and technologies (as B. F. Skinner's *Beyond Freedom and Dignity* attests). Technological power and the destruction of the sacred and of the *kerygma* do not imply forgetfulness of our roots, since our roots are our dwelling in time, and science and technology are the most rigorously consistent realization of this dwelling. To be sure, the desert grows. But the desert is time and the destiny of this growth is techno-scientific domination of the earth. All the Time-dwellers who, with Heidegger, Adorno, Marcuse, Habermas, Fromm, Ellul, Ricoeur, and many others, belong to the culture that condemns technological civilization—all those who seek to oppose the desert's growth and to defend man and his dignity inevitably fail, since they are not true to their genuine roots (that is, to essential alienation)— since they are not consistent with the essential belief that envelops them. Their aspirations and projects for a more human world are the wreckage that the desert's relentless growth leaves behind. Philosophy,

---

5   Ricoeur, ibid.

Christianity, Marxism, art, are the colossal wrecks of this ever growing desert.

Just as one cannot combat a disease by restoring the physiological conditions that originally caused it, so one cannot oppose the desert's growth by returning to traditional or archaic forms of human civilization. Essential alienation appears only insofar as does truth, with respect to which alienation is and shows itself as such. Parmenides, the most misunderstood thinker in the history of man, took the first step in testifying to truth when he said: "You shall not sunder Being from its connection with Being" (*Ou gar apotmezei to eon tou eontos echesthai*, Fr. 4). But Parmenides' testimony remains a presentiment. The gaze that sees the desert growing and that sees its authentic meaning does not belong to the desert. In this gaze being—each and every being, from the most humble to the most solemn and exalted—is originally linked to Being. In this gaze *all* things share the nature of the sun, whose existence continues to shine even when nightfall hides it from our eyes. The Time-dwellers created both the gods and the jealousy of the gods: the gods are jealous because they kept for themselves that unity with Being which is the property of *every* thing. In this gaze every being is eternal (*aion*, i.e., *aei on* or united immediately to *estin*), and the variation of the world's spectacle, the appearing of variation, is the rising and setting, the showing and the hiding of *the eternal*, in every way like the sun.

But this opens up another aspect of the question, developed elsewhere: the discourse on the hermeneutics of the appearing of Being. Here I can merely indicate its general course by saying that the belief that time is evident—the conviction that time *appears*, that the separation of being from Being *appears*—belongs itself to that essential alienation which is what time is. The Time-dwellers believe that time, the "when things are not," is *visible, manifest*. But for them it is unquestionable that when a being—say, a house—is not, not only has it become a Nothing, but it also ceases to *appear*: when a house has been destroyed and is no longer, it no longer *appears* either, to the extent that it no longer is. But this means that *on the basis of Appearing we cannot know anything* about that which, "having become a Nothing," no longer appears. In "being destroyed" and "becoming a Nothing," the house leaves Appearing; and Appearing, as such, shows and says nothing about what befalls a being that has left its horizon. Therefore having been a Nothing (when the house is not yet) and becoming a Nothing once more (when the house is no longer) cannot appear. The nothingness of being—namely, *time*—is not something that *appears*, it is not itself a "phenomenological" content. The belief that time appears is therefore the result of a hermeneutics of Appearing that, on the ground of the will that being be nothing, wills that the nothingness of being be something visible, manifest, and evident.

Outside of essential alienation, that which appears is being—immutable, the eternal. The eternal enters and leaves Appearing, just as the sun—which shines eternal—enters and leaves the vault of the sky. When being leaves the vault of what appears, Appearing keeps silent about the fate of the being that is hidden (and "when" assumes an unheard-of meaning). But the Erinyes of truth (*Dikes epikouroi*) of whom Heraclitus speaks (Fr. 94) catch up with what is hidden and remind it of its destiny: the Necessity, the *Ananke* that it remain united to its Being.

PART ONE

CHAPTER I

Returning to Parmenides

1. THE SETTING OF THE MEANING OF BEING

The meaning of Being, first glimpsed by the most ancient of Greek thought, has been progressively altered, distorted, and thus forgotten throughout the history of Western philosophy. But nowhere in this history is the alteration and forgetting less conspicuous than in the history of metaphysics itself. For metaphysics, in explicitly professing to uncover the authentic meaning of Being, calls our attention to, and exhausts it upon, the plausibilities with which the altered meaning imposes itself. Yet the history of philosophy is not, on this account, a succession of failures: we should say, rather, that philosophy's greatest achievements and conquests have occurred within an inauthentic understanding of Being.

In saying this, however, we allude to something radically different from the Heideggerian interpretation of the history of Western philosophy. The difference is radical, because Heidegger's thought is itself an alteration of the meaning of Being, and a no less serious one. For him, the most ancient of Greek philosophy saw Being as "presence"; that is, as the opening of a horizon within which each determinate feature of being can manifest itself. The direction of idealist historiography is thereby reversed. For idealism, the horizon—the "actualist" would say the thought, or the "act"—is the culmination of the development of philosophical knowledge. Yet that which is a result for the idealist is, for Heidegger, the beginning: the dazzling beginning which soon pales and abandons the field to the metaphysical-theological mystification of Being, where the horizon of any manifestation of being itself becomes a being, albeit the *Ens supremum, das Seiendste.*

The arbitrariness of Heidegger's reading is, today, unquestionable. This does not mean, however, that one should embrace that other dogmatism, which holds that Greek philosophy never became aware of the horizon of presence (it remained, that is, in a situation where thought sees Being, but does not see itself)—it means, rather, that the attempt to discern at the very dawn of Greek thought an identification of the meanings of "Being" and "presence" is historically untenable. There is, no doubt, an interweaving of the two; but, by the same token, there is also their difference. And yet the most essential—and most forgotten—word of all our knowledge is hidden in the few verses of Parmenides' poem. To rediscover it, what is called for is not the philological shake-up to which Heidegger's interpretation aspires, but rather a far more profound and arduous one: a shake-up that will allow us to understand the invincible force of a discourse which, while known and articulated for millennia, is in fact no longer understood. It is not a matter, then, of giving words new meanings (as if by tracing "Being" back to "presence" we might find ourselves before something more evident than Being), but of thinking the old meanings, of reawakening them, and in this sense, certainly, of replenishing them from their deepest sources.

Being is, while Nothing is-not (*Esti gar einai, meden d'ouk estin*, Fr. 6, v. 1–2). The words, which return in various guises throughout the poem, are always the same. Yet the great secret lies in the plain statement that "Being is, while Nothing is-not." Here, what is indicated is not simply a property of Being—albeit the fundamental one—but rather its very *meaning*: Being *is* that which is opposed to Nothing, it is this very opposing. The opposition of the positive and negative is the grand theme of metaphysics, but in Parmenides it lived with an infinite pregnancy that metaphysical thought no longer knows how to penetrate. Parmenides' "simple" opposition between Being (understood as what-is) and Nothing (understood as what-is-not) is, in fact, ambiguous; and this ambiguity gave rise to the prolific development of concepts that led Plato and Aristotle to their reflections on the positive and negative. "Ambiguous," we say, because the "simple opposition" can be understood (as, indeed, it was always to be understood) as a law—the supreme law—that governs Being, but that does so—and *here* we are at the heart of the labyrinth—only *as long as* Being is. "As long as Being is": the ambiguity has already become fatal. The meaning of Being has already set. But at sunset, as Plato well knew, shadows become particularly prominent and true to life. Where, then, is the ambiguity? Being is opposed to Nothing; but it is clear that such an opposition is possible only if, and only when, Being *is*; because, if it is-not, it is nothing and so is opposed to nothing. This discourse of the setting of the meaning of Being finds its strictest and most explicit formulation in Aristotle's *Liber de Interpretatione*: "Being necessarily is, when it is; and non-Being necessarily is-not, when it is-not. Nevertheless, it is not of necessity that all Being is, nor that all non-Being is-not. That everything that is necessarily is, when it is, is not the same as being purely and simply of necessity. The same must be said as regards non-Being" (19a 23–7). In this clear light of the setting sun, Parmenides' words themselves cannot but appear equivocal: "Being is": yes, but *when* it is; "non-Being is-not": yes, but *when* it is-not. Let us not confuse the necessity that Being is, *when it is* (*to on einai ex anankes ote estin*), with the necessity *sempliciter* that Being is (*to aplos einai ex anankes*); nor the necessity that non-Being is not, *when it is not*, with the necessity *simpliciter* that non-Being (the things that are-not) is-not! Parmenides failed to see this distinction.

Yet in this discourse the meaning of Being has already been lost: the very clarity of the discourse itself testifies that the break is irremediable. For the struggle between Being and Nothing is not like those fought in ancient days, when armies made war by day, while at night the enemy leaders drank together in their tents—enemies, therefore, *if* and *when* they were on the battlefield. This was possible because, besides being enemies, they were also men. Being, however, is such an enemy of Nothing that even by night it does not lay down its arms: for if it did so, it would be stripped not of its armor, but of its very flesh. Let us look, then, at this Being, which is *when* it is. By day it is the enemy of Nothing: when it is (when by day it is on the field), it is opposed to Nothing; and Aristotle calls this opposition *pason bebaiotate arché*, *principium firmissimum*, "principle of noncontradiction"— that principle to which everyone (even the most obstinate antimetaphysician) in the end, more or less explicitly, assents. But then night falls: when Being is-not (when it has left the field), then it is no longer opposed to Nothing—because it has itself become a Nothing. Yet it is still governed by the *principium firmissimum*, because, when Being is-not, it is-not. Being's noncontradictoriness seems to be safeguarded—in the very act in which it is most radically and insidiously denied.

For this nighttime Being, this Being that has left the field, is the Being that has left *Being*. But what, then, *is* it? In the phrase "when Being is-not," *what is the meaning of the word "Being"*? If we maintain that, when Being is-not, Being has become nothing, why do we continue to say "when Being is-not," instead of saying "when *Nothing* is-not"? But there is no difference whatsoever between a Being that is-not and a Nothing that is-not. And yet, we will not let the phrase "when Nothing is-not" replace the phrase "when Being is-not." We are unwilling to do so, because—despite the betrayal that is being perpetrated—we still intend to maintain that Being is not Nothing, the positive is not the negative. *But then*—and if there is a moment when the benumbed and torpid meaning of Being is to be roused, these words might be the occasion—*"Being that is-not"* when it is-not, is nothing other than Being made identical to Nothing, "Being that is Nothing," the positive that is negative. "Being is-not" means precisely that "Being is Nothing," that "the positive is the negative." Thinking "when Being is-not"—thinking, that is, the time of its not being—means thinking the time when *Being is Nothing*, the time of the nocturnal intrigue of Being and Nothing. That which the opposition of Being and Nothing rejects is precisely a time when Being is-not, a time when the positive is the negative.

"A time when Being is-not": in the failure to realize that assenting to the image of a time when Being is-not, one assents to the idea that the positive is the negative, Being itself has been brought to setting. What does "is" mean in the phrase "Being is," if not that Being "is not Nothing"? "Is" means "fights off Nothing," "conquers Nothing," "dominates Nothing"; it is the energy by which Being towers above Nothing. "Being is" means "Being is not Nothing"; saying that Being is-not means saying that Being is Nothing. Aristotle's argument (later to be repeated by Aristotelians and Scholastics, past and present) that when Being is, it is, and when Being is-not, it is-not, therefore states that when Being is Nothing, then it is nothing. But in this discourse, then, one fails to see that the real danger that must be avoided lies not in affirming that when Being is nothing, it is Being (and, when Being is Being, it is nothing), but rather in admitting *that Being is nothing.* The real danger lies in assenting to a time *when* Being is not Nothing (i.e., when it is), and a time *when* Being is nothing (i.e., when it is-not)—in admitting, that is, that Being *is in time.*

In this way, the "principle of noncontradiction" itself becomes the worst form of contradiction: precisely because contradiction is concealed in the very formula that was designed to avoid it and to banish it from Being. This *principium firmissimum* shuts the stable door after the horse has bolted. It is a judge who, guilty himself of more serious crimes, punishes misdemeanors which are not only unimportant, but which, in the end, no one really intended to commit.

The way of belief, which attends upon truth (*Peithous esti keleuthos [Aletheiei gar opedei],* Parmenides, Fr. 2, 4), posits instead that "Being is and may not not-be" (*opos estin te kai os ouk esti me einai,* Fr. 2, 3), and not-Being is-not "and not-Being shall never be forced to be" (*ou gar mepote touto damei einai me eonta,* Fr. 7, 1). This way diverges and departs from the path of night, "unfathomable" and "impassable" (*panapeuthea*), on which "Being is-not and necessarily is-not" (*os ouk estin te kai os chreón esti me einai,* Fr. 2, 5). But after Parmenides the impassable path was the sole route left to Western philosophy. What could be more plausible than positing Being in time, where—necessarily—it sometimes is, and sometimes is-not?

2. THE OCCASIONS AND THE FORM OF THE SETTING
(WESTERN METAPHYSICS IS A PHYSICS)

But for Parmenides, Being is not the differences that are manifest in the appearing of the world: the manifold determinations that appear are all merely "names" (*pant'onoma*). Parmenides, therefore, also bears the primary responsibility for the *setting* of Being. Since differences are not Being—since "red," "house," "sea" are not synonymous with "Being," i.e., with "the energy that repulses Nothing"—differences are not-Being, they are very much Nothing, which opinion (*doxa*) calls by many names. Thus the no-longer or the not-yet being of differences is no longer something that occurs on the impassable path: if "red"—say, the red color of this surface—is not "Being," then the phrase "when red (or when this red) is-not" no longer conveys a "sick" conception of Being, for it is now taken to be synonymous with the phrase "when not-Being is-not."

The Platonic distinction between not-Being as *contrary* to (*enantion*) Being, and not-Being as *other* than (*eteron*) Being, has been as fatal for Western thought as it has been essential and indispensable. For this distinction, which brings differences assuredly and definitively into *Being*, continues (just as Parmenides did) to leave them in *time*. But then, one must "set out"—and the way is yet to be concluded—in *search* of that Being which is outside of time.

Differences have to be taken back into Being, because if "red," "house," "sea" are not synonymous with "Being"—and this is unshakable!—they do not mean "nothing" either (i.e., they are not Being—and in this sense they are not-Being—but, at the same time, they do not mean "nothing," but rather "house," "sea," etc.). And if "red" does not mean "nothing" (or: if this red is not meaningful as "nothing," i.e., if its way of being meaningful differs from the way in which Nothing is meaningful), then Being must be predicated of it; it must, that is, be said that it is a repulsing of Nothing, that it is the energy that negates the negative. Being, accordingly, becomes the predicate of that which is *different* from it, not of that which is *contrary* to it: so that now the affirmation that not-Being (i.e., a determination) is, no longer means that the negative is the positive. Parmenidean Being has become the predicate of all determinations; rarefied positivity becomes the self-determining of the positive, the positivity of the determinate; no longer pure Being, but Being as synthesis (of essence—a determination—and existence—the "is"), Being as *on*, as Aristotle was later to call it.

Once differences (determinations) have been taken back into Being, Being—at least worldly Being—comes to be seen as that which, originally, can, and indeed must, not-be (at times, in time). For Parmenides differences are outside being, and therefore it appears legitimate that they not-be, i.e., that there be a time when they are-not (indeed, for Parmenides the time when they are is taken to be illusory). Plato, on the other hand, ineluctably shows that differences belong to Being; with the result that Being is presented as that which is-not: at least to the extent that the great stage of the world attests the coming-on and the going-off of determinations, and so attests the times when they are-not. Differences have been taken back into Being, but they continue to be thought just as Parmenides thought them: as something that can not-be, or as something of which it may be said "when it is-not." But in this way it is forgotten, once and for all, that Parmenides could allow determinations to not-be, precisely because he understood them *as not-Being*.

And so the occasion of the forgetting of the meaning of Being is provided by the Platonic-Aristotelian deepening of that very meaning. The irruption of differences into the area of Being draws attention to itself to such an extent that the very whole of the positive, or Being as such, comes to be originally conceived after the manner of worldly Being (after the manner, that is, of Being whose supervening and vanishing appears). But, it should be noted, this assertion has nothing to do with the threadbare accusations of physicism or of empiricism that have been raised against Aristotelian metaphysics. Aristotelian Being *qua* Being (*on e on*) is, unquestionably, *the transcendental*, i.e., the identity and unity *of the totality* of the manifold, just as Thales' water was intended to be. In this sense, not only is Aristotle not a "physicist," but neither was Thales. The determinations of Being *qua* Being belong, as we have said, to Being, not insofar as it is determined in a specific way (say, as sensible Being), but insofar as it is *Being*; that is, insofar as it is determinate positivity. Therefore, such determinations belong *to any* Being, they occupy the whole and do not stop at this or that particular dimension of it; and Being's transcendentality consists in this very occupation (in, that is, this overabundance with respect to the partial zones of which it is predicated and which, indeed, it fills).

In another sense, however, Aristotle must indeed be called a "physicist." But in this sense it must also be said that, after Parmenides, *all* Western metaphysics is a physics. Yet, once again, by this we mean something completely different from the analogous Heideggerian assertion. The irruption of the differences of the manifold into the area of Being led to a conception of the whole of the positive—or the positive as such—after the manner of the empirical positive (here lies the "physicism") *not because* after Parmenides metaphysical thought was unable to keep the whole explicitly in view, but because with the idea of Being that was to take shape after Parmenides, Being was seen as that which is, when it is, and which is-not, when it is-not (according, that is, to what one had occasion to observe regarding the differences that manifest themselves in experience). This idea, accordingly, left Being free to be or to not-be, and projected upon *all* Being observations made about the differences that had irrupted into Being; differences, indeed, that now are, but earlier were-not, and later, once again, will not-be.

Ontology, in this way, can no longer see *Being*—and Being, as such, is Being-that-is; and so this task has devolved to rational theology, which sets out on its wayward adventures. Contemporary Neoscholasticism has pointed out, quite rightly, that in Aristotelian-Thomistic metaphysics, rational theology springs directly from ontology itself: the very "reasons" for Being *qua* Being—it is said—lead to the affirmation of immutable Being (Being-that-is). But, as we have seen, ontology is forced to go further, in order to recover that which it has lost and which, moreover, constitutes the original "reason" for Being. Ontology sets out from an evirated Being which has "loosened its bonds" with Being (the Justice of Being, said Parmenides, does not unlock her fetters—*chalasasa pedesin*, Fr. 8, 14); its point of departure is a positive that is negative, and in its obtuseness to the meaning of Being it goes in search of that which it was unable to find within itself. That which it will find—immutable Being—is based on the most radical absurdity: namely, on the identification of the positive and the negative! And, to this day, all neoscholastic and neoclassical philosophies remain in this absurdity, though—unlike the other schools of contemporary thought—they do have the merit of explicitly undertaking to safeguard the opposition of the positive and the negative; to safeguard, that is, the non-contradictoriness of Being.

In this sense, then, we have to say that after Parmenides all Western metaphysics is a physics: because if the idea of Being upon which it is built does in fact think Being as the positive that is opposed to Nothing, it *also* thinks Being as something that exercises such opposition *only when* Being is. And so, it thinks *Being* as that which may not-be (!) (which may be *Nothing*), according to what befalls the differences that manifestly come-to-be.

If our age is to be the time of a return to the sources of the meaning of Being, we must be ready to receive the irruption of the differences of the manifold into the area of Being. This is the moment of greatest risk, since it means returning to the watershed where the truth of Being was originally diverted, and this time going down the other side, from where the true spectacle of Being is contemplated. To be ready to receive the irruption of differences! Differences—incontrovertibly manifest, no less than their supervenience and disappearance. The horizon of the manifestation of Being (the horizon of *phainesthai*) today opens up anew, at the end of a long process, cleansed of any naturalistic presupposition. (This purification constitutes one of the most significant episodes to unfold *within* the forgottenness of the meaning of Being.) That which manifests itself is not a subjective or "phenomenal" image of Being, but Being itself, which refers back to things just as they are in themselves. But, for this very reason, the ontological torpor of philosophies that today hold fast to and, indeed, purify the ancient concept of *phainesthai* is even greater and more pernicious. If Being is understood as that which stands beyond thought, the reason for the setting of the meaning of Being is clearer: Being sets because people have turned their backs on it. But the setting becomes all the more incurable and definitive the longer Being stands, in broad daylight, right before men's eyes, while they neither see its face nor grasp its meaning.

But then, if that which is disclosed is Being, is it not therewith incontrovertibly attested that Being is-not (when it is-not), and that therefore it is subject to the process of time? Does not experience attest precisely the opposite of what is prohibited by the truth of Being? And must not one begin, therefore, with that very neutralized Being (that Being which is opposed to Nothing only when it is, but which as such is indifferent to its being or not being) in which only the theological development of ontology has been able to discern immutable Being?

To this, we must immediately reply that if the aporia which has been presented here cannot, at present, be resolved, this does not mean that one may avoid it by abandoning the truth of Being and reproposing that concept of Being as indifference (to Being and not-Being) which to date has been the mainstay of Western ontology. One should, instead, take note of the radical aporia in which thought would find itself, torn between two equally intransigent calls: one should, then, take note of the reality of the absurd. But is the aporia really insoluble?

3. THE TRUTH OF BEING

Being, then, is not a totality devoid of the determinations of the manifold (as Parmenides held it to be), but rather the totality of differences, the area outside of which there is nothing, or nothing of which it can be said that it is not a Nothing. Being is the whole of the positive. And precisely insofar as there is consciousness of the whole (our discourse is witness to such consciousness), all manifest determinations—this sheet of paper, this pen, this room, these trees and mountains I see outside my window, things perceived in the past, fantasies, expectations, wishes, and all the objects that are present—appear as inscribed within the perimeter of the whole. Any determination is a determinate positivity, a determinate imposing on Nothing: determinate Being (being) [*essere determinato* {*ente*}]. This pen, for example, is not a Nothing, and therefore we say it is a Being; but it is a Being determined in such-and-such a way: this shape, this length, this weight, this color. When we say "this pen," this is what we mean. But—and here is the crux of the matter—if we say that this pen is-not, when it is-not, we are saying that this positive is negative. "Is" (exists) means "is not nothing"; and therefore "is not" means "is nothing." But—the rejoinder—this pen is-not, precisely when it has become nothing! When it is nothing, it is nothing! Language, however, in saying that a pen is-not, does not say that *Nothing* is-not; it says, quite precisely, that a *pen* is-not, i.e., does not exist. Indeed, it is *of* the great mass of "nonexistent" things (and, as things, they are determinate somethings) that one says, "they are-not." When a pen is nothing, it is, unquestionably, nothing. But what occurs when a pen is nothing? What does "when a pen is nothing" mean? It means by *no* means "when Nothing is nothing," but rather "when *a pen*—i.e., that positive, that Being that is determined in that specific way—is nothing"; it means, that is, "when Being (this Being) is nothing." Metaphysicians—the very men, that is, who claim to safeguard the positivity of the positive—have forgotten no less than this: that Nothing can be predicated only of Nothing; that "is not" can be said only of Nothing; that if the subject of a proposition is not Nothing, but is *any* determination whatsoever, then the predicate is "is," and is never "is not." The truth of Being uncovered by Parmenides is unshaken even after the Platonic "parricide" (which was the only deepening of the meaning of Being to be achieved by metaphysics after Parmenides); unshaken, that is, even when Being came to be thought not as "pure" Being which leaves determinations outside itself, but rather as concrete Being—as, that is, the positivity of determinations.

Therefore,[1] Being neither leaves nor returns to nothingness, is neither born nor dies; there is no time, no situation in which Being is-not. If it was nothing, it was *not*; if it should return to nothingness, it would *not* be (*Ei gar egent, ouk esti out ei pote mellei esesthai,* Parmenides, Fr. 8, 20). Parmenides posits the immutability of Being by means of this *single* consideration, which touches the very foundations of Being's truth: if Being comes-to-be (if it is generated, if it perishes) it *is not* (*ouk esti*). And this must be said of Being *as such*; whether, that is, it be considered as the totality of the positive, or as a plain and ordinary thing such as this pen. The young Socrates deserved reproach because he thought there could be no ideas of insignificant things (the hairs of one's beard . . .): which means, for us, that any thing, no matter how insignificant, if a thing, is eternal. This sheet of paper, this pen, this room, these colors and sounds and shades and shadows of things and of the mind are eternal—"eternal" in the essential sense attributed by the Greeks to *aion*: "that it is" (without limitations).

But, then, is it not manifest, does experience not attest that all these things "that are," earlier were-not and now already are no longer since they have given up their place to others? Is not Being that is manifest in fact manifest as coming-to-be, namely, as a process in which Being first was-not, then supervenes, and then vanishes again? Does not, then, experience attest that Being is-not—does it not attest the opposite of the truth of Being?

If at this point we continue to follow the truth of Being, it is *now* that the voice of philosophy is heard above all other voices as the most

---

1   For the exact meaning of this "therefore," cf. E. Severino, *La struttura originaria*, Ch. XV, 1st ed. Brescia: La Scuola, 1958; 2nd ed. Milan: Adelphi, 1981.

solemn and the most sacred. And the most *firm*, if it is true that philosophy, as the locus and guardian of truth, is true *science, episteme*, according to the original meaning the Greeks gave to this word (from *epistamai*): "that which lays itself upon, *that which imposes itself* and so has in itself the strength to assert itself, to repulse that which resists it, to stand *firm* in itself." Only authentic philosophy can impose itself in this way. *Everything* else (science, faith, common sense) is incapable of doing so.

Being, *all* Being, is; and so it is immutable. But Being that is manifest is manifest as coming-to-be. *Therefore* (which is to say, precisely because it is manifest as coming-to-be), *this manifest Being, insofar as it is immutable* (and it, too, must be immutable, if it is Being), *is other than itself* qua coming-to-be. Or again: therefore, *this manifest Being, insofar as it is immutable, hovers, in the company of all Being, over itself* qua *coming-to-be*. Or again: *therefore, the totality of Being* (and so also manifest Being, insofar as it is Being), *insofar as it is immutable, is gathered into and keeps to itself, thus forming a different dimension from that of Being* qua *coming-to-be*; forming, that is, the hospitable realm where Being is forever kept and sheltered from the assault of Nothing. Or once again (with our gaze always fixed upon the truth of Being): this green color of the plant outside my window is Being, and insofar as it is Being it is immutable, eternal (there is no time when it was-not or will not-be). But then, this "same" green color was born just now, when the sun began to illuminate the plant; and now, when I have moved my head and see it in a different perspective, it has already vanished. This "same" color (like the countless events that make up our experience) is therefore immutable, insofar as it is Being, *and* is manifest as coming-to-be. This means that the "same" (this color) *differentiates itself*; i.e., that *qua* immutable it constitutes itself *as* and *in* a *different dimension* from itself *qua* coming-to-be.

This difference, which is the authentic "ontological difference," is implied by the fact (for indeed it is a matter of *fact*) that "the same" is subject to two opposite determinations (immutable, coming-to-be), and so is not the same, but different (i.e., this eternal color is *not* this color that is born and perishes). Here, once again, the law of the opposition of the positive and the negative is at work, whereby the negative is not simply the pure Nothing (Parmenides), but is also the *other* positive (Plato). On the one hand (the forgotten side of the truth of Being), this law posits the immutability of Being; on the other hand, it posits the difference between Becoming and the immutable. Being was brought to setting not by the consciousness, in Plato, that the negative is also the *other* positive—on the contrary, this was the only step forward to be taken by metaphysical thought after Parmenides—but rather by the fact that this advance led metaphysics to *forget* that meaning (already grasped by Parmenides) of the opposition of the positive and the negative, for which the positive refuses to not-be, i.e., refuses to be nothing. (For in that other meaning, which was established by the "parricide," the saying that Being is-not—that Being is *not* its other and, therefore, is *not* other Beings—does most definitely belong to the truth of Being; indeed, Being is what it is precisely because, in this sense, it is-not.)

Everything that is present is therefore, *qua* immutable, different from itself *qua* coming-to-be. "Different *from itself*" signifies, here, that difference is not established between two positives, each of which is devoid of something that the other possesses. The realm of the immutable contains all Being, precisely because every Being, *qua* Being, is immutable. By this we certainly do not mean to say—nor can it be said—that the dimension of Becoming is therefore Nothing. We mean, *per contra*, to say that *all* Being, *all* the positive that crosses the inhospitable region of Becoming, is always already rescued from nothingness and always and forever sheltered and contained in the immutable circle of Being. *All* the positive, all that is positive in Becoming, *is*; it keeps to itself, in the "sincere land" that lacks nothing (*ouk ateleuteton to eon*, Parmenides, Fr. 8, 32), for if *anything*, i.e., any positive, were lacking, then that positive would not-be, i.e., would be negative. All the positive that supervenes and vanishes in Becoming dwells eternally in the company of the totality of the tension.

This is why it can be said that the immutable is "different from itself" *qua* coming-to-be and that Becoming is "different from itself" *qua* immutable: precisely because Becoming does not augment Being, but mirrors it. Plato, in fact, spoke in terms of imitation (*mimesis*) and of participation (*methexis*). But Plato's own calling to the truth of Being was betrayed by the Socratic distraction from truth. The doctrine that everything in this world has an idea that corresponds to it is rooted in the very truth of Being, for which any positive, even the most fleeting, has its permanent dwelling-place in the house of Being. But the gnose-ological-Socratic distraction led Plato to conceive the idea as the universal (which is the content of the concept), over against the indi-vidual (the content of sensible knowledge); and thus the house of Being became a refuge for survivors, an abode of phantoms. *Being* is immuta-ble not insofar as it is universal but insofar as it is *Being*, which means that every aspect of Being is immutable, the inimitable individual no less than the universal. The Platonic notions of imitation and participa-tion, like the emanatistic conception of the Neoplatonists and the crea-tionistic one of the Patristics and the Scholastics—these formidable determinations of Western metaphysics—are, then, the exclamations of a consciousness startled by the stifled voice of Being, whose truth it had forgotten. The start consists in keeping—or, more precisely, in return-ing—to the *result* reached by Parmenides, after the dualism of Platonic and Aristotelian metaphysics. Parmenidean Being (like the *apeiron* of Anaximander and the *polemos* of Heraclitus) lacks nothing: for Parmenides, the differences of the manifold have no positivity. But Plato's world of ideas and Aristotle's pure act (which is how they think immutable Being) do unquestionably lack a dimension of the positive: namely, matter, the cosmic root from which all sensible things are generated, which is not governed by the divine, but merely "persuaded" to transform itself from chaos into cosmos. The need to understand the immutable as the fullness of Being was precisely that which led the Stoics, Neoplatonists, Patristics, and Scholastics to posit the world's dependence—its absolute dependence—upon God. The immutable gives matter and the world their Being, for if they were to stand before it, independent and as its limit, then it—the immutable—would be deficient, would be open to a possible completion—would not, in short, be the immutable. If for Parmenides the immutable lacks nothing because the world is illusory, for Augustine and Aquinas the immutable lacks nothing because it contains all the world's positivity; and it can do so only on the condition that it set itself up as the free creator of the world. The affirmation of the immutable and of its ontological fullness is the call of the truth of Being, which Western metaphysics manages to hear through the mists of truth's oblivion. *Within this oblivion*, the process leading from Plato and Aristotle to Neoplatonism, Patristics, and Scholasticism has, without question, progressively purified the picture of Being of any contradiction. *Within* this forgottenness of the truth of Being, it is undoubtedly true that the law of the opposition of the positive and the negative is safeguarded only if one affirms the existence, the fullness, and thus the creativity of the immutable. But, as we have seen, here we have a truth that is enveloped in the forgottenness of truth; and so, rather than a truth, we have a *coherence*. And at the root of this coherence, an essentially *inauthentic* understanding of the meaning of Being is at work. The opposition of the positive and the negative is the driving principle, it is said, of classical metaphysics—the very principle that led to the creationistic conception of reality. "Being" means the positive that is opposed to the negative. But after Parmenides this positive, *as such*, is indifference to Being and to not-Being (=to existence and to nonexistence); a positive, therefore, that is understood as something indifferent to its being opposed to the negative—for admitting that Being is-not means admitting that Being is nothing.

The classical conception of the noncontradictoriness of Being is, then, contradictory. By no means, however, does it follow that modern and contemporary metaphysics (and modern and contemporary philosophy in general) are any better off. For, indeed, the stifled call of the truth of Being, which classical metaphysics still managed to hear, has grown progressively weaker—until today its very silence (the silence of our time) has come to be the decisive factor for an awakening and a return. A return that has the classical conception of Being not behind, but before it. Yet also this conception must be left behind, precisely because it, too, betrays the very thing it seeks to safeguard: the opposition of the positive and the negative, the noncontradictoriness of Being. Thus the results of classical metaphysics are based on a principle (the principle of noncontradiction) in which Being is contradictorily conceived, and are themselves, therefore, self-contradictory.

4. FORGOTTENNESS OF THE MEANING OF BEING IN ANY ATTEMPTED "DEMONSTRATION" OF NECESSARY BEING

The most dramatic aspect of this situation is that now thought *looks* for "necessary Being," attempting to *demonstrate* it. Does a necessary

Being exist? A Being, that is, of which it cannot be said that it is-not? The torpor of the meaning of Being leads one to question that which is the basis of any saying and thus also of any questioning. If one were to search for a noncontradictory Being and undertake to prove its existence, if one were to ask oneself, "Does a noncontradictory Being exist?," metaphysics would be outraged—and rightly so! Asking whether noncontradictory Being exists means in fact admitting the possibility that it not-exist, the possibility, that is, that Being may be contradictory. But the noncontradictoriness of Being is original, immediate knowing which, as such, does not tolerate even the possibility—the supposition—of its negation; for such a possibility implies the negation of that immediacy and originality [*originarietà*]. But what occurs when one *looks* for necessary Being? When one asks if it exists? When one attempts to demonstrate it? *Here* metaphysics (throughout the course of its history) has never been outraged—though it has had good reason to be! It began, instead, to seek what was right before its eyes. It sought, and is still seeking, necessary Being—which it has never been able to find, since it looks into the distance instead of looking close at hand. Seeking necessary Being means seeking the Being of which it cannot be said—in any circumstance, at any moment—"it is-not" ("it has gone away from—it might leave—it has not yet entered—existence"). But *here* is the great barbarity of thought—here, in asking, "Does a Being that cannot be said to not-be exist?," "Does a Being-that-is exist?" For with this one is asking, "Does a positive that is not the negative exist?"—one is *asking whether* the positive is negative and, in the asking, one admits the possibility that such is the case. Asking whether necessary Being exists means affirming Being's contradictoriness, its identity with Nothing.

And the *demonstration* of a necessary Being seeks and presumes to find a middle that joins the negation of the negative to the positive. "Being is not not-Being" (nor, indeed, is it a not-existing): the predicate, here, is the negation of the negative ("not-not-Being"), and as such it belongs *per se*, immediately, to the subject (Being). Affirming a middle between subject and predicate means not seeing the originality of this predication; it means, that is, problematicizing the very immediacy of truth and thus denying it. The demonstration of the immediate is not only a *petitio principii*, but is *negation* of the immediate, for if one feels the need of a middle, this means that the predicate is seen as something that, *as such*, can belong, or not-belong, to the subject; and if such is the case, then the negative is seen as something that, as such, can be identified with the positive (as, indeed, it can not-be so identified: but here we are interested in considering the circumstance in which the identity of Being and Nothing is allowed to subsist). Demonstrating that the positive is not negative means beginning with the identification of the positive and the negative. But in the proposition "Being is not not-Being," one denies not only that in certain cases the positive is negative: the negation is transcendental, i.e., it concerns the positive as such. So this *same* proposition also excludes the not-being of Being; it excludes, that is, any situation about which it can be said that Being is-not (and such a situation is *time*, in relation to which one mistakenly thinks it can be said, "When Being is-not"). So this proposition—which expresses the original truth of Being—excludes the existence of an unnecessary Being. Demonstrating that a necessary Being exists means demonstrating that Being is not not-Being, and thus beginning with the identification of Being and not-Being.

Thomas Aquinas sets forth five ways in which one can prove there is a God. In the third way, the existence of a necessary Being is proved as follows:

> If everything need not be, once upon a time there was nothing. But if that were true there would be nothing even now, because something that does not exist can only be brought into being by something already existing. So that if nothing was in being nothing could be brought into being, and nothing would be in being now, which contradicts observation. (*Si omnia sunt possibilia non esse, aliquando nihil fuit in rebus. Sed si hoc est verum, etiam nunc nihil esset: quia quod non est, non incipit esse, nisi per aliquid quod est; si igitur nihil fuit ens, impossibile fuit quod aliquid inciperet esse, et sic modo nihil esset: quod patet esse falsum.*)[2]

If everything were contingent, there would be a time (*aliquando*) when there was nothing. We do not intend, here, to discuss the correctness of

---

2   Thomas Aquinas, *Summa Theologiae* I, q. 2, a. 3, Blackfriars Edition.

this reasoning, but rather the *circumstance* (common to *all* metaphysics after Parmenides) in which the absurd (i.e., the identification of the positive and the negative) stands right before one's eyes and yet is not recognized as such. Likewise the affirmation *itself* that "*aliquando nihil fuit in rebus,*" or that "*nihil fuit ens*" (the affirmation, i.e., that Being is-not), is not seen to be absurd, but rather the *consequence* that stems from it; namely, the fact that even now nothing would exist, which is false (and it is unquestionably false) since Being is present in experience. And this consequence follows from the aforementioned affirmation of the strength of the principle that "*quod non est, non incipit esse nisi per aliquid quod est.*" Contemporary Neoscholasticism sees in this principle the foundation of classical metaphysics: *ex nihilo nihil.* This is correct, if by "classical metaphysics" one means that first phase of the setting of the meaning of Being, beginning after Parmenides and ending with medieval metaphysics—a setting which had already begun within the Eleatic school itself, with Melissus. He, not Parmenides, is the father of Western metaphysics; with Melissus begins that *betrayal* of Being by which metaphysics has come to dominate common consciousness, which deems it perfectly natural that things are-not (i.e., supervene and vanish). It is true that, especially today, one points to the yawning abyss separating the metaphysical-ontological outlook (the classical one in particular) for which nothing really begins and ends but everything has always existed in the divine substance, from the attitude of modern man, who does not contemplate or imagine Being, but produces and increases it. On the one hand, the contemplation of God; on the other, the practical construction of God. Yet this distinction is made from the standpoint of he who has already left the truth of Being behind. Contemporary praxism is rooted in post-Parmenidean ontology, for which Being, *qua* Being, is indifferent to existing or not-existing, and for which, therefore, one must go in search of a demonstration of necessary Being. To the extent, then, that one is not convinced of the value of the demonstration, one is left with that ontology—that notion of Being (common to Melissus, Aristotle, Hegel, Marx, Heidegger)—which allows one to affirm that Being is not an object of contemplation, but of an infinite praxis. Unquestionably, also for classical metaphysics the affirmation that the whole may be increased is an absurdity; yet this absurdity is ascertained within an ontology (an understanding of

Being) that itself represents the most serious breach of the noncontra-dictoriness of Being. In classical metaphysics only an echo of the truth of Being emerges: there remain the *results*, the mere façade of an edifice which is not only bereft of foundations, but which has deliberately been undermined. Satisfaction at the agreement about "results" is the great-est disservice that can be rendered to philosophy; for, in philosophy, not only do results count only for the way in which they are attained, but their very meanings vary according to the various ways of attaining them. Agreement about results is, in fact, agreement about different things, and is therefore disagreement. The malicious complacency which says that, after all, immutable Being exists no less for Parmenides than it does for Scholastic metaphysics, and the immutable lacks no positivity whatsoever, does nothing other than confirm the impover-ishment of philosophy in our time.

From Melissus on, classical metaphysics has founded the immuta-bility of Being (and so, *da capo*, necessary Being) upon the principle of *ex nihilo nihil*. However, this is *not*—as Bontadini would have it—Parmenides' principle, but belongs to that "classical metaphysics" which bears the primary responsibility for the forgottenness of the truth of Being. Melissus's Fragment 1 states: "Whatever was always was and always will be. If in fact it was born, before being born it must necessarily have been nothing; now, if it was nothing, nothing could have been born from Nothing, in no way" (*Aei en o ti en kai aei estai. Ei gar egeneto, anankaion esti prin genesthai einai meden. Ei toinun meden en oudama an genoito ouden ek medenos*). In these words, Western metaphysics finds the model from which it has never been able to break free—words in which the meaning of Being has already grown torpid: a torpor that is different from the one with which Aristotle was to reproach Melissus, because it is the very one that envelops Aristotelian metaphysics as well. For this torpid meaning, the *absurd* is that—if Being is-not (and, if it is generated, before being generated it must unquestionably not-be)—something is generated from Nothing. This torpid meaning is not even startled by the situa-tion in which *Being is-not* (*to on einai meden*). The darkness has already grown so thick that one no longer feels ill at ease in using the very words that indicate the *essence* of the absurd: Being is nothing. If I ask a metaphysician whether Being is nothing, "Good heavens, no!" will be his reply. But then, he has no difficulty whatsoever in admitting straightaway that Being is-not (*to on einai meden*), when, indeed, the situation presents itself in which Being (assuming it is generated) is-not (before being generated).

For Melissus and his countless legions of followers, the affirmation that Being is-not—which is to say, the affirmation that Being is nothing—*as such* does not yet contain those elements that would lead to its rejection: something else is needed. But Parmenides' discourse ends right here—it needs nothing else: Being is not born and does not die, because otherwise it is-not (before its birth and after its death). Melissus is no longer aware of the impossibility that Being not-be (that is, he no longer recognizes the identity between the statement that Being is-not and the statement that Being is nothing). Thus he comes to exclude the generation of Being not simply on the basis of the principle that, if it were to be generated, before being generated it would be nothing, but by *adding* that, if it were nothing, nothing could be generated from Nothing (*ouden ek medenos*). Classical texts have generally treated this proposition as something immediately evident. With the realization that it, too, must be further radicalized (but the perspective remains that of Melissus), the point of arrival is still the opposition between Being and Nothing: affirming that Nothing generates Being means attributing positivity to Nothing, which means, in turn, identifying it with Being.

5. SOME REFLECTIONS ON THE FORGOTTENNESS OF THE MEANING OF BEING IN NEOSCHOLASTICISM

Contemporary Neoscholasticism too is steeped in the forgottenness of the meaning of Being. Hegel, in a way, was more mindful of it when he noted that the principle of noncontradiction denies, as such, the becoming of Being. The Neo-Aristotelians, beginning with Trendelenburg, took great pains to show that the principle of noncontradiction in the Aristotelian sense is by no means the same as the principle of noncontradiction in the Parmenidean sense. And that is certainly true: but this truth in fact declares that the Aristotelian principle of noncontradiction is self-contradictory. Trendelenburg spoke of the "limit" of the principle of noncontradiction:

A is not not-A . . . The limits of its application in objective cognition derive from the very essence of the negation. Since the negation is never primary, but arises, as secondary, from the individual determination, the principle expresses nothing other than the right of the determination, which affirms itself. Hence a notion of A, usually consisting of a set of characteristics, must come first. *The principle can only defend this posited determination; it prescribes nothing about Becoming or genesis . . . If it is made into a metaphysical principle . . . it lacks ground and leads to contradictions.* It is a principle of the understanding that pins notions down . . . *Whoever, like the Eleatics, attempts to deny motion on the grounds that it contradicts this principle, is in error . . . Motion is motion, and not rest, declares the principle; but it says nothing more. Whether there can be motion or not, the principle cannot say.*[3]

Much ought to be said about this—radically incorrect—procedure, in which the determination is posited as prior to the negative relation it bears to its own negation. We, however, shall limit ourselves to saying that the authentic principle of noncontradiction, while unquestionably excluding that motion may be rest, does not stop there: it goes as far as that "more" which Trendelenburg and the Neoscholastics do not wish to accept. No doubt, in order to *see* this "more," a spell has to be broken—the authentic understanding of Being must reemerge; otherwise, the "more" is seen as something that "lacks ground and leads to contradictions"!

The opposition of Being and Nothing belongs to the truth of Being: not in the sense that Being presses upon something that resists it, but in the sense that, in the very saying that nothing resists Being, Being is thought in its relation to Nothing, and it is in this relation that it takes on meaning. The original *truth* of Being is the original *meaning* of Being. But the original truth of Being is not the simple opposition of Being and Nothing—it is the opposition of Being and not-Being, as the unification of that unchecked plurality of formulations of the "principle of noncontradiction" which is already rife in the Aristotelian texts.

---

3 Friedrich A. Trendelenburg, *Logische Untersuchungen*, 3rd edition, Leipzig: Hirzel, 1870, 174–5 (our translation, our italics).

It unifies the "logical" and "ontological" formulations of the principle as well. "Being is not not-Being" ("the positive is not the negative") is in fact the *universal*, of which the various formulations of the principle of noncontradiction are just as many *individuations*. When, accordingly, it is posited that A is not not-A, one excludes that that positive, that Being which is A, may be any of the determinations that are other than A, and indeed that are, with respect to A, the negative. In saying that motion is not not-motion (or is not rest), one is therefore saying, *in a certain way* (in this modality consists the individuation of the universality of the opposition of the positive and the negative), that Being is not not-Being. In saying that motion (or any given determination of the positive) is not nothing, one is saying—in a different way— that motion is not not-motion (for Nothing is, in its *own* way, a determination that belongs within the horizon of that which does not mean "motion"); and so, once again, one is saying *in another way* that Being is not not-Being. When one denies—and here is the "more" that Trendelenburg rejects, without realizing the force of what he is rejecting—that Being is-not, one is saying once again, *in yet another way*, that Being is not not-Being. The truth of Being is not exhausted in this or that modality of expression: precisely because it is the universal of this expressive plurality. But, precisely because it is the universal, it cannot relinquish any of its individuations, neither those recognized by Trendelenburg, nor the one that he (and everyone else) is unable to see. The denial of the not-being of Being is itself the prescription that Being not be born and not perish; it is itself the denial of Being's becoming.

If this relation between the universal and the individuation of the opposition is not held fast, even the traditional formulations of the "principle of noncontradiction" are self-contradictory. Saying, for example, that it is impossible to be and not to be (*idem simul esse et non esse, tauto einai kai me einai*) means accepting that *non esse* may be predicated of a positive: the predication *simul* of *esse* and of *non esse* is excluded, but one has no objection if, once the predication of *esse* is eliminated, *non esse* is left as the positive's only predicate. Likewise, saying that to affirm and to negate is not the same thing (*non est simul affirmare et negare*) means—if the object of the affirming and denying is Being, i.e., the existence of a positive—accepting the denial of the positive's existence: that this existence may be *simul* affirmed and denied is excluded, but one has no objection if it is only denied. And the principle of the excluded middle becomes an explicit declaration of the possibility of the not-being of Being: for that principle limits itself to the demand that it be affirmed of every being either that it is, or that it is-not. These formulations are self-contradictory if they are not maintained in relation to the universal opposition and, thereby, to the denial of the not-being of Being. Whereas if they are so maintained, the impossibility that the same may be and not-be—referring to the totality of Being *qua* immutable—indicates a *dual* contradiction: that the positive is and is-not, and that the positive is-not—where the second contradiction is part of the first. In other words: if in the exclusion that the same may be and not-be, one does not simultaneously think the fundamental contradictoriness (the positive is-not) which is included in the contradictoriness that is explicitly denied (the same is and is-not), then the *impossibile est idem simul esse et non esse* not only is not a transcendental principle (is not, that is, the law of all determinations), but is a false principle of the finite; it indicates the way in which the finite is noncontradictory from the standpoint of metaphysical thought. It becomes a transcendental principle and frees itself from the domination of metaphysics when, referring to Being *qua* immutable, it recognizes the fundamental contradictoriness which is included in the affirmation that Being is and is-not.[4]

Within the purview of Neoscholasticism—and not only the Italian variety—far and away the most rigorous position is that of Gustavo Bontadini. But Bontadini, too, works within the Melissian perspective. Indeed, he formulates it in the most radical way possible: the principle of metaphysics is given by the affirmation that "Being cannot be originally limited by not-Being"; since Becoming is precisely Being limited by not-Being, the totality of the real is not exhausted in reality-that-becomes. Here, too, the becoming of Being is seen as something that,

---

4 With reference to the concept of "individuation," it should be noted that individuation (i.e., the specificity or particular modality of the opposition) is established in a number of directions: the above-mentioned formulations of the principle of noncontradiction are individuations, as are the oppositions in which what is opposed to the negative is not the positive as transcendental or as a concrete totality of the positive, but rather as a particular field of the positive.

as such, does not manifest itself as contradictory: it is only seen as a manifest contradiction when *referring to something else*; which is to say, only if first it is seen as a negation (insofar as it is taken as the totality of the real) of the principle that Being cannot be originally limited by not-Being, and then it is seen that such a negation implies the identification of the positive and the negative: if not-Being were originally to limit Being, it would be a positivity (at least to the extent that it is able to check Being). But the positive is not the negative. Therefore not-Being does not originally limit Being. Therefore Becoming (in which Being is limited by not-Being) is not the original, but is transcended and limited by unlimited (immutable) Being. So in this discourse, too, the affirmation that Being is-not astonishes no one; and in thinking Becoming, one is brought up against just such an affirmation, since the becoming of Being (of *any* Being) means that first Being is-not and then it is, or that first it is and then it is-not. In Bontadini's discourse, too, that Being is-not (that the positive is the negative) is something perfectly natural for thought: Being becomes—which means "Being is and (then) is-not." So far—one thinks—so good, as yet there is no contradiction; in order to find it, further steps have to be taken. The principle that Being is not originally limited by not-Being must be introduced, and this principle must itself be brought back to the opposition of the positive and the negative. But this means bringing it back to that very opposition which was *denied* at the outset, and which was denied precisely because that notion of Becoming in which the positive is identified with the negative was allowed to pass as essentially noncontradictory. If one thinks the becoming of Being as such as noncontradictory, then the very contradiction that was to be superseded by the ultimate grounding of the exclusion that not-Being may originally limit Being is allowed to pass with impunity. Bontadini's discourse, too, is therefore contradictory, because in the notion of the opposition of the positive and the negative on which it is grounded, the positive is identified with the negative (precisely because here too one fails to realize that the affirmation that Being is-not is nothing other than the affirmation that Being is Nothing).[5]

---

5 Bontadini presents no analysis of the concept of "limitation." But it is clear that defining Becoming as being limited by not-Being can mean nothing else than

6. THE "VALUE" OF THE OPPOSITION OF THE POSITIVE AND THE NEGATIVE

But *why* can't this identity of Being and not-Being be affirmed? We shall dwell upon this question, since rarely has the noncontradictoriness of Being been dealt with at anything but a trivial level, whether by its defenders or its opponents.

Replying to this question means effecting the *authentic* unconcealment of the truth of Being, which is not a simple saying, but is a saying that has *value*; a saying, that is, capable of superseding [negating] its own negation (and so of superseding any particular form that negation may assume). The affirmation that Being is not not-Being must, unquestionably, be denied as long as its value is not seen. In the meantime, this affirmation is like an invincible sword in the hand of someone who does not know he has an invincible sword: such a swordsman will be struck down at the first encounter. And rightly so: a "truth" that cannot hold its ground is not a truth.

Philosophy is the locus, the guardian of truth. The original and absolute unconcealment of Being—indeed, the *truth* of Being—can occur only in philosophizing. And in authentic philosophizing. Anywhere else—in any activity or dimension that is not the original openness of the truth of Being—is a place of untruth (which is nevertheless the untruth of Being, its opening up in untruth). It is, moreover, the concern of philosophy, understood as the only thought of

---

that in Becoming, a certain dimension of Being is-not. First this sound was not there, now it is. Why is the transition from silence to sound a limitation of Being? Because once the existence of a sound has been established, it is thereby established that experience (the totality of immediately present Being), before the sound appeared, did not contain that positivity which is constituted by that sound, and therefore was, with respect to this positivity, something limited: precisely because it did not contain that positive that we now know to exist. Saying, therefore, that experience is subject to such a limit means that a certain positive (the sound) previously was-not and now is. And the totality of present Becoming is itself such a limitation of Being, precisely because the countless masses of positivity that earlier were-not, now are (or, conversely, that earlier were, now are-not: in which case, Becoming as limitation means that experience now proves to be devoid of that positivity which it previously possessed, and so, once again, proves to be limited with respect to this dimension of the positive). In thinking Becoming as a limitation of Being on the part of not-Being, one therefore thinks it as a process in which Being is-not; so that if it is allowed to pass with impunity as a noncontradictory concept, one effectively affirms—as we have said—the identity of the positive and the negative.

Being ("thought" in its strong sense, i.e., as absolute and incontrovertible knowing), to establish what relation all the other activities of man bear to Being, and it finds them all eccentric and impoverished with respect to the truth of Being. The man who lives out such activities does not live in truth, but in *doxa* (i.e., in untruth). Living them out in fact means keeping oneself closed off from the ground, and thus in groundlessness—precisely because one does not practice an absolute and incontrovertible knowing; so that whatever one asserts is unable to *impose itself* (is not *episteme*). To establish that something of the face of Being is effectively revealed in these eccentric activities (and that therefore, in this sense, they are "true"), Being's face must incontrovertibly emerge in philosophizing. Only then can it be said that in this or that "common" or "natural" conviction—in this or that form of consciousness—something is affirmed that belongs to Being. That there be *adaequatio* between such affirming and Being is only a presupposition or a faith as long as no incontrovertible thought of Being exists. Truth as simple *adaequatio intellectus et rei* refers back to truth as the incontrovertible manifestation of the *res*. This, however, is not simple phenomenological manifestation (as Heidegger would have it), but is that Appearing in which Being submits itself to the law that opposes it to not-Being. The "truth" of untruth (the adequation of eccentric activities to Being) is therefore possible only if authentic truth, authentic philosophizing, holds untruth before it and keeps it in sight.

In other words, convictions and forms of consciousness that are other than the absolute conviction and consciousness in which the authentic act of philosophizing consists can find their ground (in philosophizing) only insofar as they are subsumed in philosophizing and not insofar as they are lived out as such. Lived out as such—as we have said—they keep themselves closed off from their ground and so, as groundless, are mere opinions that can legitimately be denied. Their truth lives in them as something merely presupposed, as a faint-hearted truth that allows itself to be negated by its own negation. For a saying is undeniable only if one sees its ground; but insofar as the saying is inscribed in unphilosophical consciousness, that consciousness—by definition—does not see it in its ground (where unphilosophical consciousness—i.e., untruth—means nothing but the consciousness that does not see the ground, the value, the truth of what it says). In this consciousness, therefore, the saying exists as groundless—nor, as such, can it *be* grounded: for one does not ground the groundless, but rather that which in the grounding has become something else. Unphilosophical "truth" is therefore inauthentic truth, impoverished truth; it does not shine with its own light, but is a derivative phenomenon of truth. And philosophy, when it recognizes the "truth" of unphilosophical consciousness, neither consecrates nor sanctions this separation and detachment from authentic truth. Philosophy does not recognize the world, but demands its transformation.

How, then, must the opposition of Being and not-Being be thought, so that it may be seen in its truth? By thinking its *value*; which means, on the one hand, that the opposition is *per se notum*[6]—i.e., that the predicate (the negation of not-Being) belongs *per se* or immediately to the subject (Being) (so that the negation of opposition is negated, because it denies that which is *per se notum*, i.e., that which is the ground of its being affirmed); and, on the other hand, that the opposition is undeniable, because the negation can live *as* negation only if, in its way, it affirms the opposition. *This* is the formidable contribution made by the Aristotelian *elenchos*. If the opposition is, in *any* way, denied[7] and the negation is to *be* negation—is to hold fast as negation (i.e., as that specific negation which it is) and intends to deny in earnest and not be indifferent to its ranking as negation rather than as not-negation—then the negation *is opposed to* its negative; that is, it holds firm in that meaning for the sake of which it is negation, and differentiates this meaning from all other meaning: its positivity, its being meaningful as negation and as that specific negation which it is, consists in its differentiating itself from, and opposing itself to, its

---

6 Known by virtue of itself, through itself, on its own account (cf. Thomas Aquinas) [*Translator's note*].

7 The opposition can be denied either by saying that the positive is negative, or by saying that the positive is and is-not the negative, or in any other way in which the affirmation enters into synthesis with the negation. When one affirms that the positive is and is-not the negative, it is indeed true that the opposition is at once affirmed and denied, but, for this very reason, the opposition is denied insofar as it is posited as that which refuses to enter into synthesis, in any way, with its negation. Taking the opposition as a moment of such a synthesis means denying the opposition insofar as it refuses to be posited as such a moment.

negative (i.e., from and to all other meaning). In denying that Being is not not-Being, one must therefore *think* that the Being in which this negation consists is not not-Being (i.e., is not everything that is other than this negation). The negation is explicit, *in actu signato*, whereas the thought is implicit, *in actu exercito*: but it *is* a thought that one really *thinks*, a thought that must be realized, if one wants the negation to have that determinate meaning of negation which is proper to it and if one is not to remain indifferent to its having some other meaning.

But the Aristotelian *elenchos* must be more closely examined. First, it should be noted that the *elenchos* consists not simply in ascertaining that the negation of the opposition is also affirmation of the opposition, but rather in the ascertainment that the affirmation of the opposition, i.e., the opposition, is the *ground* of any saying, and so *also* of that saying in which the negation of the opposition consists. In all discourse and in all thought, the meaning that emerges in the saying and in the thinking is held fast in its difference from any other meaning, i.e., in its opposition to its own negative. If this opposition is not thought, no thought can constitute itself, not even that thought which consists in the negation of the opposition. In manifesting itself, that is, Being submits itself to the law opposing it to not-Being; in *any* manifestation of Being, be it in truth or in untruth—and so also in that paramount form of untruth, which is the explicit denial of truth. The opposition is the ground, in the sense that it is *that without which no* thought and *no* discourse could constitute itself or exist. It grounds its own negation as well: not, however, in the sense of making it be valid or grounding its value, but rather in the sense that if the negation did not base itself upon the opposition (that is, did not oppose its own meaningful positivity to all other meaning), it would not even exist. It exists, only if it affirms that which it denies. Indeed, denying, it denies its own ground, it denies that without which it would not *be* (or, which is the same thing, would not be *meaningful*): it denies itself. The negation of the opposition effectively includes the declaration of its own nonexistence, it supersedes itself by itself; it says, "I am not here," "I am meaningless"; and if this saying has meaning, it is only because, despite the explicit negation of the opposition (which is equivalent to the self-supersession of the negation), the opposition is held fast. The *elenchos* is precisely the ascertainment of this self-supersession of the negation;

i.e., it is the ascertainment that the negation does not exist as *pure* negation—as negation that, in order to constitute itself, has no need to affirm that which it denies. Saying that the opposition "cannot" be denied thus means ascertaining that, precisely because the ground of the negation is that which it denies, the negation consists in the negation of itself, in its superseding itself as discourse.

But a more thorough investigation into the meaning of the *elenchos* leads to the following series of considerations.

The assertion "Being is not not-Being" is the opposition *qua universal*—in the aforesaid sense of the term (i.e., it is the opposition between Being as transcendental and not-Being as transcendental, where "Being" means any positive, be it the totality of the positive or any moment of that totality). The assertion "this Being is not its not-Being" is an *individuation* of that universality. The *elenchos* shows that the negation of the universal opposition is (*in actu exercito*) affirmation of an individuation of the universal opposition. Such individuation consists in affirming that this Being (this meaningful positivity), in which the negation of the universal opposition consists, is not its not-Being. The denial of the universal opposition can be realized only if it implies, i.e., only if it bases itself upon, the affirmation of an individuated opposition between Being and not-Being (that is, only if it implies the affirmation that a certain positive is opposed to all its negative). The *elenchos* so understood does not show that the negation of the universal opposition implies and is grounded upon the affirmation of the universal opposition.

It seems, then, that whereas the *elenchos is* capable of showing that the negation of the opposition fails to be universal, precisely because there is a region in which the negation does affirm the opposition (and it is in this region that the negation holds fast as negation), it does *not* seem able to prevent the negation—insofar as it renounces its claim to be universal—from presenting itself as negation of the opposition with respect to everything that lies beyond that region. It would seem, that is, that the *elenchos* fails to prevent the negation of the opposition from re-presenting itself in the following way: "Beyond the region that is constituted by the negation and by its semantic implications, the positive is not opposed to the negative"; or, put another way: "Only in a limited region is the positive opposed to the negative, whereas beyond this region it is not so opposed. Such a region is constituted by the very discourse that denies the opposition of the positive and the negative in the residual region." In this way, the negation would no longer be grounded upon that which it denies, because that upon which the negation is grounded, i.e., that upon which its constitution depends, is the *individuated* opposition, which is now no longer denied by the negation. For, now, the negation limits itself to denying the opposition with respect to the area not occupied by the ground of the negation.

Yet, this conclusion rests upon a misunderstanding. This approach, in fact, fails to keep in mind that when the negation of the opposition, i.e., the affirmation of the contradictoriness of Being, renounces its claim to be universal, it does so *not* because it intends to supersede itself, but rather because it intends to posit itself in earnest, and thus as *non*contradictory, banishing contradictoriness from itself. Accordingly, we are faced here with something radically different from the universal negation of the opposition of Being and not-Being (or negation of the universal opposition). The Aristotelian *elenchos* effectively shows that such universal negation fails to constitute itself: for the very reason that it can constitute itself *only if* it is affirmation of the opposition (albeit of the opposition between a particular positive and its negative); and thus it denies both its own ground and itself. The *elenchos*, be it noted, does not say that the negation of noncontradictoriness is inadmissible because it is contradictory (since, in that case, it would presuppose the very thing whose value it has to show: namely, noncontradictoriness), but rather that such negation fails to live as negation, because in the act in which it constitutes itself as negation it is at once also affirmation. And so it is, most definitely, contradictory: but the negation is not superseded insofar as it is formally ascertained to be contradictory—the negation is superseded insofar as it is ascertained that it fails to posit itself as negation, unless it grounds itself upon that which it denies, and so only if it denies itself. The negation, failing to free itself from that which it denies, becomes its very bearer; not only does it fail to tear what it denies off its back, so that it can then hold it at arm's length and condemn it, but what it thinks it has before it and has condemned, actually stands behind it and directs all its thoughts, including the thought that announces the condemnation. The law of Being is the destiny of thought, and thought is always witness to this law, always affirming it, even when ignorant of it or when denying it.[8] The supersession of the negation is not, therefore, brought about by the negation's being shown to be contradictory (for the negation intends to posit itself precisely as an affirmation of contradictoriness), but rather by showing that the negation fails to live as pure negation (that is, as negation that is not grounded upon that which it denies): the negation is superseded insofar as it is shown to be self-supersession.

Now, when the negation, recognizing that it cannot live as pure negation, forgoes positing itself as universal negation and presents itself as limited negation of noncontradictoriness (i.e., as the affirmation that everything, except the positive consisting in the affirmation that some positive is not opposed to its negative, is not-opposed to its negative), then it, too, becomes a discourse that, not wanting to deny that upon which it is grounded, wants to be noncontradictory; the noncontradictoriness, here, being the very determinateness of the discourse. At this point, then, it is no longer a matter of showing the value of noncontradictoriness (i.e., of the opposition of the positive and the negative), but rather of seeing whether this way of understanding noncontradictoriness is effectively noncontradictory; of seeing, that is, whether this new type of negation, having set out to hold fast to its determinateness, manages to do so. We are no longer faced with an opponent of the principle of noncontradiction, but

---

8   In the word "destiny," which derives from the Latin *destinare*, do we not find the stem *stan* (*istano, istemi*), which forms the meaning of the word *episteme* (so that, for the Latins, *destinare* means also—or above all—*firmness* of conviction)?

[1981 note] With regard to the way in which the word *episteme* is employed in *The Essence of Nihilism*, it should be noted that, in the first chapters, it indicates, beyond its historical meaning, the "standing" [*stare*] of the destiny [*de-stino*] of truth. However, beginning with "The Earth and the Essence of Man" in *The Essence of Nihilism* (and in all my subsequent writings), *episteme* retains its most authentic Greek sense and indicates the will to keep open the immutable space to which everything that, in Becoming, leaves and returns to nothingness must submit [*sotto-stare* = stand under]. It indicates, that is, the first form, in Western history, of nihilism's deviation from the destiny of truth.

Analogously, the word "God" in *The Essence of Nihilism* indicates the immutable totality of beings, while in my subsequent writings it assumes its authentically historical meaning—i.e., that of being one of the dominant figures of the prehistory and the history of nihilism.

rather with someone who affirms it in a certain way; namely, as having a limited range. Thus in order to eliminate this limited affirmation we have but to show that it is contradictory, i.e., that it fails to be what it sets out to be. And this is so in several respects. Apart from the arbitrariness of attributing noncontradictoriness to that particular region of the whole which is itself nothing other than the partial affirmation of noncontradictoriness, we have only to observe that this affirmation divides the whole into two fields, in one of which (let it be C1) the positive is opposed to its negative, while in the other (C2) the positive is not opposed to its negative. Consequently, since C2 is the negative of C1 and vice versa, it is said (when the noncontradictoriness of C1 is to be prereserved) that C1 is opposed to C2, and (when the contradictoriness of C2 is to be posited) that C1 is not opposed to C2. The limited affirmation of noncontradictoriness is self-contradictory.

It is, however, possible for this limited affirmation to further limit itself, so as to avoid being self-contradictory in the aforementioned manner. If x, y, z is the content of C2, it *is* necessary, in order to maintain the determinateness of C1, that C2 should also be determinate— i.e., that it be opposed to C1, precisely because C1 is held fast in its determinateness, i.e., in its being opposed to C2—but it does *not* seem necessary for the determinations of C2 (i.e., x, y, z) to be opposed *to one another*: for the determinateness of C1, the determinateness of C2 with respect to C1 is requisite, but the determinateness of the terms that make up the content of C2 is not. If we give a concrete value to the variables x, y, z, it seems that judgments such as "man is trireme" (x is y), "red is green," etc., are not superseded by the *elenchos*, at least in the way it has hitherto been formulated. The negation of the opposition, now, not only renounces its claim to be universal, but consists in nothing other than the ascertainment that the determinateness of a particular field (whose confines have yet to be determined) can be exempted from the law of opposition (which, consequently, would no longer be a universal and transcendental law).

And yet the *elenchos*, in order to ascertain the self-supersession also of these self-contradictory propositions, need not alter its structure. If, in affirming that "red is green," one is in a situation where, effectively, no difference between red and green is known, present, or intended, then the law of opposition would be denied if one were to say that red is not green, and not by saying that red is green. For the opposition to be effectively denied, it is requisite that the difference—the opposition—between red and green should be known and affirmed, so that red, known as opposed to green, be denied as opposed to green. Here too, then, the affirmation is the ground of the negation of the opposition, so that the negation denies that without which it would not be negation, and so denies itself.[9]

The *elenchos* is the ascertainment of the *determinateness* of the negation of the opposition (where "determinateness" means nothing other than the positive's property of being opposed to its negative). This determinateness is proper *both* to the negation, considered as a semantic unity with respect to everything that is other than the negation, *and* to the single terms that make up the negation. If the negation does not remain distinct from its other, there is no longer negation; if each term of the negation is not distinct from every other term (as occurs when no difference is posited between red and green, i.e., when red is affirmed to be green), again there is no negation (for if the terms are not seen to be different, positing a difference between them would be a negation of the opposition). In order for there to be negation, the negation must be determinate, both with respect to its other, and in

---

9   It is interesting to observe that the negation of a content is always an affirmation, on a different plane, of this same content. If it is denied that this green surface is red, then this red surface, insofar as it is the object of the negation, is known, present, and thus is existent. But, indeed, it is present and existent in a *different* dimension from the one with reference to which the absence and nonexistence of the red surface is ascertained. If this red surface is not *affirmed* in that other dimension, it could not be *denied* in the very dimension with reference to which it is denied. Without this distinction between planes, it would occur here, too, that propositions ascertaining a content's absence from, say, the phenomenological plane, would be negations that are grounded upon the affirmation of that which they deny. But, be it noted, this distinction between planes is lacking in any type of negation *of the opposition*; such negation presupposes *sempliciter* the affirmation of that which it denies (that is, it does not limit itself to presupposing the affirmation insofar as such affirmation places itself on a different plane from the one in which the content is denied). This presupposing *sempliciter* the affirmation of that which is denied also occurs with regard to the negation of the immediately present content: the *elenchos*—but this question will be taken up elsewhere—works not only on the negation of the opposition of the positive and the negative, but also on the negation of the existence of the immediately present positive.

the terms that constitute it; and therefore it presupposes and is grounded upon that which it denies.[10]

From what has been said, it is clear that the *elenchos* works not only on the just-mentioned type of negation of the opposition, but also on the aforementioned type of limited negation, in which the opposition is affirmed in C1 and, at the same time, denied in C2. In this case, it is true that we are dealing with a discourse that wants to be noncontradictory (i.e., determinate), but which is superseded by simply showing it to be self-contradictory; but it is also true that the *elenchos* works on this type of discourse as well: and it does so by ascertaining that the denial of the positive's being opposed to the negative in C2 presupposes the affirmation of the opposition (for the same reason as that for which the denial of red's being opposed to green presupposes the affirmation of this opposition). In what follows, this will be considered in a context of greater theoretical scope.

In considering the determinateness of the negation concretely, it becomes clear that the negation can constitute itself as negation only if, on the one hand, as a semantic unity it is determinate with respect to its negative, and, on the other hand, if the terms that constitute it are themselves mutually determinate. The concrete consideration of this determinateness makes it possible to formulate the *elenchos* in such a

---

10   This occurs also when the form taken by the negation of the opposition is not "the positive is negative," but rather "the positive is and is-not the negative" (or other forms of this sort). In fact, as we have mentioned, this second form of negation does not include the affirmation of the opposition: precisely because it includes such affirmation *as a moment* in the synthesis with the negation, and therefore *denies it* insofar as it is an affirmation that does not intend to enter into such synthesis. Consequently, in thinking that the positive is and is-not the negative, one denies that the positive is not negative (once again: not simply in the sense that "the positive is and is-not the negative" includes "the positive is not the negative"—for, in this sense, the opposition is indeed denied, but is also affirmed—but in the sense that, in affirming-denying the opposition, one denies it insofar as it is an object *sempliciter* of affirmation—insofar, that is, as it refuses to become, at the same time, an object of negation). If the thought that the positive is and is-not the negative is a denial, in the sense we have indicated, of the positive's not being negative, i.e., is an identification of the positive and the negative, then we find again, at the root of this thought, that negation of the opposition which the *elenchos* supersedes by ascertaining (as in the case of the affirmation "red is green") that it grounded upon the affirmation of that which it denies.

way that the negation of the determinate is not simply grounded upon the affirmation of *a part* of what it denies (as occurs in the ascertainment that the universal negation of the opposition is grounded upon the affirmation of the opposition of that particular positive, in which the universal negation consists, to its own negative), but rather, indeed, upon the affirmation of *the whole* of what it denies. In this way, the *elenchos* is given the widest possible scope appropriate to it.

The negation states: "the positive is negative" ("Being is not-Being").[11] What do "positive" and "negative" mean in this proposition? If the meaning of "positive" is identical with the meaning of "negative," we are dealing not with a negation of the opposition, but rather with an identification of identicals, and, indeed, of the identical—as if one were to say that a building is an edifice: only if one does not know the meaning of either term can it be thought that, in saying that a building is an edifice, one has an identification of opposites. The meaning of "positive" and of "negative" is identical? Fine! Then, in this linguistic form, it must certainly be said that the positive is negative. In order to have a real negation of the opposition (and not merely an apparent one), it is necessary that the positive and the negative should first be posited as different (and so as opposites), and that one then posit the identity of the differents, i.e., that the differents *qua* differents are identical. As long as the differents are not seen as different, they must unquestionably be said to be identical; but if they are seen as different, and if, indeed, they must be held fast as different, in order that the affirmation of their identity may be negation of the opposition of the positive and the negative, then this negation is grounded upon the affirmation of what it denies; and, this time, it is no longer grounded upon the affirmation of only a part of what it denies, but rather upon the whole content that is denied. Consequently, the negation is negation of that without which it cannot constitute itself as negation, and so is negation of itself; it is a quitting the scene

---

11 This form of negation is the basis, as we have seen, of all other forms of negation. If, for example, instead of positing that the positive is the negative, one posits that the positive is and is-not the negative, this negation, in affirming and denying the opposition, unquestionably *denies* it: the opposition is denied insofar as it is posited as that which refuses to enter into synthesis with the negation of the opposition.

of the word and of thought, a declaring its own nonexistence and its own meaninglessness.

It is of the utmost interest to observe that even the proposition "the positive is not the negative," while positing the identity of the positive and the negative as superseded, knows this identity to be present (precisely because it is denied); which means that the identity exists (as the content of that knowing and that presence) and, as so existent, is affirmed. The identity of opposites can be denied only insofar as it is affirmed. The *elenchos* ascertains that the opposition of opposites can be denied only if it is affirmed; now, it has been ascertained that the opposition of opposites can be affirmed only if it is denied (i.e., that the identity of opposites can be denied only if it is affirmed). But then, are we not left in the most radical of antinomies? The answer is no, because the identity of opposites (like *Nothing* itself), insofar as it is thought, is a positive, and as positive is not negative: the identity of opposites, as existent, is a positive meaning [*è un positivo significare*] (just as nothing, insofar as it is thought, is a positive meaning), and precisely this positive meaning is that without which the opposition of the positive and the negative could not constitute itself. The identity of opposites is presupposed (i.e., is that without which the opposition of opposites could not constitute itself) not *qua* identity of opposites, but rather *qua* meaningful positivity. Just as, in positing that Being is not Nothing, Nothing is presupposed by this position not *qua* nothing, but rather *qua* meaningful positivity.[12]

Consequently, the negation of the opposition presupposes *sempliciter* that which it denies, while the negation of the identity of opposites presupposes not that which it denies, but rather the *positive meaning* of that which it denies: the opposition of the positive and the negative does not presuppose that the positive is negative, but rather presupposes the meaningful positivity (positivity that as such is not negativity) that forms the content of the identification of the positive and the negative. How, then, the identity of the positive and the negative— which is precisely that which is superseded by the opposition, and so

---

12   For a more thorough investigation of the aporia deriving from the fact that the nothing and the contradictory are positively meaningful, cf. Chapter IV of *La struttura originaria*.

is that which is-not, or is the negative—can be positively meaningful constitutes that aporia of the positive meaning of Nothing to whose resolution we have referred the reader above (q.v. footnote 12).

If one wants to *say* something—if, that is, one gives a determinate meaning to what one says—then it is imperative that the content of the saying should not deny the determinateness (that is, should not deny the opposition of the positive and the negative); for otherwise, the saying would be realized not in the way prescribed by its semantic content, but in some other way. The saying itself would be an exception to that which it says, and the exception the ground of the rule. The destiny of any type of negation of the opposition is just this: always to be the opposite of what it intends to be (precisely because the negation consists in a saying that does not respect its own prescriptions and is realized as a determinateness).

The opposition of Being and not-Being can be expressed by saying that Being is *determinate*. Being repulses that which it is not, repulses not-Being (both as the not-Being constituted by *other* determinations, and as the not-Being of Nothing), and, setting itself apart in this way, stands firm in itself, determinate. The *elenchos*, considered in the first of its two formulations (in which it is ascertained that the negation of the opposition is grounded upon an individuation of the universal opposition), is constituted by this apophantic organism: "The negation of the determinate is a determinate and thus is a negation of that determinate which is the negation itself (i.e., is a negation of itself)." In Book IV of the *Metaphysics*, Aristotle argues that the discourse on the first principle—and so also the *elenchos*—is the province of first philosophy, namely, *episteme*; it is therefore itself an *epistemonikos* discourse. But then, in Book I, Ch. 2 of the *Topics* he asserts that the consideration of principles—and so the *elenchos*—is the concern of dialectic, which is understood by Aristotle to be a moment of *doxa*. If such were the case, the discourse on the value of the principle, and therefore the *elenchos* itself, would not have absolute (epistemic) value. But the first principle is undeniable only when its value is seen. If the discourse that ascertains its value has no absolute value, then the first principle can be denied. Dialectic does not belong to *doxa*, but is an essential moment of *episteme*. The authentic formulation is the one in Book IV of the *Metaphysics*: the discourse that shows the truth of Being belongs to the truth of Being.

The ascertainment of the value of the first principle—or, more precisely, of the opposition of the positive and the negative (in which, however, the opposition is not conceived contradictorily, as opposed to all the post-Parmenidean formulations of the noncontradictoriness of Being, and so also to the Aristotelian one)—consists, on the one hand, in the positing of the immediate belonging of the predicate to the subject (the negation thus being superseded, since it is negation of that which is *per se notum*, affirmed on the basis of itself), and, on the other hand, in the *elenchos*. But then, *what* is the value of this ascertainment of the value of the opposition? If it is kept in mind that the opposition, concretely thought, is identity-opposition—which is to say, Being is opposed to not-Being because it is self-identical, and it is self-identical because it is opposed to not-Being: co-originality of identity and opposition—then the value of the ascertainment of the identity-opposition's value consists in the following: that *such an ascertainment is itself an individuation of the universal identity-opposition.* The *elenchos*, as an apophantic organism, is the union of these two assertions: "the negation of the determinate is a determinate" and "the negation of the determinate is negation of itself." Each of these assertions is an individuation of the universal identity-opposition, which means that the entire apophantic organism of the *elenchos* is, in its turn, just such an individuation. (The union of the two assertions adds nothing to their content, but is the concrete comprehension that prevents their abstract separation.) Let us consider each of the two assertions that make up the first formulation of the *elenchos* one at a time.

The first assertion, "the negation of the determinate is a determinate," means that that positive in which the negation consists is identical to itself and opposed to its negative: the determinateness is identity-opposition (henceforth referred to simply as "opposition"). In fact, when it is ascertained that the opposition is the ground of the negation of the opposition, the ground is not posited as something other than the negation, but rather as the negation's very positivity and determinateness; the ground is posited as a condition not extrinsic, but rather intrinsic to the negation. Consequently, saying that the opposition is the ground, without which the negation would-not-be, is equivalent to saying that the negation would-not-be without itself, i.e., without its being a determinate positivity. Precisely because the negation is a determinateness, the negation's determinateness is that without which the negation would-not-be: that which the negation is (its determinateness), is that without which it would-not-be. (In general: if *a* is *b*, *b* is that without which *a* would-not-be: thinking that *a* is *b* means thinking *b* as the ground—in the sense just indicated—of *a*.) With this it becomes clear that the ascertainment of the ground of the negation is the immediate referring of determinateness to that determinate positive which is the negation, and hence such referring is an individuation of the universal opposition.

The second of the two assertions that make up the apophantic organism of this first formulation of the *elenchos* runs: "the negation of the determinate is negation of that determinate which is the negation itself (i.e., is negation of itself)." The subject of this assertion is identical to a part (of the meaning) of the predicate. In fact, the predicate is the union of the "negation of the determinate" (and thus far it is identical to the subject) and of that specification of the determinate which is the negation itself (of the determinate). The synthesis of this specification and of its being a determinate is precisely that which is expressed by the first of the two assertions we are considering (i.e., by the assertion "the negation of the determinate is a determinate"). Thus in this second assertion the predicate belongs to the subject because a part of the predicate is identical to the subject. Hence the assertion contains an individuation of the universal identity-opposition (such individuation consisting in the very identity of the subject and of part of the predicate). And this individuation, in the assertion in question, is united to the other part of the predicate by means of a synthesis (the synthesis that connects the negation of the determinate to its determinateness) that is in turn an individuation of the universal identity-opposition.

Thus the first formulation of the *elenchos*, as a union of the individuations of the universal identity-opposition, is itself an individuation of such a universality.

And it cannot be otherwise: the opposition is *original* and *immediate* truth, which as such does not rest upon any other truth; if the ascertainment of the value of the opposition did not belong to the opposition itself, if it were not included in the opposition's semantic field, then the reason for the original's being held fast would be other than the original, and therefore the original would not be original, but derived. The ascertainment of the value of the original is a moment of the original. It comes about as follows: the apophantic organism in which the *elenchos* consists is an individuation of the universal opposition; and such opposition can constitute itself as original truth only insofar as it is posited *as actually inclusive* of that individuation. If the universal and its individuation are abstractly separated, then the universal is left devoid of this individuation, which thus supervenes as something other than the universal so posited; and therefore that unthinkable situation occurs, whereby the original (the universal not actually including that individuation) finds in something else (the supervening individuation) the reason for its being held fast, and is thus posited as derived. The original is the *co-originality* of the universal opposition and of this, its individuation. This individuation—in turn—like all other individuations of the universal opposition, has value only insofar as it is understood in relation to the universal of the opposition. (Saying that a sheet of paper is not a pen—or that the negation of the determinate is a determinate and so is negation of itself—has value, only if this saying is related to the universal opposition of the positive and the negative.)

It is, then, interesting to observe that the assertion "the negation of the determinate is a determinate" is not itself a self-contradictory proposition (as if one were to say that "not-red—the negation of red—is red"); for this assertion does not say that that which effectively manages to realize itself as indeterminate is determinate (in which case it would unquestionably be self-contradictory), but rather that the denial of the existence of the determinate is a determinate act. "Negation of the determinate" does not mean here "indeterminate," but rather "affirmation that Being is not-Being": the two meanings are formally distinct. The assertion says, then, that not even the negation of the determinate—to the extent that it, too, is a positive—manages to constitute itself as indeterminateness; and thus it is said to be an individuation of the universal opposition.

Such individuation is the explicitation of that determinateness which is implicitly thought in the negation of the determinate (and thus it is the explicitation of the ground of the negation). The negation, as we have seen, holds firm in its meaning; i.e., it differentiates this meaning (insofar as it holds it fast) from any other meaning (i.e., from its negative). In the negation, although this differentiation is indeed *thought*—and thus the negation affirms an individuation, i.e., is an individuation of that which it denies (and is grounded upon this individuation)—it remains *unexpressed*. The *elenchos* consists precisely in expressing, and explicitly reflecting upon, that which is already thought in the negation; it consists, that is, in *positing* that which the negation *is*—and thus it is the individuation *posited*.

The *elenchos*, considered in its widest formulation (the one, that is, in which the negation of the opposition is grounded not upon a part, but upon the whole of that which it denies), consists in the following apophantic organism: "the negation of the opposition is opposition and so is negation of itself." Here too, each of the two assertions that makes up this organism is an individuation of the universal identity-opposition, and thus the organism of the *elenchos* is itself such an individuation. Again, let us consider each of the two assertions that make up this second formulation of the *elenchos* in turn. The first assertion runs, "the negation of the opposition is (affirmation of the) opposition," or, "the identification of opposites is opposition of opposites" (i.e., "the identification of the different is differentiation of the different"). Here too, we have not a self-contradictory proposition, identifying identity and difference, negation and affirmation, but rather the ascertainment that the negation realizes itself only by joining up with the affirmation, the identification only by joining up with, or clinging to, the opposition of opposites. And this joining-up is the grounding itself of the negation upon that which it denies. The identification *of opposites* is negation of the opposition only if the opposites are known *as* opposites. Thinking the identity *of opposites* means, then, thinking the *opposition*, i.e., affirming it. The *elenchos* is the ascertainment that the identification *of opposites* includes the opposition, or, that the opposition, included in the identification, is opposition. Thus the schema of this first assertion is "*a b* is *b*" (where *a* = negation, identification; *b* = affirmation, opposition; as if one were to say, "a plane figure is a figure"—except that, in this case, "figure" is not the contrary of "plane"). If this assertion consists in ascertaining that the opposition joining up with the identification is opposition, the affirmation that the opposition is opposition is a form of individuation of the universal opposition of the positive and the negative. In fact, in this first assertion the predicate (*b*) is identical to a part of the subject (*a b*) and so the assertion *includes* an individuation of the universal identity-opposition (such individuation being precisely the identity between the predicate and part of the subject).

The second of the two assertions that make up this second formulation of the *elenchos* runs, "the negation of the opposition is negation of the negation of the opposition" (is negation of itself), or, is negation of that part of itself which is the opposition. The assertion says, "the negation of the opposition is negation of the opposition that is part of the negation of the opposition" and so, here again, the subject is identical to a part of the predicate. In fact, the predicate is the union of "negation of the opposition" and of that specification of the opposition which is the opposition as part, i.e., as a moment that is included in the negation of the opposition. (And the synthesis between this specification and the negation of the opposition is expressed by the first of the two assertions that make up this second figure of the *elenchos*, namely, "the negation of the opposition is opposition.") Consequently, the predicate belongs to the subject, because the part of the predicate that is identical to the subject is predicated of the subject. Thus also this second assertion includes an individuation of the universal opposition. And so also this second formulation of the *elenchos*, as a unity of the individuations of the universal opposition in which the assertions that make up the *elenchos* consist, is an individuation or moment of the universal opposition. The opposition is original, only insofar as it actually includes this moment (which, in turn, has value only insofar as it is held fast in its relation to the universal of the opposition).

After these remarks on the structure of the two formulations or figures of the *elenchos*, it appears that, with the exception of the first assertion of the first figure, it must be said of the other assertions of the two figures not that they coincide, but rather that each of them *includes* an individuation of the universal opposition of the positive and the negative. And this is because, in each of these assertions, the subject is identical to a part of the predicate, or the predicate is identical to a part of the subject. Which means that the predicate belongs to the subject not *ratione sui*, but *ratione suae partis*; or that the subject is not, *ratione sui*, that to which the predicate belongs, but *ratione suae partis*. And thus the belonging of the predicate to the subject is mediated by that which is part of the subject or of the predicate.[13] As a union of mediations, the two figures of the *elenchos* are, therefore, in turn, mediations.

But mediation, as such, is the unification of individuations of the universal opposition. (The assertions that constitute mediation are, that is, affirmations in which the subject is identical to the predicate, or the predicate is the negation of the negation of the subject.) Such individuations are the content of the mediation, which is a union of the individuations not in the sense that it adds other determinations to that content, but rather in the sense that it does not leave the individuations abstractly separated, positing them, instead, in their distinction and so in their relation. If the original truth of the opposition of the positive and the negative is the unity of the universal opposition and of the individuations of its universality, and if original truth is immediacy—i.e., is a saying mediated by no other saying and thus is the ground of any saying—then the mediation in which the *elenchos* consists belongs to the content of immediacy (and the entire possible development of mediation is nothing but an increase of the content of immediacy).[14] And immediacy is such only insofar as it includes mediation; insofar, that is, as it includes those individuations of the universal opposition which constitute the mediational structure of the *elenchos*. Original opposition demands that the universality of the opposition actually be individuated in a specific way: according, that is, to the modality of the *elenchos*. Such individuation (in which the *elenchos*, as a unity of individuations, consists) is therefore no accidental variant, but rather a necessary constant of the original openness of truth. In this sense the discourse that expresses the value of the universal opposition is a moment of the semantic field by which such opposition is constituted.

If the opposition cannot be denied, because its negation does not exist—and it does not exist because it is the very negation that destroys itself (and it destroys itself because, in denying its own ground, it

---

13   Cf. *La struttura originaria*, Ch. IX, paragraph XV.
14   Cf. *La struttura originaria*, Ch. IX, paragraph XIII, d; paragraph XIX.

denies itself)—this nonexistence and self-destruction still have to be carefully determined. Not in the sense that the *elenchos* is to be completed by a further discourse, but rather in the sense that it is a question of seeing *what* is effectively thought when the opposition is denied.

For Bontadini, "a thought that contradicts itself is annulled. In contradicting itself it says twice as much as it ought to say, but the result of (explicitly or implicitly) saying too much is the annulment of the thought. The supreme demand therefore proves to be that of *positivity*."[15] In *this* way, then, thought is to be freed from contradiction, and not in the way we envisioned. But what does it *mean* that a thought that contradicts itself is annulled? Does it mean that it is a thinking nothing? That there is no act of thought? That when one contradicts oneself it is as if one were conscious of nothing? Our reply must be no, for thinking that the positive is the negative, or that the positive is and is-not the negative, is nonetheless a thinking; utterly aberrant, but *living*. Is it a question, then, of an annulment of *value*? As if one were to say that a thought that contradicts itself loses all value? And indeed this is true, but, in this way, one merely asserts the value instead of concretely showing it, and thus the value itself is not seen. Contradicting oneself means saying "twice as much as one ought to say." But this is precisely the problem: what, exactly, *must* one say?

We reply to this question by showing that the negation of the opposition fails to constitute itself, which means that the opposition (noncontradictoriness, determinateness) is the *destiny* of saying—is, precisely, what "must" be said.

We asked ourselves a moment ago: what is this incapacity to exist—this self-destruction and nonexistence—of the negation? What is effectively thought when the negation is denied? If it is true that Bontadini's argument does not bring out the concrete value of the opposition, on the other hand—once this concreteness has been ascertained in the way we proposed—will not the reply to these questions indeed be that a thought that contradicts itself is annulled? Replying to this question no longer means establishing the value of noncontradictory saying

---

15   Gustavo Bontadini, in Nicola Abbagnano and others, *La filosofia contemporanea in Italia. Invito al dialogo*, Asti: Arethusa, 1958, 123–4.

(precisely because this value is ascertained in the way we proposed, through the *elenchos*); it means, rather, establishing what is thought when one contradicts oneself, what effectively occurs in that self-destruction and "nonexistence" of the negation. But we have already begun to show that a thought lives even when it contradicts itself: when it contradicts itself, it is not annulled. *Here*, then, is the crux of the matter: *self-contradicting is not a thinking nothing, but is a thinking the Nothing.* The identity of the positive and the negative (which is precisely what is thought when the negation is denied) is that which is-not: that which is—the positive—is opposed to the negative. A thought that contradicts itself looks at Nothing. Be it understood: the negation of the opposition denies its own ground and thus denies itself: that which is effectively thought, in this negation (which is also self-negation), is Nothing.

And insofar as Nothing lets thought look at it, it dons the mantle of the positive. Any contradiction—like, for that matter, the very meaning "nothing"—constitutes the positive meaning of Nothing. That Nothing should let thought look at it (and thought must do so, if it is to oppose Being to Nothing) constitutes one of the most formidable obstacles to the thought of Being. Indeed, Heidegger was to call attention to this question, but the defenders of traditional metaphysics failed to appreciate the gravity of his call. And although Heidegger stressed that the thought of Nothing makes the Nothing into a positive, instead of trying to clear the hurdle he fell back upon the facile condemnation of logic and of the principle of noncontradiction. But the opposition of Being and Nothing is not a principle of logic—it is the breath of thought. This problem, too, will command our attention.

The purpose of our present remarks, however, has been to show that self-contradicting is thinking Nothing (not a thinking nothing), contradictoriness constituting the very positive meaning of Nothing. Thus the negation of the opposition is nonexistent not in the sense that it is a thinking nothing, but rather in the sense that it is itself the first to reject its own thesis. When one says that the positive is the negative, one looks at Nothing (and Nothing is presented as this identification of opposites); and since this saying is, at the same time, an opposition of opposites, in this identification-opposition one looks once more at

Nothing (and Nothing is presented as this identification-opposition of opposites). Saying that the opposition "cannot" be denied means, therefore, referring to the *nonexistence* of the negation, in the sense we have indicated. This is the "faith" that envelops thought when it affirms the opposition. The conviction that "attends upon truth." In Parmenides' words: *Peithous esti keleuthos (Aletheiei gar opedei)* (Fr. 2, 4).

7. FURTHER REMARKS ON THE TRUTH OF BEING

Insofar as the denial of the not-being of Being (*and thus* the affirmation that Being is) is an individuation of the universal opposition of the positive and the negative, and insofar as it is held fast in its concrete relation to the universal, it participates in the originality of the logos—if by logos is meant the opposition of the positive and the negative. In the original opposition, every Being (and the totality of Being) turns in a number of directions—it enters into a plurality of relationships. For example, a tree is not a mountain, or this positive is not its negative; a tree is not a mountain, a house, or anything that is other than a tree. But when Being, any Being, turns in the direction along which it is linked to its "is" (this turning is the "true way," *alethes odos*, of which Parmenides speaks)—when, that is, one does not (only) say of a tree that it is not a mountain, but rather that it is and it cannot occur that it is-not—then that Being assumes a divine face. Insofar as this tree, with this its form and colors, is, and it cannot occur that it is-not, this tree is already divine (*theion*)—if, that is, God (*o theos*) is indeed Being in its immutable fullness. Being, all Being, seen as that which is and cannot not-be, is God. And when Being speaks of itself, it says precisely: "I am that I am" (*ego eimi o on, ego sum qui sum*, Exodus 3:14); which is the highest speculative expression of Holy Scripture. One does not arrive at God; one does not come to behold him after a time of exile or blindness: precisely because God is Being, of which the original logos says that it is and cannot not-be. God is the content of original truth, to the extent that such truth constitutes itself as an affirmation that Being is.

Being as it appears in this original affirmation (which is not the result of demonstration or mediation) is God, and God, therefore, is the content of original truth, insofar as such truth is original *logos*—but *on the other hand* the whole of Being, *qua* immutable, transcends the original *manifestation* of Being, i.e., transcends *being-there* [*esserci*]: original truth is the intertwining of the original logos and the original manifestation of Being (the horizon of *phainesthai*, the phenomenological horizon). God is not to be demonstrated; not, however, in the sense that he is immediately experienced, i.e., belongs to the originally manifest content, but rather in the sense that the affirmation that Being is constitutes the immediacy—the originality—of the logos. This immediate affirmation (in the sense of the immediacy of the logos) says that Being exists (=is; is not nothing) and cannot not-exist. But Being as it is spoken of here is *God*, for by this word is meant the whole of the positive, thought in its existing and in the impossibility of its nonexistence; or, the word "God" means Being as it appears in the affirmation, "Being is." And it is precisely this Being (which is "this" not because it is a part, but because it is the whole, seen in the impossibility of its nonexistence) that is affirmed to be immutable and thus transcendent with respect to Being-that-becomes that is manifest.

Being *qua* Being, and so the whole of Being, is; and thus it is immutable. But as immutable it hovers over Being-that-becomes, transcending it. Thus Being *qua* Being (*on e on*) possesses a twofold meaning. *On the one hand* it is Being, in its absolute fullness and intensity: of all Being, insofar as it is Being, it must be said that it cannot befall it to not-be and that therefore it is eternal, immutable, necessary. But then, insofar as the totality of Being, *qua* immutable, transcends Being-that-becomes, the very thing that from the standpoint of Aristotelian-Thomistic ontology may seem to be absurd must now be affirmed: namely, that the transcendental (Being *qua* Being) is transcendent; that the whole of the positive (which is the field to which the determinations of Being *qua* Being apply) is transcendent. *On the other hand*, the transcended is not nothing; it, too, is Being, positivity—but a positivity that is *wholly* possessed by the immutable totality of Being. And it *must* be possessed: precisely because the positive that appears is subject to the process of time, so that the horizon of Appearing does not save Being from non-Being. Being slips out of its hands—and so the inanity of Appearing can live only if Being is kept to itself, by sure hands. In Appearing, Being is in time (i.e., there is a time when it is-not); but Being is not in time; and thus all the Being that appears in time always and forever abides in blessed company with all Being, outside of time—and justice is rendered to Being, which is a victim of time's injustice. This conveys the profound meaning of Anaximander's dictum that Beings "give justice for their injustice" (*didonai diken tes adikias*)—where *adikia* is Being's temporality and *dike* its eternity.[16] Precisely because the immutable contains *all* the positive that is in Being-that-becomes, we said that the whole of the positive (the field of application of the transcendental) is transcendent. But the transcended, as we said, is *not* a Nothing, since all its positivity is precontained and forever safeguarded by the transcendent: it is nothing as *novitas* or increase with respect to God. And so we have a second meaning of *on e on*, for which Being *qua* Being refers *both* to immutable Being, *and* to Being-that-becomes (both to the transcendent, and to the transcended; both to God, and to the world). Whereas for the first meaning the whole of the positive is identified with the immutable, for the second meaning the whole of the positive "contains" the immutable—but contains it, as we said, as something that is not devoid of the positivity proper to Becoming; on the contrary, this positivity is eternally preserved. (In this sense it can be said that the world is an image of God, or, more precisely, is the outcome of an abstract comprehension of the immutable totality.)[17]

To object at this point that the denial of the not-being of Being is belied by the world, where Being supervenes and vanishes—i.e., where Being is-not—means neither more nor less than disregarding what has been said here. This tree is a positive, and as such it is and it cannot befall it to not-be, and so it is eternal. And, as eternal, it dwells in the hospitable house of Being, where all its positivity has already been, and will always be, saved. If at this point one objects that this tree is born and perishes, and so it is-not, and so there is a Being of which it can and must be said that it is-not, so that the *falsity* of the denial of Being's not-being is manifest in Appearing—if one objects in this way, one has

---

16   Cf. E. Severino, "La parola di Anassimandro," in *Essenza del nichilismo*, Milan: Adelphi, 1982, 391–411. Not included in the present edition [*Editors' note*].

17   For the concrete meaning of this statement and its content, cf. the "Postscript" which follows, and in particular 113–6.

forgotten that the positive—any positive—which appears subject to the vicissitudes of time, has *already* been rescued from nothingness (precisely insofar as the impossibility that it—that *any* Being—not-be has been ascertained). Thus there is no residual portion or dimension of the positive that, not having been saved, is abandoned to time. That which is in time is not something that is not possessed by the eternal (precisely because it must be said of *everything*—and so also of Being that appears in time—that it *is* eternally); so that the not-being of Being that is in time does not disprove that which, moreover, cannot be in any way disproved: that Being is and cannot not-be. Only if one did not affirm the immutable whole of the positive would the presence of Being in time be a negation of the affirmation that Being is and that it cannot befall it to not-be. The assertion that Becoming would be contradictory if one did not affirm the immutable has frequently been repeated by metaphysical thought: but here one wishes to attain the eternal while understanding Being originally as in time (understanding, that is, Being as that which is, *when* it is), so precluding the possibility of attaining the eternal.

Are we to free philosophy and metaphysics from this mystification of the meaning of Being? I have been proffering this invitation for quite some time. But still for too short a time, if one considers the essential transformation in philosophic consciousness that such an invitation demands.

CHAPTER II

Returning to Parmenides (Postscript)

If we are to reawaken the truth of Being, which has lain dormant in Western thought since the very day of its birth, we shall have to fathom the meaning of *this thought*, both simple and great: that Being is and may not not-be. Indeed, such a reawakening poses the greatest threat to the long winter of reason, upsetting its most time-honored practices and setting it a new task—the most essential task of all. If possible, this thought must be stifled before it comes to flower, for otherwise it alone will be destined to have the *right* to flower. There can be no turning back from the path that has been cleared: if it cannot be thought of *Being* (of all and of every Being) that it is-not, then it cannot be thought of *Being* (of all, of every Being) that it *becomes*. For if Being were to become, it would not be—before its birth and after its corruption. Thus *all* Being is immutable: neither issuing from, nor returning to, nothingness, *Being* is eternal.

The strength of this inexorable course springs wholly from its matrix: Being is. The fate of truth entirely depends on the meaning that one gives to the intertwining of these two words. Where "Being" stands for everything that is not nothing: nature and language, appearance and reality, facts and ideal essences, the human and the divine . . .; and "is" indicates *esse*, existence, Parmenides' *estin*. If "Being" is the *eon* of Parmenides—which after Plato came to include the totality of determinations or differences: the totality of whatever is not nothing— *estin* means just this not-being-nothing. "Is"—existence, *esse*—*is* not being a Nothing: that something "is" means primarily that it is not a Nothing, i.e., that it manages to keep to itself without dissolving into nothingness. Existence, then, in the sense of *ex-sistere*—in the sense, that is, of a managing to constitute itself by coming out into the light— is only a particular mode of existence in the transcendental sense, i.e., as the negation of Nothing. And, in general, the plurality of modes of existence is nothing other than a plurality of the modes of not being nothing; so that the plurality of determinations or differences of Being is itself nothing other than the plurality of modes of existence, and any single determination is a unique mode of existence. *Here*, then, we are already at the heart of Being's intertwining with its "is." This lamp which is illuminating my desk as I write is a determination of Being— it is a determinate mode of not being nothing. But there is unquestionably a distinction here between the determinateness and its not being nothing: this determinateness is that which is not nothing, and, for this very reason, it is distinct from its not being a Nothing, just as that- which-determines (i.e., the determinateness) is distinct from that which it determines (i.e., the not-being-a-Nothing). But does this distinction not amount, perhaps, to an accidental relation between this lamp and its not being a Nothing? Alienated reason is quick to affirm the relation's accidentality: when this lamp is destroyed, it will be nothing; the remembrance—the "intelligible essence"—of the thing destroyed will remain, but that which is effectively destroyed (namely this concrete lamp, as opposed to the lamp remembered or to its intelligible essence) will become a Nothing, will be no more.

"When this lamp is no more"! Will people never wake up to the *meaning* of this phrase, and of the countless analogous phrases that they think can be constructed? Just as the phrase "when the sky is cloudy" includes the affirmation "the sky is cloudy," so the phrase "when this lamp is nothing" includes the affirmation "this lamp is nothing" (albeit referring to a different situation from the present one, a situation in which one recognizes that this lamp is not a Nothing). And yet, this affirmation is the unfathomable absurd—it is the identi- fication of the positive (i.e., of that positive which is this lamp) and the negative, of Being and Nothing. Since this lamp is this lamp, and as such is meaningful, not only is Nothing, *in fact*, not predicated of it, but such a predication is *impossible*—given that the supreme law of Being is the opposition of the positive and the negative. The great devi- ation of dawning truth has led to a paradox: the very element of

Parmenides' discourse whose sacrifice was demanded by the truth of Being is, instead, held fast. Was not the Platonic "parricide" the great—and the only—step forward after Parmenides? Was not Being then to be understood as the positivity of the determinate, and no longer as the pure indeterminate? Parmenides could say, "this lamp is nothing," because for him determinations stood outside the confines of Being and as such were indeed a Nothing whose positivity was merely illusory. The Platonic parricide, however, should have *prohibited* the positing of the determinate as a Nothing, for the determinate had been brought within the confines of Being. (And therefore it should have delivered determinate Being from time—since, in time, Being—and, now, also determinate Being—becomes nothing.) But this did not occur; and Western thought drew away from the living truth discovered by Parmenides, taking with it from Parmenides thought that which ought instead to have perished.[1]

When this lamp has been destroyed, and thus annulled, is there *something* of the lamp that becomes nothing, or does *nothing* of the lamp become nothing? In the latter case, if *everything* were to remain what it is, there would be no destruction. If alienated reason wants to detach the determination from its not being a Nothing (i.e., from its existence)—if it wants to render accidental, or merely factual, the relation between a determination and its not being a Nothing—then it is compelled to recognize that, when the lamp comes-to-be or is destroyed, everything in the lamp cannot remain what it was, and that therefore *something* of the lamp must now be no more. The objection has been raised that this annulment is the *de facto* no-longer-existing of an essence that nonetheless, as an abstract intelligible essence,

---

1 This is why, in "Returning to Parmenides," paragraph II, we said that the Platonic deepening of the meaning of Being had been the very occasion for the forgetting of that meaning. And this was no "superfluous occasion," as one of my critics affirms, adducing the reason that "the empirical observation of a Becoming in general itself implies a temporal dimension of Being" (G. Bontadini, *Sozein ta Phainomena*, "Rivista di filosofia neo-scolastica," 1964, V, 443). Such would be the case only if things that become were posited *as Being* (otherwise, time would have no bearing upon Being). Parmenides, however, did not posit them that way (and was therefore free to leave them in time)—*Plato* was the first to do so (and thus in saving the determinate from nothingness he handed it back to nothingness: precisely because he—like all his progeny—took determinate Being to be in time).

eternally endures. But then—even in this way one admits *something* that, with the annulment, has become nothing: namely, the *de facto* existence of the lamp. (Indeed, if not even this *de facto* existence were to become a Nothing, then it would be unthinkable that something, which in *no* way has become nothing, has been annulled.) Now either one holds that there is nothing (i.e., no determination) that becomes, or can become, nothing, or one holds that, in the annulment of a determination, there is something that becomes nothing and, having become nothing, is nothing. Clearly, the first belief cannot be that of alienated reason, which strives to posit as a simple fact the not-being-a-Nothing predicated of the determination (a simple fact, therefore, which is seen as that which can also not be predicated of it). The second conviction expresses the utter *forgottenness* of truth—because that very *something*, which has to become nothing when a determination, such as this lamp, is destroyed—that something as such, is a not-Nothing. Envisioning a time ("when this lamp is nothing") when something becomes nothing, therefore, means envisioning a time when Being (i.e., not-Nothing) is identified with Nothing: the time of the absurd.

Not being a Nothing is predicated of this lamp insofar as it is this lamp, and therefore this lamp (or any factor or element that constitutes it) *cannot* become nothing, i.e., cannot be nothing. And vice versa: if, when this lamp has been destroyed, *something* becomes nothing, and is thus nothing (and something *must* become nothing, if one is to maintain that the lamp has been destroyed), then Being (i.e., that negation of Nothing which is this something) is identified with Nothing. Not being a Nothing cannot therefore be understood as simply belonging *de facto* to the determination (since otherwise, when the *de facto* predication ceases, that very identification of Being and Nothing would occur), but must rather be understood as that which is predicated of the determination as *such* (and which therefore cannot not be predicated of it).

The spurious subtlety of alienated reason thinks it can oppose the positive to the negative and, at the same time, affirm that Being is-not (when it is-not). But if the "is" (the existing, the *esse*) of a determination is its not-being-nothing, then thinking—of any determination whatsoever—that it is-not means thinking that it is nothing; it means denying the very opposition of Being and Nothing that was to have been safeguarded. Existence, therefore, is predicated of *every* determination of the positive precisely insofar as it is a *determination*; wherefore positing any determination whatsoever without positing it as existent is inadmissible.

It should, moreover, be noted that the "ontological argument" for the existence of God reflects one of the most typical aspects of the forgottenness of the truth of Being. On the one hand, the argument states that existence belongs, *per se*, only *to a certain determination* (the perfect being)—and belongs to it, therefore, not insofar as it is a *determination* (be it real or ideal, factual or essential), but rather insofar as it is *that* determination which it is. On the other hand, existence here is not taken in its transcendental sense, i.e., as pure not-being-a-Nothing, but is understood as *that particular mode* of existence which is existence *in rerum natura* (or extramental being); and the determination, of which existence is predicated, is understood as intelligible essence, belonging to that ideal or mental order which is to be transcended. Therefore, the ontological argument consists in the attempt to establish a connection between two different modes of existence (between, that is, the ideal and the real). For the truth of Being, however, it is not a question of going from an ideal to a real order, but rather of recognizing that *every* order (ideal or real, illusory or true, factual or necessary) is a positivity, i.e., is a not-being-a-Nothing, and as such it cannot befall it to not-be, and therefore it is eternal, immutable, imperishable: the ideal as ideal, the real as real, the illusory and the true as illusory and true, the factual and the necessary as factual and necessary.[2] It is not a question, then, of establishing an implication between two different modes of existence, but rather of positing the existence (in the transcendental sense) of *every* mode of existence (for every such mode is a determination of the positive). *Everything* is eternal, according to its own distinctive mode of existence. And so

---

2 Moreover, it should be noted that the "factual" is not that which is, but might not-be, but rather is that whose not-being is actually excluded by the single consideration that the not-being of any positive whatsoever is impossible; whereas the nonexistence of the "necessary" is excluded not only by this, but by further considerations, which find in the concept of the nonexistence of the "necessary" a self-contradictoriness beyond the fundamental one, i.e., that of the not-being of Being. It is clear, however, that this distinction between the "factual" and the "necessary" lies within that *necessity* which is of primary speculative value.

everything that appears (this lamp, the sky, the things and processes of experience)—everything whose mode of existence is testified to in Appearing—is also eternal. Just as everything that does not appear—if it exists—is eternal, according to its own distinctive mode of existence.

In the light of these considerations, one of my critics is most definitely on the wrong track if he thinks that the identity of the phrase "Being is" and the phrase "Being is not nothing" was intended, in "Returning to Parmenides," to signify the mere definition of the "essence" of Being, and therefore had no existential meaning. Now, there is no question that in positing that Being is not nothing (in positing, that is, Being in its opposition to not-Being), the meaning of Being is indicated, or—if you will—its "essence" is defined; but it is also true—and here the face of truth shines forth in all its splendor—that this definition is the very exclusion of Being's nonexistence: as long as existence is understood in its authentic value as pure not-being-a-Nothing. If Being is that which is not nothing, then Being (every Being, every thing that is not nothing) is that which exists and cannot not-exist, or, is not nothing and cannot become a Nothing.[3] That this lamp "exists in fact" (and so exists differently from the way it exists in memory or an intelligible essence) is attested by the appearing of things. But in the very act in which this modality of existence appears, the truth of Being demands that, since the existence—the not being a Nothing—of this modality has been posited, it must also be posited that this modality (which is nothing other than this lamp in its concrete form) cannot be or become nothing (since if it became nothing, Nothing would be predicated of Being).

The totality of differences or determinations of Being is not therefore, as one of my critics would have it, "the totality of essences," but rather is the totality of that which exists and which therefore includes,

---

3 Indeed, E. Severino, *La struttura originaria*, 1st ed. Brescia: La Scuola, 1958; 2nd ed. Milan: Adelphi, 1981—a book that must be kept in mind by anyone wishing to discuss "Returning to Parmenides" concretely—states quite clearly: "That Being has to be resides in the very meaning of Being; wherefore the principle of noncontradiction expresses not simply the identity of Being with itself (or its difference from other essences), but rather the identity of essence with existence (or the otherness of essence with respect to nonexistence)" (Ch. XV, section 6, paragraph II).

as a part, the totality of essences—for also essences exist (i.e., are not nothing), albeit differently from the way in which this lamp exists.

And again: it is true that a tree is—necessarily, immutably—a tree, or that the proposition "a tree is a tree" does not express a simple fact, but is necessary. But "Returning to Parmenides" intended to express a quite different thought—and one which constitutes the supremely disquieting aspect of the truth of Being. It intended to say that this tree (and every thing, however proud or humble) necessarily exists (according to the modality of existence that is proper to it). It intended, that is, to say that *existence* is not a predicate that simply belongs *in fact* to this tree (and to every thing), and therefore that the totality of Being necessarily, immutably *exists*. But then—it is the *ground* of this assertion that has to be considered and discussed! And that ground is always the same: can we think that this tree is-not (that it has been destroyed and its actual life is finished), without thinking that a positive is nothing— without thinking that Being is not-Being, and therefore without betraying the *truth* of Being? Indeed, if the thought expressing the truth of Being consists in showing that the ascertainment of the meaning of Being—i.e., the definition of the "essence" of Being—is the very exclusion of Being's nonexistence (so that Being is that which exists and cannot not-exist), how can one object that in this thought there is a "slippage" from the necessity of essence to the necessity of existence? As if, in expressing the truth of Being, it has been forgotten that the necessity that Being be Being is one thing, while the necessity that Being exist is another! And this, when the truth of Being is precisely the *identification* of these two necessities: not the forgetting of a distinction, but rather the ascertainment of the spurious subtlety of that very distinction.[4] And again: how can one reproach the thought that

---

4 The "slippage"—or so the objection would have it—occurs as follows: "Since it is necessary that Being be Being, it seems necessary that Being be, i.e., exist in fact, because in fact a Being exists and it cannot be *said* that it does not exist." But the authentic reason for the identification of these two necessities is by no means the one conjectured here. Clearly, the impossibility that something existing in fact not exist in fact may be ascertained, but it is by no means through *this* ascertainment that one comes to identify the necessity of essence with the necessity of existence: this identification is postulated by the affirmation that Being is every thing that is not nothing; and every thing (be it corporeal, ideal, real, or factual) that is not nothing, cannot become nothing, since in that case Being would become and would therefore be

expresses the truth of Being with confusing the necessity that Being is, when it is, with the necessity that Being is unconditionally? And this, when at the very beginning of "Returning to Parmenides" we explicitly considered the distinction between these two necessities as set forth in the canonical text, i.e., in Ch. IX of Aristotle's *De Interpretatione*, finding in that very "when Being is" the fundamental aberration of the thought of Being! It is common knowledge that, after Parmenides, Western thought distinguished between the necessity that Being is, when it is, and the necessity that Being is simple (*aplos*)! Indeed, we

---

Nothing. But existence, in its transcendental sense, is Nothing other than not being a Nothing, and therefore everything that is not a Nothing cannot become nonexistent. Precisely because Being is not a Nothing, if one thinks of a Being—say, this lamp—that it is-not (i.e., does not exist) (or can not-exist), then one thinks that this Being is nothing (or can be nothing). And if one thinks that—when it does not exist—it is nothing, then once again one thinks, in this "when Being is-not," that this Being is nothing. Will people never wake up to *this*, the first breath of the truth of Being?! Instead of trying—as many have done—to interpret "Returning to Parmenides" as a series of considerations which are valid as regards the "essence" of Being, but unacceptable as regards its "existence," those who wish to oppose the thought of the truth of Being would do well to reflect upon the profound and ineluctable *reason* for understanding Being as that which (precisely because it is not a Nothing) *exists*.

No doubt, such reflection will become fruitful only after the most elementary misapprehensions have been eliminated (misapprehensions, moreover, which are themselves the fruit of the way of thinking of Western man—so that the errors of the critics of the truth of Being are fully justified by that way of thinking). Have I not insisted—in "Returning to Parmenides" and elsewhere—that the abysmal difference between Parmenides and Melissus lies here: that for Parmenides the immutability of Being stems from the impossibility that Being not-be (since if it were to become, it would not-be: *ei gar egent' ouk esti*), whereas Melissus is no longer aware of the impossibility that Being not-be (=not exist) and demonstrates Being's immutability on the basis of the consideration that, if Being were-not, it could not be generated from Nothing? Here the absurd, for Melissus (as for all traditional metaphysics after him), lies not in the fact that Being is-not (does not exist), but rather in the fact that Being is generated from Nothing. Melissus, therefore, is the father of Western metaphysics precisely because, in the very act in which he intends to demonstrate the immutability of Being as such, he sees nothing improper in the supposition, as such, that Being is-not (*ei meden en*), and, to posit this immutability, feels the need to add that, if Being were-not, then nothing could be generated from Nothing—he feels the need to add that principle of *ex nihilo nihil* which, when employed in this way, is nothing but the *betrayal* of the truth of Being. Does not, then, the abysmal difference between Parmenides and Melissus (and thus between Parmenides and Western metaphysics) consist in this: that for Parmenides Being does not come from Nothing (and, in general, does not become), whereas for Melissus if Being were-not, it could not come from Nothing?

have put forward ineluctable reasons showing why the very idea of Being that is, *when it is*, has given rise to the *forgottenness* of the *truth* of Being; and I should like to invite my critics to discuss and to contest *these reasons!* The remoteness from the truth of Being goes far deeper than those contradictions which alienated reason is able to discern. Thus it is not simply a question of denying the self-contradictory affirmation that that which is lamp is not lamp, or the self-contradictory affirmation that this lamp that exists now does not exist now. Alienated reason has already formulated these negations of the absurd.

But then, such reason is alienated precisely because it has failed to discern that profound and ancient aberration which took root at the culmination of Western thought, in the way Plato led to the overcoming of Parmenides. For Parmenides, the determinate is not Being (*parex tou eontos*); but in such a way that Being and the determinate are thought as *absolutely independent* of one another, wherefore the determinate—*because* of its absolute independence with respect to Being—is posited as a Nothing. For the determinate to be posited as nothing, it is therefore not sufficient to establish its difference from Being (that is, it is not sufficient that it be posited as not-Being, as *parex tou eontos*); indeed, Plato was to hold fast to this difference (and he could not do otherwise), while at the same time denying that, on this account, the determinate has to be understood as nothing. Once again: if the determinate is to be posited as nothing there must be an *abstract separation* that posits Being and the determinate as two absolutes, as two absolutely unrelated loci. This being so, the determinate, as we said, and on account of its very absoluteness, stands outside of Being, in Nothing.

Yet Western man has *never ceased* to think Being and the determinations of Being in this abstract separation—it is how he has never ceased to think *being*, understood as the *synthesis* of Being and a determination. Plato himself failed to seize the great opportunity to think the truth of Being, for he too (and all Western thought thereafter) left this abstract separation at the bottom of the thought of beings—Plato, who claimed to have healed the rift and unified Being and its determination! In the Platonic rethinking of the relation between Being and the determination, the synthesis of these two moments was thus imposed upon two terms that were initially posited as separate (posited, that is, just as Parmenides had posited them), their subsequent synthesis being the unification of that which from the very beginning had been thought as not united. It is as if one thought a human being could be brought back to life simply by juxtaposing the parts of its dismembered corpse.

Our thesis, then, is that in the depths of Platonic rethinking lurks that same abstract separation of Being and its determination from which, on the surface, Plato wished to free the thought of Being. And yet Plato unquestionably took a great step forward, by understanding the determinate as that of which Being is predicated. The *difference* between Being and the determinate had been uncovered, once and for all, by Parmenides, and neither Plato nor anyone else could deny it; but the determinate is now presented as that *not*-Being (insofar as it is different—differently meaningful—from Being) which is not a pure Nothing, and which therefore *is*. Parmenides kept to the pure "is"; Plato recognizes the difference between the "is" and the determination (nor could he do otherwise), but he posits "is" as the predicate of the determination. But then, what of that abstract separation which we claimed to be at the bottom of Platonic rethinking? Where is it to be found?

The answer is that it is hidden in the very way in which Plato thinks the "is" as the predicate of the determination. The determination is not a pure Nothing, and therefore the truth of Being must say that it is; and thus "is" (=exists) expresses this very not being a Nothing. And not being a Nothing is predicated of the determination not insofar as it is this or that, this or that type of determination, but insofar as it is a *determination* (i.e., is not a being-meaningful as nothing). This lamp is not a Nothing—i.e., this lamp is—precisely insofar as it is this lamp; this lamp, then, cannot shake off its "is," nor will it ever be able to do so, simply because it cannot shake off its not being a Nothing. What Parmenides said of *pure* Being—"wherefore Justice loosens not her fetters to allow it to be born or perish, but holds it fast" (*tou eineken oute genesthai out' ollusthai aneke Dike chalasasa pedeisin, all' echei*)—the truth of Being must repeat of *every* Being, of every determinate positivity.

For Plato, however, the determination is prohibited from shaking off its "is" *not* insofar as it is a determination (i.e., any "what" whatsoever, that is not a Nothing), but rather insofar as it is *idea*, i.e., is *that specific type* of determination which is distinct from the sensible determination. The things that bear the seal of being "that which is" (*ois episphragizometha touto, o estin, Phaedo, 75d*) are not *every* thing (yet—quite the contrary—every thing should indeed be posited as that which is, *o estin*!), but rather are the ideal essences of visible things. And ideal essence is posited as immutable being *not* because Plato is mindful of Parmenides' truth—i.e., that Being (=that which exists, *o estin*) is not Nothing, nor can it become Nothing—but rather because Plato bases himself upon the narrow evidence of the impossibility that the beautiful, the just, the good (as opposed to things that are beautiful, just, good) not be beautiful, just, good; so that the beautiful is *o estin*, because it can never cease to be the beautiful. For something to be posited as *o estin*, it is not sufficient that it be a something, i.e., a not-Nothing: rather, it has to be that super-being which is the *idea*. If it is not *idea*, and is simply a something (and a something that is not *idea* is, for Plato, a sensible being), one clearly recognizes that Nothing cannot be predicated of it—but in the sense that Nothing cannot be predicated of it *as long as it is*, whereas *when it is not* such a predication is perfectly acceptable. Thus it is posited as something that at once is and is-not (*ti outos echei, os einai te kai me einai, Republic, 477a*), and is intermediate (*metaxy*) between idea—between the essence, *ousia*, that has rightfully to be called *o estin* (*e ousia echousa ten eponumian ten tou o estin, Phaedo, 92d*)—and Nothing (*me on*).

This means that *in the very thought* by which Plato unites the determination to its "is" (by positing it as that which is not nothing), the determination is understood as that which can be released from its salutary embrace with its Being, and thus as that which can not-be. The thought that thinks the not-being-nothing of the determination (the thought, that is, that rises above Parmenides) is the very thought that allows the determination (when it is not) to be a Nothing! It remains, therefore, in that same abstract separation of Being and the determination which had been Parmenides' own: at bottom, this thought thinks Being (*estin*) and the determination (*o*) as absolutely unrelated, and *for this reason* can understand "that which is" (*o estin*)—i.e., that which cannot be released from its "is"—not as the determination as such (the determination insofar as it is a "what," a *ti*), but rather as the determination as *idea*. And therefore the unification of the determination and Being—this great step beyond Parmenides, which affirms the being of not-Being, i.e., of that not-Being which is the determination as differently meaningful from Being—unites that which *per se* is dis-united; so that the union becomes something accidental, i.e., a fact that can be replaced by its opposite. And therefore, while one does indeed recognize that the determination as such, or any "what" whatsoever, is not a Nothing (*me on ouk en ti, Republic*, 478b), it is a not-Nothing that can also not-be, and thus that can also be nothing (*to amphoteron mete-chon, tou einai te kai me einai*, ibid., 478e). The distinction between Being and determination, which in Parmenides was an absolute separa-tion, is still an absolute separation in Plato, even though Being has now come to be predicated of the determination.

Yet Plato has become the savior of the positivity of differences, and the saving of differences was the root of the saving of phenomena (*sozein ta phainomena*). For the phenomena can be saved only if the logos does not necessitate their being posited as a Nothing. And if the Parmenidean logos did just that, the Platonic logos delivered them from nothingness by positing the not-being of determinations—and thus also of the determinations that appear—no longer as *enantion* (contrary to), but rather as *eteron* (other than) Being. Plato has become the defender of the concrete, a shelter from the Parmenidean ship-wreck. And Western thought has taken shelter here to this day, without realizing that the wolf had slipped in before the sheepfold was closed, and that the light of the truth of Being had been left outside, in sover-eign solitude. For Plato let into the fold the very thing that should have been left outside, namely, the abstract separation of Being and the determination; while he left outside that which should have been the first to go in—the breath of the flock, Parmenides' *truth*. Plato is the guardian of Western thought and in this faithless guardian Western thought has placed all its trust, even, and above all, when it has condemned him and made him the scapegoat for the antimeta-physical stance. The demands of the concrete, of history, of immanent experience, the impatience with metaphysical Platonism and the aspi-rations to a demythologized comprehension of the world of man—are not all these possible only if one is able to *think differences*? To *think*, that is, the *manifold*, the *determination*? And has not the Platonic opus been the only attempt to do so, the only shield against Parmenides?

Western thought has continued to shelter beneath this shield long after Plato's great struggle against Parmenides became a distant memory, and long after that metaphysical dimension whose salient moment was the Platonic parricide was judged to be superseded. (Thomas Aquinas, *De ente et essentia*, Ch. IV). As Aquinas says:

> Whatever is not of the understood content of an essence or quiddity is something which comes from without and makes a composition with the essence, because no essence can be understood without the things which are parts of it. Now, every essence or quiddity can be understood without anything being understood about its existence. For I can understand what a man is, or what a phoenix is, and yet not know whether they have existence in the real world. It is clear, there-fore, that existence is other than essence or quiddity, unless perhaps there exists a thing whose quiddity is its existence.[5]

In this celebrated theorem the abstract separation of Being and the deter-mination (i.e., of *esse* and *essentia*) is formulated in the most explicit way possible: "every essence or quiddity can be understood without anything being understood about its existence" (*omnis autem essentia potest intelligi sine hoc quod intelligatur aliquid de esse suo*).[6] And those contemporary Thomists who reject the truth of Being do so on the basis of this very theo-rem. Yet if we are to awaken from the great sleep of reason, the touchstone is right *here*: here is the *watershed* of Being: "and the decision on these matters rests here: it *is* or it is not" (*e de krisis peri touton en toid estin; estin*

---

5   Thomas Aquinas, *On Being and Essence*, trans. by Joseph Bobik, Notre Dame, IN: University of Notre Dame Press, 1965, 159–60. ("*Quidquid non est de intellectu quidditatis vel essentiae, hoc est adveniens extra et faciens compositionem cum essentia; quia nulla essentia sine his, quae sunt partes essentiae, intelligi potest. Omnis autem essentia vel quidditas potest intelligi sine hoc quod intelligatur aliquid de esse suo; possumus enim intelligere quid est homo, vel Phoenix et tamen ignorare an esse habeat in rerum natura. Ergo patet quod esse est aliud ab essentia vel quidditate; nisi forte sit aliqua res, cuius quidditas sit ipsum esse suum.*" *De ente et essentia*, IV.)

6   It should be noted that the meaning of the term "*essentia*," as it is employed in this theorem, is not restricted to that of "intelligible essence," abstracted from indi-viduating determinations, but rather indicates all types of determination, from the most individual (whence one speaks of "Peter's essence" [*essentia Petri*], in which "this bone or this flesh is included" [*ponitur hoc os vel haec caro*], Thomas Aquinas, ibid., II) to the most abstract. Thus "*essentia*" is nothing other than that "not-Being" which Plato has shown to be *eteron* than Being.

e ouk estin. Parmenides, Fr. 8, 15–16).[7] Is or is not the determination nothing? "*Homo*," "*phoenix*," "Socrates," "this bone or this flesh" (*hoc os vel haec
caro*)—are they or are they not nothing? To repeat in *truth* the great step
beyond Parmenides—to take it, that is, without being ensnared by the
Platonic mystification—we have to say that the determination refuses to
be a Nothing *insofar as it is a determination*; so that not being a Nothing is
predicated of the determination *as such*, and therefore is a predicate that
can never be separated from it. "Every essence or quiddity can be understood without anything being understood about its existence" (*Omnis
essentia vel quidditas non potest intelligi sine hoc quod intelligatur aliquid de
esse suo*)—*unless*, that is, one thinks its not being a Nothing, and *thus* its
esse, its existence. Where—be it noted!—existence, which *is* of the understood content of an essence or quiddity (*est de intellectu quidditatis vel
essentiae*), is not a certain *modality* of existence, but is *existence as such*—is
esse in its transcendental sense, i.e., as pure not-being-nothing. Aquinas
on the contrary thinks he can demonstrate that *Being* is not of the understood content of essence (*esse non est de intellectu quidditatis*) by pointing
out that it is possible to think what "*homo*" is and nevertheless ignore
whether he has existence in the real world (*ignorare an esse habeat in
rerum natura*). But in this way he loses sight of the transcendental aspect
of *esse* and reduces it to "*esse in rerum natura*," i.e., to a particular modality
of existence. For, in thinking "*phoenix*," it is clearly problematic if this
fabulous bird is to have the same mode of Being as this lamp, and which
allows the lamp to be touched, looked at, held in one's hand: it is problematic if it is to have *that mode* of Being which, if you will, may be posited as
a mode of "*esse in rerum natura*" (just as this lamp's assuming a modality
of existence different from the one that is actually manifest is also problematic). And in this sense it is by no means false to affirm that *esse*—
understood, however, as this *modality* of *esse!*—"is *not* of the understood
content of an essence or quiddity" (*non est de intellectu quidditatis vel
essentiae*). But while the implication between an essence and *a particular
modality* of its existence (different from the one that it actually possesses)
is indeed problematic, there is no problem whatsoever with the implication between essence (in the sense of *any* essence or determination

7   G. S. Kirk and J. E. Raven, *The Presocratic Philosophers: A Critical History
with a Selection of Texts*, Cambridge, UK: Cambridge University Press, 1957, 273.

whatsoever: unreal or real, incorporeal or corporeal . . .) and pure existence, i.e., existence in its transcendental sense. To the extent that this fabulous bird appears, and according to the modality of its appearing—and it
indeed must appear, if "we can understand what a Phoenix is" (*possumus
intelligere quid est Phoenix*)—to this extent and according to this modality
it is not a Nothing, and this not being a Nothing is immediately (*per se*)
predicated of it, in virtue of (*per*) its being a *what* that is in some way
meaningful. Just as, to the extent that this lamp appears, and according to
the modality of its appearing, it must immediately be affirmed of this
lamp, as such, that it is not—nor can it become—a Nothing.

Thus we find Parmenides' original sin at the bottom of the Thomistic
theorem as well: since "Being" does not signify "man," "house," "red,"
these and all determinations are a Nothing. And thus, even if one follows
Plato (and Plato indeed denies that the determination is a Nothing!),
one nevertheless continues to think the determination as that of which
not-being-a-Nothing is not immediately (*per se*) predicated; that is, one
continues to think the determination as something whose concept does
not include not-being-nothing. "It is clear, therefore, that essence is
other than existence or quiddity" (*Ergo patet quod esse est aliud ab essentia vel quidditate*): which implies that, if one considers "man" or "phoenix" or any other determination *by* (*per:* in virtue of) *itself*, one can
convince oneself that there is no difference whatsoever between a man
and a Nothing! For if one were to protest, insisting that such a conviction is untenable—that is, that a determination *cannot* be thought to be
a Nothing—this would mean that not being Nothing "*is* of the understood content of an essence or quiddity" (*est de intellectu quidditatis vel
essentiae*), and it would therefore be impossible to "understand what
man is and yet not know whether he has existence" (*intelligere quid est
homo et tamen ignorare an esse habeat*). "Existence [being] is other than
essence" (*Esse est aliud ab essentia*): therefore a determination is that
which, *per se* considered, could also be identified with Nothing; and
therefore the determination is *per se indifferent* to being, or to not-being,
a Nothing.[8] Behold the defenders of Being! For them, it is possible to

---

8 And, again, one cannot say that essence, as intelligible essence, is indifferent
to being or not-being *in rerum natura*: precisely because, as we have seen, in the
Thomistic theorem essence is any type of determination whatsoever, be it abstract or
individual. Is abstract essence nothing? If not, then it is eternal as abstract essence. Is

affirm that earths and seas, skies and stars, living beings, men and all things are nothing! Behold thought's sickness unto death: to the extent that one considers any given determination *as such*—to the extent, for example, that one considers this man *as such* (*hoc os vel haec caro*)—one cannot say whether it *is* or *is not* a Nothing! And one cannot do so, because "essence or quiddity can be understood without anything being understood about its existence" (*essentia vel quidditas potest intelligi sine hoc quod intelligatur aliquid de esse suo*). For, if in thinking the determination as such one were able *thereby* to exclude its being a Nothing, then *esse* (and so *eternity*) would be "of the understood content of an essence" (*de intellectu essentiae*).

To be able to affirm that existence is included in essence, i.e., that existence belongs *per se* to essence, alienated reason has recourse to a *middle*.[9] Just as for Plato not every "what" (*ti*) is *o estin*, and thus not

---

"*haec caro*" nothing? If not, then it is eternal in its being concretely individuated in this way. It is clear, however, that from the standpoint of Aquinas's theorem one *cannot* reply in this way (that is, one cannot essentially link essence to its existence), and thus essence, be it abstract or individual, is conceived as *per se* indifferent to being or not-being a Nothing.

9   The truth of Being demands that such inclusion be an *immediate implication* of existence on the part of (every) essence, and not the *indistinctness* of existence and essence, as another of my critics has objected. But the *distinction* is no abstract *separation* of the distincts which, *as distincts*, necessarily imply one another. (In other words, the alienation of "existence is other than essence" [*esse est aliud ab essentia*] consists not in the affirmation of the distinction—which is clearly unshakable—between "*esse*" and "*essentia*," but rather in the affirmation of their separation, i.e., in understanding the distinction as separation.) "Yellow" does not mean "Being," but in considering what "yellow" means, we affirm that it is not a Nothing (and therefore is, exists). Or perhaps, in thinking "yellow"—in considering this determination as such—we do not know whether we are thinking a Nothing or whether we are thinking a not-Nothing?!

Clearly, the determination of which "is" (i.e., not being a Nothing) is immediately predicated is not the determination that is separated from its "is" (and which, as so separated, is either immediately posited as nothing, as Parmenides thought, or is posited as that of which it cannot be known whether it is or is not a Nothing—as everyone else thinks, following Plato). The union of a determination and its "is" is not a union between two terms (essence, existence) that were once disunited (as was the case with Plato), and thus the determination of which it is immediately affirmed that it is not nothing is nothing other than the determination-that-is-not-a-Nothing. Hence, in *La struttura originaria* we dealt at length with the structuring of the judgment which, as such, must always be an *identical* judgment. By this, we mean a judgment in which the predicate is not predicated of the pure subject (otherwise, even in saying that Being is Being, an identity between two differents would be posited, since, in affirming that Being is Being, one says not simply "Being," but Being as predicated

every "what" is delivered from all Becoming (*to eilikrinos on*)—*only* that privileged essence (*ousia*), which is the *idea*, enjoys that prerogative—so for Aquinas existence (*estin*) does not belong *per se* to every essence (i.e., to essence as such), but only to that particular reality, *if it*

---

by Being); rather, the predicate is predicated of the subject *of* this predication, and the predicate is not the pure predicate, but is the predicate *of* the subject. Therefore *any* judgment whatsoever must be understood as the identity between the synthesis of the subject and the predicate and the synthesis of the predicate and the subject: that is, as identity of identicals (cf. *La struttura originaria*, Ch. III, paragraphs IX–XIV; Ch. VIII, paragraphs X–XIV; Ch. IX, paragraphs XVII–XXIII; Ch. XV, paragraphs I, VII).

So: is "yellow" nothing? Plato has taught us that the answer is no: if "yellow" means "yellow," no identity can be posited between "yellow" (i.e., between this not-Nothing) and Nothing. (And in order to say that yellow is not a Nothing, not only is there no need of a *mediation* that connects yellow to its not-being-nothing, but any such mediation must be rejected.) But *that which* is not nothing is not a "that," which is separated from its not-being-nothing (and can therefore, as so separated, be nothing), subsequently entering into synthesis with it. Essence and existence are not to be presupposed *by* their synthesis (precisely because essence, thus presupposed, would be presented once again as something of which it would not be known whether it is or is not a Nothing; and existence, in turn, as presupposed by the synthesis, would be the existence of nothing), but rather as distinguished *in* the synthesis, which is therefore original synthesis. Accordingly, not-being-a-Nothing is predicated of essence-that-is-not-a-Nothing. (In saying this, however, we do not mean to suggest that there can be an essence that is a Nothing, but, quite the contrary, that essence is always already in synthesis with existence and is not presupposed by the synthesis.) And therefore it can be said equally well either that existence is necessarily predicated of essence, or that existence is necessarily predicated of Being (or of being) ("Being is"—the Parmenidean formula stressed throughout "Returning to Parmenides"). Existence, then, is predicated of essence (and not of existence, as my critic mistakenly believed), since it is *of the determination* that it must be affirmed that it is not a Nothing. But essence is that of which existence is predicated; which is to say that existence is predicated of essence in its being in synthesis *with*, and not in its being separated *from*, existence—just as a marriage is consummated not between two people each alone in separate homes, but between a couple embracing under the same roof. Thus when the truth of Being affirms that *Being is*, it is not thinking of that banality which consists in referring existence to an essence already thought as existing in fact, thereby confusing hypothetical necessity (i.e., *if* an essence exists, then it necessarily exists) with absolute necessity (essence necessarily exists). The truth of Being highlights the alienation typical of the concept of a hypothetical necessity, by positing that essence, *as such*, is a not-Nothing, and therefore, *as such*, exists (and therefore necessarily exists). But precisely because essence, as such, exists, the synthesis of essence and existence is *original*; i.e., existence is not predicated of essence as presupposed by the synthesis, but rather of essence that is in synthesis, and so of essence that exists. Thus that which *per se* exists is essence that exists, and the concrete expression of this implication is given by the very affirmation that Being (i.e., essence-that-exists; essence not presupposed by the synthesis) is.

were to exist (*nisi forte sit*), whose essence is its very existence: "existence is other than essence" (*esse est aliud ab essentia*)—i.e., *esse* "is not
of the understood content of an essence . . . unless perhaps there exists
a thing whose quiddity is its existence" (*non est de intellectu essentiae . . . nisi forte sit aliqua res cuius quidditas sit esse suum*). *If*, that is,
one manages to *demonstrate* that there exists a being which demands
by its very nature—as pure act, immutable, etc.—that existence be "of
the understood content of an essence" (*de intellectu suae essentiae*),
only then will one know that there exists an essence of which, as such,
existence is predicated. In this perspective, essence, as such, does not
imply existence, and consequently the demonstration of the existence
of the immutable being (that is, of a being that postulates a relationship *sui generis* between essence and existence) is the *middle term* that
unites that supreme essence which is God to its existence—which is to
say, that unites "*esse*" to "intellectus essentiae." The knowledge of an
essence (or determination) as such is not deemed sufficient for its
existence to be affirmed: *something else* is required, on the basis of
which existence may be linked to essence. And this "something else" is
that very "middle" which allows existence to be necessarily predicated
of essence. In this way, alienated reason posits as a *result*—as something *mediated*—the very immediacy of the logos—if, that is, the original logos indeed consists in positing everything that is not nothing
(essences, determinations, Being) as not-nothing and thus as necessarily existent. Indeed, one feels the need to *demonstrate* that there
exists a being to which existence necessarily belongs, precisely because
thought is subject to such a fatal metathesis that it fails to recognize the
originality [*originarietà*] of the affirmation that any determination
whatsoever is not a Nothing, and thus that existence belongs of necessity to every determination. And thus the Thomistic identity of essence
and existence in God, as the original inclusion of existence by essence
as such, is nothing other than the most radical mystification of the
truth of Being. Aquinas most definitely recognizes that the proposition "God is" (*Deus est*) is self-evident (*per se notum*), since the predicate belongs *per se* to the subject (*praedicatum est idem cum subiecto*,
Sum. theol., I, q. 2, a. 1); but that this proposition is "*per se notum*" is
the result of a demonstration (which comes to affirm a being) in which
"*esse*" cannot be combined with essence (*facere compositionem cum*

essentia), and therefore, for Aquinas, it is not *"per se notum"* with respect to us (*quoad nos*): which means, indeed, that it is *not* immediate, but is mediated. In this distortion of the truth of Being, original truth becomes a result, and, precisely because it is not maintained as original, is denied. For the truth of Being, the *"Deus"* that appears in *"Deus est"* (that is, in a proposition in which the meaning of the subject varies according to the historical situation of consciousness) is itself a determination within the totality of determinations, and is therefore a determination that shares the fate of all determinations: namely, that it cannot not-be, and is therefore eternal. But in truth, God is this very totality of the positive, posited as that which cannot be released from its "is." And this position is the original—the immediate—which only the torpor of the meaning of Being can treat as the result of a mediation.[10]

---

10   Presenting these thoughts in "Returning to Parmenides," I in no way intended (as Bontadini claims in "Sozein ta Phainomena," 451–2) to present classical metaphysics as a popular philosophy whose purpose was to "prove the existence of God," i.e., the existence of a representation of religious consciousness. It is unquestionably true that in classical metaphysics the meaning of the term "God" is a result of the logical process that intends to supersede the contradictoriness of the world of Becoming (cf. *La struttura originaria*, Ch. V, paragraph V, note 3). Yet it is this very process that makes it possible to affirm the existence of a necessary Being. By this we mean that the necessary existence of Being (i.e., of any determination that is not a Nothing) is not regarded by classical metaphysics as an original truth—even though the affirmation that the not-Nothing is not and cannot be a Nothing *must* be original!—but rather as the *result* of a *mediation* in which a *middle* (namely, the demonstrative procedure that constructs the meaning of the word "God") is inserted between Being and its not being a Nothing (i.e., between Being and its existence). On page 50 of "Returning to Parmenides" it was stated: "The *demonstration* of a necessary Being seeks and presumes to find a middle that joins the negation of the negative to the positive": a middle between *Being* and its is, and not—as Bontadini mistakenly read it—"a middle between the subject God and the predicate 'is'" (452). This careless reading led my critic to object that, in fact, classical metaphysics did not undertake to prove the existence of God by introducing a middle between the subject and the predicate of the proposition "God is," since "the classical thinkers were well aware that here the predicate belongs to the notion of the subject." A correct reading, however, shows that the alienation of classical metaphysics (and indeed of all subsequent thought) consists in its not recognizing the immediacy of the relation between the positive and the negation of the negative; and thus that process in which classical metaphysics constructs the meaning of the word "God" (a process which is by no means a popular demonstration of the existence of God) acts as a *middle* between Being and its not-being-nothing (i.e., its existence): precisely because only when the existence of the immutable is known can one then affirm that there is a being of

The Heideggerian question of why there are beings at all rather than nothing—"Why do beings exist instead of there being nothing?" (*Warum ist überhaupt Seiendes und nicht vielmehr Nichts?*)—*by its very questioning* expresses with the utmost consistency that abstract separation between the determination and being (*einai*) which the whole of Western thought has inherited from Parmenides in Platonic form. For indeed, once that abstract separation has been posited, one must unquestionably ask why there are beings. Put in question, the totality of beings "wavers" (*schwankt*), for in posing the question one seeks the very "ground that will ground the dominance of being as an overcoming of the Nothing" (*wird einen Grund gesucht, der die Herrschaft des Seienden als eine Überwindung des Nichts begrunden soll*).[11] This, which ought to be the fundamental metaphysical question, seeks the ground of *original* truth—it seeks the ground of that which is itself the ground of all thought! Here too, one asks why there are beings, precisely because thought has sunk so deeply into forgottenness of the truth of Being that it fails to realize that the Being (*esse*, *einai*, existence) of being is its very not-being-nothing, and that *here* one is at the *bottom* of thought, at original

---

which existence is necessarily predicated. Hence it can well be said that any logical demonstration that comes to affirm the existence of a necessary being is a wishing to "seek"—i.e., to "demonstrate"—that which constitutes the *original* truth of Being: it is a being destined always to look far into the distance, and so to never find that which lies close at hand. While on the one hand, for the affirmation "*Deus est*" "the classical thinkers were well aware that here the predicate belongs to the notion of the subject" (in the sense, however, that the belonging of the predicate to the subject is *per se notum*, but not *quoad nos*), on the other hand, for the affirmation "Being is not nothing, *and thus* exists and cannot not-exist," neither classical thought, nor any other thought after Parmenides, ever realized that *here* the predicate belongs to the notion of the subject. And this is clearly demonstrated by those contemporary Thomists who, apropos of "Returning to Parmenides," declare themselves willing to accept Parmenides' truth, but then understand that truth as immediate with respect to itself (*quoad se*), but not with respect to us (*quoad nos*): thus failing to understand that, "accepted" in this way, the truth of Being has been utterly lost, just as it has been utterly lost in the Thomistic thesis of the identity of essence and existence in God.

11 Martin Heidegger, *Einführung in die Metaphysik*, Tübingen: Niemeyer, 1953, 22. Heidegger translates Leibniz's "Pourquoi il y a plûtot quelque chose que rien?" in Gottfried Wilhelm Leibniz, *Principes de la nature et de la grâce fondés en raison*, 7ème article, 602. See *Die philosophischen Schriften von Gottfried Wilhelm Leibniz*, Vol. 6, ed. Carl J. Gerhardt, Berlin: Weidmannsche Buchhandlung, 1882 [*Editors' note*].

truth, which cannot be questioned since the questioning itself is a form of its denial.

1. THE ETERNITY OF BEING AND THE APPEARING OF BECOMING

But if the truth of Being reawakens, it must be said of *every* thing that, precisely because it is not nothing, it cannot become a Nothing (nor can it have been a Nothing), and therefore it *is* and reigns eternal. Everything is eternal. *And yet* Being appears—and no less incontrovertibly—as coming-to-be. Everything is immutable; and yet Becoming appears. This shadow on a sheet of white paper was never born and will never perish; and yet it just supervened in the content that appears, and now that I have moved my hand, it has already vanished. This shadow is immutable, yet this shadow becomes; it is impossible that this shadow not-be, yet this shadow was-not, and now it is no more. Does not the truth of Being lead, then, to the most irremediable aporia, to the most irreparable rupture in knowing? If Being, *qua* Being, is immutable, the becoming of Being is impossible; but this impossibility is the very content of Appearing.

This is unquestionably the fundamental aporia to which the truth of Being gives rise. But can it be used as a *critique* that compels one to renounce the truth of Being? If thought were unable to find a way out of the aporia, could it for this reason go back and repropose the thesis that Being can be annulled, i.e., that Being can be identical to Nothing?

In setting forth the formal meaning of the aporetic situation in which the truth of Being finds itself, I observed that

> in any case truth must undertake to negate its own negation and, in relation to the negations argued for, must show that such arguments are mere *appearance* . . . If truth is *truth*, it can negate its universal negation and thus show why its negation, considered in its essence, and therefore as universality, must be negated. Truth therefore knows *a priori* that any possible argument for its negation, and thus any specific way of arguing for that negation, is a merely *apparent* argument: it is no real, *true* argument, for to be such it would have to be grounded upon that original truth which instead it intends to negate.

But while truth knows *a priori* that there can be no argument for any possible form of its negation, and that therefore any such argument is merely apparent, it must also undertake to show this mere appearance *concretely*, since otherwise that which ranks as an apparent argument would in practice be effective. For truth, an argument for its negation acts effectively only when it manages to present as mutually contradictory two assertions that belong to the apophantic structure of truth: only when—to put it another way—such an argument manages to show that an assertion q is such that it cannot be negated, and q is contradictory with respect to an assertion p that belongs to the structure of truth. But then, insofar as q belongs to or is implied by the original structure of truth, it cannot be negated: wherefore an argument for the negation of truth will be effective only insofar as it shows truth to be a saying of things that contradict one another. This corresponds to the first of the two formulations. Now, p and q are predicative moments of truth insofar as neither one of them can be negated. The question, then, is one of unmasking in the argument for the negation that element x which is heterogeneous to the original structure of truth (i.e., which stems from forms of conviction not resting on that structure) and which, assumed as an element of truth, gives rise to the situation in which p and q are presented as mutually contradictory assertions. Truth knows *a priori* that this x exists; but, as we said, it must solve for the unknown; it must concretely determine the content of x, thus showing its heterogeneity with respect to the original structure. In this task, truth may succeed, but may also fail: it may find itself in situations such that, while knowing that the argument for its negation can have no truth, it is not actually capable of concretely showing the argument's untruth. Truth, that is, may find itself in situations of aporia, from which the only way out passes through the concrete determination of x, and not through the elimination of p or of q.[12]

So then, the immutability of Being (prescribed by the opposition of Being to Nothing) and the becoming of Being (which is present in Appearing) are the concrete values assumed, in this instance, by p and

---

12   Cf. E. Severino, *Studi di filosofia della prassi*, Milan: Vita e pensiero, 1962, 39–40.

by *q*. Thus the question here, too, is one of unmasking that factor of untruth (i.e., *x*), which occasions the appearance of a self-opposition of truth. If the logos prohibits the not-being of Being, then the contradictoriness of Becoming—the contradictoriness of that which is incontrovertibly manifest—must be a merely *apparent contradictoriness*.

2. THE TRUTH OF THE APPEARING OF BECOMING AND THE NIHILISTIC INTERPRETATION OF BECOMING

The alienation of reason implies an alienated meaning of Becoming. If the impossibility of Being's not-being is not recognized, one will be left without the slightest suspicion that the authentic content of Appearing is radically altered by defining the Becoming that appears as an annulment of Being, or as Being's emerging from nothingness. *Be it noted*: if Becoming is understood, by definition, as the annulment of Being, or as Being's emerging from nothingness, then the truth of Being prohibits that Being become and proclaims it to be immutable; *but the problem, now, is another*, namely: does Becoming *appear* as such annulment or as such emergence? In other words: is the Becoming that appears a Becoming that cannot be predicated of Being? Alienated reason, as we said, tends not even to suspect the existence of this problem, and accepts the expression of the Becoming that appears in terms of Being and not-Being as definitive. From Plato onward it has been established that, in the becoming of things that appear, their not-being is not the nothingness of every thing, but rather is the not-being of *some* thing—wherefore Becoming is the transition from a certain not-Being to a certain Being—yet the Becoming that appears has been defined nonetheless as the transition from a moment in which a something *is not* (and so is nothing) to a moment in which that something *is*. This means that every thing whose Becoming appears is posited as participating in Being and in not-Being (*to amphoteron metechon, tou einai te kai me einai, Republic*, 478e)—this double participation constituting the very definition of the Becoming that appears. But does this definition faithfully express the content that appears?

This piece of paper burns quickly, and now it is ash. We say, then, that it has been *destroyed* and that the result of this destruction is its now being a Nothing. But—here is the problem—*does this nothingness appear, or does nothing more of the object appear* (nothing, that is, of the mode of Being that distinguished it before it was burned)? In other words, does it *appear that* the object *is nothing*, or does the object *no longer appear*? That the nothingness of things *appears* is the reply of those who attribute a value of truth to the cunning that makes life in the world possible—the reply of those who transform technology (*techne*) into *episteme*. It appears that the object is now a Nothing—so they say—because the flame that was consuming it and the ash that remains belong to the content of Appearing. And if we were to ask them whether the sun that disappears behind the clouds is *destroyed*, their reply would be no, because the sun can *return*; but who has ever seen a body return from its ashes? Ash remains ash, and *therefore* an object that has become ash has been destroyed and is no more. And if tomorrow bodies were to come back from their ashes just as the sun comes out from behind the clouds? Mere fancy, would be their reply, because up to now the world has gone on in the way we know. And this, undoubtedly, is the way we all think, as long as we remain intent on defending our lives in the world, and are concerned that our lives should not become ashes.

Yet from these considerations it is clear that the destruction and the becoming-nothing of things is affirmed *not insofar as their nothingness appears*—not, that is, insofar as one faithfully expresses the content of Appearing—but rather *insofar as that content is interpreted* according to the categories of the practical wisdom that hitherto has favored man's life in the world. From the standpoint of this wisdom one understands—i.e., one *interprets*—that that which nature or human art is unable to bring back (from nothingness) has been destroyed and is no more. But if, instead of keeping to the categories of *doxa* (children's toys, *paidon athurmata*, as Heraclitus called them, Fr. 70), one keeps to the categories of truth, *aletheia* (and truth does not need to be wise)—if, that is, one is careful to express the content that appears *just as* it appears—then Becoming that appears *cannot* be understood as the annulment of Being. This body burns, and this body is replaced by its ashes: Appearing attests nothing other than a succession of events: the piece of white paper—the approach of the flame—a flame that grows—a smaller, differently shaped piece of paper—a flame dying away—a piece even smaller and of still another shape—ashes. Each event is followed by another, in the sense that *a second event begins to appear when the first appears no longer*. After the fire, ashes; which means: when the fire no longer appears, ashes appear. But that something that no longer *appears* no longer *is*—*this* is not manifest in Appearing. On the contrary—it is *interpreted* on the basis of the way in which something appears and disappears. When something appears that has never appeared before, one says that it has been born and that previously it was a Nothing; when something disappears and does not return, one says that it has died and become a Nothing. And men have learned that when something appears in a certain way, it has never appeared before; and when it disappears in a certain way, it will not return.

Yet this is untruth's interpretation of Becoming: only the intervention of *doxa* compels one to posit as a Nothing (before and after its appearing) that which appears and disappears in a certain way.[13] The *veritable* [*veritativo*] comprehension of the Becoming which is the content of Appearing instead throws into relief the *silence* of Appearing regarding the fate of that which does not appear. And if Appearing as such says nothing about this fate, it is disclosed "unadorned" (*akallopista*) by the truth of Being which, Sybil with raving mouth (*Sibulla de mainomeno stomati*, Heraclitus, Fr. 92), says that Being is and cannot not-be and keeps to itself, eternal. But, in the meantime, the aporia provoked by the truth of Being has disappeared, at least in the form in which it was originally presented: for indeed, Appearing *does not attest* the opposite of that which is demanded by the logos. The logos demands the immutability of Being—it demands, that is, that Being not be nothing, and thus not issue from and not return to nothingness—and Appearing, *in its truth, does not attest* that Being does so. The apparent contradictoriness of the Becoming that appears is

---

13 Likewise, the cosmogonies of modern physics, based upon the so-called "principles of conservation," also reflect the doxic point of view; for when one postulates the "conservation" of "matter" or of "energy," one accepts the destruction of everything that such matter or energy constituted. Also those who posit Becoming as "accidental" or "subjective" betray the testimony of Appearing and the truth of Being, since it can neither be said of the accidental or subjective that they are-not, nor that they appear as an issuing from and a returning to nothingness.

superseded *not* by introducing the absurdity of a creator god who identifies Being with Nothing (as if the not-being of Being would no longer be absurd if it were caused by a god), but rather by freeing oneself from that definition of the Becoming that appears which stems from the illegitimate intervention of *doxa*—this definition being the very x that gives rise to the apparent opposition between p, the immutability of Being, and q, the presence of Becoming: the two apparently opposed moments of truth. This spurious definition of existent Becoming (and that Becoming of which existence *must* be affirmed is the Becoming that is manifest) is present also in the passage of Aristotle's *De Interpretatione* considered above; and it is natural that the new Aristotelians see the value of this Aristotelian discourse (i.e., Being is when it is, and is-not when it is-not) precisely in its allegedly being disclosive of experience.[14]

---

14   The "Aristotelian discourse is such that not only can it be formulated, insofar as it corresponds to the report of *phainesthai*, but indeed it must be formulated, since experience cannot be set aside" (G. Bontadini, "Sozein ta Phainomena," 446). *Here* is the spurious definition, right here in this belief that the moment in which Being is-not (=when Being is-not), and thus the moment in which Being is nothing, "corresponds to the report of *phainesthai*"—corresponds, that is, to that evidence which would posit the emergence from nothingness and the annulment of Being— and therefore is something that "must" be affirmed, "since experience cannot be set aside." But manifestation (*phainesthai*) says nothing with regard to Being that does not appear, and there remains only the ontological torpor, without foundation, that says of Being: "when it is-not." Bontadini goes on to say that this Aristotelian discourse, "furthermore, is a discourse that 'has already been formulated.' Indeed, it was formulated the very moment we semantized *Being* in its original opposition to Nothing. This semantizing Nothing is, precisely, the not-being of Being; it is that not-Being which is evidenced in Becoming. Thus the Aristotelian discourse is assured both semantically and apophantically" (ibid.). But—to the contrary—since the not-being of Being is by no means evidenced in Becoming, the Aristotelian discourse not only is not assured apophantically (indeed, it is belied by the truth of Being, which prohibits that Being not-be), but in it—and above all in Bontadini's interpretation of it—the semantics of Being vanishes completely. Since that Nothing which was to have semantized Being does not appear, and its Appearing was to have been the ground of the semantization of Being, Being, in this Neo-Aristotelian semantics, turns out to be a meaningless word. It is, moreover, quite natural that, due to nonfamiliarity (*asunetheia*) with the truth of Being, one fails to recognize the mystification at work in the definition of existent Becoming in terms of Being and not-Being. But this semantization of Being leads to results which are unacceptable even from the standpoint of classical metaphysics itself. Indeed, if Being is meaningful only in its opposition to that not-Being which is allegedly manifest in the experience of Becoming, then the meaningfulness of Being would be merely a *fact*, since the

Thus what appears is not Being's issuing from and returning to nothingness, but rather its appearing and disappearing. This appearing and disappearing need be *interpreted* as the being and not being of things, only if one affirms that the totality of Being coincides with the Being that appears. In that case, entering and leaving Appearing unquestionably mean becoming Being and becoming nothing. Here too, however, the annulment of Being is *interpreted*, not observed. The truth of Being, then, destroys the ground of this interpretation, since *all* Being—even Being that appears no longer, overtaken by events and times and histories—even that piece of paper and the fire that enveloped it—even the last tongue of flame—*all* Being *is*; immutably keeping to itself, it extends beyond that of itself which it uncovers in Appearing, like the sea, which uncovers and recovers the edges of its sandy bed only along its shoreline. The Becoming that appears is not

---

becoming of things is itself merely factual. And thus it cannot be ruled out that the observed restlessness of Becoming should come to rest in a still spectacle, in which there remains neither memory nor suspicion of the not-being of things that appear and in which, therefore, the word "Being" would no longer be meaningful. In this way, classical metaphysics admits that the logical positivistic doctrine of the nonsense of metaphysics may become a truth.

However, that Being is meaningful only in its opposition to Nothing (and vice versa) remains unshakable. When it is affirmed that Being is that which is opposed to Nothing, one indicates not simply a property of Being—albeit the fundamental one—but rather its very meaning: Being is that which is opposed to Nothing. The opposition has a protagonist (="that which" is opposed), and the meaning of the protagonist is given by the opposition. Thus the semantics of Being coincides with the original self-revelation (*apophansis*) of the logos: *the operatio prima intellectus* (i.e., that which posits the meaningfulness of Being) is realized *only* in the *operatio seconda intellectus* (that which opposes Being to Nothing) (cf. *La struttura originaria*, Ch. IV). But the semantizing Nothing is not something that can be found in the manifestation of Becoming; on the contrary, it is absolutely other with respect to any positive, the totality of the positive or, which is the same thing, the totality of the meaningful: it is the not being any of the determinations that constitute the totality (not even the one expressed by the word "nothing"!). Moreover, as an absolute negativity this Nothing is a condition not only of the finite comprehension of Being (i.e., of a consciousness that has to limit itself to abstracting Being from the experience of Becoming), but must be posited by an absolute and immutable consciousness of Being as well. For, if Being *is not* Nothing—and if this "not being" is the very meaning of necessity (*ananke*)—then thinking Being without thinking Nothing is equivalent to not thinking Being: precisely because Being is, of necessity, the negation of Nothing, and not thinking Being as this negation means not thinking Being (just as thinking a triangle, but not thinking it as having three sides, means not thinking a triangle).

the birth and the death of Being, but rather its appearing and disappearing. Becoming is the process of the revelation of the immutable. (Indeed, Ch. XV, paragraph XXVI of *La struttura originaria* is entitled "Becoming as Appearing of the Immutable.") But let us not lose sight of the *force* of the arguments that have been put forward: *Being*, as such, and in its totality, is immutable (it cannot be thought that it is-not); the *becoming* of Being that is the content of Appearing does *not* appear as an issuing from and a returning to nothingness on the part of Being, but rather as an appearing and a disappearing *of Being*, and thus as an appearing and disappearing of that which is, i.e., of the immutable, which *is* eternally even when it has not yet appeared and even when it has disappeared. Thus: if Becoming is defined in terms of Being and not-Being, then the truth of Being proclaims Being's immutability; but if Becoming is defined according to the determinations that authentically belong to it as the content of Appearing—if Becoming is defined as the process of the revelation of Being—then Being's immutability and its Becoming no longer rank as mutually contradictory terms.

The authentic meaning of the *doxa* of Parmenides remains a problem. If *doxa* is understood as the very appearing of the manifold and of Becoming, and if the untruth (*ouk eni pistis alethes*, Fr. 1, v. 30) of *doxa* is understood as being constituted by the opposition between the content of Appearing and the content of the veritable logos, then the responsibility for the alienation of the meaning of Becoming goes back to Parmenides. For it can be affirmed that the Becoming that appears is opposed to the logos that proclaims the immutability of Being *only if* one believes that Appearing attests Being's emerging from and returning to nothingness—which is to say, only if one *inauthentically* interprets the Becoming that appears. From this point of view, there would be a substantial solidarity between Parmenides, who posits the untruth of Becoming, and all those who, later, were to undertake a "salvation" of Becoming: both interpret Becoming in terms of Being and not-Being. But once Becoming has been interpreted in this way its salvation becomes a desperate undertaking, since that which it claims to save is the *absurd*—i.e., the not-being of Being. While the meaning of Parmenidean *doxa* may be a problem, all subsequent thought unquestionably saw in Parmenides a denial of the becoming of experience (i.e., a denial of its value of truth) on account of the opposition between the truth of Being and manifest Becoming; Parmenides, then, was seen as the first to define Becoming in terms of Being and not-Being (Becoming thereby appearing as the opposite of the logos, which affirms the impossibility that Being not-be). Both classical metaphysics, which intends to save Becoming alongside the immutable, and the immanentistic tradition of modern philosophy, which tends to save Becoming while rejecting the immutable, derive from the conviction that Becoming is to be defined in the way that Parmenides is believed to have defined it. The myth of the salvation of the phenomena thus becomes one of the fundamental ways of expressing the alienation of the meaning of Being: post-Parmenidean thought, precisely because it is unable to rise to the truth of Being, is faced with the desperate undertaking of saving Becoming, defined as emergence from nothingness and annulment of Being. Indeed, both the Platonic affirmation of a middle ground (*metaxy*) partaking of Being and not-Being (an affirmation that will find its systematic explicitation in the Aristotelian theory of Becoming as the unity of potentiality and act) and the Hegelian affirmation of Becoming as the unity of Being and not-Being are equally abandoned by the truth of Being.

REMARK

But is the authentic meaning of Parmenidean *doxa* really the one set forth above? In Parmenides' poem, most of the passages that determine the meaning of *doxa* leave the question unsettled. Fragment 19 states:

> *outo toi kata doxan ephi tade kai nyn easi*
> *kai metepeit' apo toude teleutesousi traphenta*
> *tois d'onom' anthropoi katethent' episemon ekastoi.*

Thus, according to opinion, these things [that appear: *ta aistheta*, as Semplicius puts it] are born, and now exist, and from now on will grow and come to their end. Men have given them a name, a distinguishing mark for each.

If this text is read without introducing the categories of alienated reason, then it affirms that *doxa consists in believing that things that appear are generated and corrupted*, i.e., issue from and return to nothingness. And thus it is *not* stated there that *doxa* consists in the *appearing* of the generation and the corruption of Being (i.e., in the appearing of its issuing from and returning to nothingness)—in which case the untruth of Appearing would consist in the opposition between the content that appears and the content of the logos—but rather that *doxa* consists in *opining* that things that appear issue from and return to nothingness. That this opposition has no truth—*this* is the truth of Becoming. Only the torpor of the meaning of Being—and thus of the meaning of Becoming—can lead one to suppose that by positing this issuing from and returning to nothingness as *doxa* one thereby posits as *doxa* the manifest becoming of things. While it is true that the becoming of Being incontrovertibly appears (in the sense of Being's supervening in and departing from the circle of Appearing: the transition from not being-*there* [*esserci*] to being-*there* and vice versa), this commerce of Being with Nothing does not appear. Positing the affirmation that Being issues from and returns to nothingness as *doxa* is therefore something essentially different from positing the manifestation of Becoming (as it effectively appears) as *doxa*. Fragment 19 states *not* that the appearing of things is sick, but that the sickness lies in *believing* that things that appear (*tade*) issue from and return to nothingness. These are Parmenides' words and this is the truth of Becoming.

But when Parmenides denies Becoming, defined in terms of Being and not-Being, is he aware that this denial, besides being a rejection, is also an affirmation of Becoming, understood as the appearing and disappearing of Being? Admittedly, there is no trace of such an affirmation in what remains of Parmenides' poem. We know that Parmenides denied that which it was just to deny—i.e., Becoming, understood as issuing from and returning to nothingness (and justice, here, is the justice both of the truth of Being and of the truth of Appearing). But his words say nothing about that which it was just to affirm—i.e., Becoming, understood as the appearing and disappearing of Being (and here, justice is the justice of the truth of Appearing). And it was also this silence that led subsequent thought to interpret the Parmenidean denial of Becoming as a denial of the content of

Appearing. After Parmenides, thought kept to that definition of Becoming which had been explicitly formulated in Parmenides' poem (the Becoming, that is, which Parmenides had justly denied); but in doing so, it mistakenly came to believe that Becoming, so understood, is the content of Appearing and therefore, as such, *cannot* be denied. Accordingly, after Parmenides, alienated reason set out to save the phenomena, and so to save that Becoming (understood as issuing from and returning to nothingness) which, besides being prohibited by the truth of Being, does not even appear.

Parmenides' silence concerning that which is to be affirmed (i.e., the authentic meaning of Becoming) accompanies verses 38–41 of Fragment 8 as well:

> ... *toi pant' onoma estai,*
> *ossa brotoi katethento pepoithotes einai alethe,*
> *gignesthai te kai ollusthai, einai te kai ouchi,*
> *ai topon allassein dia te chroa phanon ameibein.*

Wherefore all these are mere names which mortals laid down believing them to be true: being born and perishing, being and not-being, change of place and variation of bright color. (After Kirk & Raven, *Presocratic Philosophers*, 277)

Here too, the fragment is clear: the *conviction* that things are born and perish, are and are-not, and really undergo change, has no truth (and thus is *doxa*). Here too, Parmenides does not state that manifest things have no truth; rather, he posits as untruth that which effectively has no truth (and which therefore does not appear): i.e., Becoming, understood as a process in which Being is at stake. And, just as in the last verse of Fragment 19, he throws into relief that sickness of language which reflects the inauthenticity of opining: being born and perishing, being and not-being, the transformation and corruption of things have no truth (indeed, such is the authentic report of Appearing), but are only the way in which words and language have come to be slaves of the untruth of Being.

In these passages Parmenides says nothing about the value of the manifestation of things, and limits himself to explicitating the valuelessness of that way of thinking which understands Becoming as a process in which Being is at stake. Thus the invitation, in Fragment 7, to make use of the logos (*krinai de logoi*) and not the senses, instead of being read as an affirmation of the untruth of Appearing as such, may be taken as an awareness that the meaning of Being is given not by Appearing, but by that supreme justice (*Dike*) of Being which prohibits that Being not-be. Appearing as such says nothing about the meaning of Being; incapable of establishing anything about the fate of that which has not yet been revealed and of that which is no longer manifest, it limits itself to disclosing and concealing Being. And this inability of Appearing could well be expressed by the word *askopon*. Referring to the eye (*omma*), which—together with "echoing hearing" (*ekheessan akouen*) and the "tongue" (*glossan*)—is not to be used in the examination of Being, *askopon* would thus not signify (deriving it from *skopeo*) the mere valuelessness of that which manifests itself to the senses, but rather (deriving it from *skopos*) the unfitness of sensible manifestation to set itself up as a judge (*krinai*) of the meaning of Being.

On the other hand, if Parmenides denies the manifold—and while the extant fragments by no means definitively confirm this, Plato and Aristotle did understand him in that way—then the appearing of the manifold would unquestionably be doxic: *doxa*, that is, would have to be understood as Appearing itself, and not as an erroneous interpretation of it. And, in this case, the thesis concerning the appearing of Becoming would also be affected: for if Being is the simple, then the appearing of the becoming of the manifold has no truth, precisely because the manifold itself has none. Parmenides' silence regarding the necessity of affirming the Becoming that appears could in that case be explained by the implicit impossibility of giving a value of truth to the Becoming that appears, precisely because of its being the becoming of the manifold. But how sure can we be that Parmenides intended to deny the manifold? There can be no doubt that Plato's intervention was needed in order to posit the manifold, but the question here is another: *did* Parmenides explicitly intend to deny the manifold? If he did not, then his silence regarding the Becoming that appears would again become a problem.

The "world" is the dimension in which beings, becoming (in the nihilistic sense), or being [*essendo*] as that which could not-have-been, are a Nothing. Metaphysics began to "see" the "world" at the very dawn of its history: not in the sense that the "world" let itself be seen, but rather in the sense that metaphysics *imposed* the "world" upon things that let themselves be seen. In this way, the "world" became the *a priori* of any vision, and metaphysics convinced itself that the "world" stood before it as something seen—indeed, as the "seen" par excellence. Was this Parmenides' view (if so, he would have posited as untruth that which he believed he saw)? This question may well be destined to remain unanswered. But it was the Eleatic school itself that, perhaps for the first time, rigorously and definitively expressed the faith that the "world" stands before one as the "seen."

In Fragment 8, Melissus demonstrates that only the one is (*en monon estin*), while the manifold is-not.[15] The manifold (*polla*) is everything that we "see and hear" (*oromen kai akouomen*), that "appears" or "seems" (*dokei emin*), and that we say that we "understand" (*sunienai*) and "know" (*ginoskein*): "earth and water," "air and fire," "iron and gold," "things living and dead," "black and white," "and all the other things that men say truly exist" (*kai ta alla, osa phasin oi anthropoi einai alethe*). Yet all these things *show themselves* to us as subject to change (*panta etepoiousthai emin dokei kai metapiptein ek*

---

15   "If there were a plurality, things would have to be of the same kind as I say that the one is. For if there is earth and water, and air and fire, and iron and gold, and if one thing is living and another dead, and if things are black and white and all that men say they really are—if that is so, and if we see and hear aright, each one of these must be such as we first decided, and they cannot be changed or altered, but each must be always just as it is. But, as it is, we say that we see and hear and understand aright, and yet we believe that what is warm becomes cold, and what is cold warm; that what is hard turns soft, and what is soft hard; that what is living dies, and that things are born from what lives not; and that all those things are changed, and that what they were and what they are now are in no way alike. We think that iron, which is hard, is rubbed away by contact with the finger; and so with gold and stone and everything which we fancy to be strong, and that earth and stone are made out of water; so that it turns out that we neither see nor know realities. Now these things do not agree with one another. We said that there were many things that were eternal and had forms and strength of their own, and yet we fancy that they all suffer alteration, and that they change from what we see each time. It is clear, then, that we did not see aright after all, nor are we right in believing that all these things are many. They would not change if they were real, but each thing would be just what we believed it to be; for nothing is stronger than true reality. But if it has changed, what is has passed away and what is not has come into being." (Melissus, Fr. 8. Trans. Kirk & Raven, *Presocratic Philosophers*, 304–5).

tou ekastote oromenou). It *seems* to us (*dokei de emin*) that things undergo change; that is, change *appears* to us, it *manifests itself*. In fact, it appears to us that "what is warm becomes cold, and what is cold warm; that what is hard turns soft, and what is soft hard; that what is living dies, and that things are born from what lives not." *But, for every thing, its undergoing change means that being perishes and that non-being comes to be* (*en de metapesei, to men eon apoleto, to de ouk eon gegonen*). The changing of things *appears*, which means that it *appears* that beings pass from their existing to their existing no longer (this is the "perishing" of beings), and from their not yet existing to their beginning to exist (and this is their "coming to be"). In the most explicit way possible—thus leaving the Master's ambiguity behind—Melissus affirms the appearing of the "world"—the appearing, that is, of the nothingness and nihilation of beings. And it is precisely because he is convinced that the "world" *appears* that—when he considers the appearing of the "world" in the light of the principle of the immutability of Being—he comes to affirm the untruth of Appearing: *ouk orthos eoromen* ("we do not see aright"); *mete oran mete eta onta ginoskein* ("we neither see nor know that which truly is"). The affirmation of the *being* and therewith of the eternity of things "does not agree" with the appearing of their undergoing change—*ou toinun tauta allelois omolonei*—since the changing of beings appears as their issuing from and returning to nothingness. "Nothing is stronger than that which truly is" (*tou nar eontos alethinou kreisson ouden*); and yet the "world" is the spectacle of the weakness of things. Or, in the words of Aeschylus: "*Techne* [i.e., the process by which things are turned into 'world'] is weaker by far than necessity" (*techne d'anankes asthenestera makro*, *Prometheus Bound*, v. 514). The growth of the power of technological civilization tacitly posits the constitutive weakness of that which is "technical": i.e., Being. For Melissus the affirmation of the "world" has no truth; for Plato and Aristotle, on the contrary, this affirmation is the content of "science." And "science" establishes the difference and the "agreement" between what-becomes and the immutable; i.e., between *techne* and necessity. But the vision of the "world" is common to Melissus, Plato, and Aristotle. Indeed, this vision has become the West's unchallenged evidence, and remains its dominant thought.

3. THE ETERNITY OF BEING AND OF ITS APPEARING

But if the totality of Being is immutable, then by positing that Becoming implies the not-appearing of Being rather than its not-being, does one not simply shift the aporia brought about by the truth of Being that was instead to be resolved? For—the objection runs—is not the entrance into Appearing itself a determination of the positive? But in that case, before something appears and after it has disappeared, that positive which is its appearing *is-not*. And thus, even if one were to affirm that Becoming is not the annulment of things, does it not remain unshakable that Becoming is the annulment (or, conversely, the emergence from nothingness) of *that* thing which is the appearing of individual things that appear?

In considering this objection, we have first to establish what value it accords to the position of Becoming. When one objects that, in understanding Becoming as an appearing and disappearing of Being, the not-being of that Being which is the *appearing* of Being is nevertheless posited, the following question arises: is the objection based upon an *observation* of the not-being of Appearing (i.e., upon an observation of the becoming of Appearing, where Becoming is observed to be an issuing from and returning to nothingness on the part of that Being which is Appearing), or is it based upon a *deduction* or inference of that which Becoming must be, *once* it has been understood as the appearing-disappearing of Being? In other words: the truth of Being says that in Becoming it is not *Being* that is at stake, but the *appearing* of Being; the objection points out that, precisely because Appearing, too, is Being, then in Becoming, that *Being* which is *Appearing* is indeed at stake (hence the impossibility of not defining Becoming in terms of Being and not-Being). But, once again, we ask: does the objection point this out on the basis of the *observation* that Appearing issues from and returns to nothingness, or rather on the basis of an inference that *deduces* how Becoming remains a question of Being and not-Being, even if it is understood as the appearing-disappearing of Being? An exposition of these two possible bases of the objection will suffice to bring out the valuelessness of the objection itself.

The basis of the objection cannot be an *observation* (i.e., cannot be the *appearing* of the annulment of Appearing), since that which was said earlier with regard to the burning paper also holds for the super-vening and vanishing of the *appearing* of that piece of paper and, in general, for *any* determination whose becoming appears. Saying that, of *this body*, it appears that first it is and then it is-not, can now mean only this: it appears that first this body *is there* (appears) and then it *is not there* (does not appear). And saying that, of the *appearing of this body*, it appears that first it is and then it is-not, can mean only this: it appears that the appearing of this body (i.e., its entering into Appearing) first appears and then does not appear. Just as it does not appear that this body, as it burns up, becomes nothing, so it does not appear that the appearing of this body, as it vanishes, becomes nothing. Becoming is the appearing and disappearing of *every thing* whose becoming appears. And if this is the *de facto* constitution of the Becoming that appears, the truth of Being demands that it be the *de jure* constitution of Becoming as such: for it is the truth of Being itself that excludes the very possibility of the appearing of that annulment of Being which in fact does not appear.

But the truth of Being does something more: it *a priori* renders valueless any possible *deduction*—this was the second possible basis of the objection—of the necessity of continuing to understand Becoming in terms of Being and not-Being, even if Becoming is posited as the appearing-disappearing of Being. To the objection that affirms, "if Being disappears, then Appearing is-not" (where this "if . . . then" ranks as a logical deduction and not as an observation), the truth of Being counters: "Since Being is not and does not become a Nothing, then any possible demonstration that comes to affirm that Being is-not is a priori or originally valueless (i.e., its value is merely apparent); and therefore the proposition 'if Being disappears, then Appearing is-not' has a merely apparent value." For the very reason that original truth is (or, more precisely, includes) the opposition of Being and Nothing, a demonstration that comes to affirm the identity of Being and Nothing is merely an apparent demonstration. Since this demonstration claims to establish a necessary implication between a moment of original truth (viz., Becoming) and a factor that denies another moment of original truth (and this other moment is the opposition of Being and Nothing, i.e., the immutability of Being), here too there is an x—to be unmasked—that gives rise to the appearance of that necessary implication. If this *x* cannot actually be unmasked, this does not mean that one should therefore abandon that which moreover *cannot* be abandoned: on the one hand, the truth of Being, which prohibits that Being not-be, and on the other the truth of Becoming, for which the Becoming that appears is not the Becoming of Being (a process, that is, in which Being issues from and returns to nothingness), but rather its appearing and disappearing. Just as, in general, if the aporia brought about by the truth of Being—Being is immutable, but at the same time Being becomes—cannot actually be resolved, this does not mean that one should therefore abandon the two moments of original truth: the immutability of Being and the Becoming that appears. For in a situation of this type, it is nevertheless *known*—albeit indeterminately— that these two moments *cannot* be incompatible, even if one is unable to indicate the determinations that concretely give rise to the apparent incompatibility. Since the appearing of Becoming is *not* the appearing of the birth and death of Being, but rather that of its appearing and disappearing, the aporia, considered in its general formulation, is thus resolved: Appearing does *not* attest the opposite of the truth of Being. But now the question is this: *how* is one to understand the supervening and vanishing of Appearing, so as to avoid a recrudescence of the aporia as a result of the objection that such supervening and vanishing imply the not-being of Appearing?

This question will remain unanswered as long as one is unable to achieve a comprehension of the authentic structure of Appearing; as long, that is, as one fails to realize that *something can appear only if its appearing*—i.e., its being included in Appearing—*appears*. But as a rule, Appearing ("thought," "consciousness," the "subject") is represented as that which does not necessarily have itself as its content: Appearing—so one thinks—can be the appearing of things, without being the appearing of their appearing. The appearing of Appearing is thus held to be a figure that is realized only *if* one reflects upon the appearing of things. And yet Appearing is a predicate that *necessarily* belongs to things that appear: not in the sense that every thing that appears cannot not-appear, but rather in the sense that, whenever anything appears, Appearing is necessarily predicated of it (just as redness is necessarily predicated of this surface which is red, and if this surface ceases to appear red, it does so not insofar as it is *this*, but rather insofar as it is a permanence underlying the red and the not-red surfaces alike). But if one determination (P) is necessarily predicated of another (S), then, if S appears without P's appearing, S does not appear: precisely because S is that of which P is predicated. If P is necessarily predicated of S, S appears only if P appears (just as, if it has been demonstrated that lightning is necessarily accompanied by thunder, if lightning were to appear without thunder, then that which appears would not be lightning: precisely because lightning is that which is accompanied by thunder). Now, if this lamp (S) appears, but the appearing of this lamp (P) does not, then this lamp cannot appear. And if instead of this lamp something else (S') comes to appear, this something else, for the same reason, can appear only if its appearing appears; and thus any attempt to let something appear, without making the appearing of that which appears appear, would be an attempt to realize the unrealizable. The appearing of Being is at once, necessarily, the appearing of itself: the content that appears necessarily includes its own appearing. And this is so, even if common consciousness (i.e., the untrue attitudes of Appearing) remains unaware of the essential presence of Appearing.

Thus, if the appearing of this lamp necessarily implies the appearing *of its appearing* (i.e., of its being included in the horizon of Appearing), then if this lamp begins to appear, its appearing begins to appear as well; and if this lamp no longer appears, its appearing no longer appears either. Something's becoming, then, is not simply the transition from its not-appearing to its appearing, but is at once the transition from the not-appearing to the appearing *of its appearing*. *In the very act* in which something passes from not-Appearing to Appearing (or from Appearing to Disappearing), *in this same act* its *appearing* passes from not-Appearing to Appearing (or from Appearing to Disappearing).

In light of this, let us reexamine this insistent objection: even if Becoming is an appearing and a disappearing of Being, it is still the case that, in Becoming, that Being which is Appearing *is-not* (when something has not appeared or when it appears no longer). Now, in objecting in this way one affirms the not-being of that which *has already been posited* as a not-Appearing: one demands, that is, that that which *has already been expressed* in terms of Appearing and not-Appearing now be expressed in terms of Being and not-Being. In other words: it is only because one fails to realize that something's appearing and disappearing is *at once* the appearing and disappearing *of its appearing* that, in relation to the position of Becoming as the appearing and disappearing of Being, one feels entitled to infer that if something appears and disappears, then its appearing is-*not* (or, respectively, is-not-yet and is-no-longer). If, on the other hand, one realizes that something's becoming—taken here according to its authentic definition—is also the becoming *of its appearing*, there is no longer any way to attribute Appearing with a Becoming that is inauthentically defined in terms of Being and not-Being. Or again: it is no longer possible to *resume* the discourse and conclude that, if Being appears and disappears, *then* its appearing is-not: precisely because its appearing has itself already been posited as something that appears and disappears. In short, the objection arises because one wishes to perform inauthentically that which has already been performed authentically.

If there is no consciousness of Appearing (i.e., if Appearing, which is necessarily the appearing *of Appearing*, not only has no awareness of this self-reflection, but has no *self*-awareness whatsoever—a self-ignorance typical of all untrue forms of Appearing), then the becoming of things cannot but be understood as the transition from not-Being to Being and vice versa. And the same thing occurs if one fails to realize that the appearing-disappearing of things is at once the appearing-disappearing of their appearing: here too, it will be said that the becoming of their appearing is the transition from the being to the not-being, and vice versa, of their appearing.

Any Becoming that appears is thus a transition from not-Appearing to Appearing; and only an inability to grasp the authentic structure of Appearing can lead one to the conclusion that, if Becoming is appearing-disappearing, then Appearing is-not.[16]

---

16   If Becoming is the process of appearing-disappearing, and if the existence of Becoming is affirmed because Becoming appears, then the appearing of Becoming is a form of self-consciousness. This form of self-consciousness must be distinguished, however, from that self-consciousness according to which Appearing is realized, insofar as Appearing is the appearing of something. As we have seen, if something appears, then its appearing appears (i.e., Appearing always has itself as its content); and if something begins or ceases to appear, then its appearing begins and ceases to appear. The appearing of this beginning and ceasing is the appearing of Becoming; but this Appearing, precisely because it is the appearing *of Becoming*, neither begins nor ceases with that beginning and ceasing whose appearing it is. The

4. TRANSCENDENTAL APPEARING AND EMPIRICAL APPEARING

But the Becoming that appears is always the becoming of a particular, or "empirical," determination of the content that appears: it is the becoming of this burning paper, or of the appearing of this or that

---

appearing of Becoming does not become (it is not involved in the becoming of that Becoming whose appearing it is); and thus there is one Appearing that begins (to appear) and ends, and another that witnesses this process (of which it is the appearing). If this latter Appearing were to be involved in the process whose appearing it is, then the process itself would not appear. If, that is, the appearing of Becoming were to begin when what-has-become [*il divenuto*] begins, then the become could not appear *as become*. For the become to appear as become, that with respect to which the become supervened would have to appear; but this condition could not be fulfilled if Appearing were to begin when the become begins: in this case, the become would appear not as a *result*, but as an *immediate* (as occurs in all those situations in which one is *in* Becoming, but Becoming is not *posited*: here, one passes from an unawareness to an awareness of something, but this transition is not *posited*, i.e., is not reflected, is not allowed to appear).

Thus there is a self-consciousness in which the content of Appearing is the process of appearing-disappearing; and there is another which comes about because the appearing of something implies the appearing *of itself*. In the first case, the content of Appearing is not itself, but rather Appearing that becomes (Appearing-that-becomes is the content of Appearing-that-does-not-become); in the second case, Appearing has itself as its content. (From this it follows that, precisely because Becoming appears, this not-becoming appearing of Becoming appears; and thus, here too, the second of the two cases is realized.)

However, what we wish to bring out here is that, if the appearing of Becoming is not involved in the becoming whose Appearing it is, it *can* be involved in another Appearing. First the clear sky, then clouds; or, first the clear sky appears, and then the clouds: the appearing of this Becoming does not become, in the sense that it does not begin with the beginning of the appearing of the clouds (and does not end with the ending of the appearing of the clear sky). But the appearing of this change in the weather also becomes (although it is involved in a different Becoming from the one whose appearing it is): before the change in the weather appeared, there appeared a remembrance of the previous day, and after the appearing of the change, there appeared an apprehensive melancholy for the morrow. The appearing of Becoming can become, but this Becoming comes about within a broader field of Appearing, which can, in its turn, become, and so on until the *total horizon* of the actual Appearing is reached. This total horizon, however, as will be made clear in the text, not only *does not* but indeed *cannot* appear as coming-to-be.

But here, once again, we stress that it must be affirmed of *any* Becoming that it is a transition from the not-appearing to the appearing of something: where something's beginning-to-appear is at once the beginning-to-appear (the supervening) in Appearing of its very appearing. And this is the case, whether the something be a color, a sound, a feeling, or whether it constitute itself as the appearing of something or as the appearing of something's becoming.

determination. As we have seen, the becoming of everything that appears as coming-to-be is an entering into and departing from Appearing. However, if we consider Appearing not as a particular or "empirical" determination, but rather as the transcendental event, i.e., as the horizon of all that appears (and thus as the horizon in which determinations that become supervene, and from which they take their leave), we see that the becoming of Appearing so understood *does not* and indeed *cannot* appear. If, that is, Appearing is considered as the transcendental event, then its supervening in and departing from the transcendental event does not and cannot appear.

For supervening to appear *as* a supervening, there must appear the "earlier" with respect to which it constitutes itself as such; and for vanishing to appear *as* a vanishing, there must appear the "later" as a no-longer-including that which has vanished. And thus the horizon that includes every earlier and every later that appear—and this horizon is Appearing as the transcendental event—*cannot* appear as supervening and vanishing (i.e., *cannot* appear as something that enters and leaves Appearing). Or again: if the rising and setting of Appearing were to appear, then the appearing of that whose rising and setting appears would be an empirical determination, and not Appearing as the spectator of this process, i.e., as the total horizon of Appearing. The transcendental event, then, can be said to become, *only* in the sense that its *content* becomes: the transcendental event appears as coming-to-be *not* in the sense that its rising and setting appears, but only in the sense that there appears the rising and setting of the particular determinations of the *content* of Appearing. Something's appearing and disappearing—i.e., its becoming—has therefore to be understood as its entering and leaving the fixed, transcendental dimension of Appearing. (And thus this firmament of Appearing, in coming to include something, comes to include, in this very act, this inclusion; that is, it comes to include the *appearing* of something—for, as we have seen, something can appear only if its appearing appears.)

This consideration is of fundamental importance in establishing the meaning of the aporia brought about by the truth of Being. Whereas, with respect to the particular determinations of the content that appears, the aporia *can* constitute itself (i.e., *does* gain the semblance of a contradiction within truth), since the becoming of such determinations appears, on the other hand the aporia *fails* to constitute itself (i.e., *cannot* be formulated) with respect to the transcendental horizon of Appearing. And this is because, while the truth of Being demands that every positive, and thus also the transcendental horizon, be immutable—eternal—the transcendental horizon *does not appear* as coming-to-be: there is not even the *appearance* of Appearing's denying the logos. The transcendental event is eternal (like all positives) and does not appear as coming-to-be. Nor can it even be *supposed* that the transcendental event is-not (i.e., might not-have-been or might be-no-longer), since such a supposition is the scandal of reason—it supposes that a positive is a Nothing.

It can be supposed of the particular determinations of the content that appears that they no longer appear, or that they might not-have-appeared (just as, in fact, one observes that first they did not appear, and then they no longer appear); but it cannot be supposed that everything has ceased to appear or might no longer appear, because in that case one would suppose that that positive which is the appearing of Being—that positive which is the total horizon of Appearing—might have been or might be a Nothing. If one is to be true to the truth of Being, which prohibits that *any* positive may be a Nothing, it must then be proclaimed that the immutable *necessarily* reveals itself in the actual Appearing. Everything is eternal, and Becoming is the appearing and disappearing of the limbs of the eternal, their entering and leaving the light of Appearing. But *Appearing*—this eye of light in which God shows himself—is that moment of the eternal which not only refuses—like every other moment—to not-be, but which by its very refusing is a lamp eternally lit to God that *cannot* be extinguished: if nothing of the eternal appeared, Appearing (i.e., that Being which is Appearing *qua* transcendental event) would be the appearing of nothing and therefore would-not-be, i.e., would be a Nothing. While, as we have seen, particular determinations of the immutable can not-appear (and thus the appearing of this or that determination, or Appearing *qua* empirical event, can not-appear), *every* such determination always and forever keeps to itself and its not-appearing does not imply the annulment of the total circle of Appearing. If not all the guests in the house of Being come out into the light, there *is* always someone who appears at the threshold and, as the light is cast upon him, enables it to live. But if everyone were to stay inside at Being's banquet, the light, illuminating nothing, would no longer live and would itself be nothing. And since the light too is a guest in the house of Being, its annulment would create a lack in the divine chorus—which this time *would* be jealous.[17] If the appearing of Being is the essence of man, man is this eternal gaze upon Being: of necessity the soul is ungenerated and immortal (*ex anankes ageneton te kai athanaton psyche, Phaedrus* 246): but preeminently with respect to other Beings, which are no less ingenerable and incorruptible. For while these other limbs of Being can conceal themselves, *Appearing* (*psyche*) is the eternal sign of God, the eternal scene of a divine spectacle. (Wherefore Aristotle says of the intellect in act that it *always* thinks—and it is not the case that it sometimes thinks and at other times not [*all ouk ote men noei ote d'ou noei, De Anima* III, 430a 22]—it alone is immortal and eternal [*kai touto monon athanaton kai aidion,* ibid. 430a 23].)

5. "HE NEITHER SPEAKS OUT NOR CONCEALS, BUT GIVES A SIGN": THE APPEARING OF THE PART AND THE ONTOLOGICAL DIFFERENCE

The appearing of Being is therefore an eternal *sign*. As we have seen, the immutable necessarily reveals itself: its appearance in the dwelling of Appearing, which eternally receives it, cannot not-occur. Yet the immutable does not reveal itself *completely*—and thus its self-manifestation is a sign. In the words of Heraclitus, "The lord whose oracle is in Delphi neither speaks out nor conceals, but gives a sign" (*o anax, ou to manteion esti to en Delphois, oute legei oute kruptei alla semainei,* Fr. 93, Kirk & Raven trans., 211). The immutable does not conceal itself completely, since such coyness would mean the not-being of Appearing; nor does it reveal itself completely, since some of its limbs disappear when others appear and appear when others disappear. Precisely because the appearing of the immutable is a process, the immutable reveals as it conceals and conceals as it reveals. If a gust of wind stirs outside my window and rattles to come in, the shadowy

---

17 Cf. Aristotle, *Metaphysics,* 983*a*, "We should not believe in divine jealousy."

silence of the room no longer appears: the lamp, this page, my books, the flowers now appear together with that wind and thus with their face and meaning changed. Precisely because the new voice of the wind has entered Appearing, the quiet room—this unmistakable timbre of Being—no longer appears: now another timbre appears, new and equally unmistakable. Appearing is disappearing and disappearing appearing: for something to appear (i.e., enter Appearing) another must disappear, and vice versa. Again, Heraclitus: in Becoming, everything lives the death and dies the life of its other (*zontes ton ekeinon thanaton, ton de ekeinon bion tethneotes*, Fr. 62).

Precisely because the appearing of the immutable is in process, the immutable reveals itself *in part*. This means that the part does not reveal itself in the whole; that is, it does not appear in the blissful company it keeps, and that it *essentially* keeps. In other words, being in the whole is no *accidental* property of the part: just as the part cannot cease to be, so the whole cannot cease to envelop it, for the contrary would entail that which the truth of Being prohibits, namely: that Being (in this case the being of the part or of the whole) is-not. The part is that which is in the whole; i.e., the meaning of the part—flower, house, star—necessarily has as its predicate being in the whole. And therefore if the part appears, but the whole in which it dwells does not, then that which appears is *not* the part in the concrete meaning that is proper to it as dwelling in the whole, but rather is a *different* meaning.

This fundamental principle, which encloses the very essence of the dialectic, is transcendental in scope (indeed, it was utilized above in our grounding of the assertion that something's appearing necessarily implies the appearing *of* its appearing). We formulated it above by saying that if a predicate necessarily belongs to a meaning (i.e., to a positive), and if that meaning appears without this predicate's appearing, then that which effectively appears is a meaning that is *different* from the meaning considered. The meaning is *different*, we said, not simply because first it appears with the predicate and then it appears alone, but because it is different from the meaning itself *as* distinct from the predicate that necessarily belongs to it. And thus this distinct meaning, as related to the predicate, is itself, as such, different from the meaning that appears alone and which therefore is no longer simply "distinct," but indeed is something "separate" from the predicate. In other words, letting s be the meaning (the part) and p the predicate (being in the whole), if s appears without p's appearing or if σ indicates s in its appearing without p, then σ is not different from s only because s is different from sp, but because σ is different from s as distinct from p: and this because s means s only *insofar as* it is related to p; and not appearing in this relation it no longer means s. If we say that the part is the abstract (and the whole is the concrete), the appearing of the part without the appearing of the whole is an *abstract comprehension or manifestation of the abstract*: it is a not seeing the abstract as it is, i.e., in its authentic form, and thus that which effectively appears (the abstract in its being sundered from the envelopment of the whole) is the *outcome* of an abstract comprehension of the abstract.[18]

The eternal appears (and cannot not-appear), but, since it appears in process, it appears in part; i.e., that of the eternal which appears does not appear in its being in the whole, and therefore the part that appears is *not* the part as enveloped by the whole. In "Returning to Parmenides," this *not being* was called the authentic "ontological difference" (46). This is not the difference between two beings, each of which lacks something that the other possesses: the part that appears is not a positivity that is not included in the immutable whole, for, insofar as that which appears is a positive, it dwells, like every other positive, in the all-enveloping circle of the immutable. But insofar as the part appears as not dwelling in the enveloping whole—insofar as the *concrete* relation of part to whole does not appear—the part does not appear *as it is*. And since nothing can appear that is not in the eternal, the part appears in a *lack*, i.e., in its being lacking in that which it possesses (or in that which passes through it), as part, *as* enveloped by the whole. As so enveloped, the part, as distinct from that which envelops it, is nonetheless "traversed" by it (just as a living body, while distinct from life, is nonetheless "traversed" by it: life courses through it, distinguishing it from a corpse, which may look like a living body only insofar as it is observed carelessly). And it is *in* this being-distinguished that the part is determined (or "traversed") by that from

---

18   This fundamental theme was developed analytically in Chapters I and XII of *La struttura originaria* and was taken up again in *Studi di filosofia della prassi*, II, Ch. I, paragraph IV.

which it is distinguished; but insofar as it appears alone, and thus does not appear in this being-distinguished (in this being-determined), the part is *altered*, and this alteration can be nothing other than its impoverishment and its paling with respect to its true face, which shines out in the blissful company of the immutable.

The part that appears alone differs from itself as enveloped by the whole, in that it comes to lose (=to conceal) something of itself as so enveloped. Which is to say, that which withdraws from Appearing is not simply the dimension that *exceeds* the part, but owing to this withdrawal there is also a withdrawal *in* the part that appears, which thus appears withered. However, the following objection may be raised about this institution of the ontological difference. The alteration of the part that appears abstractly (i.e., alone, as not enveloped by the whole) must be understood as a lack in the part, since *all* Being is immutable, so that the part that appears in solitude can differ from itself as accompanied by the whole, only in the sense that in solitude it lacks something that *is* present in the company of the whole. In other words: σ differs from s, only in the sense that σ lacks something (in σ a dimension of positivity does not appear) that *is* to be found in s: and this because, if σ were to differ from s in the sense that in σ there were a positivity not to be found in s or in the envelopment of s on the part of the whole, then the positivity contained in σ and not in the immutable whole would be a dwelling *only* in the sphere of Appearing, wherefore its appearing and disappearing would be its emerging from and returning to nothingness—would be, that is, the denial of the truth of Being. Yet—*and here is the objection*—the content of Appearing is not a Nothing: if σ is a lack with respect to s, it is not, however, a total lack—it is, nonetheless, a *Being*. And if every Being is immutable, σ too is immutable, and thus the appearing of σ—even if understood as the abstract manifestation of s—is the *adequate* appearing of a moment of the immutable. Which is to say: whereas that moment of the immutable which is s appears inadequately (it appears, that is, in solitude and not in its being enveloped by the whole)—that of s which *does appear* (namely σ) is a moment of the immutable that adequately appears, i.e., is in the whole just as it appears. The ontological difference is thereby reduced to the fact that that which appears is a part of the whole, and this part appears *as* it is.

This spurious way of understanding the ontological difference derives from nothing other than the failure to bear in mind that s is the mode in which σ exists as concretely enveloped by the whole, and that σ is the mode in which s appears whenever s appears in solitude and thus as not enveloped by the whole. This means that the existence of σ, as enveloped by the whole, cannot be said to be different from s. Being (i.e., the immutable) appears. Let us call that which appears σ. But, since the appearing of Being is in process, Being appears in part (and σ this part that appears). Thus the part does not appear as it is, i.e., in its authentic form, since it does not appear according to that determination which essentially belongs to it, namely: its being enveloped by the whole. Let s be the part as thus concretely enveloped, i.e., the part as it is: we affirm that σ differs from s and that this difference is an impoverishment of s, or is lacking something that is to be found in s. This lack is certainly not a Nothing, for it is in and by this lack that the Being that appears (i.e., σ) is realized. But from this it by no means follows that, since *all* the positive (and therefore σ as well) is immutable, then σ appears as it is: it does not follow because σ, as it *is*, and thus *as* enveloped by the whole, is s—wherefore that which appears does not appear as it is (nor, in this self-differentiation, can it add any positivity to the whole, and thus it differentiates itself as a lack: not for the simple reason that what appears is the part, not the whole, but rather because the very part that appears is impoverished with respect to the part as it is).

The same faulty reasoning that leads to the spurious conception of ontological difference we have just considered can also give rise to a different, but equally spurious, conception of such difference. It can, that is, give rise to the following objection: if, when s appears isolated from the whole, that which appears is σ, then also σ appears isolated from the whole, and therefore that which effectively appears cannot be σ either, but something different from σ—say, σ'. Yet σ' too appears alone (i.e., is abstractly manifest) and therefore that which appears cannot be σ' either, but something different from σ'. But *any* content that one presumes to posit as that which effectively appears will necessarily appear in solitude and therefore as other than that which it is, and thus Appearing will not be the appearing of any content whatsoever. Here too, the original flaw lies in the failure to realize that σ, as enveloped by the whole, is not something different from *s*, but is *s* itself. If this is not comprehended, then σ, as concretely enveloped, comes to be hypostatized as something different from *s*, and, of this "something different," one is then compelled to say that, if it were to appear alone, it could not appear as σ (precisely because σ is the mode in which *s* appears when it appears alone, and therefore σ cannot be the mode in which that hypostasis appears, if it were to appear alone). When, that is, one says that σ *also* appears isolated from the whole, it is tacitly posited that, if σ were to appear in its concrete relation with the whole, it would be something different from *s*. But quite the contrary— *s* is nothing other than σ as concretely related to the whole; and thus in affirming that σ cannot appear *either*, one does nothing but *repeat* what has already been posited through the affirmation that, if *s* appears alone, then that which effectively appears is not *s*, but σ. One repeats the same, while positing it as other: and therefore the conclusion derives from a self-contradictory proposition.

Nothing, of that which appears, appears as it is in the whole; and everything that appears *is* immutably in its concrete dwelling in the whole. Not even *Appearing*—i.e., the abstract comprehension of Being—appears *as* it dwells in the whole: the abstract comprehension of Being abstractly comprehends itself as well. Appearing—in which Being necessarily reveals itself—does not grasp its own concrete relation with the whole. *Everything* that appears (and thus also *Appearing* itself) therefore *differs* from Being: but in the sense that that which appears is Being itself as abstractly manifest—is *Being* in its concealing itself *in* its self-revealing. This is why in "Returning to Parmenides" we said that that which appears is the "outcome of an abstract comprehension of the immutable totality" (82). That which appears adds nothing, then, to Being (i.e., to the immutable): precisely because that which appears *is* Being. And yet that which appears *differs* from Being: precisely because Being, appearing, does not reveal itself in all its fullness.[19]

---

19 The abstract manifestation of Being gives rise to a difference between Being, as the outcome of abstract manifestation, and the "same" Being, as concretely enveloped by the whole; but the *limits* of this difference cannot be foreseen in the actual Appearing or, more precisely, they suggest a boundless region open to speculative investigation. If certain features of a pretty face do not appear, those that do appear

The ontological difference is thus the difference between Being and Being-there, i.e., between Being as such and Being as abstractly manifest. The world (that which appears) is God insofar as he reveals himself in finite consciousness (whose finitude is precisely its ranking as an abstract appearing of Being). But finite consciousness (the actual Appearing), precisely insofar as it is not a Nothing, is itself a moment of the immutable and, indeed, is that moment which is not only immutable, but which—as the totality of Appearing—*does not even appear* as coming-to-be. It is such that its becoming can be understood as nothing other than the appearing and disappearing of its particular contents: as receiving, and taking leave of them. The ontological difference is an event within the immutable: the actual Appearing—in which the eternal discloses itself—is a moment of the eternal.

6. BACKGROUND AND VARIANTS

And the eternal cannot not disclose itself, since otherwise Appearing, as the total horizon, would not be (i.e., would be a nothing). But here it must not be forgotten that whereas it is impossible that Being actually not-appear, this necessary Appearing is not the appearing of the concrete totality of Being. For Appearing to be, it is necessary that Being reveal itself, but it is not necessary that it reveal itself totally: *in fact*, Being, revealing itself in process, does *not* reveal itself in its totality, and this could not be the case if it implied the not-being of Appearing. Necessity cannot be belied by a fact. The absurd is that which cannot occur.

For Appearing to be, that of Being which must necessarily appear is not the concrete whole of Being. We shall call the necessary content of Appearing the "persyntactic field" (cf. La *struttura originaria*, Ch.

---

are not the "same" as those that merge with all the others in the complete appearance of the face; and thus the expression that appears in this limited manifestation may be as pathetically bearable as it is utterly monstrous. If only certain tracts of the "plain of truth" (*to aletheias pedion*) appear, then the face of God becomes the face of the world, which is indeed the face of God, but in its letting certain essential traits remain concealed.

XII, paragraph XXIX), or, simply, "background."[20] But Being-that-appears becomes; that is, new determinations of Being always appear, joining up with and concretizing the meaning of the background. We shall call such determinations "variants." Precisely because variants supervene in the content that appears, Appearing exists even before the supervening (i.e., appearing) of variants, which thus do not belong to that minimum content (the background), without whose appearing Appearing, as the transcendental event, would not exist. Even if one is not actually in a position to determine the content of the background concretely, the becoming of the content that appears essentially implies the distinction between a necessary content of Appearing (the background) and a simply factual content of Appearing (variants).

On the other hand, the background and variants may be related in two different ways: 1. the appearing of the background does not necessarily imply the appearing of variants, and thus their appearing is a *fact*; 2. the appearing of the background necessarily implies the appearing of variants (which therefore, while not an initial requirement for Appearing to be, are subsequently a necessary requirement for that which *is* initially required for Appearing to be).

In the first case, variants appear, but might not-appear, or might have not-appeared: Being reveals itself "freely," albeit in relation to that

---

20 The determinations that make up the background are not indifferent; i.e., for Appearing to be, it is not a matter of indifference that one content manifest itself rather than another: as if Appearing, to be, were indeed to require the manifestation of certain determinations—but that it was a matter of indifference whether these determinations rather than others should manifest themselves. The passage from *La struttura originaria* referred to in the text sets forth a series of considerations, on the basis of which it is demonstrated that if *certain* meanings (or "categories," if one prefers) did not appear, then nothing could appear. The fundamental (but not exhaustive) complex of these meanings is formed by meanings such as "Being," "not-Being," "totality," "Appearing." Now, since it has been demonstrated that, if certain meanings did not appear, nothing could appear, then, when one concludes that something must appear, since otherwise Appearing would not be, this something cannot be just any set of determinations, but must primarily be constituted by *those* meanings whose not-appearing would imply the disappearing of every determination. But this something must not only be "primarily" constituted by just those meanings—it must be constituted *by them alone*: since every other meaning is such that its not-appearing does not imply the annulment of Appearing. And thus the something—i.e., the background—that must appear, for Appearing to be, can be constituted by nothing but *those* meanings which form the transcendental content of Appearing.

dimension of Being which is constituted by variants. In the second case variants could not have not-appeared, and therefore everything that is revealed of Being necessarily reveals itself (where "necessity" indicates the self-contradictoriness of any affirmation opposed to a "necessary" affirmation).

7. "HISTORY" AND THE ALIENATION OF THE MEANING OF BEING

From the standpoint of the actual structure of truth, these two cases are equipollent. Neither of them, that is, actually shows itself to be a negation of this structure, even if from the standpoint of alienated reason either one could appear as such a negation. On the one hand the history of the world is said to be a necessary process that takes place within the immutable; while on the other, this process is posited as not-necessary, although, here too, history and Becoming are understood as a moment of the immutable. But then—did classical metaphysics not resolve this contradiction when it rose from the Neoplatonic concept of emanation (in which Being comes once again to be understood as a moment of the immutable) to that of creation? And then, is this returning to Parmenides not ultimately just another form of immanentistic metaphysics?

Yet, as we have seen, after Parmenides both the metaphysics of transcendence and immanentistic metaphysics alike reflect the forgottenness of the meaning of Being; they share, that is, that alienated meaning of Being, for which Being is seen as that which, as such, can not-be. Due to this forgottenness, thought can convince itself that the Becoming that is the content of Appearing is a process in which Being is at stake: precisely because thought is convinced that this process is the content of Appearing, it can therefore undertake to "save" Becoming so understood. The oblivion of Being compels thought to save the monstrosity to which it has given birth. For classical metaphysics, Being-that-becomes (i.e., Being that issues from and returns to nothingness) is thinkable only if immutable Being exists. The development of modern immanentism ultimately leads to the conviction that Being-that-becomes (i.e., Being that issues from and returns to nothingness) is thinkable only if immutable Being does *not* exist. But modern immanentism is a natural development of classical ontology. Both are rooted in the mystification of existent Becoming, understood as the birth and death of Being. On this basis, classical metaphysics is right to reject the claim of certain forms of immanentistic metaphysics to posit Becoming as a moment of the immutable: if in Becoming Being is imperiled, then the immutable cannot become. Neoplatonism denied Platonic-Aristotelian dualism (in which the independence of prime matter with respect to the divine places the divine, i.e., the immutable, in a sort of potentiality, and therefore becoming, with respect to prime matter) precisely in order to avoid positing the immutable as coming-to-be. And for the very same reason, Patristic-Scholastic creationism was then to deny Neoplatonic emanationism (in which the necessity of producing the world that becomes ends up by positing the product as necessary to the producer, wherefore Becoming constitutes itself as an essential determination of the immutable). But in classical metaphysics the affirmation of the immutable does not follow Parmenides along the way of truth: thought, once it has lost the truth of Being, attempts to *demonstrate* the existence of the immutable (making use above all of that distortion of the truth of Being which is the Melissian principle that Being cannot be generated from Nothing). And not only classical, but also modern metaphysics attempts to *demonstrate* that immutability of Being, which can never be attained precisely because one is unable to see it *in* the original truth of Being. And therefore it follows that every possible demonstration of the immutable is grounded upon an alienated meaning of Being. The development of the immanentistic demand, which leads to the rigorous negation of immutable Being (be it Aristotelian pure act or Hegelian idea), unquestionably rights the wrong in the inauthentic way in which metaphysics (both transcendentistic and immanentistic) has continued to posit the immutable. But no one is right when everyone is wrong: due to the conviction that the birth and death of Being appear—due, that is, to the alienation of the meaning of Being, which produces in its turn the alienation of the meaning of Becoming—due to the conviction that Being appears as a "self-realization," as "history," one reaches the conclusion that this effective increase of Being would be impossible if Being were already wholly realized in immutable reality. "History," understood as substantial innovation of Being, is the incontrovertible "datum"; and the immutable, posited as the sphere in which Being is already wholly or essentially realized, is the negation of this incontrovertible "datum."

Within the logic of alienated reason it is no doubt self-contradictory to affirm that the immutable becomes, or that Becoming is a moment of the immutable: precisely because, here, Becoming is understood as contradictory with respect to immutability. But if one brings the truth of Being alive, then the becoming of the immutable means that the immutable appears and disappears. Becoming, here, is no longer the contradictory of immutability, a process in which Being is at stake, but rather is a process in which the *appearing* of Being is at stake. And, in this process, everything that appears and disappears *is* eternally (or, everything that appears and disappears in this moment of God, is eternally in God).

And, primarily, the *background* is eternal—those traits, that is, of the face of Being which are the destiny of Appearing: those determinations of Being, without whose appearing the transcendental event of Appearing would not be. From the moment, however, that variants are superimposed upon the background, the background as pure background has already vanished: not in the sense that there no longer appears that without which Appearing would not exist, but rather in the sense that, *since* with the supervening of variants the background *continues* to appear, it no longer appears in that solitude which was proper to it before the supervention of variants. (The transcendental event, even if it endures, is no longer the same—indeed, it is no longer the same *insofar as* it endures: insofar, that is, as it remains identical in its self-differentiation.) But if the solitude of the background disappears with the onset of history, it still *is* eternally in the company of all Being; just as *all* the expressions progressively assumed by the content of Appearing, however durable or fleeting they may be, eternally dwell in the house of Being. In the inhospitable realm of Appearing things come into the light only if others go into shadow, and therefore the face of Being that appears can assume one expression only if another is laid aside. But in the house of Being all guests are equally welcome and the most contrasting of worlds live together. In the first case, for day to appear night must disappear; in the second, day and night live together eternally: God is day and night, said Heraclitus (*o theos emere euphrone*, Fr. 67). Being, that is, eternally contains the history of the finite mode

of seeing Being: and eternal Being, which eternally shows itself in
Appearing, eternally contains the history of this, its self-manifestation
(the history, that is, that grows on the *background* of Appearing),
together with all those possibilities (even the beards of the Melissians)
that the course of history progressively sweeps away.

And thus while there is a moment of the immutable—namely, the
actual Appearing—in which the immutable reveals itself in process,
this Becoming is no longer incompatible with the immutability of
Being. For in this Becoming, which is no longer understood according
to the alienated definition of the untruth of Being, nothing of Being is
lost, nor, therefore, can anything be lost of that Being which is the
appearing of Being. The becoming, the history, the vicissitudes of the
world neither augment nor diminish Being, precisely because
Becoming is the appearing and disappearing of Being. But must it not
at least be said that the *content* of Appearing increases and decreases?
Yes; but in excluding the increase and decrease of Being, one also
excludes the coming-to-be of something that previously was not and
the ceasing-to-be of something that previously was; while in recognizing the "increase" and "decrease" of the content of Appearing, one only
affirms the appearing of something that previously did not appear, and
vice versa. Take this feeling of contentment: it has just appeared. Yet it
always was and always will be. It is just that it *has not always appeared*,
it was not always included in this moment of the immutable which is
the abstract consciousness of the immutable. But then—here is something that *begins to exist*! Does not, that is, *this actual appearing* of this
feeling begin to exist? And yet the answer, once again, is no. For, as we
have seen, when something begins to appear—when, that is, it comes
into the transcendental horizon of Appearing—its appearing—its
inclusion in transcendental Appearing—also begins to appear. And
thus not only this feeling, but also its *appearing* always was and always
will be, even if it has not always appeared. And there is nothing more
to say: there is no *progressus in indefinitum*, since this latter Appearing,
which is the appearing *of* the something's appearing, is its *very* appearing. In the two propositions, "something begins to appear" (let a' be
this Appearing) and "the appearing (a') of something begins to appear"
(let a'' be this latter Appearing), a' and a'' *are the same*. Wherefore, once
it has been posited that something, and therefore also the appearing

(a') of something, begins to appear (a''), one cannot prolong the discourse and conclude that a'' is something that previously was not: one cannot do so, precisely because a'' is that very a', in relation to which it has already been posited that first it did not appear and now it begins to appear. Appearing that begins (or ends) has itself as its content, which means that beginning-to-appear structurally excludes beginning-to-be.

Everything that enters and leaves the circle of Appearing *is* eternally. Just as the circle itself is eternal: as the transcendental event, it has always awaited the coming of the Guest. And it can do so only insofar as the Guest has always already come and has shown himself along the broad furrows of the background, in which variants grow to make up the history of the world. That history be the process of the revelation of the immutable, in which beginning-to-appear structurally excludes beginning-to-be, is possible, therefore, only insofar as this self-revealing (the actual Appearing) is an eye eternally open on God—for what Plato, in the *Phaedrus*, said of the slothful soul cannot be said of the essence of man: that lacking the strength to follow the celestial path of the gods, it "did not see" (*me ide*, 248c).[21]

---

21   For the becoming of Being to be its entering Appearing, it is necessary that Appearing be to await that which supervenes. For *everything* that supervenes and vanishes (and thus also for the semantic face that the transcendental event progressively assumes in Becoming), Becoming *presupposes* transcendental Appearing, as the dimension that Being enters and from which it takes its leave. And the *being* of this dimension demands the necessary revelation of Being; for if nothing had appeared or if nothing were to appear, that Being which is transcendental Appearing would not have been or would not be: it would have been, or would be, nothing. Thus it is inadmissible to argue that, as in the case of empirical Appearing (i.e., Appearing that begins and ends), so in the case of transcendental Appearing one may suppose that it might not have appeared. It is also true that transcendental Appearing—like every Being—is eternal (it too, that is, must be said to be eternal, as is everything that enters and leaves it); but if transcendental Appearing had not *appeared*—and since its *de facto* becoming is, as we have seen, categorically excluded, its becoming can only be *supposed*—if, that is, nothing of Being had appeared, then Appearing, in its actuality, would not be and thus would be a Nothing. Unlike the appearing of this or that particular determination of the content that appears, it must be said of transcendental Appearing that its not-appearing would be its identification with Nothing: everything that enters and leaves the circle of Appearing *is* eternally, but if the circle itself did not appear it would be nothing. When this color does not appear, it *is* all the same, forever; to actually appear it has to enter the circle of actual Appearing, which thus must be to await it. Now if of this circle too one were to say that, even if it had

In "Returning to Parmenides," the "ontological difference" was introduced by saying that, since all Being is immutable and nonetheless the becoming of Being appears, then Being, *qua* immutable, is *other* than itself *qua* coming-to-be (paragraph III). If this discourse is interpreted through the categories of alienated reason, one must unquestionably conclude that, in it, a dimension of Being is abandoned to the absurd: the dimension, that is, of Being-that-becomes, i.e., of Being that is-not. If, that is, Becoming is understood in terms of Being and not-Being, then the ontological difference between that which becomes and the immutable (i.e., the affirmation of the existence of Becoming alongside that of the immutable) unquestionably affirms the existence of a dimension of Being that is dominated by the absurd. Correctly interpreted, however, the introduction of the ontological difference means that, since all Being is immutable and since Being becomes—i.e., *appears and disappears*—Being, as subject to the process of Appearing, is *not* Being as it is in itself: Being, as abstractly manifest, is not Being as concretely enveloped by the whole. Being, as abstractly manifest, is nothing other than Being-that-becomes, since Being, becoming, appears in part and therefore does not appear concretely in the whole; and Being, as concretely enveloped by the whole, is Being that does not become (i.e., that does not appear in part). Thus in affirming that Being, *qua* coming-to-be, is not Being, *qua* immutable, one affirms that Being, *qua* abstractly manifest, is not Being, *qua* concretely enveloped by the whole. In "Returning to Parmenides" we

---

not appeared (and thus nothing had appeared), it would still be always, and forever in the immutable, then we would have to respond that, for it to actually appear (for it to become the actual content of itself) it is necessary that the actual Appearing *be*—and it is impossible that this Being, like every other Being, not-be. But if nothing had appeared, that Being which is the actual Appearing would not have been.

On the other hand, if Being has always already appeared—if man always already receives God—this does not mean that Being is devoid of the positivity of the actual Appearing. Only in immanentistic metaphysics does the part possess a positivity that is possessed by the whole exclusively insofar as it includes the part. Appearing is indeed a part of Being. But since Appearing manifests *abstractly* everything that appears (it does not let that which appears appear in its being concretely enveloped by the whole), and thus also manifests *itself* abstractly, we must conclude that whereas *everything* that appears (and therefore also Appearing itself) is, in itself, differently from how it appears, on the other hand Being in itself—the concrete—includes all the positivity of that which appears—the abstract—and therefore includes the positivity of Appearing itself.

concluded: "This is why it can be said that the immutable is 'different from itself' *qua* coming-to-be and that Becoming is 'different from itself' *qua* immutable: precisely because Becoming does not augment Being" (47), but mirrors it, i.e., is the process of its manifestation. Being-that-appears, since it appears as coming-to-be, is a *part* of Being (in the sense that whereas the whole, unquestionably, appears, precisely insofar as the term "whole" is meaningful, on the other hand the whole does not appear in its concrete content, and, in this sense, it is said that Being appears in part); but since Being-that-appears does not appear in its concrete relation to the whole, Being that appears is *different from itself qua* concretely related to the whole.

The nature of the ontological difference therefore imposes that distinction between the two senses of Being *qua* Being (*on e on*) set forth in "Returning to Parmenides" (80–81). Being leaves nothing beyond itself, and since Being is immutable, the immutable leaves nothing beyond itself: Being *qua* Being extends just as far as does the immutable. But the immutable appears in process—i.e., becomes—and therefore Being-that-appears *differs* from Being that is in itself: not, however, in the sense that something appears that is not in itself, but rather in the sense that that which appears (and therefore Appearing itself) appears devoid of a quantity of positivity that is proper to it insofar as it is in itself. Nothing of Being appears *as* it is in itself (even if all Being that appears is in itself). And thus it must be said that Being leaves "beyond itself" its own appearing, or that Being *qua* Being "includes" the immutable: for, besides Being, it includes Being-that-appears (and that which appears—we repeat—is Being in itself, but since it appears in process it does not appear as it is in itself: it *differs*, in the sense we have indicated, from Being in itself).

These two aspects of Being *qua* Being—which are, at the same time, two aspects of the idea of "totality"—are determined by the circumstance that, in the ontological difference, one of the two differents lacks no positivity whatsoever (and in this sense it coincides with the whole and with the field of application of Being *qua* Being); wherefore the other different adds no positivity to the first—and this is possible because the second *is* the first as abstractly manifest, and therefore differs from it as a lack of Being. And thus the affirmation of these two senses is not an affirmation of two mutually contradictory theses (the whole coincides with the immutable, the whole includes the immutable), for the subjects of the alleged contradictories are *different*. In the first case, the subject ("whole") signifies Being as such, or that different which lacks nothing; while in the second, it signifies the synthesis of Being and its appearing, or the ontological difference itself.

On the next-to-last page of "Returning to Parmenides" we stated:

> To object at this point that the denial of the not-being of Being is belied by the world, where Being supervenes and vanishes—i.e., where Being is-not—means neither more nor less than disregarding what has been said here. This tree is a positive, and as such it is and it cannot befall it to not-be, and so it is eternal. And, as eternal, it dwells in the hospitable house of Being, where all its positivity has already been, and will always be, saved. If at this point one objects that this tree is born and perishes, and so it is-not, and so there is a Being of which it can and must be said that it is-not, so that the *falsity* of the denial of Being's not-being is manifest in Appearing—if one objects in this way, one has *forgotten* that the positive—any positive—which appears subject to the vicissitudes of time, has *already* been rescued from nothingness (precisely insofar as the impossibility that it—that *any* Being—not-be has been ascertained). Thus there is no residual portion or dimension of the positive that, not having been saved, is abandoned to time. That which is in time is not something that is not possessed by the eternal (precisely because it must be said of *everything*—and so also of Being that appears in time—that it *is* eternally); so that the not-being of Being that is in time does not disprove that which, moreover, cannot be in any way disproved: that Being is and cannot not-be. Only if one did not affirm the immutable whole of the positive would the presence of Being in time be a negation of the affirmation that Being is and that it cannot befall it to not-be.

In other words: do we really affirm—and it *must* be affirmed!—that *everything* is immutable? If so, then we *cannot* take Becoming to be a Being that is-not, since, like all Being, it would have to be immutable. We cannot do so because, in this way, we would show that we have not posited *everything* as immutable, but only a part. And this part would become the whole only if that very being of Becoming were to be added to it which, at the same time, one believes cannot be so added. It cannot be said: since there is Becoming, not everything is immutable. But it must, rather, be said: since everything is immutable, Becoming cannot belie the immutability of the whole (and at the same time: since there is Becoming, the immutability of the whole *cannot* belie the being-there of Becoming). Therefore, once the immutability of the whole has been posited, it can be affirmed that Becoming belies this immutability only if one forgets that *the whole* has already been posited as immutable. If the whole is immutable (and it *is* immutable!), then Becoming—and Becoming, too, insofar as it appears, cannot be denied—*cannot* rank as a decrease and increase of Being. This tree is eternal; its becoming, then, *cannot* mar its Being. In saying this, however, we do not arbitrarily embrace the thesis of Being's immutability to the detriment of its becoming; on the contrary, our discourse alludes to the necessity of reconciling the two theses. A reconciliation, we repeat, that would be excluded from the outset if the immutability of the whole were denied on the basis of the observation of Becoming (just as it would be excluded from the outset if one were to deny the Becoming that appears, on the basis of the affirmation of the immutable). Thus, in concluding "Returning to Parmenides," we affirmed that if the whole of Becoming is immutable, the Becoming that appears *cannot* compromise Being. This, however, is only the negative side of the matter. It is a question, at this point, of introducing that positive determination which will allow Becoming to be understood as a process that does not compromise the immutability of the whole; and this positive determination is—as we have seen—Becoming as appearing-disappearing of Being. Indeed, on that next-to-last page of "Returning to Parmenides" we did not dwell on this positive determination. However, on that occasion, we recalled that "the world is an image of God, or, more precisely, is the outcome of an abstract comprehension of the immutable totality": we recalled the principle that the content of Appearing is the immutable (as abstractly manifest), i.e., that Becoming is the appearing-disappearing of the immutable (as is specifically determined in Ch. XIII, paragraph XXVI of *La struttura originaria*).

8. THE PROBLEM OF FREEDOM

Thus the relation between background and variants, as set forth in section 6, remains a genuine problem: whereas the background cannot not-appear, the manifestation of variants may be understood, from the standpoint of the actual structure of truth, either as necessarily or as not-necessarily implied by the manifestation of the background. As long as this problem remains unresolved, one cannot determine the essence of man. The fundamental contribution of philosophical anthropology consists in positing the essence of man as the appearing of Being. But is the history of the content of Appearing—the superimposing, that is, of variants on the background—a history of necessity or of freedom? The freedom of Appearing to not-be and thus of Being to not-appear is a form of the forgottenness of the meaning of Being. But does *all* the content that appears belong to the destiny of Appearing, or does a dimension of Being offer itself in Appearing beyond all destiny, as a pure gift? The philosophical-theological interpretation of the sacral meaning of "creation," developed by the whole of Western culture, is steeped in the forgottenness of the truth of Being. If "creation" is interpreted in terms of Being and not-Being—if, that is, it is interpreted as implying the possibility of not-being (whereby it may be said of a certain dimension of Being that it might not-have-been or might not-be: *vertibilitas in nihilum*)—then the concept of creation is an explicit negation of the truth of Being. But if creation is interpreted as a determination that concerns the appearing and disappearing of Being, then creation is a genuine *possibility* of the truth of Being. A possibility—and thus a *problem*: the problem of the relation between the background of Appearing and the history of the content of Appearing. From the standpoint of the truth of Being, the possibility of creation is the possibility that in the eternal spectacle of Appearing there may appear that which might not have appeared; or, that in that moment of the eternal which is the actual Appearing, the eternal reveals more of itself than is destined to appear. But, as we have seen, this possibility actually coexists with its opposite, i.e., with the possibility that history be the necessary development of the revelation of the eternal. These two possibilities—and their conceivable interweavings—contend for the meaning of man. (And if the development of the content of Appearing were a history of freedom, what, then, would be the concrete system of the categories that constitute the *background* of Appearing? And does that which is commonly called "human reality"—this set of physical and psychical determinations, this bundle of sensations, feelings, volitions, and thoughts—belong to the background of Appearing, or does it belong to that possible dimension of Being which appears, but which might not have appeared or might no longer appear? And must it not be said, therefore, that "creation" is primarily the emergence of the self-consciousness of the background— the acquiring of self-consciousness on the part of eternal man? And all this bound up with a specific empirical situation, namely, corporality, sensitivity? The acquiring, that is, of that self-consciousness which would be precluded if man were an eternal gazing upon Being and thus an eternal self-beholding, and only in time became aware of this, his self-beholding? And in the history of freedom, to what extent would freedom be freedom of Being, and to what extent freedom of Appearing?)

PART TWO

CHAPTER I

The Path of Day

"Here is the gate that divides the paths of Night and Day."
entha pulai Nuktos te kai Ematos eisi keleuthon

Parmenides, Fr. 1, 11

1. METAPHYSICS AND WESTERN HISTORY

The advent of technological civilization has met with widespread condemnation. But what our age has failed to understand is that each of its attempts to reject or overcome the civilization of technology is rooted in the very way of thinking from which this civilization springs and of which it is the culmination. This is also the case in the Heideggerian interpretation of the meaning of technology. For Heidegger, metaphysics is the protagonist of the history of the "Occident"—the land of the "setting" of the "truth of Being"—while technology is the way in which metaphysics manifests itself today. But the meaning Heidegger assigns to the truth of Being is itself completely dominated by the "technical" way of thinking that, for him, came to represent the deepest oblivion of Being.

Yet the history of the West is a metaphysical experiment. Any historical reconstruction worthy of the name must attempt to penetrate the metaphysical secret of the West. Metaphysics has by no means been reduced to a mere mode of thought that was once effective in the limited sphere of cultural phenomena and is now in decline even there. On the contrary, it has progressively extended its sphere of influence to the point of determining and guiding the entire course of Western history. And this is more so today than ever before, both because metaphysics has come to dominate all aspects of life, and because Western civilization is in the process of supplanting every other form of civilization. Technological civilization is in fact the latest manifestation of metaphysics itself. It expresses the spirit of the age—of that single age known as "Western history"—against which all opposition is in vain unless a new age can be opened.

The possibility of a new age must be kept alive. For if metaphysics is the dominant spirit of our civilization, this very domination has led the West into the remotest distance from the truth of Being. Metaphysics, as it witnessed the dawning of this truth, also brought it to its setting. Indeed, the history of the West—and not only the history of Western philosophy—is the development of that *forgottenness* of Being, which has progressively—and now wholly—come to determine every aspect of our lives.

The fact that these same affirmations (as the Heideggerian interpretation shows) may also express a completely different meaning of the historical development of the West—the fact, that is, that forgottenness of the meaning of Being has taken possession of the very words that denounce it, in order to indicate forms of "decadence" that are not the *authentic* decline of the West—simply serves to show the abysmal depth of the alienation in which this age lives. We are so far from the truth of Being that, even if called in its own language, it does not awake.

2. POIESIS

By introducing a middle ground (*metaxy*) between Being and Nothing (*Republic* V, 477–80), Plato sealed the fate of the West, unleashing the thought that was to become the ever more demanding protagonist of Western history: the affirmation of a dimension containing that which is born and dies—that which, partaking of Being and Nothing, was-not and will be-no-longer, was a Nothing and will be a Nothing again. In short, Plato bequeathed the "world" to men.

Only insofar as there is "world," and one concedes that something (*ti*, i.e., a not-Nothing, a Being—"something" is always said of something that is—*to ti ep' onti legomen ekastote, Sophist*, 237d) could have been nothing and could become nothing again—only then can one set out to guide the "production" and "destruction" of Being. The controlled production and destruction of reality are the fundamental categories of technological civilization. Plato was the first to expressly set them forth: "Any cause that makes a thing pass from Nothing to Being is production (*poiesis*), and thus the actions performed in all the arts (*technais*) are productions and all artificers are producers" (*e gar toi ek tou me ontos eis to on ionti otooun aitia pasa esti poiesis, oste kai ai ypo pasais tais technais ergasiai poieseis eisi kai oi touton demiourgoi pantes poietai, The Symposium*, 205b–c).

Heidegger translates the phrase "from Nothing to Being" (*ek tou me ontos eis to on*) as "*aus dem Nicht-Anwesenden in das Anwesen*" ("from 'something' is always said of something that is the not-present to presence"), identifying Being (*to on*) with presence ("*Unverborgenheit*"):[1] since the Being of beings (i.e., of that which is) is the presence of what is present ("*Anwesen des Anwesendes*," ibid., 252), *poiesis* is not an *efficere*, a fabricating, but rather a bringing to and maintaining in presence. In this way, however, the not-present is identified with Nothing: it cannot be said that it "is," since in that case Being would signify not the Presence of what is present, but that which can be either present or absent. And thus bringing to presence (*poiesis*) is still a making pass from Nothing to Being. Heidegger's translation was designed to restore to *poiesis* the meaning it had lost through centuries of techno-metaphysical distortion; but in fact he defines it according to the very way of thinking that was first expressed by Plato, and which today invisibly sustains not only our civilization itself, but even the diagnoses of the unknown sickness of our time.

3. OCCIDENT AND ORIENT

Plato founded not a theory of the "world," but the "world" itself. Before Plato there was neither "world" nor production and destruction: they had been waiting, in concealment, to be called into the light. For the "world" (the *metaxy* between Being and Nothing) to come to light, Being and Nothing had first to be called forth from concealment. But this is not to say that they *emerge* from a total concealment—since

---

1 Martin Heidegger, *Vorträge und Aufsätze*, Pfullingen: Neske, 1954, 19.

Being and Nothing always already appear:[2] rather, "calling forth" expresses the need to bear witness to that which eternally appears. Parmenides was this witness. Thus only the West was to call the "world" into the light; yet in evoking the "world," at the same time it abandoned the truth of Being dawning in the testimony. The "world," as a middle ground between Being and Nothing, appeared on the horizon only because of the attention paid to Being and Nothing; but with the supervention of the "world," the *truth* of Being and Nothing was abandoned.

The Orient did not testify to Being and Nothing and was thus unable to found the "world." This does not mean, however, that the Orient has remained immune to that alienation of the meaning of Being in which the history of the West, as a history of the "world," was lost. On the contrary, it means that the Orient, as such, never reached the parting of the ways where the road followed by the West, the path of Night (*Nuktos keleuthos*), branches off from the uncharted, mysterious path of Day (*Ematos keleuthos*). Approached but never travelled, the path of Day still beckons, waiting for the West to follow the truth of Being.

Through inertia, the Orient has continued to pursue the nonmetaphysical way of Life that was superseded by Parmenides' testimony at the very outset of Western history. Thus it continued to live in the constant possibility of setting out on the path of Day. Today, however, with the Westernization of our planet as a whole, this possibility has definitively been lost. The Orient has not been saved: it has not yet been lost.

4. THE BAD SHEPHERD

The Platonic "parricide" led determinations (i.e., beings) into Being from the nothingness to which they had been relegated by Parmenides, and thereby gave rise to the "world." Having guided the flock into the fold of Being, Plato divided it in two: on one side the privileged company of divine beings, ungenerated and immutable, and on the

---

2 Cf., the "Postscript," paragraph VI.

other the company of sensible beings (i.e., the "world"), whose birth and death would seem to be attested by their very appearing: "that which always is and never becomes, and that which is always becoming but never is" (*ti to on aei, genesin de ouk echon, kai ti to gignomenon, on de oudepote, Timaeus, 28a*). The bad shepherd had already taken the path of Night. Plato failed to seize the opportunity offered him of committing parricide without being stained. Might such an opportunity—the possibility of reawakening the truth of Being—be offered again in our time?

The parricide had to be committed, since determinations are not a Nothing (an opposite—*enantion*—of Being), and therefore "are." Being is not the pure indeterminate but the concrete totality of determinations. And *any* determination, insofar as it is a something-that-is, is a *Being*: *to on* is now the synthesis of the determination and its "is."

But Plato, in the very act of opposing Being, thus concretized, to Nothing, also leaves Being identical to Nothing. He thinks determinations (and thus the not-Nothing, i.e., beings) as *per se* indifferent to their being or not-being (i.e., to their existing or not-existing, to their not-being or being: a Nothing). To maintain them in existence—and understand them as ingenerable and incorruptible—he must in fact go in search of a *ground*; a ground, however, that grounds only the privileged region of universal determinations while abandoning empirical determinations to annulment. Evoking the "world" thus means evoking "God," understood as the privileged region of Being. The "ground," therefore, is theology: with Plato it begins its now age-old attempt to reach the affirmation of a Being-that-is by setting out from a mode of thought in which Being—the not-Nothing—is posited as *per se* indifferent with respect to its being or not-being a Nothing (i.e., with respect to its existence or nonexistence).

Today the West knows that God is dead. But it does not—and cannot—know the cause of his death. For the West is in fact still afflicted by the same sickness that caused his birth. What Zarathustra teaches is that *men* are the creators, not God. If God existed, man could not create. But creation is common to the old God and the new Man.

For Plato *poiesis* was primarily divine: the creator (*o demiourgos*) produces the things of the "world" by making them pass from nothingness to Being. The creationistic conception of medieval metaphysics was later to radicalize the productivity of divine *poiesis*, removing the limit (and the ambiguity) of Platonic *chora* and Aristotelian prime matter.

For modern immanentism, by contrast, *o demiourgos* is man. Man, in history, produces himself and the world. Today natural science and technology have endowed him with a creative capability never possessed before. The possibility of creating the *Übermensch* now looms on the horizon. Biology and cybernetics are moving precisely in this direction.

Yet throughout the history of the West the dominant thought—dominant to the point of not even being expressed—has continued to be the ancient thought of Plato: Being (i.e., determinations—which after Parmenides are no longer posited as Nothing) is essentially unstable: it is (i.e., is not a Nothing), but might not-be (i.e., might have remained a Nothing); it is, but earlier was-not, and later will be no longer and might be wholly annihilated. Confronted with this instability of Being, modern technology endeavors to ward off the annihilation of values (i.e., of things that are deemed to be values). Today Western man rejects metaphysics, since it leads to the affirmation of an immutable Being which makes visible human creation impossible. Yet he continues to think metaphysically, since he continues to "see" the "world" as the absolute horizon of Being, within which the emergence from nothingness and the annulment of Being (increasingly controlled by man) seem to stand before his very eyes.

5. THE TRUTH OF BEING AND THE REPETITION OF THE PARRICIDE

In *seeking* a Being that is immutable and eternal, metaphysics identifies Being with Nothing. For in seeking to ground the existence of an eternal Being, it admits that Being, as such, might be a Nothing: just as it "sees" that the Beings of the "world" have been, and return to being, nothing:

> When we say of something that it "is not," does this not signify merely the absence of Being from that of which we are saying that it is not? In saying that something is not, do we mean that in one sense it is not

and in another sense is? Or are we using the phrase "is not" without qualification, to signify that the thing which is not is not in any sense whatsoever and in no way Participates in Being? Thus, that which is not cannot be, nor can it in any way participate in Being. But what, then, is "coming to be," or "perishing"? Is the former anything else than acquiring Being, and the latter anything else than losing it?[3]

When thought affirms the possibility that something (i.e., a not-Nothing) not-be, and thus that it acquire and lose its being, it affirms that the not-Nothing is nothing—it posits the identity of Being and Nothing. For indeed, it is not of a *Nothing* that thought affirms that it is not, and so is nothing—no, it affirms this of a *not*-Nothing, and thus of *something* that, as such, is Being: "'something' is always said of something that is" (*to ti ep' onti legomen ekastote*).[4] The history of the West is grounded on this identification of Being and Nothing, and is therefore the history of nihilism.

The parricide had to be committed; it had, that is, to be affirmed both that "not-Being" is (*estin ex anankes to me on, Sophist, 256d*), and that "Being" is not (*to on ouk estin*, ibid., 259b). For "Being," in these formulae, is not yet the synthesis of the determination and its "is"—rather, it is *only* this "is," i.e., pure Being, which differs from any determination. "Being," here, is that which for Parmenides (the Parmenides of the Platonic-Aristotelian interpretation) exhausted the semantics of Being, whereas now, for Plato, it has come to be a moment of this semantics. And therefore it must now be said of "Being" that it "is not," precisely because it differs from—i.e., has not the same meaning as—determinations, which constitute the other moment of this semantics. And determinations, in turn, as different from "Being" so understood, are "not-Being"—but are that "not-Being" of which it must now be affirmed that it "is."

But this "not-Being" in which every determination (i.e., every something, every *ti*) consists is not a Nothing, and for this very reason

---

3   Parmenides 163c–d, after John Warrington, New York: Everyman's Library, 1961, 59–60.

4   Cf. "Returning to Parmenides," secs. 1–2, and the "Postcript" (Recapitulation).

that which Parmenides affirmed of pure indeterminate Being ought to have been affirmed of *every determination* and thus of the *concrete totality of determinations*: that it neither is born nor dies—neither issues from nor returns to nothingness, since before its birth and after its death it would then be a Nothing. It is eternal.

If this had been affirmed, the parricide could have been committed without the West's staining itself with the identification of Being and Nothing. But this was also the thought essentially *not* thought by Plato and by the entire history of nihilism. To think *this* thought means committing the West to the path of Day—destining the truth of Being to dominate the future, just as Plato was the first to destine the untruth of Being to dominate our own time.

6. PARMENIDES AND MELISSUS

Plato was the first to do so, for his identification of Being and Nothing refers not to abstract indeterminate Being, as was the case with Melissus, but to Being understood as a synthesis of existence and the determination.

The identification of Being and Nothing was, however, already present in Eleaticism. Melissus, in Fragment 1, excluded the generation of Being, since "if it was born, before being born it must necessarily have been nothing. But if it was nothing, nothing could have been born from Nothing, in no way":

> *Ei nar egeneto, anankaion esti prin genesthal einai meden.*
> *Ei toinun meden en, oudama an genoito ouden ek medenos.*

To deny the becoming of Being, Melissus—like all metaphysical thought after him—feels a need to introduce the principle of *ex nihilo nihil*: the affirmation that Being was a Nothing (*anagkaion esti prin genesthal einai meden*) is not seen as that which, as such, is a negation of the truth of Being. The nothingness of Being is not seen as the absurd, since to reach the absurd Melissus needs to hypothesize that Being is generated from Nothing—which means that the Melissian exclusion of this absurd is grounded on an acceptance of that authentic and fundamental absurdity which constitutes the nihilistic substance of Western thought: i.e., the nothingness of Being.

The nothingness of Being: which Parmenides rejected when he excluded the generation of Being on the basis of the abysmal simplicity of the consideration that, if Being were to be generated, it would not be:

> *Ei gar egent, ouk esti* (Fr. 8, 20), i.e., it would be nothing.

7. THE AMBIGUITY OF PRE-ONTOLOGICAL LANGUAGE

Before Plato there was no "world," since Becoming was not thought as an annulment of Being, nor was there "production" and "destruction," since the activity of nature and man was not considered to be a making things pass from nothingness to Being and from Being to nothingness.

Yet this is not to say that we know what the "world" replaced. Primitive man, and nonmetaphysical existence in general, stand before us in an essential ambiguity. This ambiguity, however, shows itself only within the nonalienated comprehension of Being. That is the meaning of primitive language—a language that has not yet measured itself against the explicit meaning of Being and Nothing. In the Vedas, in the Brahmana, in Genesis, in Homer and Hesiod, what is the meaning of the words we translate as "Being," "not-Being," "generate," "produce," "be born," "die"? Any hermeneutics of primitive language formulated by Western culture is always guided by the untruth of Being, and therefore—in whatever language it interprets—it can find only the categories of untruth. And yet it never throws these categories into relief, since they constitute the common element and unchallenged horizon enclosing both interpreter and interpreted.

The affirmation of the ontological ambiguity of nonmetaphysical language is primarily phenomenological: it rests, that is, on the *fact* that a given language does not include the explicitation of the meaning of Being. The relation between a language of this type and the explicitated meaning of Being is therefore always a comparison between two different languages and never simply an interpretation of the former.

Nor can the implicit ontological meaning of a language be inferred from its explicit semantics. The semantics that is explicit is not ontological (for the ontological semantics is absent from the explicit); that which is explicit is only the ambiguous ontological meaning, which can only serve as an ambiguous basis for the inference. It could provide a nonambiguous basis, only if that which one wished to infer were already explicit; but in that case there would no longer be any need to infer the ontological meaning.

But the ontological ambiguity of metaphysical language must be affirmed in another sense as well—where, however, it is no longer a fact (i.e., is no longer phenomenological), but is a *possibility*. In the first sense, the ambiguity arises with respect to the *actual* appearing of Being; with respect, that is, to the nonalienated comprehension of Being which, knowing both the path of Day and that of Night, realizes that it is impossible to establish whether nonmetaphysical man (i.e., that particular phenomenological content which is nonmetaphysical existence) treads one path rather than the other. In the second sense, the ambiguity arises also with respect to the inactual appearing of Being, whose existence cannot be immediately denied, and which is therefore a possibility (i.e., a problem). Can it be excluded that Being also manifest itself beyond the actual Appearing (beyond, that is, that Appearing in which "I" consist)? Or that languages different from "mine," and thus also primitive languages, may express Being, insofar as Being appears in an Appearing different from the actual Appearing?

8. THE ETERNAL AND ITS TESTIMONY

But in Appearing as such (and thus also in any possible appearing of Being that is different from the actual Appearing) "Being" and "Nothing" are part of the eternal spectacle (since Appearing too, like all Being, is eternal). In Appearing there are things that come and go, and others that always and forever appear and without which nothing could appear. Among these things that eternally appear (in the "Postscript," paragraph VI, they are called the "background" of Appearing) we find, together with Being and Nothing, also the *truth* of Being and of Nothing.

This house appears and is not a Nothing. However, if its "not being a Nothing" did not appear, the house itself could not appear, since it is, as such, a not-Nothing. And if the "not-Nothing" does not appear, nothing else can appear instead of the house, since *any* something is, as such, a not-Nothing. If things do not appear as Being—as not-Nothing—nothing appears. And again: Being as such is the negation of Nothing; and thus if Nothing does not appear, Being does not appear either. If "Nothing" did not appear, nothing would appear. And again: since Being, as such, is not-nothing, Being neither issues from nor returns to nothingness (i.e., cannot have been, and cannot re-become, a Nothing). The *truth* of Being is the affirmation of the *immutability* of Being (i.e., of the concrete totality of Being). Since Being as such is immutable, it appears only if it appears as immutable. If the truth of Being does not appear, nothing can appear.

Forgottenness of the truth of Being, in which the West has lost its way, thus does not mean that the Appearing in which Western man consists has been emptied of its eternal spectacle. And primitive man, who has not reached the parting of the ways where the path of Day branches off from that of Night, is not an Appearing that has yet to look out on this eternal spectacle. Man always and forever has the truth of Being before him, never-setting. In this sense, he is not a creature who, having emerged from nothingness, prepares himself, in time, to enter eternity (or to return to nothingness): man is the eternal appearing of the truth of Being. Time and history stand within this Appearing and constitute the process of the revelation of the whole.

The way in which man interprets "the divine spectacle" (*to theion aphoronta*) belongs to this process. Man stands eternally before the truth of Being; yet the West alone began to testify to this truth. And the testimony, "due to the brightness of the place" (*dia to lampron tes choras, Sophist*, 254a), was altered at the very moment of its birth. As a result, to this day we do not know what we are (we are not aware of what we know). Today technology has undertaken the construction of man. Man, as an object of production (*poiesis*), is thus the rigorously consistent result of metaphysics, i.e., of the alienated explicitation of the meaning of Being. Here, forgottenness of the truth of Being is the expression or interpretation that alters the truth which eternally appears.

Primitive (or, in general, nonmetaphysical) language, by contrast, does not explicitly bring to light the meaning of the truth of Being, which nonetheless stands before it; but neither does it bring to light the alienated meaning of Being. For us, accordingly, it remains essentially ambiguous, since we are not in a position to establish whether the meaning of its words expresses or betrays the truth of Being, before which the language grows. One can establish the syntax, but not the ontological semantics of a language that does not make explicit the meaning of Being and Nothing. Western metaphysics represents the only explicitation of this meaning in the history of man. And this very explicitation allows us to discern in the West (in the "land of setting") the setting of that which does not set (i.e., the alienated interpretation of the never-setting).

On the other hand, every language grows before the glow of Being, referring to it even when unable to express it. Every language intends to express it (and in this sense every language sinks its roots in the truth of Being), but no language has been able to do so. For either its expression reflected the glow but altered it, or else stood speechless before that which it saw, naming only things while saying nothing about the *truth* of things, thus remaining, with respect to this truth, an essentially ambiguous saying.

9. THE WEST AND THE SACRED

The evocative force of nonmetaphysical language lies, as we have seen, in its essential ambiguity, which reaches the fork where the two paths divide without going beyond it. Resolving the ambiguity through a hermeneutics means entering a different dimension from the one to be elucidated. The language interpreted, instead of revealing its hidden intentions, is transformed into a different language—which, in Western hermeneutics, is always the alienated language of the truth of Being. The ambiguity is resolved, only because one leads the language beyond the fork and forces it to explicitate the meaning of Being according to the categories of alienation. Thus the beginning of the Bible Story became the book of *Genesis*, and with the word *genesis* metaphysics definitively took possession of the way in which the West listens to the Sacred.

The West was incapable of receiving the Sacred. The metaphysical experiment of the West—i.e., the extension of metaphysics' dominion beyond the confines of philosophic thought—began with this failure to encounter the Sacred.

Today, the encounter with the Sacred has been turned into a simple question of "subjectivity." The transformation began with Kierkegaard. It is only a matter of "having faith." And, unquestionably, the Sacred is the way in which faith leads Being into Appearing. But subjectivity (faith, goodwill) is not what is lacking in the constitution of the West. Kierkegaard was able to note such a lack in the Hegelian professors of his day, and Nietzsche to rail against the guile of modern Christian faith; yet we are unable to affirm Western man's constitutional impossibility to have faith. On the contrary, it is the authentic meaning of "objectivity"—and therefore the authentic meaning of the Sacred— that is, by its constitution, precluded for him.

In the encounter with the Sacred, whoever holds fast to the moment of subjectivity alone assumes that the individual can decide his own destiny independently of the direction taken by the history of peoples (independently, that is, of the objectivity that emerges in history). The individual is saved even if the world (as objectivity) goes to perdition. He has to live the few years of his life as best he can (and that means applying his subjectivity, his goodwill, etc.), then death definitively settles accounts with the world. It never even crosses his mind that the individual is always and essentially involved with the history of the World—i.e., with the history of the appearing of Being—and that therefore he cannot remain indifferent before man's remotest past, his most distant future, or the way in which, in the past and the future, man encounters the Sacred.

And yet, the history of peoples determines the measure of man's relation with Being; it brings to light the earth upon which every man must walk. The way in which Being appears, and is destined to appear, to the individual depends upon the way in which peoples bring to completion the total appearing of Being. The individual is not left behind by this completion, or, more precisely, that which is left behind is the individual *qua* empirical determination. I am not an empirical determination, but the actual and eternal appearing of Being;[5] and every completion is reflected in the content of the actual Appearing, for while Being may be enclosed by other lights besides the light of the actual Appearing, the actual content is determined by the way in which being is disclosed by the totality of lights.[6]

Like a captain who guides a ship, the philosopher guides the completion of the appearing of Being. It is clear that, in bringing the ship to safety, the captain's actions also bring the captain himself to safety. Yet there are gestures that save, and others that lead to perdition: just as peoples can approach the never-setting by following either the path of Night, or the path of Day.

Commitment to the universal and objective is thus the most radical form of existential and subjective commitment. Kierkegaard failed to see the existential commitment of world history (*Weltgeschichte*). Authentic *Weltgeschichte*, however, is no mere comprehension of what has already been disclosed: in grasping the meaning of the past, it looks out on the future. Revolutionary Marxism, too, explicitly intends to prepare the future, but its aim is to deliver the objectivization of man in his work from alienation—where "objectivization" is always understood in the sense of Platonic *poiesis*. (For Marxism too, alienation is not simply *poiesis*—i.e., action dominated by the metaphysical

---

5 Cf. the "Postscript," paragraph IV.

6 It is true that other people's experiences do not belong to my experience; but if mine is an experience among others, its content can be neither indifferent to nor independent of the way in which the totality of experiences is brought to completion. If other people's experiences exist, the actual content is not the same as the content that would manifest itself if such experiences did not exist (and only the "behavior" of others existed). If the experiences of others exist, the content of the actual experience is related to these other experiences (and to the way in which, in them, Being is brought to light)—if only because it exists together with them; and this being related is something that must be discernable in the actual content. If other experiences exist, this something must be here before us. But we do not yet know whether it is there, nor what it is. Only if we already knew that experiences different from the actual experience existed could we then say that this something is the empirically ascertained set of other people's behaviors. Nor is there an incontrovertible inference by which we can affirm the existence of other people's experiences on the basis of the behavior "of others" belonging to the content of the actual Appearing.

And yet, the existence of a plurality of experiences is a possible truth: given this possibility, the individual cannot remain indifferent before the history of peoples taken as the disclosure of Being, brought to completion by a constellation of lights.

mode of thought—but is the existence of those social conditions which deprive the *demiourgos*, who now is man, of his own product, i.e., himself. Communism and capitalism are but two different modes of organizing the object of production, and thus also that object which is man. Their opposition—like all the oppositions in Western history—is realized within a fundamental solidarity.)

As he guides the millennia of the World—thus preparing the future house of man—the philosopher also prepares his own dwelling. Plato prepared the houses of Night (*domata Nuktos*, Parmenides, Fr. 1, 9), and it is here, in this perennial Night, that the West encounters the Sacred. The history of Christianity is the history of metaphysics' domination of the Sacred. Christianity made its peace first with philosophy, then with science and today with technology, i.e., with the various historical configurations assumed by metaphysics. And it is perfectly natural that Christianity keep in step with the times: from the very beginning it has let the guiding spirit of Western history take it by the hand. But the critics of Christianity also cling to that same hand.

10. YBRIS

Along the path of Day the encounter with the Sacred may be repeated. Yet it already takes place in the act in which thought invites the West to retrace its steps and return to the parting of the ways.

This invitation comes not from just any thought, but from the thought that actually constitutes itself as absolute, incontrovertible knowing, the negation of any presupposition and therefore it alone truly *episteme*—if, as its derivation from *epistamai* indicates, *episteme* is that which imposes itself and dominates, and therefore cannot be contradicted—it alone the locus and guardian of truth. *Episteme* is not *Ybris*. *Ybris* is the presumption and overweening pride of that which wants to assert itself beyond (*y=yper=epi*) its own power (*Brithein*); while *episteme* is the power or firmness (*istamai*) of the actual saying that imposes itself on (*epi*) any other discourse. This means that the appearing of Being may constitute itself as knowledge (*episteme*) or as opinion (*doxa*), but only *episteme* is able to negate any negation of that which appears. The truth of Being appears in both, but only *episteme* can bring it to light and assert it; *doxa* attends not to its precious load but to other things, and whatever it says can be denied.

When *doxa* presumes to say the incontrovertible, it is *ybris*. Since the incontrovertible cannot constitute itself independently of the testimony to the truth of Being, the history of philosophy is a history of *ybris*, where the very figures of the incontrovertible become the most radical forms of the alienation of the meaning of Being. Thus the opposition of Being and not-Being becomes the "principle of noncontradiction," which denies that Being is Nothing—but does so only *as long as* Being is. For Being, in this principle, is understood as that which can become nothing and, having become nothing, can be nothing. And phenomenology, in turn, states the "principle of all principles," which affirms everything that appears, and to the extent that it appears—but *that which* appears, i.e., Being, is understood as something that, when it does not appear, might be a Nothing. Both the empiristic critiques of metaphysics for going beyond the given and the idealistic elimination of presupposed realism come together in the principle of phenomenology. The insistence upon presuppositionlessness (*Voraussetzunglösigkeit*) inevitably leads to the demand to ground the existence of that which does not appear—i.e., to ground it differently from the way that that which appears is grounded. For idealism, such a grounding is impossible and the appearing of Being is its very "production," since Being, in entering consciousness, leaves nothingness, and in leaving consciousness, enters nothingness; while for phenomenology—which, as such, cannot accept the categorical rejection of a reality that does not appear—entering and leaving consciousness *might* be a leaving and entering nothingness. But in both idealism and phenomenology alike, Being is understood as that which may be nothing.

As an opposition between the incontrovertible and the controvertible, *episteme* and *doxa* are, respectively, truth and untruth. "Truth," here, means a saying that shows its invincible force. That which is said is the truth of Being. In one sense, accordingly, "truth" is *that which* is said in *episteme* (and in this sense one speaks of the "truth of Being"). In another sense, however, "truth" is *episteme* itself, understood as incontrovertible saying (a saying that contains within itself the positing of the relation between *doxa* and *episteme*). Due to this duality of meaning, there is no contradiction in affirming that the truth of Being is the content not only of *episteme*, but also of untruth, i.e., *doxa*. In *doxa*, the truth of Being is either unexpressed, i.e., not testified to—in which case the ontological semantics of *doxa* is essentially ambiguous (as in primitive language or in certain forms of religious or poetic language)—or, when *doxa* is *ybris*, it is explicitly denied. The history of the West is the progressive conforming of *doxa* to the categories of *ybris*.

11. INTERPRETATION AND LANGUAGE

A set of empirical facts (signs, sounds, etc.) is a language, only if they are interpreted in a certain way. That the signs of the Greek language correspond to certain meanings is a convention, and is no less one for being accepted by everyone who has anything to do with that language. Similarly, it is a convention that the words of everyone who "speaks the same language" are coordinated with certain meanings. The coordination of the signs and sounds of a language with certain meanings is a set of rules, whose application then allows particular groupings of signs and sounds, given *de facto*, to acquire a sense.

The confines of a language too are a convention. If, in applying a set of rules to a given grouping of signs, no sense is obtained, then it may simply be said that the grouping has no sense. But it may also be said that the set of known rules does not include the rules that would make sense of that which is apparently senseless; just as it may be said that the grouping belongs not to the language considered, but to an altogether different language.

The ambiguity of a language can only be affirmed if one accepts the mass of conventions that make the interpretation and delimitation of that language possible. The adoption of these conventions belongs to *doxa*. The historical sciences are grounded on a whole system of such adoptions and, as in the physico-mathematical sciences, this system itself belongs to those groups of postulates that are the basis of scientific inquiry (which, accordingly, operates wholly within *doxa*).

Every historical "interpretation"—even the one that interprets the history of the West as a journey on the path of Night—is therefore grounded on conventions (or more precisely, is grounded on those fundamental interpretations which, on the basis of certain conventions, furnish the set of meanings that historical science then "interprets" at a higher level by referring them to broader semantic categories). From the standpoint of *episteme* different conventions, i.e., different coordinations between signs and meanings giving rise to different interpretations of languages, cannot simply be rejected. Similarly, a convention that treats the signs of languages just as one treats the arrangement of leaves on trees cannot be rejected out of hand: the position, size, and shape of the leaves is not (but could be) coordinated with a system of meanings (in which case a tree or group of trees would become a language).

Every convention is an act of faith. However, by adopting the conventions upon which the interpretation of historical languages is usually based, sets of meanings are disclosed that would otherwise have remained concealed; and these sets of meanings are in fact of incomparably greater interest than others, obtained on the basis of other interpretations. While, moreover, the coordination of a sign with a meaning is but one convention among an infinity of possible conventions, it is also true that there is that set of conventions which is a *fact*. That which is agreed upon [*convenzionato*] (hypothesized, supposed, decided) has no ground in truth—and thus cannot even be a fact that belongs to the content that appears (wherefore it is said that it is merely the content of a faith, i.e., of *doxa*). But the agreement upon [*convenzionare*] and thus the interpretation of historical languages in a certain way is a *fact*: that way by which we coordinate the sign "*anthropos*" with the meaning "man," and the sign "man" which we find in the *Divine Comedy* with the meaning "man."

It is to this fact—i.e., to the way in which historical languages are interpreted *in fact*—that we refer when we say that the West is the setting of the truth of Being. Given the way in which historical languages are interpreted in *fact*, the West is this setting. A fact that— like all facts—might be replaced by others. But any other fact would still be a convention: whether one decides to interpret the empirical events that constitute languages differently, or whether one decides not to interpret them at all.

To the extent that truth is not yet able to affirm that Being appears even beyond the actual Appearing, the signs of historical languages may be coordinated either exclusively with their actual meanings, or also with worlds of meanings belonging to possible consciousnesses different from the actual one. In the first case a language has no meaning "in itself," but is the means by which a field of meanings that would otherwise have remained concealed is disclosed in the actual Appearing. (Even if a historical language were to include the rules of coordination of its signs and meanings, in indicating these rules it would give rise to other signs, which in turn would have to be interpreted.) Only in the second case do we encounter the problem of the existence of rules of coordination different from those which coordinate the signs of a historical language with their actual meanings.

12. THE SACRED AND THE LANGUAGE OF DAY

Truth's encounter with the Sacred is primarily the relation between truth and an ontologically ambiguous language, which is already prey to metaphysics but may also become prey to truth. For this to occur, the language of the Sacred has to be wrested from metaphysics; that is, it must be understood as a saying that speaks the tongue of the truth of Being. But even in this way violence is done to it, since it is not *found*, but rather *willed* in the company of the truth of Being. If the language of the Sacred goes along with metaphysics, it becomes an alienated language; but left to itself it returns to a position of equilibrium between truth and the negation of the truth of Being, which, in turn, can only take possession of it by forcibly upsetting this equilibrium. But while metaphysics takes possession of it, convinced that the language of the Sacred reflects its own mode of thought (i.e., failing to see the language's ambiguity, metaphysics finds it already prone to let itself be conquered), truth knows that it can take possession of this language only by an act of will. Truth knows, therefore, that instead of compelling the Sacred to speak its own tongue, it may limit itself to delivering it from alienation, leaving it in a position of equilibrium.

But if truth compels the Sacred to speak the tongue of Day, then the Sacred says things that are unknown to truth and that stand before it as a *problem*. As long as the language of the Sacred maintains itself in the equilibrium of ambiguity, it is not yet a problem for truth, but may lapse into alienation, or else *become* a problem for truth. Here, it is not yet a problem, for the problem is that of *establishing* what it says; whereas, now, it is precisely *what* it says that presents itself as a problem. The Sacred says that God lived as a man among men. This becomes a problem for truth, only if it is understood as a saying that speaks the tongue of Day. And the very same words, spoken in the tongue of Day or in that of Night, take on different meanings. The Sacred also says: through him all things were made (*panta di' autou egeneto, omnia per ipsum facta sunt, John* I, 3). Metaphysics never even suspects that the meaning of this *gignesthai* may be different from the one with which it is familiar—and thus "creation" becomes the absurdity of a region of Being (*panta*, created things) which might have been, and might re-become, nothing.

13. THE IMPOSSIBILITY OF THE APPEARING OF ANNIHILATION

The truth of Being demands that *all* Being be immutable and eternal. Experience does not attest the annulment of Being, i.e., its becoming, or having been, nothing (cf. the "Postscript")—not even when a nuclear explosion destroys a city. This is not to say that the becoming of things is mere illusion (as Spinoza thought), and thus that the appearing of change is merely phenomenal; rather, it means that the changing and becoming of things do not appear as an annulment of Being. The error lies not in Appearing, but in the way Appearing is interpreted. So deep is the forgottenness of the meaning of Being, that one believes one sees what is not there—one believes that that which does not appear appears. One thinks one sees the "world" and yet the "world" was never *there*, but was superimposed by alienated reason upon the veritable content of Appearing. Forgottenness of the truth of Being is, at the same time, forgottenness of the truth of Becoming. "Birth" and "death," "growth" and "change," "generation," "corruption," and "destruction" are the various ways in which Being *appears* and *disappears* (i.e., are the various aspects assumed by Being in its appearing and disappearing). The becoming of Being, as contained in Appearing, is the process of the appearing and disappearing of eternal immutable Being.

Alienated reason is convinced that the annulment of things appears. But when a city that has been destroyed by a nuclear explosion is annihilated—does it continue to appear? Has it become a Nothing—yet it still continues to appear? Here, alienated reason itself is forced to admit that that which is annulled disappears: to the extent, that is, that it is annulled. That which has become nothing is also that which has disappeared. But how, then, can the annulment of that which no longer appears *appear*? If something no longer appears, its having become nothing or its continuing to exist cannot be determinations that appear.[7]

Appearing says nothing about the fate of that which no longer appears (or has not yet appeared), but the Justice of Being (*Dike*) always catches up with everything that does not appear and prohibits it from becoming, and from being, a Nothing.

Thus that which is born is that which has never appeared before, and that which dies is that which has not reappeared. Today, Western common sense too has fallen prey to metaphysics, and even an illiterate, faced with a man's corpse, knows that the set of expressions,

---

7   If these determinations cannot be affirmed on the basis of their appearing, the only basis for affirming them will be the *logos*. The opposition between the two determinations (some Being is annulled, all Being is immutable) is not an opposition between experience and reason, but rather between alienated reason and veritable reason, i.e., between untruth and the truth of Being. The truth of Being belongs to the original structure of truth (cf. E. Severino, *La struttura originaria*, 1st ed. Brescia: La Scuola, 1958; 2nd ed. Milan: Adelphi, 1981), i.e., to that structure of immediate protases upon which alone incontrovertible knowing can grow. Any possible discourse that, on the basis of the original structure of truth, presumes to *demonstrate* that some Being is annulled, is therefore known a priori to be *absurd*, whatever its degree of plausibility: demonstrating the negation of truth on the basis of truth is impossible. Nor can the negation of truth (i.e., the affirmation that some Being is annulled) belong to the original structure of truth: the affirmation that all Being is immutable cannot be co-original with the affirmation that some Being is annulled, since it is the negation of the latter.

All this means that the annulment of Being (or of some Being) can be posited neither as a phenomenological content—i.e., as something that appears—nor as something incontrovertibly demonstrated or mediated. Nor can it belong to the immediacy of the logos. It belongs, on the contrary, to the untruth of Being, i.e., to that mode of thinking and living which, from Plato onward, deems it perfectly natural that things (the earth, plants, stars, animals, feelings, and thoughts) be Nothing (i.e., can become a Nothing and, having become a Nothing, be a Nothing).

movements, looks, and words which made up the living man has become a Nothing. And yet—everything that is dead, like everything not yet born, always and forever dwells in the company of all Being.

14. THE TRUTH OF APPEARING

Appearing is not appearance; appearances too, like realities, appear. Unlike appearance, which conceals, Appearing uncovers and brings to light. In this respect, Appearing is a drawing back, or aside, just as the curtain is drawn aside to let the show be seen. Except that in Appearing there is no trace of that which is drawn aside: Appearing is an awakening, or rather an always already being awakened with the curtain raised: hence, a negativity. Aristotle himself had pointed out the purity and indeterminateness of intellect, or *nous* (*De Anima*, 429a 18–21): the very meaning of Appearing precludes it from having eidetic dimension, it is not "mixed" (*ananke . . . amige einai*)—where "mixing" is the addition to the pure meaning of Appearing of other determinations (which would thus constitute the dimension). If Appearing as such were determinate, its having a particular meaning would cover and conceal that which has to appear, "for anything foreign hinders and obstructs it" (*gar koluei to allotpion kai antiphirattei*). As in the case of the Kantian "phenomenon": its eidetic dimension, understood as an essential component of Appearing, is a covering that conceals the thing in itself in the very act of letting it appear. But then, the eidetic dimension of the phenomenon appears (the objects of experience appear), and in the Kantian discourse this Appearing implicitly enjoys that condition of purity and indeterminateness which is proper to authentic Appearing.

This drawing aside is, however, only the negative aspect of Appearing, which cannot be indeterminate and pure to the point of being nothing. While Heidegger did understand Appearing as "nothing," he also stressed that this "nothing" is not a *nihil absolutum* (indeed, so far is it from being a *nihil absolutum* that, for him, it is "Being" itself). The purity and indeterminateness of Appearing thus mean that it is *nothing other than* Appearing (not, therefore, a Nothing, but rather nothing beyond its being Appearing), or, that the meaningfulness and particular determinateness of Appearing exhaust themselves in its being Appearing (manifestation, presence, openness of Being).[8]

And yet, the authentic meaning of Appearing constitutionally eludes Western philosophy. From Aristotle to Husserl, phenomenological reflection has been able to grasp the "unmixed" character of Appearing only in the abstract. And this is due to the fact that metaphysics has always mixed Appearing with the "world." In fact, Appearing here is no pure letting things come forth, but rather a letting the "world" superimpose itself upon things that come forth—it is a receiving things in the altering eidetic dimension of the "world." Precisely insofar as one is convinced that the "world" appears, the "world" brings about an inevitable phenomenization or subjectivization of the things that appear. Except that the "world," as an a priori category, is attributable to the structure of man as enveloped by metaphysical alienation. In modern philosophy, epistemological phenomenism and the theory of intentionality that is opposed to it are but two faces of phenomenism itself, understood as an essential component of metaphysical nihilism. The authentic meaning of Appearing can be grasped only in the light of the truth of Being.

15. WE LIVE ETERNALLY ALL THE LIVES WE MIGHT HAVE LIVED

But is the Being that appears and disappears all destined to appear and disappear, or is the epiphany of Being the freedom of Being?

If Being did not appear, Appearing would be nothing. It is

---

8   It may be objected that in this way no progress has been made, since if Appearing exists, then the conditions that make its functioning possible must also exist, and so far we have found no trace of such conditions. (And these conditions as such are not in themselves Appearing—wherefore that "mixture" which above was excluded now seems unavoidable.) But this objection stems from the hypothesis (typical of the techno-scientific mode of thought) that everything that exists is a sort of manufactured article or apparatus, about which one can sensibly ask how it can exist or function; and if everything that exists has been "manufactured," then it should in principle be possible to trace the conditions of its functioning, or the elements that constitute it. To test the truth of this hypothesis, however, would require going back to the *original* truth, in which Appearing is assumed in its pure meaning—the truth that provides the only basis for verifying a hypothesis.

therefore necessary that Being appear, and thus that those determinations appear whose appearing is a condition for the appearing of every thing. Such determinations constitute the "background" of any further manifestation of Being. On the other hand, those determinations of which it is not yet known whether they belong to the background or not (in the "Postscript" they are called "variants") give rise to the problem of freedom. Is there freedom in Being? This question means: do variants follow a necessary destiny in the process of their appearing and disappearing, or do they appear, but might not have appeared, and disappear, but might not have disappeared? (The "eternal return" is one way of thinking the necessary manifestation of the eternal. As long as freedom is only a possibility, then so also is the eternal return. A possibility, however, not as it is understood by metaphysics, which with Nietzsche thinks an eternally returning from nothingness and to nothingness, but rather in the sense of the possibility that the eternal reappear as it once appeared, i.e., return to a previous Appearing.)

If the language of the Sacred is made to speak the tongue of Day, then the "making" (*gignesthai*) contained in "through him all things were made" (*panta di' autou egeneto*) signifies the *appearing* of all things that appear: not their becoming Being, from the nothing they once were or might have remained, but the enduring coming out of their concealment. The actual appearing of Being is theophany; and the word "creation," pronounced in the tongue of Day, signifies theophany. It is here that the Sacred becomes a problem for truth: the problem of freedom in the appearing of Being. Is Being "Master" of its appearing, or does everything that appears necessarily appear? The background necessarily appears, and the "I" is this eternal place where worlds are born. But might these worlds have remained concealed, or are they driven into the light by necessity?

Like "creation," in the language of metaphysics "freedom" too becomes absurd: the absurdity of a certain Being—a *decision* (i.e., an act of will, the will's determining itself in a certain way)—that might have been nothing. "Freedom" begins to become a problem only when it is thought as the possibility of the not-appearing of the Being that appears. It is only within this problem that the problem of human freedom becomes concrete. The life I live I have always lived, and shall always live. Always and forever I live the lives I might have lived: if lives exist that I might have lived, I *live* them eternally, since they cannot have remained a Nothing. Possibility is not in Being, since a possible Being is a Being that is in some way nothing (i.e., the "reality" of that which is only as possible is nothing). From the standpoint of metaphysics, "possibility" signifies that it is not contradictory for what-is-not to be, which means that its becoming Being is its having been nothing; this not-Nothing (which now is) has been nothing, and precisely because it was nothing as real Being, it was able to be that not-Nothing which is possible Being.

Possibility is not in Being, but in the appearing of Being (i.e., does not belong to Being insofar as it is, but to Being insofar as it appears). I live eternally all the lives I might have lived, I have always already decided everything I might have decided—and yet only *this* life that I live enters Appearing. But is this so because all my other lives are concealed, or because no other life of mine exists? Or again: do other lives of mine exist, besides this one, that appears? And if they do exist, might they have appeared instead of this one that appears? The ground of the freedom of man lies here, in this possibility; thus man can be thought as free only if he is thought as eternally living all the lives that he could possibly live.[9]

16. THE POSSIBILITY OF LANGUAGE "IN ITSELF"

That God live among men is by no means problematic: since the forgotten essence of man is the appearing of Being (and this forgotten-ness is an aspect of the forgottenness of Being itself), man is the *locus* where God—i.e., Being—shows himself (and it is only Being that can show itself). But when the Sacred announces that God lived as a man

---

9   The reasons for which freedom cannot be posited as immediately evident are set out in the second "Study" of E. Severino, *Studi di filosofia della prassi*, Milan: Vita e pensiero, 1962—where, however, such terms as "existing," "not-existing," "reality," "unreality," "contingency," "possibility," and "capacity" must no longer be understood as determinations of Being, but as determinations of Appearing. It still holds, that is, that freedom can be thought only as a form of contingency—but of "contingency" understood as a modality of *Appearing*, i.e., as the appearing of something that might have remained concealed. And that that which appears might not have appeared is not immediately evident but rather, as we have seen, is a problem.

among men, it alludes to an exceptional sojourn, to a different synthesis of the human and the divine. This becomes a problem for truth, only if the words "man" and "God" are thought in the light of the truth of Being. Thinking them in this light, truth *wills* that the Sacred speak the tongue of Day; but then, it is the Sacred that, speaking, makes itself heard and announces something which truth is unable to deny or to confirm, and which is therefore a problem.

In the meantime, however, it is also possible that the language of the Sacred, like any other historical language, does not become language only when its signs are coordinated with actual meanings, but that it already be language independently of this coordination; i.e., that it already be coordinated with meanings, independently of its coordination with the actual dimension of meaning. If certain rules are adopted for the coordination of signs with actual meanings, certain physical events become a language, and it is possible that only then do they begin to be language. In this case language has no meaning "in itself," independently of its coordination with an actual meaning, and interpreting it in a certain way is equivalent, purely and simply, to *willing* that it have a certain meaning. But it is also possible that a language already has a meaning of its own, independently of this *will* that it have meaning, and that it therefore expresses Being, insofar as Being comes to light in an Appearing different from the actual Appearing. Since the language of the Sacred is ambiguous with respect to the truth of Being (not expressing it, not even to deny it), it is therefore possible that the language of the Sacred *already* speaks the tongue of Day, and that while it does not speak *of* Day (i.e., of the truth of Being), that its every word is dedicated to the prodigious announcement. This announcement says nothing about the truth of Being; but it envelops truth with the problem, it is itself the problem.[10]

---

10   This problem stands at the apex of a ramification of problems, for when truth says, "Perhaps God has lived among men," it says this at the apex of the following considerations: "Perhaps the language of the Sacred exists (i.e., perhaps this language is not only willed, but is itself already the expression of an appearing of Being, different from the actual Appearing); and perhaps the way in which its words are actually interpreted corresponds to the way in which they were constructed; and perhaps it speaks the tongue of Day; and perhaps that which is said in this tongue (i.e., that God has lived among men) is true."

17. THE CONTRADICTION OF TRUTH AND THE SACRED

Truth is an already having resolved, in practice, that which nevertheless continues to be a problem.

Every Being is, necessarily, part of the whole: it cannot annul itself and leave the whole, nor can the whole cease to envelop it. The whole is in fact the totality of eternal Being. Thus no Being can appear if it does not appear as part of the whole. If the whole does not appear, nothing appears. (The whole is a determination of the "background" of Appearing; indeed, it is the very background as such.)

Yet precisely because Being appears and disappears, the whole does not appear in its fullness. Thus the whole, while appearing as whole, is not the whole. The whole is the completed richness that lacks nothing, but if it enters Appearing while leaving this richness concealed, then that which is not the whole is posited in Appearing as whole. If, that is, only the form of the whole appears, but not its content (precisely because the content appears only in part), then the form becomes content; but the form is not the whole (precisely because it is *only* the form of the whole), and thus that which is not the whole is meaningful as "the whole." This contradiction arises not because the part is falsely identified with the whole, but because there appears only a part of that to which the meaning "whole" refers, wherefore the part (including even the formal reference to everything that does not appear) is meaningful as "the whole."[11]

The actual Appearing as such is constituted according to this contradiction, and likewise untruth and truth, which are the two

---

This last problem would remain, however, even if all the conditions that gave rise to the previous problems were to fail, leaving only the actual meaning of that which has been posited here as problematic. Every language might disappear and every man fall silent, all remembrance of what has been written or said might fade away— and yet, for truth to be engaged in the problem of the truth of this pure thought, that God has lived among men, it would suffice that the thought appear and be thought in the tongue of Day. Truth is the *locus* in which a problem can authentically constitute itself; and when, in truth, it is said of something that "perhaps it is true," this means that one is not actually able to exclude—nor, therefore, to affirm—the existence of a nexus that, once brought to light, would show how the negation of that something is the negation of truth.

11   Cf. *La struttura originaria*, Ch. XII.

modes according to which the content of Appearing is determined. Truth is contradiction. There would no longer be contradiction, if all Being were to come out of concealment.

Insofar as truth is contradiction, the incontrovertible is controvertible; not, however, in the sense that what truth says must be denied, but rather in the sense that what it says abstractly must be said concretely. Truth's saying, *qua* saying, remains at the bottom of its concretization, and is therefore superseded (and hence denied) not insofar as it says, but rather insofar as it is a not-saying (i.e., insofar as it is an abstract saying that says the whole abstractly, and which is a contradiction not *qua* saying, but rather insofar as it is not a saying the whole, and is thus a not-saying). Abstract saying is incontrovertible precisely insofar as it has to remain at the bottom of its every concretization. Hence the incontrovertible is not in the same respect (*sub eodem*) controvertible. The supersession of truth that resolves the abstract in the concrete, and which is therefore the very concretizing of the incontrovertible, is thus essentially different from the negation of truth that denies truth insofar as it is saying.

Acceptance of the Sacred *may* be the key that leads to the greatest disclosure of Being possible for truth—liberation from the entire mass of contradictions from which it is possible for truth to be liberated. But acceptance of the Sacred may also bring on the desert, the deepest concealment of Being.

Truth cannot not compromise itself, since neutrality with respect to acceptance or rejection is itself a way of not accepting that which might be the salvation (or the perdition) of truth. Truth cannot live otherwise than as untruth, *episteme* cannot live otherwise than as *doxa*, since in whatever way truth takes up a position with respect to the Sacred, in truth something occurs that has no truth: it is not known where it will lead. The prisoners in the cave do not free themselves before reaching the sunlight—they see the sun while still in chains. The going down of the sun (*katabasis ek tou eliou*) is not an event that occurs after its coming up (*anabasis epi to elion*) has been completed, but coming up is a having to remain where one began. Truth lives in untruth, and it is in truth so understood that the truth of Being is testified to: not in the sense that this testimony has no truth, but in the sense that the testimony inevitably goes along with untruth, i.e., with faith. This, in essence, is the practical resolution of the problem of the Sacred.[12]

18. SALVATION

The thought that invites the West to return to the parting of the ways is thus already an encounter with the Sacred: a different encounter from that which took place along the path of Night, where it was an alienated civilization that related itself to the Sacred. The thought of the truth of Being is just at the beginning of the path of Day (just as the metaphysics of Plato, insofar as it remains in the abstract element of philosophic thought, is just at the beginning of the path of Night). It is only the trace. But the trace prepares the future of the West—the encounter of a nonalienated civilization with the Sacred. Nonalienation consists not in acceptance of the Sacred, but in the purification of the place where acceptance or rejection of the Sacred can occur.

The relation with the Sacred is, primarily, a relating of truth to the Sacred. The problem of salvation regards, primarily, the salvation of truth. If man, in his essence, is the eternal appearing of Being, what may be seen arising in this essence? In speaking of the salvation of the "individual," one more or less consciously refers to the irruption of infinite happiness into Appearing. But what is happiness? And something that cannot incontrovertibly be known to be genuine happiness, which cannot be lost—can that be happiness? A paradise can establish itself only as the content of truth (since only truth is incontrovertible knowing), and for truth the necessary condition of any paradise is the resolution of contradiction. (Unhappiness, pain, etc., are a being in contradiction;[13] the resolution of which is also the supersession of untruth, since any form of untruth—error, faith, not-appearing, a problem—is a contradiction.) Salvation is primarily this resolution of contradiction, and is thus a bringing of Being to its greatest possible disclosure in truth.

---

12   Cf. *Studi di filosofia della prassi*, 65–115.
13   Cf. ibid., 109.

Which is the way to this disclosure? Truth relates to the Sacred, precisely insofar as it thinks the Sacred as that which may be the way of salvation—and thus also the way of perdition. These two ways are the two possibilities of truth, and therefore of the path of Day itself, which may grow on truth. The path of Day too is a possibility of truth: in the sense that just as the West has grown on the tree of metaphysics, so the future of the West might grow on the tree of truth. But, as we have seen, it is truth as such that has to go along with untruth—and therefore also with the untruth of the Sacred: it is truth as such that has to bind itself to that which may be its salvation—but may also be its perdition. This bond exists between truth and every untruth that is a problem. (Truth is forced to go along with a decision that, however it be determined, decides something that might save truth, but might also be its perdition; it is forced to decide upon that which *might* be its perdition, not that which it knows to be perdition.)

The Sacred is a problem in a dual sense. For not only is it uncertain whether the acceptance of the Sacred will lead to truth's greatest disclosure of Being, but it may also be that this disclosure is the greatest only insofar as Being is presented in it according to the determinations that form the content of the prodigious announcement of the Sacred. It may, on the one hand, be supposed that truth's greatest disclosure of Being is possible only insofar as the truth of the Sacred announcement appears. (Just as, on the other hand, it may be supposed that such a disclosure is possible only if it does *not* include as truth the determinations announced by the Sacred.) The possibility that the Sacred may be truth—and indeed, may be the greatest openness of Being that is possible for truth—is the possibility of a nexus between the Sacred and truth, such that the negation of the existence of that which is announced by the Sacred necessarily implies the negation of truth.

Truth accepts the Sacred. This acceptance is a pure fact, wholly without ground (if by ground one means the nexus with truth). If truth were to reject or to be indifferent to the Sacred, this rejection or indifference too would be a pure, groundless fact. But the proposition "Truth accepts the Sacred" is not identical to the proposition "I accept the Sacred." "I" am the appearing of Being, and Being may appear in truth or in untruth (i.e., the content of Appearing may assume the determination of truth or of untruth). Acceptance of the Sacred may thus be performed in two ways: by me as truth, or by me as untruth (by me insofar as I am the Appearing whose content is presented in the determination of truth, or by me insofar as I am the Appearing whose content is presented in the determination of untruth). Truth accepts the Sacred, because it hopes to save itself as truth, but it recognizes that this acceptance may also be its most abysmal perdition, i.e., may bring about the most incurable concealment of Being, the desert in Appearing.

Truth, being bound to the untruth of faith, also knows that it poses as a problem that which at the same time it experiences as a certainty. It is possible that having faith in the announcement of the Sacred may be the salvation of truth: possible, that is, that truth be saved as truth by binding itself to this faith, and that in this way it free itself as far as possible from the full weight of contradictions by passing through the Good Friday that is the contradiction of having faith. For when truth binds itself to faith (i.e., lets itself be accompanied by faith), the same content in Appearing is the object both of certainty and doubt, i.e., appears as both affirmed and not-affirmed, and Appearing is therefore contradiction.

Nowadays it is often said that believers cannot be philosophers, nor philosophers believers. If being a philosopher means being in truth, there is a genuine incompatibility between being in truth and being in faith. The effort to deny this incompatibility on the basis of the Thomistic doctrine of the reciprocal autonomy of reason and faith is destined to fail. Aristotle himself saw that there cannot be *episteme* and *doxa* with regard to the same object (*phaneron ... oti oude doxazein ama to auto kai epistasthal endechetai*, *Posterior Analytics*, 89*a* 38 ff.). And the Sacred is, for *episteme*, a problem, whereas for *doxa* it is a certainty.

The incompatibility, however, between *episteme* and *doxa* insofar as they refer to the same object means not that their union cannot be realized, but rather that such a realization entails a being in contradiction on the part of Appearing. Being is not contradictory (is not not-Being), but Appearing is always in contradiction. Being is noncontradictory, but man contradicts himself. There is thus a real contradiction between truth and untruth (reason and faith, *episteme* and *doxa*); but there is also the possibility that being in this contradiction may clear the path that leads to the resolution of all the contradictions from which truth may be freed. Just as one may be convinced that only by going through the darkness of the wood can the light of the summit be reached. The philosopher cannot be a believer—yet that is precisely what he is, whatever his creed may be. For liberation from the contradiction between reason and faith may also be won by deciding to have no faith at all; but until it can be excluded that truth is freed from all the contradictions from which it may be freed precisely by entering this contradiction, then deciding to no longer have faith is also a faith that truth has not been freed from being in this contradiction. Just as, not knowing where the wood may lead, one's deciding not to enter its darkness is the faith that a greater light will not be encountered by going through it.[14]

19. THE PATH OF NIGHT AND NIHILISM

But truth already knows this: its salvation cannot occur independently of the way in which peoples bring the appearing of Being to completion.

There appears in truth the Being that has been brought to light along the path of Night. Not only the works of man (cities, industries, states, economic, political and religious relations, everyday actions, etc.), but also the things of nature (seas, continents, planets, the remotest galaxies) now fall within the project of the domination (i.e., production-destruction) of Being. Thus all things stand before man, in Appearing, enveloped by the shadow of the alienated meaning of Being. Nor does my way of living escape alienation—quite the contrary; in my deepest feelings there wells up an invincible repugnance for the path of Day, which heralds the demise of this technological civilization of which I am a product. The thought that invites the West to return to the parting of the ways merely approaches the path of Day. It is only the trace, nor can we know whether there will be the earth upon which the new path can be cleared. For the trace is enclosed by the *old* earth— by the Being that has been brought to light along the path of Night.

---

14   To look further into this topic see *Studi di filosofia della prassi*, 65–115.

Truth affirms the eternity of Being—of every Being—but the Being with which truth primarily deals (the Being that appears) is now the Being that ought not to have appeared, since it is brought into Appearing by the determination of Western man to guide the creation and annulment of Being.

Being is eternal: the Justice of Being (Parmenides, Fr. 8, 13–15) allows it neither to be born nor to perish—not even when the West undertakes to dominate the creation and annulment of Being. *Poiesis* fails to realize that which cannot be realized; the West can neither create nor annul that which can neither be created nor annulled. *All* Becoming is an appearing and disappearing of Being, and therefore *every* action is always a disclosing (or a letting be disclosed) of Being that was concealed, or contrariwise is a leading of Being out of Appearing, into concealment (or a letting it withdraw from Appearing). When, however, the basis of all action is the conviction that one is producing and destroying Being (drawing it from, and returning it to, nothingness), then something *different* is disclosed from that which would be disclosed were one to act in the knowledge that all acting and all doing is a disclosure of eternal Being. This different is brought to light by alienation; hence it is the Being that ought not to have appeared—if error is that which must not be brought to light.

The alienation of truth has brought to light the Being that ought to have remained concealed. The West is this very Being, in its progressively swallowing up every other Being that had come into Appearing. Alienation itself, in its very origin—i.e., in its having called the "world" out into the Light—was a letting appear of that which, superimposing itself upon things that appear, prevented man from seeing Becoming as an appearing and disappearing of Being, while leading him to the conviction that the annulment of Being is something immediately given in Becoming. The "world" too, then—this soul of the West—is eternal; but it is that eternal which ought not to have appeared. (Just as "evil" cannot be an invention of man or of the devil, but rather is a letting appear of that which, eternal, ought to have remained eternally concealed.)

The alienation of the West brought to light the Being that dwells in Appearing. And, as long as this Being dwells there and holds sway, truth cannot hope for its own salvation. Truth cannot hope to free itself from contradiction (i.e., from untruth) as long as the earth is ruled by the negation of truth. Today, the most resistant contradictions are not those that may be resolved by an act of knowledge, but those whose resolution demands the disappearing of Western civilization and the appearing of a new one. It is not enough to unmask metaphysical alienation, if the civilization produced by metaphysics continues to live. The metaphysical way of thinking has become stone, iron, the custom of peoples. Precisely because abstract thought (i.e., a "way of thinking") has succeeded in dominating the works of the West, this thought now possesses a strength that cannot be mastered by the abstract exercise of philosophic thought alone. Rather, its overcoming demands the abandonment of the path of Night, and thus the profoundest transformation in the history of man.

Nor can truth hope to save itself by fleeing the earth. Forgetting the earth (i.e., the concrete, historical negation of truth) means leaving the negation of truth in place. And for truth, to let its own negation live—to let it continue to appear on the earth—cannot bring it salvation; just as one cannot be saved by closing one's eyes in the face of the enemy.

When nihilism is only a way of thinking (i.e., when it is metaphysics), the negation of nihilism consists in the denial that Being is nothing. But when nihilism becomes praxis, then a *civilization* appears. And it appears precisely because praxis is dominated by the thought that Being is a Nothing. Nihilism is now this civilization; and the negation of nihilism can no longer be accomplished simply by recognizing that this civilization is an identification of Being with Nothing. If one stops here, while letting this civilization continue to appear, nihilism is not negated (i.e., its negation is merely formal)—truth still coexists with its own negation. This negation has become the appearing of Western civilization, which means that truth, as the negation of its own negation, implies the disappearing of this civilization.

As long as peoples do not bring this disappearance to completion—as long, that is, as they do not bring to completion the appearing of Being along the path of Day—truth lives as the negation of itself, it lives in error, and its salvation is constitutionally precluded. But only if truth begins to cry out in the desert, denouncing the betrayal of Being, can peoples travel the path of Day.

20. FINITE APPEARING AND INFINITE APPEARING

The whole does not appear in truth, since that which appears is only the *form* of the whole, filled by a part of the whole's concrete content. This contradiction—where that which is not the whole is meaningful as "the whole"—would be resolved if the concrete whole were to appear; that is, if in Appearing in its truth the content were to become adequate to the form, and truth were to become omniscience. On the other hand, the negation of nihilism demands the disappearance of Western civilization: truth can constitute itself as truth (as negation of the negation) only if this civilization disappears. Similarly, all maturation entails the disappearance of the blossoming that preceded it: the fruit appears, the blossom disappears; day appears, night disappears; the man appears, the child disappears; the later appears, the earlier disappears. This by itself makes it abundantly clear that historical development cannot lead the whole into Appearing. It is true that when the fruit appears, remembrance of the blossom persists, and thus the blossom continues to appear; but, remembered, it appears differently from how it appeared at first. And thus, when the fruit appears, there is something of the blossom that no longer appears (and something that, remembered, continues to appear—and on the basis of which it can be affirmed that something of the blossom no longer appears).

Everything must appear (for truth to be freed from contradiction), but the civilization of nihilism must disappear (for truth to constitute itself as truth). Everything must appear, but the history of Appearing is the history of the disappearing of Being.

That the earlier disappear when the later appears is, however, merely a *fact*, which might be absent in a different configuration of the Being that appears: one and the same tree might appear with fruit while continuing to appear with blossoms. Not in the sense that the same individual might appear affected—contradictorily—by two opposing determinations, but rather in the sense that what we call "individual" might be revealed in its authentic ontological constitution. It might be revealed, that is, as the *unity* of a plurality of individuals (the tree with blossoms, the tree with fruit, etc.), such that the historical appearing of this unity might lead to the simultaneous manifestation of that plurality. The historical development of Appearing might thus preserve everything that progressively appears, and preserve it not simply as an object of memory, but as having that mode of Being which is proper to it in its first appearing.[15] The negation of Western civilization might thus concretely be accomplished without implying this civilization's disappearance (i.e., its continuing to appear simply as an object of memory), since its concrete overcoming would arise from the appearing of the path of Day. Nihilism would be preserved in its being concretely overcome and the movement towards the disclosure of the whole would not be hindered by the disappearance of a moment of the whole.

But even if this hypothesis were to prove true, the whole could never enter Appearing.

Finite Appearing cannot become the infinite appearing of the whole. For the whole already infinitely appears, and thus appears in an Appearing different from the actual Appearing. The actual Appearing is the finite appearing of the infinite (i.e., of the whole). If finite Appearing alone (actual or inactual) were to exist—if, that is, finite Appearing were the supreme viewpoint—then finite Appearing would at once be and not be, *sub eodem*, truth (i.e., the incontrovertible). It would not be truth, since it would be in contradiction (i.e., would be a finite positing of the infinite): since Being is noncontradictory, contradiction not only is the controvertible, but is that which

---

15 It has been objected that, if all Being were eternal, then, in the eternal, contraries would contradictorily inhere in the same individual. In time, Socrates is first young and then old; but eternal Socrates is eternally young and eternally old. And yet, one recognizes that Socrates, *qua* man, is identical to Plato, *qua* man. In this case, the same (man-ness) is as Socrates and as Plato, i.e., is an identity individuated in two different and therefore opposing determinations. The identity that subsists between those two differents which are the young and the old Socrates is greater than the one that subsists between Socrates and Plato, but it is still the identity of a plurality of different determinations (or individuations). And just as it is not absurd that man-ness be at once as Socrates and as Plato, so it is not absurd that Socrates-ness be at once as young Socrates and old Socrates (and as an infinite plurality of individuations). For this reason, it is merely a *fact* that the appearing of the old Socrates implies the disappearing of the young one: a fact—not a necessary condition of the ontological structure of the individual. (And memory is not a retention in the mind of that which no longer exists, but is a coming back into sight of the eternal, which might even reappear just as it appeared at first.)

has to be resolved. And, at the same time, it would be truth, for if a viewpoint higher than the finite did not exist, then that higher viewpoint would be the impossible—the absurd—and if the supersession of the finite viewpoint were the absurd, then the finite viewpoint would be truth, i.e., the incontrovertible. Everything that is appears eternally in the infinite appearing of Being (which is infinite precisely because there is nothing that does not appear in it). Finite Appearing— and thus, primarily, the actual Appearing—is the eternal place in which the stars of Being rise and set eternally. (And every thing— including the path of Night—belongs to the constellation of Being.) No extension can enable finite Appearing to become infinite: finite Appearing cannot become an always having been the appearing of the whole. The immutable becomes, insofar as it appears and disappears in finite Appearing. But, in infinite Appearing, the immutable is also the unbecomable (i.e., does not rise and does not set). Finite Appearing cannot become that which cannot become (cannot become the unbecomable).

This means that the resolution of the contradiction in which Appearing *qua* finite consists is an *infinite* resolution. Finite Appearing—and thus truth itself—is an infinite contradiction: the place in which Being infinitely discloses itself is also the place in which Being is destined to remain infinitely concealed.

It is in relation to this structure of finite Appearing that the problem of the salvation of truth acquires its most appropriate meaning. This is the problem of the way in which the greatest disclosure of Being possible for truth can be brought to conclusion (where this greatness may consist either in a determinate limit, or in the supersession of every determinate limit). Since the disclosure cannot become total, this problem is, at the same time, the problem of that which must remain concealed and of that which must disappear, for the greatest disclosure of Being to come about in truth (i.e., for truth to attain its greatest possible concretion). That the civilization of nihilism has to disappear if the West is to travel the path of Day is therefore not an aporia: not only because the disappearance of that which is superseded is a fact, which might itself be superseded by a different structuralization of the historical process (the later might begin to appear, while letting the earlier continue to appear), but above all because Being is *destined* to conceal itself, however great may be the extension of the content of finite Appearing.

21. THE PATH OF DAY AND ITS APPEARING

The existence of infinite Appearing is the existence of the supersession of *every* contradiction. If a single contradiction were to remain unresolved, then finite Appearing would be the supreme viewpoint (i.e., *sub eodem*, controvertible and incontrovertible). In the whole every contradiction is eternally resolved. This means that the path of Day exists, and perhaps waits to be brought into Appearing. It is in fact the concrete supersession of the path of Night—of this abysmal contradiction which is the living negation of truth and which truth is forced to take into its own house.

The path of Day is eternal—and yet, its entering Appearing is a possibility: the path of Day is the eternal supersession of the path of Night, and yet it is only a possibility that this supersession appear. It may be that, in Appearing, Being has already reached its greatest possible limits, and it is impossible for truth to free itself from its bond to alienation. But, for this very reason, it is also possible that the salvation of truth consist in a situation different from that which actually exists, and that it may be possible for truth to move, for a certain distance which includes the path of Day, along the eternal supersession of contradiction.

In relation to this possibility, the appearing of one path rather than the other is not equipollent.

In other words, it is inadmissible (i.e., absurd) to conjecture that the appearing of alienated civilization occasion the salvation of truth. It is absurd that the negation of truth, as such, should free truth from its own negation—absurd that living in alienation be the price to pay for the salvation of truth.

Similarly, the acceptance of the Sacred (or of any problematic content) is also a contradiction. This contradiction, however, *may* be the price to be paid for truth's salvation, since in this case it is not assumed that contradiction as such may be the salvation of truth (for indeed, it is impossible that contradiction as such should be a liberation from contradiction). Rather, this supposition refers to the content that is made to appear by accepting the Sacred (which is formally distinct from the contradiction provoked by the Sacred's being accepted by truth). On the other hand, it may *not* be affirmed that the appearing of alienation includes certain contents—such as nature, poetic feeling, love—whose appearing might be the salvation of truth and that would no longer appear with the disappearing of alienated civilization. If in fact the appearing of nature were necessarily linked to the appearing of alienated civilization, to suppose that it should save truth would mean, once again, supposing that the negation of truth should be a liberation from the negation of truth. But if the appearing of such contents is not necessarily linked to alienation, then it is indeed possible that their appearing may be the condition of the salvation of truth. But only if the alienation that envelops these contents were super-seded could such a salvation occur: only, that is, insofar as they are preserved, and thus transformed, along the path of Day.

If the salvation of truth lies in a situation different from the actual one and if the path of Day can appear, then truth's salvation is possible only through the concrete supersession of Western civilization. (Given if the disappearance of this civilization—the disappearance of aliena-tion—is itself a contradiction; just as it is also a contradiction that the path of Day should continue to remain concealed.) But then it is origi-nally [*originariamente*] absurd that salvation be attained by passing over the path of Day, i.e., via the appearing of alienated civilization or the contents that are necessarily bound up with it.

Will the path of Day appear? The answer to this question lies in an occurrence whose time has not yet come: nihilism must reach its completion for the West to begin to act in the light of the truth of Being.

22. APPEARING AND THE "I"

The actual Appearing is the transcendental event which contains within itself every thing that appears and thus also every particular Appearing. It is not, therefore, a temporal present, situated between past and future, but is the horizon that includes the totality of time. In a dual sense Appearing is not in time: for, like every Being, it is eternal, and secondly the rising and setting of Appearing itself cannot appear (instead, that which can appear is only the rising and setting of the appearing of a particular determination of Being). That which appears and disappears—that which at first did not appear and then no longer appears—is in time; but Appearing, as the transcendental event, cannot come into and out of itself.

Appearing is the appearing of Being, yet it is distinct from the Being that appears. Appearing is not "my" activity: *I* am Appearing, insofar as Appearing and Being are distinct.

The spectacle that eternally invades me is *this* spectacle that stands before me. That which I have always seen and which I shall always see is *this* which I see: not in the sense that what I see neither flows nor changes, but in the sense that all flux and all change—and thus also the journey along the paths of Night and Day—are variations in the constant *background* of Appearing. The *varying* determinations (i.e., "variants," which enter and leave Appearing) can increase and diminish, but the background endures. The spectacle can diminish to the point of including only the essential bareness of the background. But how far does the barely essential extend? Does the very consciousness of my eternity perhaps stand outside it? Philosophy, as *episteme*, is the true messenger of Being: it announces that the background, which stands before me, is that which stands before me eternally (and the fact that the background stands before "me" means, as we have seen, that it is contained in Appearing).

Philosophy, however, still cannot establish the confines of the background, nor can it establish the relation with the background of that which I call "my body" and "my feelings." My body and my feelings live among the things that appear, but this still does not mean that Being can appear only if my body and my mode of feeling appears. "I have a body" means that, in fact, the things that appear sometimes include pleasure and pain (as determinations of a definite locus in space). In speaking of "other people's pain," one alludes to something that is presumed to be analogous to the pain that effectively appears. Just as "my" pain and "my" pleasure are the pain and pleasure that appear, so "my" feelings (desires, thoughts, states of mind, etc.) are the feelings that appear. "My life" is the relation of "my body" and "my feelings" with the other things that appear. In affirming that all the lives I might have lived are eternally lived, one means that any corporeity and affectivity that might appear as "mine," besides those that in fact appear as "mine," are already eternally related to all the things with which they can be related. I, like everyone else who can say "I," am the eternal place in which my eternal lives can come together. But any nexus between Appearing and the empirical determinations (physical, organic, or psychical) that constitute my life is only a *fact*—which may thus be replaced by other facts.

However, the usual mode of saying "I" presupposes a necessary nexus between the empirical determination and Appearing.

In its formal meaning, the term "I" primarily signifies self-consciousness, i.e., a going towards that from which one sets out (a "circle," as idealism described it). But one "goes toward" in such a way that what one encounters is recognized as that from which one set out, so that in setting out one comes forward for the encounter—in such a way, that is, that the point of arrival is recognized as the very point of departure, so that the encounterer sees himself in what he encounters and, seeing himself, can thus say "I." Insofar as Appearing has as its content the appearing of Appearing, this identity, which constitutes the content that appears, is that which is meaningful as "I."

Idealism is only able to grasp the formal meaning of the "I," since alienation of the meaning of Being is, at the same time, alienation of the meaning of Appearing and therefore of the meaning of the "I": Appearing becomes the creator of Becoming, and the "I," the original self-creative act. Outside of idealism, however, not even the formal meaning of the "I" emerges: here, "I" signifies not pure consciousness of self, but consciousness of self as an empirical determination that necessarily implies the openness of consciousness. The dominance of metaphysics then leads one to understand this implication as a "production" of consciousness on the part of the empirical determination. And thus "I" signifies consciousness of self as the author or protagonist of having consciousness—it signifies consciousness insofar as it assumes as object something that, moreover, is held to be the author of consciousness. Here too, then, we find the figure of the circle, but the point of departure (and hence the point of arrival) is understood not as the pure act of consciousness, but rather as empirical determination which is also posited as productive of the act or of the reflexive movement of consciousness.[16]

23. THE "WORLD" AND THE IMMUTABLES

Only when Plato began thinking Being as identical to Nothing did things first appear in the "world." Prior to him there was no "world," and the sky, the earth, and the living creatures did not appear in the "world." With Plato, things first came to light in the *Night*, and colors and sounds, the sun and the moon, life and death, war and peace were all new: not simply because all these things received their being in the "world" (while remaining, in the world, just as they had appeared at first), but because, being in the "world," things themselves put on a different face. Colors shine differently, the sun follows another course in the sky, and mortals know another death and another mourning.

Plato also lead the works of nature and of men into the "world." From the outset, however, nature and men are not simply *left* to work in the "world," but *are made* to do so. Plato *lets* the winds and rains work in the "world," but he resolves to *make* the tyrant Dionysius work in the "world." In the first case, working is seen as that which leads from nothingness to Being, but the working itself is not occasioned by the "world"; in the second case, working not only is contained, but is also occasioned by the "world," i.e., by forgottenness of the meaning of Being. In the latter case, the worker works while looking at the "world"—or, looking at the "world," he makes others work; while in

---

16 This position is a necessary condition for the constitution of the circle—even if common consciousness is unaware of the position's very existence (just as, for the most part, common consciousness has no awareness of its own ultimate criteria of judgment). If something were the author of consciousness and had consciousness of self, but had no consciousness of its being the author of consciousness, then it, encountering itself, would not address itself as "I" but would name only the determinations that constitute it (like the old bonze who, seeing a mirror for the first time, mistook it for a venerable image of a bonze and placed it among the sacred objects of the temple). This is the case with children and immature individuals who refer to themselves in the third person, or with those who, to give greater credibility and authority to what they say, treat their own speaking as something autonomous and refer to themselves in the third person.

the former, the worker is only looked at in the "world." Alexander the Great was among the first to make peoples work in the "world": not only did he guide the Greeks in the "world," he attempted to lead the East there too.

Culture, Empire, the Church, states, science, and technology are the forces that in Western civilization make man work in the "world." Each of these forces, looking at the "world," works and makes man work in the "world." In each of them, metaphysics opens the ultimate horizon within which the workings of man and of nature are then guided in various ways. The dialectic between bondsman and lord (the struggle for life, the instincts for self-preservation and domination) is also introduced into the "world" by metaphysical forces—which, ultimately, lead Western common sense too into the "world." This means that the masses are no longer merely guided in the "world" by outside forces but become a metaphysical force in themselves. The "world" no longer stands behind their backs and above their heads, but right before their eyes. Initially, metaphysics takes possession of culture and education (*paideia*), and then through theology, law, politics, poetry, science, and historiography it becomes the ground upon which Empire, the Church, national states, and the political and ideological movements that most directly determine the action of the masses are built. The West is the Republic founded by Plato.

The same forces that bring man and nature into the "world" also bring him to, and take him away from, "God"; for "God" is understood as either a necessary condition of the "world," or that which makes the "world" impossible. The lord is understood as either the condition that makes possible the bondsman's life in the "world," or that which impedes this life. Natural law or natural morals are understood as either the condition of, or an impediment to, the positive laws established by man for his life in the "world."

And the principles of the conservation of mass and of energy are understood as either the condition of, or an impediment to, the transformation of the universe.

In general, the unmodifiable is understood either as something different from the "world," or else as belonging to its structure. But the thought that posits the unmodifiable (be it "God," natural law or morals, lordship or the quantity of mass or energy) is the thought that posits the modifiable as "world." In the history of metaphysical thought, "God" is initially thought as that without which the "world" could not exist; but later it was realized that "God" himself could not exist, since he would render the existence of the "world" impossible. For the things of the "world" can really have been a Nothing and can really re-become nothing only if they are not precontained in "God" (only, that is, if no divine dimension exists, with respect to which the nihilation and creation of beings—held to be an evident given—would be unreal).

A similar fate befalls the unmodifiable, understood as an element of the "world," or as a projection of "God" into the "world." Soul, lord, monarch, church, state, property, the (physical, moral, economic) laws of nature, while initially thought as indispensable conditions of life in the "world," are then denied precisely because of the realization that they render this life impossible. In the history of modern Europe "freedom" means liberation from the unmodifiable, so that the modifiable may be modified according to man's historical purposes and not according to presuppositions and immodifiable parameters (whereby the movements of the bondsman are contained and limited beforehand in the order given by the lord, and the actions of men by natural laws). The perception (or that which is experienced as a perception) that human working (*poiesis*) is creative—this "fact" of human creativity and destructivity—is itself the supreme proof that the unmodifiable has been modified and is thus nothing more than an impediment to the expansion of man. Science and technology have abolished all limits to this expansion. Technology can already herald its own capacity for the working production and destruction of the whole of reality.

In contemporary culture this radical abolition of all limits has been widely condemned. Technology has been condemned in the name of "spirit," or of "values," and even in the name of the "truth of Being." But the controversy concerning technology is but one of the many conflicts that, in the course of Western history, have arisen within metaphysics itself. Technology, which overturns all natural orders as it undertakes to create man, the soul, the *Übermensch*, and "God," is the pure liberation from the "world"; it is metaphysical nihilism, not only in its most thorough formulation (already to be found in the various forms of historicism, immanentistic antimetaphysicism, humanism, atheism, etc.), but in its most rigorous actualization. Yet the spiritualistic condemnations of technology, or of its excesses, are themselves also grounded on a way of thinking that places man and nature in the "world"; and therefore such rejections of technology are limited to keeping alive those unmodifiables rendered untenable by the logic of the "world." Antimetaphysicism and antitechnicism are but two sides of a single misunderstanding.

24. "WORLD" AND SPINOZAN ACOSMISM

Being is thought in the "world," even when it is affirmed that only "God" exists. In the first line of his *Ethics*, Spinoza defines "self-caused" (*causa sui*) as "that of which the essence involves existence" (*id, cuius essentia involvit existentiam*). But, as had been the case in Scholastic metaphysics and in Plato, this "*id*" which cannot be thought as nonexistent is not every not-Nothing, but is that privileged being which is "God." Spinoza too begins his discourse by thinking Being as that which can not-exist, and thus by identifying Being with Nothing. In fact, he too undertakes to *demonstrate* the existence of a Being that "necessarily exists" (*necessario existit*), i.e., of a Being in which "*essentia involvit existentiam*." And this demonstration is based on the principle that "One substance cannot be produced by another substance" (*una substantia non potest produci ab alia substantia*, Prop. VI), and therefore (Prop. VII) is "its own cause" (*causa sui*); is such, that is, that in it "essence necessarily involves existence" (*essentia involvit necessario existentiam*). Thus thinking the not-Nothing is insufficient to rule out the possibility of its becoming a Nothing: the basis for demonstrating the existence of a being that cannot become nothing is the very nothingness of the not-Nothing. Hence Spinoza too can hold fast to the traditional theorem that "the essence of things produced by God does not involve existence" (*rerum a Deo productarum essentia non involvit existentiam*, Prop. XXIV)—the theorem that posits explicitly the very identification of Being and Nothing that had implicitly been the basis for demonstrating the existence of "God."

And, like the "God" of medieval metaphysics, Spinoza's "God" too is *poiesis*, with the difference that the medieval "God" can not-produce, while Spinoza's—like the "God" of the Neoplatonists—produces necessarily: "Nothing in the universe is contingent" (*in rerum natura nullum datur contingens*, Prop. XXIX). Spinoza's "acosmism" too is therefore a thinking of Being as Being in the "world": for the "world" is the identification of Being and Nothing, the very identification that provides the basis of Spinoza's demonstration of "God"—wherefore "God" himself is thought in the "world."

"God" and technology are the two fundamental modes in which the West brought to light the *poiesis* within the horizon of the "world."

25. METAPHYSICS AND MODERN SCIENCE

The divorce of modern science from traditional metaphysics is the precursor of the controversy concerning technology. Galileo came to deny the ingenerability and incorruptibility of the celestial bodies. Yet this radical rejection of Aristotle's physics left the Aristotelian meaning of generation and corruption intact. Galileo maintained that the celestial bodies too are generated and corrupted, but for him (as for all of modern physics and science after him) generation and corruption retain the very same meaning given them by Aristotle.

Today, the myriad differences between the Aristotelian categories and those of modern science are self-evident. And yet this masks a fundamental blindness which can neither know nor discern the common ground on which both Aristotle's discourse and that of modern science grow.

This blindness contrasts the Darwinian concept of the "origin of the species" with Aristotle's notion of the species as immutable and inoriginate. The "origin of the species" intended to revolutionize the Aristotelian conception of nature, bringing about a transformation in zoology and botany analogous to the one that had taken place in astronomy and the other sciences. Galileo affirmed the generability and corruptibility of the celestial bodies, Darwin the generability and corruptibility of the species. But the revolution was only superficial, since in the very concept of an *origin* of the species the fundamental thought of metaphysics, and thus also of Aristotelian metaphysics, is held fast: "origin" means a process of generation as absolute innovation and thus as an arising into positivity by emerging from nothingness. The "origin of the species" is but one of the ways in which metaphysical nihilism lives in modern science. The fact that for Aristotle the species or the celestial bodies could not be modified, whereas for modern science they can be, or that the transformations considered by Aristotelian physics were only qualitative, while for modern physics they are quantitative, or that modern physics can rely on a methodic instrument capable of controlling the production of things, while in *poiesis* such production was almost exclusively entrusted to craftsmanship—all these things and many others are, unquestionably, important differences in Western history. And yet, these very differences constitute the moments of the history of nihilism. They are moments of the fundamental—and the only—way of thinking and living in the West.

26. TECHNE AND EPISTEME

Within this fundamental unity, the opposition between modern science and metaphysics manifests itself primarily in the renunciation by "science" of any claim to be *episteme*. Science is able to dominate nature only insofar as it abandons the attempt of metaphysics to set itself up as incontrovertible knowing. In this sense, modern science has been *techne* from the very beginning, since cognition interests it not as a comprehension of truth, but rather as an instrument that makes possible the transformation of the accordance with man's purposes. As long as it can transform the "world," science will concede the hypotheticity of its own knowledge. Metaphysics, when its own knowledge was not hypothetical, tolerated being a pure contemplation of reality. But science sees nothing hypothetical in its being an activity that transforms the "world," since it never posited the "world" hypothetically—where "world" is understood as the dimension of the transformable. The essence of metaphysical theoreticism is the heart of the praxistic hypotheticism of science.

Not only is modern science *techne*, but so is modern philosophy, which posits cognition itself as productive. For Greek and medieval philosophy, cognition still intended to limit itself (albeit unsuccessfully) to recording the productions and destructions of nature and human action. In modern philosophy cognition produces the "world"; first the subjective and phenomenal "world," later, with idealism, the "world" *sempliciter*. This means that phenomenism, gnoseologism, and idealism represent the dominance of metaphysics in the sphere of modern gnoseology. This domination is expressed not only in the principle that the phenomenal world is a product of the cognizing subject, but in the very principles according to which the phenomenal world is realized. (In the first analogy of his *Analytic of Principles*, Kant explicitly applies the principle of metaphysical nihilism to phenomena: "Nothing can be born of nothing, nothing can be resolved into nothing" [*Gigni de nihilo nihil, in nihilum nihil posse reverti*].[17] Except that here the "permanent" is time, as a schema of substance, and within this permanence phenomenal determinations pass from nothingness to existence and vice versa.)

Techne in the modern age abdicates its claim to be *episteme* in order to dominate reality. Yet the very development of *techne* inevitably compels it to make a fresh bid for the scepter of *episteme*. When technological civilization succeeds in freeing man from all limits, it will then come up against that insuperable limit which will force it to modify its relation with *episteme*: since modern science is a hypothetical knowing, any realm founded by *techne* will be a hypothetical realm that may be swept away without warning. All happiness and liberation from limits that *techne* attains are constantly enveloped by the possibility of their disappearance. This possibility becomes an even more radical limitation the greater the number of limits from which *techne* liberates man. The supersession of this possibility (which is destined to become the anxiety of future technological man) cannot come about on the basis of a hypothetical knowing: the possibility ceases to be a limit and an anxiety only insofar as it is superseded by a knowing that is absolute and incontrovertible. Such knowing is *episteme*, as the locus of truth. And the question, then, is: "What truth is there in the realm of *techne*?" And thus: "What is truth?"

For *techne* to turn into *episteme*, the West must travel the entire path of Night and technological civilization must reach the height of its triumph. Perhaps this is the only way, for the West, to set out on the

---

17   Kant quotes from Persius, *Satires* 1, 111, 83 [*Editors' note*].

other path. If this be so, then the appearing of alienation on the earth would be the indispensable condition for the appearing of the path of Day.

27. SCIENCE AND TRANSCENDENTAL APPEARING

The essential relation between modern science and metaphysics is not only a historically documentable fact, but also a necessary consequence of the methodic approach that has characterized science from Galileo to the present day. Science intends to speak of nothing other than empirically observable particular events, or of events that can be referred back to such events. This means that, whereas science speaks of things that appear, it *never* speaks of the *appearing* of things. And this, as we said, is by no means accidental, but is a necessary consequence of the methodic delimitation according to which science has been realized. While science may well speak of psychical processes, human cognition, perception, mind, will, empirical observability, and the like, it inevitably treats these determinations as empirically observable particular events. Appearing, as the horizon within which any becoming of reality appears and which therefore dominates, as the transcendental event, all Becoming and every history of universes and peoples, is constitutionally excluded from the circle of the possible objects of science.

Idealism—that of Giovanni Gentile in particular—brought to light the transcendental, rather than psychological or anthropological, character of Appearing. Yet Appearing is understood as "thought" or "act," in which alone each and every thing can exist; and thus becoming the content of thought and no longer being its content is the process in which things issue from and return to nothingness. This is the deepest meaning of the "creativity" of thought. (In contemporary philosophy, it may be said that Heidegger alone has reflected on the transcendental meaning of Appearing. For him, Appearing has no creative power, but is a letting things be. But since "Being" means nothing other than "Appearing," it occurs here too that the entering and leaving Appearing of things ends up being the process of their creation and annulment.) Idealism too understands science as an absorption in the things that appear, while forgetting their appearing. Hence science is simply a specific application of naturalistic realism, in which thought sees only things but does not see itself. For Heidegger, forgottenness of Appearing is the very forgottenness of the meaning of Being, in which one deals with things only in their immediate usability; science and technology are a preeminent aspect of this use.

Yet the decisive aspect of the methodic approach of science—this having eyes only for things, while forgetting their appearing—necessarily eludes idealism. In fact, both modern science and idealism are rooted in the soil of metaphysical nihilism. Idealism cannot comprehend the fact that, precisely because science brackets Appearing, it is *forced* to understand Becoming as an issuing from and returning to nothingness. This constraint determines the essence of scientific knowing. Becoming, in its truth, is the appearing and disappearing of Being, its entering and leaving Appearing. But if Appearing is excluded on principle from the field of objects of which science speaks, then the language of science is *forced* to express Becoming in terms of the creation and nihilation of things. The "no" in "no longer" and the "not" in "not yet" can no longer express the concealment (the not appearing) of things, but must express their nothingness. Science cannot forgo such concepts as motion, time, generation, corruption, process, transformation, development, and history. In these concepts, "no longer" and "not yet" are ineliminable determinations. And in a language whose methodic self-limitation makes it impossible to speak of Appearing, the "not" is necessarily the Nothing—even when one avoids using the words "Being" and "Nothing."

And this is the case not only in the languages of natural science but also, and with greater rigor, in formal (logical-mathematical) languages. In such languages, the "not" is identified with the Nothing in the strictest way possible due to the greater rigor of their methodic self-limitation, itself due to the exactness of the indication given by the primitive terms (the rules of the formation and transformation of propositions) that control the entire development of the language. No calculus is possible without rules of transformation, for calculus is itself a transformation of premises. Once the rules of transformation have been formulated, the consequences are already implicitly contained in the premises. But a calculus is an explicitation of the implicit, and any explicitation inevitably entails historical-temporal development. Moreover, this historicity is a consequence of the fact that every explicitation is partial, wherefore the calculus can always be prolonged. The development in which every calculus consists is also realized as a "not yet" and a "no longer" (not yet explicit, no longer implicit). If *p1* indicates a certain level reached by a calculus and *p2* the successive level, *p2* was not yet explicitated in *p1* and, in *p2*, *p1* is no longer implicit with respect to *p2*. When *p2 is not yet* explicit, the explicitness of *p2* cannot be posited, within the formal language, other than as a Nothing (the "not" indicating the nothingness of the explicitness); and when *p1 is no longer* implicit with respect to *p2*, the implicitness of *p1* cannot in turn be posited, within the formal language, other than as a Nothing (the "no" indicating the nihilation of the implicitness, i.e., of that confirmation of the calculus which does not yet contain the explicitation of *p2*).

In all kinds of science, development cannot be the appearing and disappearing, but must necessarily be the nothingness and nihilation of everything that progressively emerges in such development. This is the only meaning that "development" can assume within scientific language. If science abstained in earnest from speaking of Being and Nothing, neither could it speak of such concepts as motion, development, time, and history.

Yet science continues to speak of them, and in so doing it inevitably identifies Being with Nothing.

For this identification to come about, it is thus not necessary that *poiesis* be determined according to those concepts of "production," "cause," "force," and "energy" which were roundly criticized by Humian empiricism. Contemporary epistemology and science share this understanding of causal relations as a concomitance of events, not as the influence of one thing on another. But the opposition between the "metaphysical" and the "scientific" concepts of cause is a distinction within metaphysics itself; in drawing it, that is, one remains within the "world," where the creation and annulment of Being are thought either as determined by the action of a cause, or as events concomitant with other events. "Production," as *poiesis*, thus takes place even when one forgoes speaking of the causal influence of one thing on another and limits oneself to preparing the conditions required for a particular event to take place. In this case too, science continues to speak of Being and Nothing, in a discourse that ineluctably identifies them.[18]

28. ON NONSCIENTIFIC LANGUAGES

Since this ineluctability is due to the methodic assumption of science to speak only of things (thus implicitly excluding Appearing from the body of objects spoken of), any language that does not delimit its own field of objects reveals the meaning of its relation to the truth of Being only historically. Even prescinding from the historical evidence of the essential relation between metaphysics and science, it must be said that science, as it has been realized in the West, is the identification of Being and Nothing. It is precisely the methodic self-limitation of Western science that makes it a paramount form of nihilism. Yet there are also languages that do not reflect this self-limitation. That such languages are forms of nihilism cannot therefore be affirmed a priori, but only on the basis of historical evidence. Since nonscientific languages are not exact, they may be ambiguous languages (languages, that is, in which it is structurally impossible to grasp either the recognition or the negation of the truth of Being). The *Divine Comedy* is not an exact language, but neither is it ambiguous: its poetical thought is completely enveloped by metaphysical thought. This bond with

---

18   Any attempt to posit the words "Being" and "Nothing" as meaningless ends in a vicious circle, since the distinction between the meaningful and the not-meaningful is the selfsame distinction between Being and Nothing. Being is every not-Nothing, i.e., everything that is in some way meaningful; while Nothing is that which stands beyond all meaning, i.e., absolute meaninglessness. That the "not-meaningful" is itself meaningful—this constitutes the aporia of the Nothing: insofar as the Nothing is spoken of and thought, it is turned into a not-Nothing. For the resolution of this aporia, cf. *La struttura originaria*, Ch. IV. Here we shall limit ourselves to recalling that the meaningfulness of the meaningless—i.e., the positivity of the negative—is itself also part of the totality of meaning, i.e., of the positive. Hence the Nothing is a self-contradictory meaning: precisely insofar as it is the synthesis of absolute negativity, or meaninglessness, and positivity, or the positive meaning of negativity. The Nothing is opposed to Being not insofar as it is itself this synthesis, but rather insofar as it is a moment of the synthesis; insofar, that is, as it is held fast as that absolute negativity or meaninglessness which has already been distinguished from its own positive meaning.

metaphysics leaves its mark on poetry: just as it leaves its mark on science. Western poetry and science appear as they do because they are guided by metaphysical thought. The relation between Dante's poetry and Scholasticism, or Goethe's and Spinoza, has been historically established. The background of both Dante's and Goethe's poetry is the "world"—and therefore time, Becoming, birth, and death are here determinations of the "world." This, however, cannot be said of the language of Homer or of the Bible, nor of the *dicta* of Anaximander and Heraclitus. Here, on the contrary, the meaning of Being remains completely unexpressed. It is thus possible that the background of such saying is not the "world," and that therefore determinations such as "time," "birth," and "death" express the appearing and disappearing of Being.

But once metaphysics has taken possession of culture, can it still be thought that in the poetical and religious language of the West, islands untouched by metaphysical alienation (islands of ambiguity) may emerge?

29. METAPHYSICS AND TECHNOLOGY

Technology does not go beyond the horizon established by the methodic self-limitation of science; it simply produces and destroys the objects of science (the objects of the "world"). An object is "technical" only if it can be scientifically controlled. If technology thinks the things it produces and destroys just as they are thought by science, then technology, like science, leaves Appearing aside, and "production," "destruction," and "consumption" necessarily acquire the meaning of a making things pass from nothingness to Being and from Being to nothingness. War too, as it is waged within the horizon of technology, takes on the unequivocal meaning of a destruction that has definitively settled accounts with what has been destroyed.

Like ambiguous language, ambiguous working (and working is itself a form of language) is also brought to completion outside the horizon drawn by the methodic self-limitation of science. Hence war too, as an ambiguous event, is different from war as a techno-metaphysical event. In ambiguous working, killing and destroying are still an averting of danger, and historical interpretation is faced with the problem of the meaning of this averting. In technological working, on the other hand, war and killing no longer present this problem, but unequivocally represent, within the "world," preeminent modes of the nihilation of Being.

Today technology has become the most powerful of metaphysical forces. Common sense itself is no longer dominated by religion and politics, but by the way of thinking and acting of technology. This is still the metaphysical way of thinking and acting, but it is now capable of transforming the earth; it does not limit itself to guiding the natural processes of production and destruction but replaces them with artificial processes. The "world" itself is no longer simply the horizon, but is also the object of *poiesis*: it becomes, as a whole, that which in a scientifically controlled plan can be produced and destroyed.

Things have appeared in the "world" since Plato brought the "world" to light. From that very moment nature itself appeared alienated and human *poiesis* began to deposit in Appearing the works of Night. The spreading of these works has ultimately swallowed up the works of ambiguity, which technological civilization has definitively left behind. The West brings into Appearing a new nature and a new working of man. In condemning the provocation and devastation of nature that culminate in technology, one fails to realize that this nature was brought to light for this very purpose. It does not suffer violence, since it is itself predisposed to provocation and destruction. The endless stream of manufactured goods that are progressively exhausting space and time, far from deflecting man from his authentic relation with nature, is itself a result of the very attitude by which the West first brought nature to light. Technological civilization makes explicit the nihilism of its essence in the very concept of manufactured or consumer goods, which has now become the transcendental category of Being. While St. Augustine could still affirm that something is all the more good the less it is consumable, today the "consumer good" finds itself in a position of equilibrium: it ceases to be a good both by being too consumable, and by being not consumable enough. In any case, its consumption is demanded by the principles of production; and terror in the face of the earth's possible nuclear destruction is accompanied by a satisfaction at possessing a means capable of destroying that which shows itself to be insufficiently consumable.

Today, there is an interdependency between the principles of production and the needs of technological man, who is driven to consume what is produced. If the "world" is full of things that were made to be destroyed—if the very "world" as a whole is an article to be consumed—then the fundamental need of man in the "world" can be nothing else than that of consuming the "world," and the faster the increase in consumer goods, the quicker the consumption. On the one hand, then, technological civilization simply satisfies the needs that it itself has created.

On the other hand, however, technology is seen as a liberation from all human want: from the hunger and the pain man has suffered throughout his history and which are thus not caused, but eliminated by technology. It is now unquestionable that technology represents the only means for the elimination of pain from the earth. Industrialization brings liberation from hunger, and psychotherapy from all anxiety and remorse. It is intrinsic to the logic of the West that any protest from the viewpoint of spiritualistic decadentism will be left by the wayside. Remedies of the "spirit" for earthly pain are given within the "world" without the ultimate consequences of *this* fundamental circumstance being drawn: man is in the "world" and thus the "world" has to be treated as "world." Technology treats the "world" as "world"; the other metaphysical forces that act in the name of the "spirit" (such as Christianity and Marxism) think and guide man in the "world," but refuse to exploit to the full the worldliness of man.

30. PAIN (CONTRADICTION) AND THE TWO PATHS

The way in which the West has come to liberate the earth from pain is nonetheless a result of the alienation of the meaning of Being. The path of Day, as the supersession of alienation, is at the same time a supersession of the way in which the West frees itself from pain. The "problems of humanity" are but a superficial aspect of the fundamental problem of the West, which eludes us even now. The great international and national organizations and the forces of culture are treating a disease they do not know—a throng of carpenters and workers seeking to repair the equipment of a sinking ship, without knowing if, or where, there is a leak. On the sinking earth, technology can multiply its prodigies to infinity; but only the truth of Being can bring salvation. This truth does not itself allay the evils of our civilization, but shows the way in which liberation from that sickness which is the essence of the West can be won.

Nor must it be asked how man's life along the path of Day is to unfold: just as Plato was not to be asked how Western civilization would develop. Plato sowed the seeds of Western civilization; but how they were to germinate, only the harvest could reveal. Thus the thought of the truth of Being traces the path of Day, but it is future history that will have to tread it.

The affirmation that the only way of freeing man from pain is the way followed by the West is a presumption analogous to that which deems no other nature or human working possible besides those experienced in the West. And yet the earth, the stars, the works of the truth of Being still wait to be called out into the light. The path of Day is not a return to barbarism (which is a form of ambiguous language and working). Indeed, the notion that number, space, time, quantity, motion, body, mass, and energy can be understood only in the form typical of Western science and technology is one of the fundamental presumptions that prevent man from discerning any other solution to the "problems of humanity" than the one offered by the techno-scientific capabilities of the West.

Yet is not the very way in which the "problems of humanity" are posed (problems such as hunger, war, and pain) determined within the alienation of the meaning of Being? The ways in which the West and the East intend to resolve these problems are, in fact, different. Western civilization is not far from bringing its type of solution to completion. But this completion is the very completion of alienation, which is thus presented in its greatest radicality and power.

The path of Day does not have to resolve the problems of the West: precisely because these problems have first to find their authentic formulation in the language of the truth of Being. Pain is pain only insofar as it is contradiction; and only insofar as it is contradiction does it have to be superseded by truth. Yet the West cannot know what *contradiction* is, even though the "principle of noncontradiction" and "dialectical contradiction" are fundamental determinations of nihilism. The attitude that identifies Being with Nothing is constitutionally incapable of grasping the essence of contradiction. This means that Western civilization is constitutionally incapable of resolving contradiction and thus of freeing man from pain. Never before has man been so comforted, understood, cared for, and helped; but, in our civilization, anxiety keeps pace with the therapies perfected for it.

31. THE POSSIBILITY OF THE APPEARING OF DAY

And yet, the supersession of every contradiction exists eternally. Eternal the contradiction, eternal its supersession. Eternal the stars of Night, eternal the stars of Day. But the stars of Night are in the Night, and the stars of Day in the Day. Since all human pain is contradiction, all pain has always already issued forth in joy. Liberation from pain and redemption of evil are always already entirely accomplished. The path of Day belongs to the eternal supersession of contradiction. It comes to light when peoples act in the truth of Being. Then, acting knows the eternity of every thing: the "world" sets and action is no longer poiesis, but leads the eternal into the light. The Being that thus comes to light is different from the Being that comes to light along the path of Night. That which appears when one undertakes to make Being issue from and return to nothingness is different from that which appears when action knows it is a disclosure of the eternal. That which appears when one undertakes the impossible is different from that which appears when the object of one's undertaking is the possible. The path of Day is not a flight from the "world," but is the working that leads the "world" to its setting. This path leads to the most radical transformation in the history of man, because it knows that transformation is never a consumption of Being, but is the history of its showing itself in Appearing. The most radical historical transformation comes about because action abandons its claim to be a production and destruction of Being and becomes the invitation that calls Being into Appearing.

Being can accept the invitation and the eternal stars of Day come forth, only if thought comes to testify to the truth of Being. Philosophy again becomes the most important occupation of man. A superabundance of actions and initiatives conceals the absence of thought. But the philosophical force of the philosophies of our time has come to be inferior to the philosophical force of the actions of our time, in which the fundamental thought of metaphysical alienation is realized in the most rigorous way possible. The power of metaphysical thought is no longer to be found in the books of philosophers, but rather in the great collisions of world forces, in the tensions produced by the possibility of nuclear holocaust, in the transformation of the world. One speaks in fact of the crisis of philosophy, but as if the Suitors had spoken of the crisis of Ulysses' bow. Philosophy, as the thought of the truth of Being, once more becomes the most important occupation of man. "Here is the gate that divides the paths of Night and Day."

CHAPTER II

The Earth and the Essence of Man

1. THE BODY AND BEING AS TECHNE

"How, with the death of a man, is the soul not dispersed and this not the end of its Being?" (*opos me am apothneskontos tou anthropou diaskedannuetal e psyche kai aute tou einai touto telos e, Phaedo*, 77 b). This is essentially a *metaphysical* problem. Not because it considers the relation between the "here" and the "beyond," but because it admits the possibility of the "end of Being" (*telos tou einai*), i.e., its annihilation. It is a specific way of asking whether a certain being continues to exist even when a certain other being exists no longer. Thus the fundamental presupposition is that beings *can* not-exist, and so also can exist no longer, i.e., can "end."

For metaphysics, things "are." Their "Being" is their not-being-a-Nothing. Insofar as they are, they are said to be "beings" [*enti*] or "Beings" [*esseri*]. But being, *as such*, is that which *can* not-be: both in the sense that it might not-have-been or might not-be, and in the sense that it begins and ends (was not and is no longer). Metaphysics is the assenting to the not-being of being. In affirming that being is not—in assenting to its nonexistence—metaphysics affirms that the not-Nothing is nothing. Precisely because the fundamental notion of metaphysics is that being, *as such*, is nothing, metaphysics must seek *reasons* to support its thesis that certain privileged ("divine") beings are exempt from birth and death, and so cannot be said to not-be. These "reasons" alone enable it to recognize the essential not-nothingness of certain beings; without them, being as such appears to it as a Nothing.

Today we no longer believe in the metaphysical reasons for the immortality of the soul. And yet, with the latest developments of science, the project of practically constructing precisely that which metaphysics was unable to demonstrate grows ever more determinate and consistent. But this project too—like the entire history of the West—grows within the fundamental notion of metaphysics. For the construction of being can be undertaken only if being is thought as that which begins and ends, or, in general, as that which can not-be.

Western culture can set no limit to technology's aggression against being. The project of constructing man's body is now inseparably accompanied by the project of constructing mental facts. Human happiness is thus no longer seen and pursued as a transcendent condition, determined by man's moral conduct during his life in the world (or by the combination of such conduct and divine grace), nor as an imminent result of historical dialectic. Happiness is seen today as the product of a technology whose success derives from its being rooted in physico-mathematical knowledge. Western culture can set no limit to this aggression against being since the *essence* of such culture is metaphysical nihilism, whose most radical and consistent realization is technology itself.

From the very dawn of metaphysical thought, Being has been *techne*. In the *Sophist* (247*d–e*) Plato defines Being as *dynamis* (power): that which is (*to on*) is that which has the power to make or to be made (*dynamin eit' eis to poiein eit' eis to pathein*). "To make" (*poiein*) signifies to bring into Being (*eis ousian*) that which previously was not (*oper an me proteron on*); "to be made" (*poieisthai*) signifies to be brought into Being (ibid., 219*b*). But power is the very essence of *techne*, because if *techne* can be divided into productive *techne* and acquisitive *techne* (*poietike techne, ktetike techne*), the acquisition of beings—such as money-making, property-holding, hunting, fighting, knowledge—is nothing but an ordering of what has already been produced in the various forms of *poietike techne* (ibid., 219*c*). The distinction between divine *techne* and human *techne* (*theia techne, anthropine techne*, ibid., 265*b–e*) is therefore the supreme difference between beings. *Theia techne* produces all the beings of nature, *anthropine techne* produces all the beings that are brought from not-Being to Being in human arts. Being is *techne* since it is essentially enveloped by the horizon of making and of being made—since, that is, it essentially belongs to the process of bringing and of being brought from not-Being to Being (*aitia tois me proteron ousin ystepon gignesthal*, ibid.). If something is not *technikon*—if it does not produce or is not produced, or is not part of the process of producing-being produced—then it *is not*: it is a Nothing. Today, *theia techne* has been supplanted by *anthropine techne*, but the meaning of Being has remained identical to the one established by Plato once and for all in Western history. God and modern technology are the two fundamental expressions of metaphysical nihilism.

2. THE ETERNITY OF THE BODY AND THE SPECTACLE OF ALIENATION

Authentic untimeliness is the overcoming of the essence of the West.[1] But, above all, it testifies to the truth of Being, which says that Being is and cannot possibly not-be (*e men opos estin te kai os ouk esti me einai*, Parmenides, Fr. 2, 3). Here, "Being" means everything that is not a Nothing. But only *the Nothing* is nothing. "Nothing" cannot also be predicated of a "something" that is, at the same time, presumed to be meaningful as not-Nothing (and any meaning whatsoever is meaningful as a not-Nothing), and relegated to the limbo of nonexistence—for it is posited as "something" (namely, a not-Nothing) that, when it is not, is nothing. Thus thought that testifies to the truth of Being cannot admit that with the death of the body the soul continues to exist—not because it claims that, when the body no longer exists, the soul cannot exist either, but rather because both body and soul are *eternal*. Like *every* being. The soul cannot exist without the body, just as it cannot exist without *any* being, for the destiny of *all* being is to exist. ("*Aeternus*" is a syncope of "*aeviternus*," and "*aevum*" is *aion*, "always being," the impossibility of not being. But this impossibility must refer to the totality of Being, not to a privileged being—which means that the Greek *aion* is the very expression of metaphysical nihilism.)

The body's disintegration is not its annihilation, but is the way in which it stably leaves the horizon of the appearing of Being. History is the process of the appearing and disappearing of the eternal. Dialectic is not the essence of Being insofar as it *is*, but of Being insofar as it *appears*. *Being* cannot be altered by the onslaught of technology. Unscathed, it uncovers the spectacle of the alienation of the meaning

---

1   "Untimeliness" is here opposed to that of Nietzsche [*Translator's note*].

of Being—the spectacle of our time. Today, man believes he can attain unlimited control over the creation and annihilation of Being. This faith is the basis of every work he performs, which means that every work brings into Appearing the spectacle of alienation. If we were convinced that by opening and closing our eyes we caused the birth and the annihilation of visible things, we could no doubt develop a way of living based on this conviction; but the reality that would appear and the life we would live would be different from the reality that would appear and the life we would live if we were free from this form of alienation. Like this movement of the eyes, Western technology too is an art of disclosing Being. But this art brings into Appearing a different content from the one that would appear if the West were free from the alienation in which metaphysical nihilism consists. The technological construction of man does not invent man, but is the disclosing of eternal man. Technology, however, in its failure to see that technological action—like all action—is essentially a *revealing*, discloses a different humanity from the one that would appear in the light of the truth of Being. It discloses the humanity of alienation.

3. THE COHERENCE OF TECHNOLOGY

Everything is eternal. Hence also the *appearing* of Being is eternal. But while in Appearing there are things that appear and disappear, Appearing itself, as the total horizon, cannot appear and disappear. If it appears and disappears, then it is only the appearing of a part of what appears, while Appearing, as the transcendental event, is the locus in which every thing (and so also the appearing of certain things) begins and ceases to appear. But in the truth of Being it cannot even be *supposed* that everything has ceased to appear (or might never have appeared), for in that case Appearing (i.e., a not-Nothing) would become a Nothing. Being is destined to appear. In this destination lies the essence of man. The original meaning of "soul"—of "mind," "thought," "consciousness," etc.—is its positing itself as the appearing of Being. And "I" signifies Appearing insofar as it has itself as its content; that is, it expresses in condensed form the identity of form and content.

Not only is man eternal, like every being, but he is also the locus in which the eternal eternally manifests itself. The metaphysical alienation of the West is inevitably accompanied by an inability to comprehend the meaning of man. Appearing is understood either as an empirical determination (a being among the beings that appear), or as the transcendental horizon. In the first case, man too is a being that issues from and returns to nothingness. His consciousness is conditioned by birth and death; during his life it is kindled and extinguished incessantly, as sleep and the phenomena of "loss of consciousness" traverse it. Hence technology can undertake the construction of a consciousness free from these conditioning factors. For idealism, on the other hand, consciousness is the transcendental horizon, containing time within itself; and therefore it is eternal. But, in this case, eternity expresses the ontological privilege of thought with respect to beings that are thought, just as Plato's Idea is privileged with respect to sensible beings. Thus, like every metaphysical demonstration of the existence of an immutable being, idealism's grounding of the eternity of thought is destined to fail. And the technological projecting of man can therefore legitimately undertake the construction not only of particular mental facts, or of consciousness understood as one of the particular facts of experience, but can also undertake the construction of thought's transcendental horizon itself and its incorruptibility.

Any philosophical-metaphysical protest raised by Western culture against these alleged excesses of technology overlooks the fact that technology simply takes the fundamental thought upon which both the protest and all Western history rest to its logical conclusion. In undertaking to transform man into superman and God, technology nonetheless operates within the horizon that, opened up for the first time by metaphysics, encloses the entire development of our culture. Technology takes to its logical conclusion the meaning of the metaphysical horizon by which it too is enveloped—the horizon constituted by the thought that being can be a Nothing. This thought has been the basis of every metaphysical affirmation of immutable being. It is therefore perfectly consistent with this basis that metaphysics, *qua* technology, should undertake the practical construction of the immutables and the immortals that metaphysics *qua* contemplation has been unable to ground. Except that, in so doing, metaphysics no longer brings to perdition mere modes of reasoning, but the entire civilization of men on earth. Metaphysics *qua* technology has in fact transformed everything that appears—the customs of peoples, houses, plants, the stars—into a spectacle of perdition.

4. THE NEVER-SETTING AND PHILOSOPHY

Within the horizon of everything that appears, the great stream of determinations that appear and disappear is held in by never-setting banks: they accompany those beings whose Appearing is necessarily required for the appearing of any being. These beings are the never-setting "background" of any disclosure of Being, the eternal spectacle in which all time—and so also the history of the alienation of the West—unfolds.

The appearing of a being is necessarily required for the appearing of another being when the first being is a necessary determination of the second. Originally [*originariamente*] the necessary determination of Being (and so also of the Being that appears) is the truth of Being. Truth is the incontrovertible position (positing) of its content. It says of the content what it is necessary to say—and is the original openness of the meaning of "Necessity." Truth is the incontrovertible appearing of the totality of Being, insofar as that totality is dominated by the Necessity that opposes Being to not-Being. Since truth is the structure of the necessary determinations of whatever can be affirmed with truth, no Being can appear without the appearing of the truth of Being. A being—this book, for example—is not its other (is not other than what it is): being the negation of its other is a necessary determination of this being. But this can be so only if the possibility of calling into question the position of such being and of its predicate has been superseded, and only if the incontrovertible meaning of Necessity is manifest. A necessary connection is such only insofar as it is inscribed in the original structure of the truth of Being, which accordingly—as the structure of the necessary determination of Being—is the never-setting background that accompanies and envelops each and every manifestation of Being.

Philosophy does not guard a truth that man happened upon at a certain moment in his history: man is the eternal appearing of the truth of Being. And philosophy is the emerging of this essential hearing—which is the very essence of man—once every other hearing has been relinquished. Philosophy does not present us with new things, previously unknown, but is the conspicuousness assumed by that which has always stood before us, when attention is no longer focused on that which supervenes and vanishes. Not only are we eternal, but—since the eternity of Appearing belongs to the truth of Being—we eternally *know* we are eternal. The history of man—and so also the history of the West, as the history of the abandonment of the truth of Being—can unfold only within this immutable appearing of the truth of Being. Distraction from truth is possible only insofar as truth continues to appear. For men, "oblivion of the sacred spectacle" (*lethe on tot' eidon ieron, Phaedrus,* 250*a*) is a concealment of truth, in the sense in which it can be said that the sky conceals itself from a countryman watching birds in flight or falling stars: the sky of truth appears eternally, but the things that cross it call attention to themselves and become all-important. Then, language has words only for what is important and life runs its course, as if truth had set and only things remained.

5. THE OCCURRENCE OF THE EARTH

The beings crossing the never-setting sky of the truth of Being are the occurrence. The background does not occur, but is the still place that receives the occurrence. Being eternally appears in its truth and, in this Appearing, the flowering of Being occurs. In the clear silence of truth, the occurrence is the prodigious. However long awaited, it is in fact the unexpected. Since it receives the occurrence, Appearing is not the infinite appearing of Being, the epiphany in which the completed totality is disclosed and in which, therefore, no further revelation can occur. As finite Appearing, eternal truth is contradiction. While it lets all things appear in the whole, the whole in which it envelops them is not the completed totality of Being, but only the formal meaning of this totality. Thus that which is not the whole is made to appear as "whole."

This contradiction could be resolved only if finite Appearing should become infinite.

The eternal appearing of the background is the manifestation of a contradiction, which could be resolved only in an occurrence. But truth also knows that the whole cannot become an occurrence (cf. "The Path of Day," paragraphs XVII, XXI). Thus, in its essence, truth awaits the occurrence granted it: the measure of its liberation from contradiction. In this measure lies the salvation of truth (i.e., the truth of salvation). However long awaited and however much truth knows of it, the occurrence is the unexpected. If truth knew everything of it, the occurring of the occurrence could add nothing to such knowing, within which the occurrence would therefore have always already occurred.

The prodigious occurrence is the earth. Joy and pain, war and peace, feelings, stars, thoughts, and actions all belong to the earth. The earth is Being's offering. Being has always inhabited Appearing, but the earth is the guest's long-awaited gift. Truth accepted the offering. In the beginning, truth willed the earth, and this will encloses and sustains all mortal willing.

In the life of man, philosophy is an unusual event. Man normally lives in untruth, looking after the problems of the earth—the problems, that is, of his daily existence, and those raised by religions and ideologies, by science and art, and by philosophies themselves. But the life of man is, in its essence, the eternal appearing of Being; and Being can *only* appear in its truth, since the truth of Being is the background whose Appearing is necessarily required for the appearing of any thing. However deep the untruth in which he lives may be, man is still the eternal manifestation of the truth of Being. Living in untruth cannot, therefore, be thought to be an oblivion that leads to the disappearing of the truth of Being. For untruth is possible only *within* this truth: not insofar as it is "a part" of truth, but insofar as it belongs to the occurrence that comes to light in the eternal appearing of the truth of Being.

Solicitude for the earth, in which untruth consists, is grounded primarily on the truth of Being's acceptance of the earth. We can will something—a house, food, love—only insofar as we first will the horizon within which the individual things that we will can appear. The occurrence of the earth is the originally willed horizon in which any thing that we will is willed. But this original will would not be possible if the eternal appearing of truth had not accepted from Being the offering of the earth. This receiving of the earth, performed by the truth of Being, is the same original will that acts in the solicitude that untruth feels for the earth. But—in untruth—the receiving of the earth unites with the *conviction* that the earth is the whole with which, assuredly, we deal. In this conviction, Being that occurs is *isolated* from the truth of Being. Untruth is possible only insofar as the occurrence brings with it, in the eternal appearing of the truth of Being, both the receiving of the earth and the isolating conviction. For receiving the offering belongs to the offering: it is the way in which the occurrence occurs. But the isolating conviction too belongs to the offering. If the background is indeed the *truth* of Being, error (the isolating conviction) can (and must) belong *as negated* to the background; so that, *as posited*—as that of which one is convinced—it cannot but occur with the occurrence of the offering.

As willed by truth, the earth stands out against the background. Truth, in its receiving of the earth, wills that the earth continue to appear. Receiving a guest means willing that he remain. In willing the continuation of its occurring truth does not treat the occurrence as the unexpected. The occurrence, as such, is the unexpected, but *willing* the occurrence means no longer treating the unexpected as unexpected; it means giving the unexpected what it does not have. This giving—namely, the will that the occurrence continue to occur—is the conspicuousness of the earth. To the *earth*, as projected into the future (into the place where it continues to occur), is given what it does not have.

But however much the earth may stand out against the background, the receiving of the earth cannot conceal the background—cannot, that is, conceal the truth of Being. The earth is received in the light of truth: in the eternal appearing of the truth of Being, Being flowers, this flowering is the earth, and the receiving of the earth is the way in which the flowering is spread out in Appearing. But for that *distraction* from truth to arise in which untruth consists as the normal condition of the life of man, something else is required besides the receiving of the earth. Untruth is solicitude for the earth, united with the conviction that the earth is the dimension with which, assuredly, we deal, and beyond which there is total darkness. Since the appearing of the truth of Being is eternal and never-setting, that *other* which (for untruth to arise) is required besides the receiving of the earth cannot be the setting—i.e., the disappearing—of truth, but must rather be the very *conviction* that the earth is what surely appears. In other words, the *other* is the appearing (i.e., the occurring) of this conviction within the never-setting appearing of truth. For Hegel, like Plato before him, truth (namely, that which from the viewpoint of metaphysical aliena-tion is the truth of Being) only appears in the philosophic conscious-ness. In other forms of consciousness (the forms of untruth), either truth is altogether absent or it appears in a process, determining the dialectic transition to higher forms of consciousness. The myth of the cave corresponds to the phenomenology of spirit: truth, as a unitary totality, only appears at the end of a process. But the truth of Being neither rises nor sets, and in its eternal Appearing lies the essence of man.

Man, insofar as he lives in untruth, is thus the appearing of a *contention*: between truth, which eternally appears, and error, which accompanies the occurrence of the earth and sees in the earth the sure ground. In the appearing of the truth of Being, Being flowers and error belongs to its flowering: it is one of the beings that begin to appear. But it appears as at once denied and affirmed, rejected and accepted. Appearing, which as appearing of truth is negation of error, at the same time lets error stand free in Appearing as not negated, and therefore as accepted. In so doing, it becomes the scene of a conten-tion: the appearing of a contradiction. Truth, which as such is already contradiction (since it posits as "whole" that which is not the whole: since it is the finite appearing of the infinite), here finds itself involved in a broader contradiction, in which truth and error contend for Appearing.

But error's freedom in Appearing—its eluding the dominance of truth—remains an enigma. Is the appearing of the truth of Being itself responsible for this freedom, or is the rebellion against truth part of the destiny of Appearing? Can error be "freely willed" by Appearing, or is the toleration of error—and so the existence of untruth—estab-lished by the Necessity of Being?

6. THE GROUND OF THE POSSIBILITY OF SELF-CONTRADICTION

Appearing, as the total horizon, is certainty (conviction, affirmation) in its transcendental aspect. Any uncertainty, doubt, incredulity, question, or problem are part of the content of transcendental certainty: they are the mode in which the content enters the horizon of Appearing. Uncertainty is the transcendental certainty—the appearing—of a problem that still cannot be resolved. But both problem and solution alike are part of the content of transcendental certainty. Doubting is the appearing of doubt, affirming is the appearing of affirmation, denying is the appearing of negation, self-contradicting is the appearing of contradiction: all the modalities of saying are the appearing of a certain mode, according to which what is said is said. The transcendental modality of certainty (conviction, affirmation) is the horizon of any modality of saying.

But the appearing of contradiction cannot be simple certainty of thesis and antithesis at once. Contradiction's modality of appearing cannot be pure contradiction. Being certain of the thesis means in fact not being certain of the antithesis. Therefore, being at once certain of the thesis and of the antithesis means being and not being certain of the thesis (and of the antithesis). But the truth of Being, as the impossibility for Being to be not-Being, is therewith the impossibility for certainty of the thesis (or of the antithesis) to not be certainty of the thesis (or of the antithesis). If contradiction's modality of appearing were pure contradiction, then the appearing of contradiction would be impossible (would be a Nothing): self-contradiction would be impossible. If self-contradiction is a pure being convinced of thesis and antithesis at once, then one cannot contradict oneself.[2] Self-contradiction is possible only if contradiction appears *as* an essential unrest, i.e., *as* what must be superseded (negated). This Appearing as what must be superseded is the necessary modality of the appearing of contradiction, and as such is that which makes self-contradiction possible. Self-contradiction is not a being-convinced of thesis and antithesis at once, but rather is a being-convinced of the negation

2   Cf. E. Severino, *Studi di filosofia della prassi*, Milan: Vita e pensiero, 1962, 181, footnote.

(supersession) of the identification of thesis and antithesis. But insofar as one is incapable (insofar as the capacity does not occur) of concretely negating this identification, then both thesis and antithesis are left as not-superseded within the supersession of their identity. One contradicts oneself, not insofar as one is convinced of contradiction (this conviction is impossible), but rather insofar as—though convinced of the necessity that contradiction should be negated—one lacks the reasons that would make the thesis prevail over the antithesis (or vice versa). Consequently, thesis and antithesis appear equal in power and thus as struggling against one another for possession of Appearing. Only in this sense can it be said that self-contradiction is being-convinced (certain) of thesis and antithesis at once: namely, in the sense that both are present as not superseded, because, even though their identification appears as superseded, neither of the two is capable of prevailing over the other. Living in untruth is the appearing of that paramount contradiction which is the contention between the truth of Being and error (the conviction that the earth is the sure ground). Insofar as Appearing is the appearing of the truth of Being, error occurs as superseded: it is negated from the moment when it begins to appear. But insofar as Appearing is not the infinite appearing of the whole, the truth of Being does not exhaust the possibility of Appearing. In infinite Appearing, nothing appears but the truth of Being, in which every contradiction is overcome (cf. "The Path of Day," paragraph XXI). Finite Appearing, by contrast, *as* finite is open to the irruption of error. Error irrupts in Appearing not insofar as it appears as negated by truth, but rather insofar as it appears as equal in power with truth. The power of truth is its incontrovertibility. The power of error is a pure being-convinced, a pure certainty of error; i.e., it is *faith*. Error is not and cannot be sustained by anything else than having faith in it. The power of error is the very *fact* of its succeeding in maintaining itself in Appearing, where it contends against truth. Since the truth of Being cannot disappear, but appears eternally, the distraction from truth, in which living in untruth consists, is possible only as the appearing of the contention between truth and error. It is possible, that is, only as the appearing of a contradiction, which appears as that which has to be resolved, but which at the same time does not let itself be resolved, since the contenders are equal in power.

7. THE STRIFE OF TRUTH AND ERROR

Truth wills the earth; error thinks the willed earth as the surely existing whole. The conspicuousness of the earth against the background thus becomes the earth's isolation, its separation from truth. Isolation is not the appearing of the earth without the appearing of the truth of the earth, but rather is the appearing of the thought that posits the earth as the sure ground. The earth appears always linked to truth, since nothing can appear if the truth of Being does not appear. But, in Appearing, error too appears; error, which thinks the isolation of the earth, i.e., which recognizes only a part of what appears. Thus truth and error contend for the earth. All the things of the earth—men, plants, actions, feelings, bodies, thoughts—appear, in untruth, as objects of this contention. The distraction from truth, which is untruth as the normal life of man, is the appearing of the beings of the earth as objects of contention between truth and error. Here, every thing appears pulled in opposite directions (drawn, that is, towards an opposite meaning), appears, that is, as an essential restlessness that makes it pass beyond itself—beyond what is nonetheless taken to be one of the sure things. This restlessness of meaning is the world in which habitually we live.

Error takes advantage of the way in which truth relates to the earth. Truth, in willing the earth, makes it stand out against the background, and error heightens the relief, uprooting the earth from the background and positing it as the whole that surely exists. Language—which also belongs to the occurrence of the earth—then prepares to name the things of the earth, which stand before it as isolated from their truth. But the language of untruth bears the traces of the abysmal profundity that is manifest even in the plainest and most ordinary moments of man's life in untruth. Just as in untruth the truth of Being nevertheless appears and contends with error for the things of the earth, so the language of untruth is never simply a speaking about food, heat, cold, houses, or love. The words of untruth sink into the truth of things.[3] They are like the arrows that lose themselves in the

---

3   *Affonda il suo cenno* (=gesture, sign) *nella verità delle cose.* "Words," accordingly, as the "gesture" of language that passes through the (false) "background" which the things of untruth claim to be (they claim to be sure things of the earth), "lose themselves" in the ground, i.e., in the truth of Being [*Translator's note*].

ground beyond the target: they can lose themselves in the ground because the target (things thought as isolated) is only the claim to be the background. If the aim of language is to indicate what is manifest, then the language of untruth mirrors in its every word the contention between truth and error.[4]

8. WILL AND CERTAINTY

Metaphysical alienation understands the will—be it of "God" or of "Man"—as one supreme force that makes beings issue from and return to nothingness. In Western civilization, dominated by metaphysics, man now wills only in this way, and he sets himself up as the true creator and destroyer of Being. But thought that frees itself from this domination knows that the will leads Being into Appearing. In *all* cases. Even when one wills metaphysically, to will is always to lead Being out of its concealment.

Whether there is a *necessary* link between willing and the occurrence of what is willed remains an unresolved problem. The metaphysical formulation of the relation of cause and effect is an expression of nihilism; but even when the effect is no longer understood as a coming-out of nothingness, but rather as a coming-out of concealment, the relation of cause and effect, *qua* necessary relation, remains a problem (i.e., a determination of which we do not know whether it belongs to the truth of Being). I *will* to light the lamp: my arm reaches out and the lamp comes on.[5] Is it *necessary* that the appearing of decision should be accompanied by the appearing of the arm that reaches out and of the lamp that comes on? As long as this necessity cannot be established (and Appearing, as such, cannot establish it, but can only let what has

---

4   See, as a possible confirmation of the manifestation of such a contention, what is said in "On the Meaning of the 'Death of God,'" paragraph II, about the word *theos.*

5   *Voglio accendere it lume* normally signifies quite simply "I want to light the lamp." But what is here (and throughout this section) clearly at issue is *willing* [*il volere*] and the *will* [*la volontà*], which is explicitly opposed to desiring, wishing, wanting: hence the highly unorthodox expression "I *will* to light the lamp." See, however, in the Oxford English Dictionary, under the entry "will": 1710 J. Clarke, "If I will to move my Arm, it is presently moved" [*Translator's note*].

been established appear), the will leads Being into Appearing in the sense in which a guest is led into one's home: the will invites Being into Appearing, and the works of the will are the way in which Being responds to the invitation. The will as such is an invitation; but when the will is dominated by metaphysical alienation the invitation comes to be understood and experienced as a constraint that makes Being issue from and return to nothingness. Here again, Being responds to the invitation, but its response is the works that come to light in aliena-tion. The West is the *work* of alienation.

Insofar as the will is an invitation addressed to Being, the essence of the will is certainty. It is this essence that constitutes the invitation. Since Appearing (as the total horizon) is transcendental certainty, Appearing is the transcendental constitution of the will. Language too refers the will back to certainty: *certus* also signifies "decided" (i.e., having left behind uncertainty as to such-and-such: *certus eundi*, decided to go), and *krino* (*cerno*) signifies both "to decide," "to choose," and "to believe," "to be certain."

On the other hand, certainty, as the essence of the will, finds itself in a plurality of relations, only some of which are called "will," but not others. There is certainty (i.e., appearing) of what eternally appears, and certainty of the occurrence and of its continuation; certainty whose content is truth, and that whose content is untruth, or error, or what has yet to manifest itself as truth, or as error; certainty of the occurrence of something whose occurring is held to depend, or not to depend, on us, or is judged to be for good or for ill, or is hoped or feared. In these and in all other possible structures of that of which one is certain, "certainty" varies, but the selfsame essence is repeated, namely, being certain of something.

If the word "will" is commonly used to indicate only some of these cases, it is, moreover, introduced in the conviction that willing differs from certainty. And yet, what is thus qualified as willing is a mode of being certain. Will is usually understood as will of the future (i.e., of the continuation of the occurrence). I will to turn on the lamp that is now off; I will to go, I, who am now still. What occurs when I will to light the lamp? In what does this decision consist? Willing, in its essence, is here the pure certainty that now I will light the lamp, the pure certainty that something—the reaching out of my arm and the coming on of the lamp—is to occur. Willing to light it is the very thinking: "Now I (will) light it"[6]—provided that this thinking means no longer having doubts or uncertainties about the occurrence of what is thought.

If the future is the possibility of the occurrence and of its continuation, willing the future means having faith in its coming. Faith is certainty insofar as its content is the controvertible: that my arm should reach out and the lamp come on is only a possibility, a hypothesis (and accordingly is something that can be doubted, something uncertain). Faith, in removing any character of possibility or hypotheticity from its content, treats the controvertible as incontrovertible; i.e., it is certainty of that which, to truth, appears as uncertain. The opposition of faith and works is the opposition of two types of faith: faith without works is having faith in something, without having faith in the occurrence of works; works without faith are a faith in an occurrence, without that faith's being accompanied by a certain other type of faith.

Insofar as will is certainty, it differs from any form of desire, aspiration, wish, etc., whose common trait is uncertainty of the occurrence of what is desired. A sick man's desire to get well is the conviction that, *if* he should get well, he would not be accompanied by the sadness that now afflicts him. Getting well, here, is the content of a more or less probable hypothesis, not of a certainty. Whoever limits himself to desiring does not know whether he will be able to obtain what he desires; whoever *wills* something that he does not yet have is, *per contra*, convinced of being able to obtain it, or, is convinced that something (the willed) is to occur. Anyone who says, "I don't know whether I shall be capable of walking, but I will to walk," actually does not will to walk, but wills to try to walk, i.e., he wills the attempt: he is certain that the attempt is to occur, but he is not certain that it will succeed. And anyone who says, "I am certain of dying but I do not will to die," does not really *will* to be immortal, but desires it: he is convinced that he would be happy *if* he were free of death and so found himself in that state in which he was certain of not dying. But in fact dying is the very thing that he wills; and every act of his life is a preparation for death.

---

6 The Italian employs a present indicative: *ora lo accendo; ora lo (voglio) accendere* [*Translator's note*].

Not in the sense that he seeks death on all occasions, but rather in the sense that he avoids dying in such and such a way *within* a fundamental orientation towards death. He does not live as an immortal, but as a mortal.

Since certainty is the *essence* of the will, will and certainty are not two different determinations in a relation of—albeit necessary—implication. If will and certainty are thought to necessarily imply one another while still remaining two different determinations, this is because willing is deemed capable of *producing* what is willed: certainty is contemplation, willing is productive action. In metaphysical alienation producing is always a making what is produced pass from nothingness to Being. (Even when one admits that the material—clay, for instance—pre-exists the product—the clay pot—metaphysical thought must still insist that the *synthesis* of material, in which the pot consists, before being produced was nothing. If *nothing* of this synthesis, or unification of material, had been nothing, but every aspect, every moment of the unification already existed, then it could not be said that something has been produced.) In the very definition of the will as *appetitus* (*orexis*) it is thought to be productive activity, since a "tendency" is such only if in some way it modifies its surroundings. Outside of metaphysical thought, action as a necessary link that leads from the appearing of willing to the appearing of the willed remains a problem. But even if one knew that in certain situations the appearing of willing is necessarily accompanied by the appearing of the willed, willing would nonetheless be certainty of the occurrence of what is willed. Sometimes, the will—say, to move my arm—is accompanied by the conviction that the movement depends on my willing; but at other times the will to move my arm is not accompanied by this conviction, and willing exhausts itself in the pure faith that the movement is to occur. The will is said to be the ground of faith, because faith is an assent determined not by the evidence of its content, but by the will. It must be said, on the contrary, that when one has faith, the will *consists* in having faith.

If something is not destined to occur, but its occurrence is a possibility, then willing its occurrence means trusting in the revelation of Being. Trusting in Being's revelation is the way in which one invites it into Appearing; a lamp that comes on and the mountains that move are the way which Being accepts the invitation. But when we will some thing, we do not will *only* that thing, but we will it in a context. When I will to light the lamp, I will that it should come on here in my study and illuminate my desk and my movements and so accompany, like a discreet servant, what I am doing and thinking. Here, willing to light it means willing to insert it in the horizon of beings that appear, which means willing to bring this horizon before one so that it may join company with the new determination that has been willed and envelop it. The will to light the lamp is thus only a moment of the will that my world should continue to appear. And this, in turn, is a moment of the original will with which the eternal appearing of the truth of Being wills the earth. Individual beings are willed within the original will that wills the earth.

In the eternal appearing of the truth of Being, the earth occurs; and, in this Appearing, its occurrence is received. Truth wills that the earth should continue to appear in the truth of Being: the willed is not simply the earth, but rather the link that unites it to the truth of Being. Willing to light the lamp is being certain that lighting it (will) occur;[7] willing the continuation of our world is being certain that it (will) continue to appear; willing the earth is being certain that its occurrence, as the horizon of any occurrence, (will) continue in the eternal appearing of the truth of Being. The certainty is the Appearing itself: with the occurrence of the earth, what appears in truth is not only the background and, against it, the earth, but it also appears that the earth will continue to occur. The willed is thus the very totality of whatever appears.

But the truth of Being does not rule unchallenged over Appearing: truth and error, which isolates the earth from the truth of the earth, contend for Appearing and so contend for the will. Insofar as man lives in untruth, the earth is willed as at once linked to and isolated from its truth. The certainty that the earth (will) continue to occur in the appearing of the truth of Being struggles against the certainty that the earth (will) continue to occur in the isolation that constitutes it as the whole with which, assuredly, we deal. The most commonplace of

---

7   The Italian employs (here and below) a present subjunctive, . . . *che accada l'accenderlo* [*Translator's note*].

volitions—for instance, willing to light a lamp—is rooted in the abysmal profundity of the willing that wills the earth in its link to the truth of the earth. But error isolates the willed earth from the truth of the earth, and so this volition is also a moment of the will that wills the continuation of the earth's solitude. In untruth one wills opposing continuations of the same, because volition of something is taken in two opposing contexts (viz., in the truth of Being and in error which isolates).

The works of untruth are Being's response to an ambiguous invitation (to an invitation that is in conflict with itself). And the very response—i.e., the work—is ambiguous, since like any being that appears in untruth, it is inscribed in the two opposing contexts of truth and of error. But the earth itself, as Being's response to the ambiguous invitation that wills it, is the work of untruth—the work within which any work of untruth is carried out.

9. PHILOSOPHY: REMAINING AND TESTIFYING
TO THE TRUTH THAT ETERNALLY APPEARS

The root of untruth is the isolation of the earth from truth. It is the faith that the earth is the region with which, assuredly, we deal. In this way, the things of the earth are understood to be capable of showing themselves by themselves, without requiring the accompaniment of any other. Yet the other—the truth of Being—stands eternally before us; it is the locus that receives and accompanies the earth, thus making possible both the earth's appearing and the appearing of the faith that posits the earth's isolation.

But error does not remain this pure faith. From this original faith, a multitude of faiths (i.e., of certainties) develops in various ways. Error, accordingly, does not limit itself to willing the continuation of the earth's solitude. In fact, it wills the earth in accordance with the determinations that derive from the earth's isolation, thus peopling the earth with the works of untruth. Error does not remain the pure faith in the earth's solitude; nor does it remain the organism of belief that rests upon such faith. Rather, it enters the work in which the lives of the earth's peoples are objectified. Operative error invades Appearing and forms the concrete aspect of the earth's solitude, and thus the concrete determinateness according to which error contends against truth for the earth.

But this contention prevents error (or truth) from completely taking possession of the earth. No work is a pure work of error (and, in untruth, no work can constitute itself as a pure work of truth). Being never responds to the call of error alone, nor (in untruth) to that of truth alone. A work is always—in untruth—the response to contending calls. In the humblest as in the proudest of works that can be performed in untruth, a trace remains of the working of truth—the trace, that is, of the work's positing itself as a response that Being grants also to the call of truth.

There is also, to counter error, a slow reflux that crosses Appearing invaded by error and brings error into the past—bringing it, in a certain sense, outside of Appearing. What passes disappears, in the sense that it assumes, in Appearing, a different determination: it presents another aspect of itself, letting its primitive aspect disappear. Error becomes something past, first of all with the disappearance of its being posited as a point of view, i.e., as the ultimate form of the conviction that envelops its content. It is as a point of view that error first contends against truth, which is the eternal point of view: error is primarily the certainty whose content is the negation of truth. What passes is this certainty (the point of view), not its content, which truth keeps linked to itself as superseded (negated). (The negation of truth appears eternally as superseded in truth, which is the negation of its negation.) And if the earth's isolation (i.e., error) becomes something past, then also the will that wills the continuation of isolation can become something past; and ultimately the earth itself, as a work of untruth, and all the works of untruth that grow upon it, can become something past as well. The occurrence of the earth is stirred by two opposing currents: the invasion of Appearing on the part of the earth's isolation, and the slow reflux which brings isolation into the past. Error that invades Appearing is not only a conviction, but is the provocation to which Being responds in the works of untruth: in untruth, the earth itself and the works which are performed on it bear the mark of error's provocation. Error therefore, in order to enter the past, must not only pass *qua* conviction (i.e., as the ultimate form of certainty) and *qua* provocation (i.e., as the will that obtains in the works of untruth, Being's response to its call for the continuation of the earth's solitude)—it must also pass as the mark that provocation leaves on the works of untruth. The earth itself must pass as a work of untruth.

Error passes at first in its most abstract form (which is itself the root of the concrete), i.e., as conviction. When error begins to become something past, we begin to remain what we eternally are. Philosophy is primarily this "remaining": it is the truth of Being itself, which remains, after the setting of the isolating conviction, what it has always been. The philosopher's patient concern for the truth of Being is not an "act of thought" or a series of such acts, which are added to and then replaced by others. It is, rather, that *eternal* act which is the essence of man, as the eternal appearing of the truth of Being. In the setting of the isolating conviction, what remains is what has *always* appeared—just as at dusk, when the noises of the valley die away, the mountains remain what they have always been, and no new forces are needed to sustain them. When the earth's solitude begins to set, what remains here before us, in philosophy, is what *eternally* stands before us: the selfsame spectacle, contemplated in the selfsame act that traverses and dominates the eons of time. Philosophy is at this point not yet action, but is the setting of those actions which envelop the earth in solitude. Only with this setting can we begin to give a name to the unnamed truth of Being. So begins that *action* of philosophizing which *testifies to* the truth of Being. What now appears is no longer only the truth of Being, but also that which testifies to it and so, first of all, the words that name it.

In philosophy, the truth of Being presents itself in a process: philosophy belongs to the offering of the earth. But this process is not the growth, in Appearing, of the truth of Being—it is, rather, the gradual disappearance of the actions of isolation. The truth of Being has always been here before us in its entirety; it seems to draw nearer a little at a time, because it is the earth's solitude that moves away a little at a time. Has the solitude of the earth moved away to such an extent that *all* the truth of Being that eternally stands before us is now present? Is the truth to which words testify all or only a part of what is eternally here before us? These questions remain unanswered. In this sense, therefore, it must be said that we have not yet *realized* what is eternally revealed to us, and so we have to *seek* what has always been our own. In order to "realize" and to "find," we must first witness the complete setting of the isolating conviction and so make it possible to give a name to that of the truth of Being which is still unnamed. Meanwhile, it must be said that everything to which we are gradually testifying as belonging to the truth of Being stands always already before us. The spectacle that we eternally contemplate is these very traits of the truth of Being to which philosophy testifies. Eternal life is in this actual life, just as evergreens live in the midst of trees that follow the rhythm of the seasons.

Philosophy, as testimony, brings the eternal spectacle to language: with the setting of the conviction that isolates the earth, there is time to give a name to the traits of the truth of Being. The testimony is not part of the eternal spectacle, but rather of the occurrence of the earth. Every language addresses itself to the truth of Being, but, in untruth, its words are aimed at naming the sure things of the isolated earth. Philosophy, therefore, in testifying to the truth of Being, has to use words consecrated to the earth—has to use, that is, a work of untruth. Indeed, the aim of the "perfect languages" of the logical positivists is to perfectly express the solitude of the earth. (Just as their formalisms are concerned with the formal structure of that solitude.) Giving a name to the traits of truth is already a work of truth—a work which prepares the purification of language and its consecration to the truth of the earth.

Since the eternity of the actual Appearing belongs to the truth of Being, man is the eternal consciousness of his own eternity. We lose this consciousness—which is everlasting, and the whole truth of Being—only in the sense that it comes into conflict, in untruth, with the isolation of the earth. Thus when man's reflections on his essence are based on isolation, it is inevitable that he should see himself as one of the things of the earth, i.e., as one of the things that come and go. However hard he may try to explore his past, he only encounters himself up to a certain point; and he can see even less of his future. Yet this consciousness of our transiency never exists in a pure state, but only in the conflict with the truth of Being (without which *nothing* can appear—neither the earth's isolation nor the consequent fleetingness of human life); and in the appearing of the truth of Being man recognizes his own eternity.

In *La struttura originaria* it was still asserted that the content of philosophy does not belong to the "background of Appearing" (i.e., to the "persyntactic field," Ch. XII, paragraph XXIX). But if something belongs to the background, because it is the necessary predicate of every being (so that nothing can appear unless this predicate appears), the only locus in which a necessary predication—and the very meaning of Necessity—can constitute itself is the truth of Being (and the "original structure" is Nothing other than the original structure of the truth of Being). The truth of Being is the predicate of each and every being: not in the sense that being is outside the truth of Being, but rather in the sense that the truth of Being is predication itself, i.e., is the veritable unity of being and its predicate, where the subject lives *only in* this unity with its predicate. The truth of Being—which is the content of philosophy—is therefore the background of all Appearing, or of Appearing as such. In the most commonplace, as in the most anomalous of human situations—in the remotest distance from the truth of Being—what stands before us, never-setting, is that very content which the philosopher, as guardian of the truth of Being, brings to language. In *La struttura originaria* it was asserted that Appearing "attests" the existence of human situations in which the structure of the truth of Being is not present (Ch. XII, paragraph XXIII). This "attestation" then induces one to seek the conditions permitting such an absence (ibid., paragraphs XXXIII, XXXIV). "Attestation," assumed as ground, is the principle of phenomenology. But phenomenology belongs to the history of metaphysics. For Husserl, the "principle of all principles" states that everything that appears is "a legitimate source of knowledge": every thing must be affirmed "as it 'gives itself', though only within the limits in which it 'gives itself'" (*Ideen*, 24). Yet, even here, the limits of the given are marked out by the isolation of the earth: the ground of the assumption that affirms everything that appears, and to the extent that it appears, is constituted by the conviction that the earth is what surely appears. Phenomenology does not testify to everything that appears, but to that which from the outset has been isolated from the whole that appears and posited as the whole that appears. If the testimony to the truth of Being still lets itself be accompanied by the principle of phenomenology (which is just what occurs in *La struttura originaria*), then it will *inevitably* be affirmed that Appearing "attests" the existence of human situations, i.e., of an Appearing, in which the structure of the truth of Being does not appear. Once the earth has been isolated from that which, by its appearing, makes the appearing of any thing possible, it is inevitable—even though one is testifying to the truth of Being—that whenever one undertakes to indicate what appears, one affirms that at times the earth appears without the appearing of the truth of Being.[8]

10. THREEFOLD ALIENATION

Let us review the fundamental traits in which the essence of man is revealed.

Being is eternal, and it eternally appears in this actual Appearing—which is not "mine," but which I myself am. Man has always been and will always be the revelation of Being, a satellite that forever accompanies the constellation of Being. Since the actual Appearing cannot not-exist (for it is itself a Being), Being is destined to appear—and therefore to appear in its truth, since the appearing of the truth of Being is that without which no Being can appear: it is the never-setting background of any thing that appears. Being eternally appears linked to its "is" by dominant Necessity; accordingly, the veritable and concrete meaning of necessity's dominance—of the structure of the truth of Being—appears eternally. As the eternal revelation of the truth of Being, man lives, in this sense, "the life of the gods" (*theon bios*, *Phaedrus*). But the "plain of truth" (*to aletheias pedion*, ibid.) stands gathered and still before him, and in this still spectacle man dwells

---

8　With reference to the specific determinations of E. Severino, *La struttura originaria* (1st ed. Brescia: La Scuola, 1958; 2nd ed. Milan: Adelphi, 1981): while in that work the background is understood as consisting of "persyntactic constants" and the content of philosophy (the truth of Being) as consisting of the set of "metasyntactic constants" (Ch. XII, paragraph XXXIII)—which accordingly can be absent from Appearing—the difference between these two types of constants *must be superseded*, and the "persyntactic field" identified with the truth of Being.

forever. Contemplation is not a *periodos*, outside of which man has a home to which he can return (*oikad' elthen*, ibid.): his home is the truth that eternally stands before him.

Yet his original dwelling-place is an infinite unrest. Any being that appears, appears included in the totality of Being, but this totality only appears formally: the concrete fullness of Being remains concealed. The eternal appearing of the truth of Being is the finite appearing of the infinite, where what is not the whole (because it is only the formal meaning of the whole—it is only this meaning, "whole," without being the concrete to which this meaning refers) is made to appear as the whole. In the eternal appearing of the truth of Being, the totality and every determination of Being appear as contradiction. The appearing of the truth of Being is the original being in contradiction. Being has always shown itself in Appearing, presenting itself in its truth. But Being with all its determinations does not enter Appearing. The occurrence of the earth testifies to the finitude of the primitive appearing of Being (everything that occurs is what has not yet appeared). In this primitive Appearing, therefore, the seal, guaranteeing that everything has definitively appeared, cannot manifest itself. This means that the truth of Being, which eternally appears, includes finitude, namely, the essential contradiction of its own Appearing. This contradiction is the constitutive alienation of the essence of man. Resolution of this contradiction is the *absurd*: finite Appearing that becomes what it *cannot* become, namely, the infinite appearing of Being (cf. "The Path of Day," XVII).

If this first alienation forms the essence of man, the occurrence of the earth brings with it a second and a third form of alienation. The second form is the occurring of the earth's isolation. Its conflict with the truth of the earth opens up the horizon of man's living in untruth. This conflict gives rise to a second sense of being in contradiction, namely, the contradiction between the constitutive contradiction (in which the appearing of the truth of Being consists) and the earth's isolation. This second contradiction is man's life in untruth, his fallen existence. The third form of alienation is metaphysical alienation— namely, the history of the West. Here, the most gigantic effort is made to testify to the truth of Being. But the basis of this testimony remains the earth's isolation, which is just what in the authentic—and still unattempted—testimony should have been left behind, as past. Greek metaphysics addressed itself to the truth of Being, but did so without relinquishing the conviction that the earth is the region with which, assuredly, we deal. If the earth is the sure region, then the becoming of beings and the very occurrence of the earth have to be thought primarily as the process in which being has been, and returns to being, nothing. Metaphysics inquires into the conditions of the thinkability of Becoming so understood, which is to say, into the thinkability of the unthinkable. The history of the West has thus become a celebration of the solitude of the earth, and the West's gods are the gods of this solitude.

There is a fundamental difference, however, between the first form of alienation and the other two. This is due less to the fact that we do not know whether the other two forms also belong to the essence of man, than it is to the fact that, in them, contradiction means something different than it does in the first form. The first form is a contradiction not on account of what appears, but of what does *not* appear in it; not on account of what is said, but of what is *not* said. What is in fact said there—what appears—is only a part of Being, not the whole. Accordingly, the supersession (which moreover cannot occur) of such alienation would be the appearing of the whole: it would mean saying concretely *that very thing* which in alienation is said abstractly—and which *for this reason* appears as contradiction. By contrast, in the other two forms contradiction emerges on account of what *is* said in them. In the second, the isolation of the earth is the negation of the truth of the earth and this negation is held fast together with that truth. Here, there is not a not-saying, but rather a saying no to truth. Likewise, in the metaphysical alienation of the West there is not a not-saying, but a saying and a doing in the light of the thought that posits Being as identical to Nothing. One does not rid oneself of these other two forms of alienation by positing concretely that which, in them, is posited abstractly, but rather by negating it. In passing beyond the first form, it is the position of the content *qua* abstract that must become something past; in passing beyond the other two, what must become something past is the position of the content as such.

But metaphysical alienation has now become the dominant trait of the earth's isolation. The works of isolation have been overwhelmed by the works of metaphysics. Western civilization has become the supreme concreteness of the way in which the truth of Being is contested, and the occurrence of the earth made an object of contention between isolation and truth.

11. THE EARTH'S ISOLATION AND THE MORTAL

The isolation of the earth—which dominates the decisive Moment of Western thought: the Platonic "parricide"—led metaphysics to think Being (determinations) as identical to Nothing; and it is upon metaphysical nihilism that Western civilization has been built. The civilization that today leads the peoples of the earth is grounded on the very event that brought about their fall into untruth. The earth's peoples have always been the dwelling-places where the truth of Being gathers. But when the isolation of the earth came into these dwelling-places, they became the houses of untruth. Which peoples have fallen into untruth?

Untruth is traceable primarily in the way in which the actual Appearing lets Being appear. I live in untruth. Which is to say in the actual appearing of Being, the isolation of the earth continually counters the truth of Being. Only at times does the earth's solitude begin to set and let me begin to remain what I eternally am. The solitude soon returns, full-force and with all its consequences, so that all my decisions and works become decisions and works of untruth.

But the earth is always before me laden with the fruits of metaphysical alienation that were called out into the light by the people of the West. The works which appear on the earth can in fact be interpreted as Being's response to the calls of peoples. Today, however, the works of the people of the West—the products of technological civilization—have overwhelmed all other works. Yet in *any* work—including those of the West—there is a trace of the truth of Being. In the works of untruth, there is also a trace of the earth's isolation. But we still have to learn how to uncover these traces. We know that any work can preserve the opposing traces of truth and of isolation, but what *are* these traces? What are the traces of truth? And what are the traces of the earth's isolation?

Metaphysical nihilism, within which Western history unfolds, is the trace of the solitude in which Western man has enveloped the earth. We can realize that the people to which we belong have fallen into solitude, because we know that metaphysics is the dominant spirit of the West. For metaphysics, being, as such, is nothing. This is the sign that metaphysical thought grows on the solitude of the earth. Isolated from its truth, the earth in fact is a Nothing. Isolation, which posits the earth as the surest region of being, is in its truth the nihilation of the earth. Indeed, affirming that the earth is the sure thing means, in truth, affirming that the earth is nothing. Metaphysics is the truth of isolation: it is the testimony to the nothingness of the earth. It betrays the truth of Being, precisely because it looks at that truth through the solitude of the earth. Accordingly, it posits the totality of Being just as the earth itself is posited in isolation. The isolation of earthly things thus becomes the transcendental determination according to which metaphysics posits the totality of beings. As isolated from their truth, all beings are Nothing; and it is *precisely because* from the very beginning metaphysics thought being as a Nothing that it can explicitly affirm that being, as such, can become a Nothing. (For being as such is not incorruptible and ungenerable, but being insofar as it is a privileged being—insofar as it is one of the gods of the West.)

Isolated from its truth the earth is a Nothing, because if the earth can appear only insofar as its truth appears, then the appearing of the earth (or of any being whatsoever) without the appearing of that being's truth is that which cannot be, and is therefore a Nothing. Untruth is the fallen existence of mankind. It is rooted in the conviction that the earth is the sure region of being: the earth is the sure thing, because *the earth* is what appears. For the things of the earth to appear, nothing else is required but their Appearing itself. What a house, a man, a tree, joy, or suffering is, is told by the thing itself in its unfolding and interweaving with the other earthly things that appear. For also in untruth beings are affirmed because they appear. Why do we affirm that the sky is blue, that we heard a voice, that the lamp is on the table (and so forth with the countless affirmations that make up the world in which Being appears in untruth), if not because the blue of the sky, the voice, and the lamp on the table *appear*, or we believe that they appear?[9] Even if what is testified to is but the content of Appearing and not Appearing as such, also in untruth the content is affirmed because it appears.

But untruth does not limit itself to affirming the earth. It also posits the earth as the thing that assuredly is, and so sees in it the totality of the content that appears. In this way the earth is isolated from its truth (i.e., from the background that eternally appears and without which nothing can appear). Thinking, therefore, that the earth is the sure region of being means thinking, in truth, that the earth is a Nothing, since—when referring to the earth—being the sure region means being a Nothing. For the earth is only a part (the part that occurred) of what truly is the sure region, and the part, when posited as the total content of Appearing, is a Nothing. (Furthermore: the part, thought without that in virtue of which it is—i.e., without its truth—is a Nothing.) In untruth, what is thought and therefore willed is the earth's nothingness: the things of the earth are treated as a Nothing in the very act in which they are posited as the sure region of being. Hence in any work of untruth a trace of the nihilation of things can be uncovered: every work bears the sign of the conviction that it is a Nothing. And so when language, as a work of untruth, intends to name the things of an earth left in solitude, its every word names the Nothing. That the earth should be in uncontested solitude is, however, only an intention: the truth of the earth is the contrasting background that eternally appears, coming to light in every work and in every word of untruth.

Alienation, which makes man become a mortal, is the root of metaphysics. When he posits the earth as the sure region of being, man becomes a mortal—he becomes, that is, one of the things of the earth, whose nothingness is thought and willed. Metaphysics is the testimony to the nothingness of the earth. Isolated from the truth of

---

9 But also in the case of what is believed to appear, something is affirmed because it appears. One affirms, for example, that also the unseen parts of a lamp exist. To be sure, they do not appear as the visible parts do (the specific error of naturalistic realism consists in the identification of these two modes of appearing); yet, in some way—and in any event according to a modality different from that of the visible parts—also the nonvisible parts appear precisely insofar as one speaks about them and is aware of them. It will be said that they appear as "ideal" determinations. So be it: but at the same time it is clear that, even in this case, their existence is affirmed on the basis of the appearing of such a modality of existence.

Being, the earth stands before man as a Nothing. Metaphysics testifies to what stands before us and affirms that being, as such, is a Nothing. But metaphysics testifies to solitude not because it knows that isolation is the fall into untruth, but rather because it knows how to express the result of the fall. It does not express the fall as a fall (for this comes about in the truth of the untruth of Being), but rather as that which, as a result of the fall, lies before us (and before us lies the earth's nothingness). Thus metaphysics is not simply a false thinking—it is the consciousness that man *must* have of the meaning of Being and of himself, since he has become a mortal.

The affirmation of the nothingness of being is not the only sign that metaphysics grows on the solitude of the earth. Metaphysics is the explicit affirmation that the earth is the content of immediate knowing—and this is an explicit affirmation of the earth's solitude. The earth is in fact *ta physika*, for *physis* is the region of Becoming and reality-that-becomes is the totality of what immediately appears. Precisely because it "draws from Becoming to Being" (*olkon apo tou gignomenou epi to on, Republic, 521d*), metaphysics posits the region of Becoming as that which, certainly, has to be transcended, but which, for this very reason, is the unquestionable dimension from which knowing must proceed (and with which man, in his present life, originally deals). This is the fundamental property of every type of metaphysics, whether *physis* be understood as a being outside the mind, or as the content of the *cogito* or of phenomenological description; whether metaphysics, in transcending the region of Becoming, comes to affirm an immutable being (a being that transcends Becoming), or else comes to identify reality-that-becomes with the totality of Being, positing the original content of experience in the form of thought. The Indo-European root of *kosmos* is *kens*: "to announce with authority" (Latin *censeo*). For metaphysical thought *kosmos* is *physis*, understood as the region of Becoming; which means that the earth is the sure place, the region that announces itself with authority (and silences the voices of myth). The "world" is the earth as the sure place and so as solitude. In the untruth of pre-metaphysical man, the nothingness of the earth is the invisible thought that (countered by truth) guides his every step. This thought leaves its traces in man's works, but metaphysics alone has testified to it and made it visible. Metaphysics is thus the uncovered trace of the fall of man; and the history of the West is that dizziness from the fall, which is the West's awareness of its own dominant thought.

The West, in receiving the earth, enveloped it in solitude and fell into untruth. Metaphysical domination is the trace of the fall. This trace is lacking in the works of nonmetaphysical peoples, where all testimony to the truth of Being is silent. Their works too (like all works) preserve traces of truth—which stands eternally gathered before *all* peoples—but they do not testify to it. We do not know how other peoples received the earth. We may suppose that they, too, whose works testify only to earthly things, saw and experienced the earth as the sure ground—as the only thing that *can* be testified to—and therefore that they, too, fell into the untruth of Being. It may be supposed that the fall is part of the essence of all peoples. But these suppositions still cannot be evaluated. Do only mortal peoples inhabit the earth?

12. THE EARTH'S ISOLATION AND THE "PARRICIDE"

Western civilization is the only testimony in man's history to the truth of Being. But the West addressed itself to the truth of Being while grounding itself on the solitude of the earth, and truth's only testimony became its most abysmal betrayal. Isolation, which nihilates the earth, determines the relation that metaphysics establishes between the things of the earth and their *Being*. Throughout the course of its history, metaphysics has attempted to think the Being (the existence) of what is originally seen as a Nothing. Seeing the nothingness of things in fact means positing them as isolated from their Being and recognizing the essential accidentality of their relation with Being (i.e., of their existing). It is therefore inevitable that, while explicitly opposing being to Nothing, metaphysics also comes to explicitly affirm that being is nothing (when it is-not and insofar as it can not-be).

The earth's solitude also envelops he who first named the truth of Being. All antiquity attests that Parmenides affirmed pure Being, while denying the existence of the determinations of the manifold. Acting at the root of this negation is the absolute separation—the isolation—of determinations from Being (cf. the "Postscript" to "Returning to

Parmenides," 71 ff.). Isolated from Being—thought, that is, in their separation from Being and so from the truth of Being—determinations must necessarily be understood as Nothing. Parmenides posits them as a Nothing, not because he does not yet know the Platonic distinction between other (*eteron*) and opposite (*enantion*), but precisely because he isolated them from Being; and thus, in isolation, the *eteron* must be posited as the opposite of being (*enantion tou ontos*). But the determinations of the manifold are primarily the determinations-that-become of the earth, and their separation from pure Being—i.e., from that of the truth of Being to which Parmenides did testify—expresses the way in which Parmenides keeps the earth isolated from the truth of Being. The way in which the manifold things of the earth are thought (the way of solitude) thus determines the way in which the manifold in general is thought. Hence it is *precisely because Parmenides too* is convinced that the earth is the sure ground that, when he measures the earth against the trait of the truth of Being to which he had testified—and this trait is the pure whose dazzle tries to ravish the witness from the earth—he is compelled to posit the untruth (the opinions of mortals "in which is no true belief"; *ouk eni pistis alethes*, Fr. 1, 30), the illusoriness, the unsureness and, ultimately, the nothingness of the earth.

And the very link with which Plato unites Being to its determinations is forged in the solitude of the earth. In its truth, Being is not pure Being, but rather the union of pure Being and a determination. Plato is the witness to this union, but he unites to Being that which also for him is originally understood as absolutely isolated from it. Plato too isolates the earth (and then the totality of determinations) from Being, and therefore he too must take the earth and, in general, determinations, to be a Nothing. It is this very Nothing—i.e., this non-Nothing which, isolated from Being, must be posited as a Nothing—it is this very non-Nothing, now understood as nothing, that he unites to Being (i.e., to its being a non-Nothing). For Parmenides Being is the pure "is"; a determination (such as "house"), isolated from its "is," must be posited as a Nothing. Plato, *per contra*, knows that Being is a determination-that-is (for example, a house-that-is), since "is" means "is not a Nothing," and a determination, e.g. "house," is not a Nothing (is not a meaning-nothing). But in forging this link between a determination and its "is," Plato—like Parmenides before him—from the outset isolates the determination from its Being and so, from the outset, has to understand it as a Nothing. Thus he unites to Being (i.e., to not-being-a-Nothing) that which is destined to be thought as a Nothing. Insofar as a determination is already thought as a Nothing, metaphysics deems legitimate the accidentality of its union with Being. Once this has been admitted, it cannot but be affirmed that a determination "is when it is, and when it is not, it is not," and that therefore its coming-to-be is a process in which it (the non-Nothing!) has been, and returns to being, a Nothing. Even the Idea (*ousia ontos ousa*—and each of the gods of the West), *qua determination*, is a Nothing. In fact, in order to posit it as Being—as that Being whose fate is never to be a Nothing and which therefore is "beingly being" (*ontos on*)—Plato and all Western thought thereafter have had to resort to *reasons* that are different from the *true*—and unthought—reason, which is the *truth* of the earth. If the earth comes out of solitude and determinations are no longer isolated from their Being and from the truth of their Being, then it is the determination *as such*—every determination of Being—that must be posited as *ontos on*, i.e., as that which can never have been, nor ever return to being, nothing. God—by contrast—is the result of the will to posit as Being (*ontos on*) that which is originally thought as a Nothing.

The dominant thought of metaphysics is the identity of Being and Nothing—yet metaphysics explicitly undertakes to safeguard and preserve their opposition. The Hegelian dialectic is one of the paramount forms of metaphysical thought; but the identity of Being and Nothing, which constitutes the first triad of Hegelian logic, is by no means a formulation of the dominant thought of metaphysics. Hegel in fact stresses that the identity of Being and Nothing is not the identity of determinate Being (*Daseyn*) and Nothing (as if it were "the same whether I am or am not, whether this house is or is not, whether these hundred talers are, or are not, part of my fortune"), since that which is identical to Nothing is *pure* Being, Parmenides' pure "is," isolated from determinations.[10] Therefore, according to Hegel, common sense has no call to be astonished at the identity of Being and Nothing—it would,

---

10   G. W. F. Hegel, *Science of Logic*, trans. by A. V. Miller, London: George Allen and Unwin, 1969, 85.

rather, have good reason to be astonished at their difference, as in fact Trendelenburg was, and therefore it is not a matter of indifference, according to Hegel, whether something determinate is or is not.[11] Like Plato and Aristotle before him, Hegel defends the noncontradictoriness of being: he too undertakes to safeguard the opposition of not-Nothing and Nothing. But, for this very reason, Hegel too identifies Being and Nothing: not in the sense of the first triad of the *Logic*, but rather in the same sense in which Plato and Aristotle did so. In the very act in which it affirms the opposition of being and Nothing, metaphysical thought allows being to be a Nothing. Hegel opposes being (*Daseyn*) to Nothing, but he distinguishes finite beings, whose destiny is to be born and perish—to have been, and return to being, nothing—from privileged being, which is itself the eternal becoming of the finite (so that the nothingness of finite being is the condition for the eternity of privileged being). Here too, the determinate, as such, issues from and returns to nothingness, because the basis also of Hegelian metaphysics is the isolation of the earth—and, therewith, of determination as such—from the truth of Being.

The fundamental metaphysical doctrine, designed to clarify the meaning of the isolation of determinations, is the Hegelian doctrine of abstract understanding. And yet, this epic struggle against the isolation of determinations is guided by a thought that is completely enveloped by the solitude of the earth. Hegel's *Logic* intends to be the overcoming of the abstractness of pure Being (the "is"), which, as isolated from determinations, is (in its turn) a Nothing. Indeed, dialectical development is the determinate mode according to which the synthesis between pure Being and the totality of determinations is instituted. But the ultimate meaning of this Hegelian synthesis is still the Platonic one. From the outset a bottomless abyss (the abyss which isolates the earth from the truth of Being) yawns between pure Being and determinations, so that the union of the two sides is the synthesis of that which from the outset was destined to remain divided. In dialectical development, pure Being determines itself (i.e., it unites with determinations). But the determination—as *empirical*, and not privileged, determination—maintains in its synthesis with Being the character

---

11   Cf., for example, ibid., 86.

that from the outset belongs to it as separated from Being—namely, the character of being a Nothing. It is united to Being, but continues to be a Nothing. It is thus inevitable that Hegel should treat the determination as a Nothing and affirm its synthesis with Being to be accidental, and that it is therefore destined to be born and to perish (i.e., to have been, and return to being, nothing)—only that privileged being, which is the very accidentality of the synthesis, remaining eternal. (In Hegel, the synthesis between pure Being and *categorical* determinations is indeed intended to count as necessary and not as accidental. But this necessary synthesis—the organism of categories, the Idea—is once again the privileged structure that, as in Plato, makes the becoming of empirical determinations possible; i.e., that makes possible the institution of the accidental synthesis between the categorical and the empirical.)

Aristotle himself had reproached Parmenides with isolating Being from determinations (*Physics*, 186a 22 ff.), stressing that Being is other than determinations as *distinct* (*to einai eteron*), and not as *separate* from them (*ou gar e choriston*). Distinctness does not imply the nothingness of determinations (*outhen etton polla ta leuka [=polla ta onta] kai ouk en*), precisely because what is other than Being is distinct from it in meaning, but is not something isolated from it (*allo gar estai to einai leuko [=onti] kai to dedegmeno, kai ouk estai para to leukon [=on] outhen choriston*). And yet, the isolation of determinations, with which Aristotle reproaches Parmenides, is the very basis of Aristotelian—and Platonic, and Hegelian—metaphysics. Precisely because determinations, isolated from Being (and from the truth of Being), are a metaphysical thought can it be admitted that, coming to be, they have been nothing (and return to being nothing): "For what is generated is what is-not" (*gignetai gar to me on*, *Metaph.*, 1067b 31). Indeed, for metaphysics the greatest difficulty lies in thinking that a thing is not a Nothing.

13. THE SALVATION OF TRUTH

Pure contradiction is the original dwelling-place of man. The eternal manifestation of the truth of Being is the primordial structure of contradiction. Any other contradiction is grounded on this structure. Coming-out of primordial contradiction is an occurrence, since such contradiction is the attitude that has always been assumed by the never-setting background, which is the place where every occurrence can be received. The "life of the gods," which the peoples of the earth lead in their original dwelling-places, has therefore always awaited its salvation. Salvation lies in the occurrence. The true meaning of salvation—i.e., the truth of salvation—is in fact the salvation of truth. Since man is the eternal guardian of the truth of Being, the true meaning of the salvation of man is the salvation of truth. And for truth salvation means passing beyond the contradiction that has always penetrated it.

The occurrence is a coming-out of the motionless unrest of the never-setting. One does not come out of, i.e., one does not escape the never-setting; rather, one comes out of the primordial contradiction in which the never-setting finds itself, due to its not being the completed manifestation of every trait of Being. While the never-setting does let every being appear in the "whole," it cannot bring out into the light all the concrete richness of things that the meaning of "whole," by appearing, demands be brought out (and thus that which is not the whole is made to mean "whole"). Since the never-setting background is that without whose appearing nothing could appear, contradiction does not belong to the background in the sense that, without contradiction, nothing could appear. For contradiction is the attitude assumed by the background insofar as it does not contain the concrete whole of Being. Contradiction is not that without which nothing could appear; rather, the background is invested with contradiction, due to the not-appearing in it of the whole. Salvation is the completion of that revelation of Being which is granted to the eternal appearing of the truth of Being.

The occurrence is unique. If in addition to the earth something else occurred—heaven, the beyond—then both would constitute the content of the occurrence. Therefore the occurrence occurs in the occurrence of the earth; and salvation lies in the occurrence. But the occurrence is also the greatest of perils—the possibility of abysmal perdition. Being offers the earth to the guardians of the truth of Being. And the offering is accepted. The receiving of the offering belongs to the offering: it is the way in which the occurrence occurred. Receiving the offering means willing the continuation of the occurrence to the completion of its occurring. Its total completion gives the measure of the disclosure of Being that is granted to the essence of man, thus giving the measure of the liberation from contradiction: the measure of salvation. But is the earth the measure granted, or is this measure given by a different completion occurrence?

The guardians of truth received the offering while leaving it in solitude. We have no means of shedding light upon man's fall into the solitude of the earth. But insofar as the earth's solitude is a fact, it has no need of light. Since the truth of Being eternally appears, man's life in untruth is possible only as a conflict, in Appearing, between the truth of Being and the isolation of the earth. The distraction from truth is manifest not only in our everyday existence (which seems concerned with anything but the truth of Being), but also in Western civilization itself—the civilization that today rules the earth. Yet it could not appear if isolation had not occurred. But why did the earth's peoples, when they received the offering, envelop it in solitude? Any answer to this question is, even now, only a possible interpretation.

The alienation opposed to the one in which the peoples of the earth have fallen is the rejection of the earth, i.e., the will that the occurrence not continue. No trace has been uncovered of this form of alienation. Suicide (which in our culture has become a form of metaphysical nihilism) is one of the events that occur within the receiving of the earth. Rejection of the earth is a form of alienation, since only the occurrence can bring salvation. If the isolation of the earth is a negation of the truth of Being, so is the rejection of the earth: for the rejection of the earth is the rejection of salvation. Salvation may be rejected, because in the occurrence which brings it one fears abysmal alienation. One may enclose the earth in solitude, because it is believed that the only salvation possible lies in the way in which the occurrence of the earth stands before us. If salvation disappoints, one attempts the supreme feat of forgetting the *ground* of the disappointment—namely, the truth of Being. And the only way in which man can do so is by isolating the earth. But how can the value of this interpretation be established?

In fact, truth—as testified to in philosophy—does not even know whether the history of salvation is a development necessary to the never-setting background of Appearing (i.e., an epiphany of Being, which, like the appearing of the background, is ineluctable), or whether it is a history of freedom. The offering of the earth, the receiving of the offering, the fall into solitude, the metaphysical alienation of the West, and all the ways of the occurrence—are these the steps of freedom or of inevitable necessity? And the truth of Being, which eternally appears—what does it know of the measure of its own salvation? For even if, in philosophy, the truth of Being does remain here before as with the setting of the isolation of the earth, we do not know whether, in testifying to it, we are testifying to the whole that eternally appears.

14. REPETITION OF THE ACCEPTANCE OF THE OFFERING

And yet philosophy, as the guardian of the truth of Being, is the repetition of the supreme moment of the history of salvation. The slow reflux, which in philosophy carries the earth's solitude to its setting, once more places the truth of Being before the offering of the earth and allows it to repeat the receiving of the offering. In the primordial receiving, the earth's peoples brought the earth to encroachment. Their fall into untruth made the earth itself a work of untruth. The West has become the leader of untruth, its bearer and dominant witness; and thus the earth has become a work of the West. Yet the only testimony to the truth of Being is in the history of the West. The possibility of repeating the receiving of the offering was granted to Greek thought. And in fact the Greeks came close to such a repetition. Greek thought looked out on the testimony to the truth of Being, but without stopping there it continued its course, leading the West along the path of Night, into the remotest distance. Will the West's wandering star approach the testimony anew, making it possible to repeat the receiving of the earth?

In philosophy, the truth of Being again encounters the offering of the earth. Untruth's rampant dominance is crossed by a reflux that slowly carries it towards its setting and allows the truth of Being to reemerge. The earth places itself anew, uncontended, before the eyes of truth, whose guardian is philosophy. The truth of Being is testified to in philosophy, since the conviction that isolated the earth and contends for it against truth has set. But the earth still lies before us laden with the fruits of its long solitude. Truth calls it back from exile, but the voice of truth now finds the earth in various guises, for it is laden with all the time and all the works of alienation. And yet in philosophy the possibility for the history of the salvation of peoples to begin anew is safeguarded. We are faced with the supreme test, on which the completion of the occurrence and the conclusion of the history of salvation depends. Thought that testifies to the truth of Being may once more be swallowed up by the solitude of the earth, and the peoples of the earth may definitively move away from the truth of Being. Yet all hope lies in the glimmer that thereby opens up.

Untruth is such, not because it wills the earth and the earth's continuation, but because it isolates what is willed. This willing, as such, is the same original will with which the eternal appearing of the truth of Being wills the earth and its continuation. The earth's peoples accepted the offering. This is affirmed, precisely because the earth and its continuation in fact appear as willed. The repetition of the receiving of the offering is therefore not a new always-occurring of what has always occurred since Being offered the earth to man. Ever since the offering occurred, the earth has appeared in the truth of Being, which since then has also been the truth of the earth. Untruth is a conflict not between the pure truth of Being (to which the earth is not yet linked) and the isolation of the earth, but rather between the truth of Being, which is also the truth of the earth, and the isolation of the earth. Thus it is a conflict between the truth of the earth, which wills the continuation of the earth in truth, and the isolation of the willed earth, in which willing becomes the will that the earth continue in solitude. The repetition of the receiving of the offering is, therefore, the setting of the conviction that isolates the earth; so that, with this setting, not only do we remain what we have always been, but we also remain what we have begun to be ever since the offering of the earth occurred—we also remain the receiving of the offering.

Philosophy is not a return to the silence of man's original dwelling-place, for philosophy preserves the occurrence of the earth in the truth of Being; rather with the setting of the isolating conviction, the earth is called by the pure voice of truth. Yet the earth—unsetting work of the West's untruth—remains indifferent to the voice of truth. The voice of solitude sets, but the works it called forth do not, and ever more vertiginous is the West's race towards the constellations of Night. The earth, as a work of the West's alienation, appears in the truth of Being; so that philosophy—insofar as it is our remaining what we have always been and what we have begun to be since the offering of the earth occurred—is the contradiction in which solitude and nihilism are superseded (in which they set) only in the abstract element of thought, while their works are left as not-superseded. This contradiction is the way in which man is faced with the supreme test, to which the completion of the history of salvation is linked. Since the true meaning of salvation is the salvation of truth—i.e., the completion of that revelation of Being which is granted to the eternal appearing of the truth of Being—any other meaning of salvation can be accepted only if it can be conjoined with this, original meaning. If it is true that the proclamation of salvation (*kerygma*) can save in this original sense, it is also true that theology, especially today, realizes that the conditions for hearing the *kerygma* are lacking. But theology too is dominated by metaphysical nihilism: its accusation that such hearing is impossible in our time is grounded on that same dominant thought—i.e., the nothingness of being—which itself prevents true hearing. The only hearing in the history of the West has been metaphysical hearing, in which everything is made to pass through the solitude of the earth and where, therefore, no Advent and no *kerygma* can bring salvation.

Philosophy, insofar as it witnesses the setting of the isolating conviction, makes true hearing possible. But if salvation is to occur, the road to salvation must pass through the setting of the works of solitude and so through the setting of the West, which is the dominant witness to solitude. Awaiting this setting, philosophy looks out on the supreme possibility of the peoples of the earth. Only if, in philosophy, the isolating conviction does not counter the truth of the earth, can the earth be brought to setting as a work of untruth. For the earth to become a work of truth, it is first necessary that the truth of the earth not appear countered by the isolating conviction. This is why philosophy brings us back to the parting of the ways, which once opened up before the original dwelling-place of man: to the right, the untrodden path of Day, where the earth becomes a work of the truth of Being; and to the left, the path of Night, which leads the earth into solitude. Is philosophy the dawn of Day? Or is it the swan song before the truth of the earth is definitively caught up in its conflict with the isolating conviction and the West resumes its precipitous course, never looking back?

Nor can the individual save himself independently of the history of the West, i.e., of the way in which peoples bring to completion the occurring of the earth. As long as philosophy is the contradiction in which the isolating conviction sets but the works of solitude do not, no well-being (*eupraxia*) can bring salvation: it falls on a sick ground and becomes sick itself. Any single individual's resolve to save himself independently of the configuration that historical objectivity assumes will be merely pathetic. But insofar as the individual is the guardian of the truth of Being, he is the good shepherd who calls his peoples back to the parting of the ways and shows them the path of Day.

Taking this path—bringing the earth as a work of the West to its setting—means resolving the contradiction of philosophy and thus bringing philosophy toward its completion. Philosophy is contradiction insofar as it is only our remaining what we eternally are and what we have begun to be since the earth was offered to us. But on the path of Day philosophy is the earth, which becomes the uncontested work of truth. And so it is the completion of the occurrence: Being's assent to the will that the occurrence continue and be accomplished in the truth of Being.

15. THE TESTIMONY TO THE SOLITUDE OF THE EARTH

Technological civilization is the way in which, today, the West testifies to the solitude of the earth. Science is in fact the supreme operative criterion of technology, and is the basis of modern science in its strict fidelity to the methodic assumption of positing the earth (the occurrence) as the only sure ground of investigation. Science attends only to the things of the earth: they are the dimension with which, assuredly, we deal. As far as science is concerned, metaphysics fails because its object is the unsure.

Yet metaphysics testifies to the truth of Being—to the never-setting region that is other than the occurrence of the earth. It does so, however, from a viewpoint that brings about not only the earth's isolation, but also that testimony to isolation which is reiterated in the methodic assumption of modern science. The ground of science is thus the metaphysical testimony to the solitude of the earth. But— unlike science—metaphysics recognizes the impossibility of testifying to solitude without at the same time testifying to "Being," "not-Being," the "thing," "Being," the "occurrence," "Becoming," the "immutable," the "this," the "other," "sureness," "unsureness," and all the other determinations with which it expresses the solitude of the earth. Metaphysics knows that to think the earth as the sure region it is necessary to think the categories that give meaning to the isolating thought. These categories are the fragments of the truth of Being which are employed by metaphysics to express the isolation of the earth from this truth itself. If metaphysical thought did not have before it the *whole* truth of Being it could not think the earth's isolation; but metaphysics, in expressing (i.e., testifying to) isolation, brings into its expression only fragments of Being's truth, such that the unification of these fragments assumes a configuration different from the true one. In this unification being, as such, is posited as a Nothing. Isolated from truth, the earth stands before man as a Nothing, and the nothingness of earthly things becomes the transcendental determination by which metaphysics thinks being as being. In metaphysics, the nothingness of being is explicitly enunciated—even though it is accompanied by the equally explicit intention of opposing being to Nothing.

Metaphysics, by bringing into its testimony the fragments of truth, is made to venture beyond the sure confines of the earth: the meaning of these fragments compels it to seek the conditions for the possibility of the earth in a wider dimension. This dimension is broached not only when one affirms "pure act" or "absolute spirit," but also when one identifies the earth with the totality of being or with the totality of meaning. Modern science, *per contra*, undertakes to investigate the earth without going beyond its confines. But, inevitably, when science explicitly affirms the sureness and thus the isolation of the earth, it thinks isolation, making use of the very categories whose testimony leads metaphysics to venture into unsure regions. Science is thus completely dominated by the metaphysical mode of thought which, in scientific investigation, dispenses with explicit reflection on the supreme conditions of the thinkability of the earth and limits itself to describing and forecasting the behavior of the earth that appears, once the earth has been brought within its categories.

Thus science too sees the earth as a nothing and, as testimony to isolation, expresses in its language and its works the nothingness of the earth. Science, in undertaking to ignore whatever does not belong to the earth, is the methodic development of a thought that abandons the truth of Being (and thus the truth of Becoming and of Appearing). As a result, the occurrence of the earth and of earthly things is inevitably understood by science as their issuing from and returning to nothingness. To mortal eyes, the earth appears as a Nothing. Metaphysics—and, in its wake, science, technology, and the whole of Western civilization insofar as it is dominated by metaphysics—testifies to the thought of mortals; it testifies, that is, to the nothingness of the earth, and calls it "sureness of the earth." But when metaphysics expresses the meaning of the occurrence, it dismisses all reticence and, in affirming that the earth issues from and returns to nothingness, explicitly enunciates the earth's nothingness—it *says* that the earth has been, and returns to being, a Nothing. Science, too, is compelled to say this: even when it avoids using the words "Being" and "Nothing." The eternity of being *qua* being appears—never-setting—to mortals; but man *becomes* mortal because he isolates the earth from the truth of Being, and his isolating thought ignores this truth. One can isolate the earth only if the truth of the earth appears, but isolation (i.e., the earth, posited as the sure region) *distinguishes* itself from the truth of the earth, which in isolation is therefore absent or ignored. It is inevitable that science—as metaphysical testimony to this isolation, in which the truth of the earth is ignored—should think the formation and destruction of the universe as its progressive issuing from, and progressive returning to, nothingness.

When science refuses to be understood in this way and attempts to align itself with phenomenological method, declaring that something's Becoming is its empirically observed transition from not-Being to Being, then science reverts to that very explicitation of the categories it employs in which the specific activity of metaphysical thought consists. But what becomes of a something, before and after it has been empirically observed? What becomes of empirical observation itself before and after it has been performed? Phenomenology offers no answers to these questions, and thus admits the possibility that a thing, before and after it has been empirically observed, is a Nothing, and that empirical observation itself, before and after it has been performed, is a Nothing.[12] And if no answer is given to these questions because one claims that the words "Being" and "Nothing" have no meaning whatsoever, then one definitively places oneself on that very plane of metaphysical testimony to the categories employed from which science intends to prescind. Modern science is not logical positivistic metaphysics (even if metaphysical thought indeed holds sway in science and logical positivism alike). Logical positivism identifies experience with meaning, affirming the meaninglessness of metaphysical terminology. Yet even the logical positivist recognizes the fact that his formulation of the principle of verification tacitly posits, in the very act that denies it, the meaningfulness of metaphysical categories.[13] Metaphysical thought is itself the basis of any antimetaphysical critique in Western thought. The opposition of meaning and meaninglessness is a way of expressing the opposition of being and nothing. (Privation of meaning is nothing other than privation of positivity: something is meaningful to the extent that it is not a Nothing and it is not a Nothing to the extent that it is meaningful. "Meaninglessness" itself, insofar as it is meaningful as meaninglessness, is not a Nothing—for the positive meaning of meaninglessness is not a Nothing, but meaninglessness as such. And so in denying that the term "Nothing" has a meaning, one recognizes the meaningfulness of not having any meaning, which is to say, one recognizes the meaningfulness of that which moreover would posit itself as meaningless.) Therefore, something's supervening in experience (identified with the totality of meaning) is an absolute beginning: beginning-to-be-experienced is a beginning in every sense, since it is a beginning to be meaningful. And no-longer-being-experienced is an absolute ending, since it is the dismissal of all meaning. Logical positivistic empiricism is in fact a form of idealistic immanentism, despite its attempt to distinguish itself from it.

---

12   "We all see that scientific knowledge is of things that are never other than they are; for as to things that do admit of variation cannot, if they are outside the field of our observation, discover whether they exist or not" (Aristotle, *The Nicomachean Ethics*, 1139*b* 2C ff., trans. J. A. K. Thomson, London: Penguin Books, 1953).

13   Cf. *Studi di filosofia della prassi*, I, part iii, Ch. 1.

16. NOTHINGNESS AND SURENESS OF THE EARTH

Insofar as modern science is the supreme operative criterion of technology, technological civilization is the way in which, today, metaphysics testifies to the solitude of the earth. Today metaphysical nihilism is not only the manufacture and consumption of industrial products, but is all the things of the earth—the sun, the moon, the remotest of galaxies, man's body and his feelings, plants, sounds, and colors—insofar as they come within the technological project to dominate the processes of the universe and are thus essentially related to the products of technology. The thought that makes man fall into untruth and become a mortal is the energy that, once testified to, constitutes the history of the West and now guides everything that happens on the earth. But if the setting of the West is also the setting of technological civilization, does not salvation of truth demand that man give up all the things by which he has freed himself from pain and from the fear of life? Is not, then, the path of Day a return to more primitive forms of human existence?

To be sure, technological civilization resolves problems that primitive man is wholly incapable of dealing with. But it does so not by passing beyond the act that raised them, but by taking it to the extreme. Man, enveloping the earth in solitude, becomes a mortal—he becomes one of the things of the earth, which, isolated from its truth, stands before him as a Nothing. Technological civilization resolves the problems of mortals while maintaining itself within the isolation of the earth—that is, while reinforcing, in the most rigorous and radical manner, the thought that makes man mortal. Technology may well be able to keep man from dying, but man is destined to live this form of liberation from death within his original mortal essence, of which technology is the most powerful expression to date. Future technological humanity, freed from pain and death, is the completed manifestation of the mortal essence of man. The path of Day does not have to resolve the problems of mortals, because man will set out on it when he begins to live as an immortal—when, that is, he repeats the receiving of the earth in the truth of Being, and brings to setting the solitude of the earth. The earth's peoples will go forth on the path of Day with the setting of the will to die that makes man become a mortal and confronts him with the problems of mortals.

The earth can appear only against the background of the truth of Being. This is to say that the appearing of the earth, without the appearing of the background, is not, i.e., is a Nothing. Thought, which posits the earth as the sure region, i.e., as the totality of what appears, isolates the appearing of the earth from the appearing of the background, and in so doing thinks the Nothing. Which is not to say that it thinks nothing: it thinks *the Nothing*: Nothing is the ultimate meaning of the content of isolating thought. And the Nothing, which stands before it, is posited as the surest of beings. Things, coming onto the earth, are out in a sure place; but before teaching and after leaving the earth, they are exposed to the perils of annihilation. Man becomes a mortal when—having before him the nothingness of the surest of beings, and the earth as a shelter from the perils of annihilation, and the nothingness of that shelter—he himself appears as one of the beings of the earth, and thus as a sure being that cannot hide its own nothingness, its being sheltered by a Nothing, its being exposed to the perils of annihilation.

When the mortal leaves the shelter of the earth, it is therefore his prerogative to seek out what can save him from annihilation, and what can reinforce this very shelter whose sureness cannot prevent the emergence of its nothingness. When man invokes the gods to save him from annihilation, it is a *mortal* voice that reaches them. Mortal is the voice of any metaphysical demonstration of the immortality of the soul. And mortal is man's disappointment because the gods ignore his call (and mortal, therefore, any metaphysical denial of, or agnosticism about, the soul's immortality).

The thought that, by countering the eternal appearing of the truth of Being, envelops the earth in solitude, is the *will* with which man, when he leaves his original dwelling-place, wills to become a mortal. When man wills the solitude of the earth, what he in truth is willing is his own mortality. This will is nothing but the mortal essence of man. It is the basis not only of the way in which mortals live on the isolated earth, but also of their biological conformation itself, as the development that from birth leads to growth, to ageing and to death. Birth and death, wakefulness and sleep, youth and age, health and sickness are determinations of the way in which man lives in untruth—of the way, that is, in which the isolated earth enters and withdraws from Appearing. They determine the way in which the earth's isolation counters the eternal appearing of the truth of Being. Hence the concern of mortals for the earth is not due to their biological development—on the contrary, it is precisely because they envelop the earth in solitude that such development is possible. (This development is a parabola, in which incipient awareness of the earth, extremely poor in content, is progressively enriched until it comes to a peak, at which point it is impoverished once more until it is totally spent; and where the whole parabola is composed of a series of parabolas, whose rhythm is the alternation of wakefulness and sleep, and where the regularity of this rhythm may be altered by the various forms of "loss of consciousness.") If, in isolating the earth, one posits it as the sure region, then the poverty and the wealth of its content are experienced as the poverty and wealth of content as such. The lover has eyes only for his beloved: if she avoids his gaze, for him it is as if the whole world had vanished and only its ashes remained. It is because he has identified the world with his beloved that the loved one's reticence leaves him in poverty. Only if he posits the earth as the sure region does the mortal find before him the spectacle of poverty, which, in the torpor of his earliest years, in sleep, in sickness, in death, brings him face to face with the ashes of the earth. Man is not mortal because he is born and dies: he is born and dies because he is mortal. Death in the biological sense is thus not the completion of mortal life: man can continue to live as a mortal even if he is biologically extinct. The mortal life of man reaches its completion only if the mortal essence of man is brought to setting—only, that is, if the will to die (the isolation of the earth) definitively leaves the eternal appearing of Being.

The eternal guardian of the truth of Being becomes a mortal because, in isolating the earth, he convinces himself of his own nothingness and of his being exposed to annihilation. But dominant Necessity forbids that Being be annihilated: the mortal is convinced of that which cannot occur. (The occurring of this conviction nonetheless determines the way in which he leads his life in the isolation of the earth.) Thus the truth of death concerns the law governing the earth's entering and withdrawing from the eternal appearing of Being. The two ultimate possibilities of the earth are either its totally and definitively abandoning the eternal appearing of the truth of Being, or its continuing to appear along the path of Day.

The first is the possibility of a return to the original dwelling-place of man. If the earth disappears *in toto*, any remembrance of it disappears as well, for remembrance of the occurrence belongs to the occurrence. With the disappearance of the earth, the thought that envelops the occurrence in solitude also disappears (for also the earth's isolation belongs to the earth). The history of salvation would thus be an episode that leaves no trace in the essence of man, which returns to that which man has always been: eternal appearing of the truth of Being and to eternal consciousness of his own eternity. But the recovery of the original dwelling-place is also the recovery of the pure contradiction in which that dwelling-place consists (cf. paragraph XIII).

The other ultimate possibility is the setting not of the earth, but of its solitude and of the mortal essence of man: not, that is, of man's stay on the earth, but of the mortal himself. With this setting, the eternal guardians of the truth of Being dwell on the earth as immortals. The setting of the works of solitude is, then, also the setting of "life" in the biological sense, i.e., as the effort (*bia, vis*) to keep to the shelter of an isolated earth—for "life" is one of the most primordial works of solitude. But this does not mean that the only possible way of living on the earth is the way constituted by biological development, that colors and sounds, forms, fragrances, and pleasures can only appear within such development, and that the birth and death of the body can only enclose all the spectacles of the earth between an initial and a final darkness.

Man has always attempted to escape from biological development as the only way of living on the earth. Nourishment and sexual intercourse, dwelling and tending the fire, hunting, festivals, work, war, and peace were experienced by primitive peoples within a sacred time, where man lived as an "immortal" and left the profane time of biological development behind. When the peoples of the earth were no longer capable of experiencing sacred time, men became mere mortals and the sacral activities of life became *technai*, whose principal task was precisely that of ensuring biological development. This task is now performed by technological civilization which, nevertheless, aims in its turn at a form of transcendence of the biological conditionings of human existence: the expansion of *techne* can indefinitely prolong man's life and give a different meaning to his birth. But *techne* infinitely prolongs *mortal* life: in preventing biological death and satisfying all desires, it modifies the dimension grounded on the mortal essence of man, but does not bring to setting the ground of being mortal. Technological man wills to free himself from death, while maintaining himself within the original will to die. Neither do we know whether and to what extent archaic peoples were able, in sacred time, to bring to setting their mortal essence. Myth and poetry, which in the archaic festival testified to sacred time, say nothing about the truth of Being. Only with the setting of his mortal essence along the path of Day can man live at last as an immortal on the earth.

These two ultimate possibilities—either that the earth definitively abandon the eternal appearing of the truth of Being, or that its manifestation along the path of Day be the total setting of its solitude—enclose all the intermediate possibilities: among them, that the solitude of the earth be the destiny of man, or that traces of solitude be destined to remain also on the path of Day.

Philosophy, as the guardian of the truth of Being, cannot remain indifferent to the world of possibilities. Truth does not know which possibility is the one according to which the occurrence of the earth is accomplished; yet truth also has before it the possibility that there be a link between its own salvation and its way of grasping Being—i.e., its way of *willing* Being. In philosophy, truth is confronted with the offering of the earth, uncontaminated by the isolating conviction. If this first step in the purification of the offering is not taken and preserved, the path of Day cannot enter Appearing. But the path of Day remains a possibility even if the first step is taken. This possibility is also the possibility that the history of salvation be linked to the way in which, in philosophy, truth receives the offering of the earth, thus taking a position with regard to the world of possibilities. In philosophy, truth trusts that its salvation will not be prevented, but rather granted by its trusting in salvation; i.e., it wills that its salvation be granted by its will to salvation. Truth trusts that the offering of the earth will become the offering of Day, if Day is evoked and awaited. The waiting is the trust in, and so the will to, the advent. In philosophy, the setting of the mortal essence of man remains uncertain; but, in philosophy, truth wills that the earth enter upon the path of Day, and that man live as an immortal on an earth no longer bereft of Day. Truth is not disappointed with what is offered, because in the offering it does not see the measure of salvation. And, not being disappointed, it does not give in to the desire to forget itself—as the ground of the disappointment—in the solitude of the earth, but awaits the completion of the revelation of Being.

17. CONSCIOUSNESS OF SELF-CONSCIOUSNESS

The truth of Being is the undeniable. The Being that appears belongs to the truth of Being, because it is undeniable. But the Being that appears is undeniable only insofar as it is *known* to appear; that is, only insofar as its appearing appears. If Being alone—say, this lighted lamp—appeared, while its appearing did not, there would be an equilibrium between the affirmation and the denial of this lamp's being lit. The equilibrium is upset—affirmation is able to negate its negation—insofar as it is *posited* (i.e., insofar as it *appears*) that the lighted lamp appears. The affirmation of the Being that appears can belong to the truth of Being, only if the *appearing* of such Being is posited (i.e., appears). (*Affirming* that this lamp is lit is the very *appearing* of its being lit. The appearing of Being is original saying; and the originally said forms no intermediate zone—such as the dimension of the mind, or the dimension of the proposition or of the judgment—between the saying and the Being that appears. Rather, the originally said is itself the Being that appears. "It is affirmed that the lamp is lit, since it appears that the lamp is lit" means "this affirmation is the very appearing of what is affirmed." The affirmation of the Being that appears, in order to be undeniable, need not be referred to anything other than itself; and therefore it is a moment of the original structure of the truth of Being.)

But the undeniability of the Being that appears requires the positing not only of the appearing of Being, but also of the belonging of Appearing to that dimension whose appearing it is. This dimension is the totality of the Being that appears. In the original structure of the truth of Being, the Being that appears includes its *own* appearing; not only is Appearing posited, but it is posited as the content *of itself*, i.e., this sameness of Appearing and its content is posited (i.e., appears). The Being that appears is undeniable insofar as its appearing is posited; but *that* Being appear is itself an undeniable determination, only insofar as its appearing (i.e., the appearing of the appearing of Being) is posited. *If this positing is understood as subsequent to* the position of the appearing of Being, then this position is not *originally* undeniable—and neither, in this case, is the Being that appears. Nor can it subsequently become so, because, so becoming, the Being that appears would itself become something *grounded, derived*—yet it belongs to the *original* truth of Being. And the ground of this grounded—that is, the position of the appearing of the appearing of Being—would present itself in turn as something groundless (deniable), for *that* the appearing of Being appear is itself an undeniable determination only insofar as its appearing (i.e., the appearing of the appearing of the appearing of Being) is posited. The undeniability of the Being that appears would thus be deferred *in indefinitum*, and therefore essentially compromised.[14] But in the original structure of the truth of Being, the Being that appears *originally* includes its own Appearing: the position (i.e., the appearing) of the appearing of the appearing of Being *is already* the position (i.e., the appearing) of the appearing of Being, or, is already *self*-position, and therefore is not something that has subsequently to be grounded.[15]

"Position of the appearing of Appearing" means "consciousness of self-consciousness." But the consciousness whose content is self-consciousness is the very consciousness that is contained in self-consciousness. "Consciousness of self-consciousness" does not indicate, then, a stratification of three different dimensions, as if there were an Appearing in which only such things as houses, plants, mountains appear (but where Appearing itself does not appear), and then another Appearing in which the first Appearing appears (but the appearing of the Appearing does not), and finally a third Appearing in which the appearing of Appearing appears. Given such a stratification, the undeniability of the Being that appears would be deferred *in indefinitum*. In the original structure of the truth of Being, Appearing is consciousness

---

14   Cf. *La struttura originaria*, Ch. II, paragraphs XI–XV.
15   Cf. ibid., Ch. II, paragraphs XVI–XVII.

of self-consciousness, but such consciousness is that very consciousness of Being which is posited in self-consciousness. Indeed, the
appearing of the appearing of Being (self-consciousness) is affirmed
because it appears, but this latter Appearing (which is itself consciousness of self-consciousness) is that very appearing of Being which is
originally included in the Being that appears. Here, "because" does not
indicate the arising of a *regressus in indefinitum*, but rather the circular
structure of Appearing. If with A1 we indicate the appearing of Being,
A1 originally belongs to the Being that appears. Let A2 indicate A1 as
belonging to the totality of what appears: A2 is nothing other than A1,
but A1 is the appearing of Appearing (it is the appearing of A2), so that
A2 is this very appearing of Appearing. Let A3 indicate this latter
Appearing. Since A2 is nothing other than A3, the relation between
A2 and A3 is self-consciousness and A1 is consciousness of self-
consciousness; but since A1 is nothing other than A3, A3 is consciousness of self-consciousness (and since A2 is nothing other than A1,
"also" A2 is consciousness of self-consciousness). Accordingly, the
structure of Appearing is not an infinite stratification, for while A3 is
indeed consciousness of self-consciousness, it is *that very* consciousness of self-consciousness in which A1 consists. And while self-
consciousness is indeed affirmed because it appears (that is, because it
is the content of consciousness), this Appearing is nothing other than
that A, which is undeniable by virtue of its original belonging to the
Being that appears. The absence of an infinite stratification in the
structure of Appearing is, at the same time, the absence of a regress *in
indefinitum* of the undeniability of the Being that appears.[16]

---

16 Truth constitutes itself, insofar as *Appearing itself* belongs to the Being that
appears. (Appearing "belongs" to or is "included" in the content that appears, in the
sense that a house, the sky, a plant are not Appearing—which, accordingly, is "among"
these determinations; while, on the other hand, the Appearing that appears is the
very appearing *of* all the determinations that appear, and in this sense is not "among"
them, but envelops or embraces them, positing itself therefore *not* as a simple part of
the content that appears, but rather as the very horizon of that content.) As belonging
to the Being that appears, Appearing dwells in it *as Appearing*; that is, as that which
is not merely something posited, but is positing itself and is therefore self-positing.
Precisely because Appearing itself appears—i.e., is self-positing—the self-posited is
self-positing. For positing to posit itself, the posited must not simply be a positing
other things—must not simply be consciousness; otherwise, the "self" could not
constitute itself, or, self-positing, positing itself, would have before it a positing-other

18. THE "I" AND THE BODY

In the truth of Being, Appearing is consciousness of self-consciousness. Being inhabits this absolute self-reflection of Appearing. The eternal appearing of the truth of Being is thus eternal consciousness of self-consciousness, eternal self-reflection in which being dwells.

The eternal appearing of truth is primarily the *actual* Appearing. The actual consciousness of self-consciousness, according to which the truth of Being structures itself, is the original meaning of the word "I." "I" means: "This eternal self-reflection of Appearing, in whose truth Being has always dwelled."

I received Being's offering of the earth and enclosed it in solitude. The earth, occurring in solitude, brings with it this mortal body, where pain and pleasure appear, and which lingers among the nearest of things seen; the occurrence of the earth also brings the feelings and thoughts that come and go in my mortal soul. Isolating the earth, I become one of the things of the earth, I *appear* as one of them. As consciousness of self-consciousness, I forever am; but in me there occurs the isolation of the earth, and it is there—in my mortal soul— that I appear as an earthly thing: as pain and pleasure, joy and anxiety,

---

and not that positing-itself in which self-positing consists, and thus there would be no self-positing. Self-positing is realized only if the "self" of self-positing is itself self-positing, i.e., self-consciousness. Appearing enters *wholly* into its content; it appears there without residue: absolute subjectivity is absolute objectivity. Only the presupposition of the non-objectiveness of thinking leads to the belief that, when one thinks, although a spectacle does indeed take shape within thought, the *appearing* of such a spectacle is not part of the spectacle itself, but rather stands behind it, like a light source that illuminates other things while itself remaining in darkness. Quite the contrary—that which stands behind is that which also stands before, the vault above our heads is the ground beneath our feet, the source that illuminates accompanies the things illuminated.

In the truth of Being, Appearing is therefore not simple consciousness (a positing that is not a self-positing) but *self-consciousness*—which is to say, consciousness of self-consciousness. A1, A2, A3 are the terms by which consciousness of self-consciousness structures itself. But, precisely because Appearing is a positing-itself, *each* of these terms is consciousness of self-consciousness: not in the sense that the same is repeated three times, but in the sense that the act by which each includes the other two is *the very act* with which each of the other two includes the two that remain. If this sameness is not held fast, the self-transparency of Appearing multiplies into an infinite series of self-reflections and the original undeniability of the Being that appears is indefinitely deferred.

thought, and the unity of these determinations and of others as well. Metaphysics, in testifying to solitude, also comes to understand the "I" as self-consciousness and to distinguish the "empirical I" from the "transcendental I"; but it is a thought based upon conviction that the earth is the sure region. Idealism's absolute self-consciousness is the self-reflection of the mortal essence of man.

I, as eternal appearing of the truth of Being, am the original will that wills the continuation and the completion of the occurrence of the earth, in order that salvation be accomplished. In isolation, this will to salvation becomes the will that wills the continuation of the isolated earth and, on it, the continuation of pleasure and of joy. The relation between myself, as eternal appearing of the truth of Being, and the body, as a determination of the isolated earth—as the mortal scene of pain and pleasure—is the will that in the continuation of the earth's isolation pleasure be perpetuated and pain be eclipsed. ("My" body is the locus in space in which pleasure and pain appear. Yet I *believe* that pleasure and pain also appear in a different Appearing from the actual one, and I *believe* that someone else's body is the locus where—in that different Appearing—pleasure and pain appear. But then, pleasure is not a simple quenching of thirst, but is also the green of a spring and the clearness of water, thoughts and feelings that for a moment soothe and console, and thus the whole earth gathered together in a gesture.) We do not know if there ever appeared a golden age, when the offering of the earth was not yet enveloped in solitude and when pleasure, pain, and joy, sounds, colors, and shapes meant something essentially different from that which they mean in solitude (since they did not stand before mortal eyes, but made up the life of immortals on the earth). And thus the relation between the "I" and the body, of which we may speak, passes through the solitude of the earth, in which the body continues to appear and in which the will to the continuation and the completion of the earth is enveloped. The path of Day is now the only way in which the advent of a golden age may be granted. But what traces of solitude are destined to remain on that path? And might man's mortal essence be destined never to set? Insofar as I will the earth, I also will the body (for it is part of the offering of the earth). But I willed them in solitude and now they stand before me as a work of solitude. The path of Day is the possibility of their becoming a work of the truth of Being. If the will with which I willed and isolated the earth is free (if, that is, the history of salvation is not part of the necessary revelation of Being), then the relation between myself and the body is constituted by my freedom, which means that my bodily life is part of the total response that Being grants to my freedom.

19. THE INDIVIDUAL AND APPEARING

The history of metaphysical thought includes both the thesis of the necessary implication between the human individual and Appearing, as well as the opposing thesis of the nonexistence of such an implication. The human individual has been understood, at various times, as "soul" or incorruptible "monad," "body," "unity of body and soul," "*res cogitans*," "empirical phenomenon," "phenomenological determination," "empirical I," "single individual," "worker," and "machine." And Appearing has been understood as *nous*, "mind," "consciousness," "spirit," "subject," "transcendental I," "experience," "thought," and "Appearing." Nihilism is the horizon within which metaphysics thinks the implication and the nonimplication between the human individual and Appearing.

When Marx dissociates himself from Hegel, maintaining that one must not descend from heaven to earth, but rather mount from earth to heaven, he is reproposing the Aristotelian definition of man as *animal rationale* (*zoon logon echon*). This definition has given rise to one of the most deeply rooted convictions of Western common sense: namely, that consciousness is something possessed and produced by the living human individual, an activity which is performed by him— an activity, that is, of which he is the protagonist and author. For Marx, in fact, to mount from earth to heaven means that an authentic consideration of reality must set out from concretely living individuals. Consciousness is exclusively to be understood as *their* consciousness, i.e., as something determined by their real life on earth and not as an autonomous dimension which purports to set itself up as the determining principle of life. This Marxian reaffirmation of common sense will reappear, identical, in Kierkegaard's repeated anti-Hegelian protest that it is I who am thinking, this very flesh-and-blood man, and not "pure speculation."

Feuerbach, on the other hand, stands with Hegel. The divine trinity of man, i.e., the supreme forces—reason, will, and heart—that constitute man's essence, are "above" the individual, who cannot be said to "have," or "possess" them but who, *per contra*, is possessed and ruled by them: I do not possess reason, it is reason that possesses me. And Heidegger echoes Feuerbach when he proposes to overturn the Aristotelian definition of "man," positing *physis* (Appearing) as "being holding man" (*logos anthropon echon*)[17]—and understanding the feeling that reveals the Nothing not as something felt by me or by you, but as an impersonal feeling: *one* feels ill at ease.

But these contrasting positions all move on the common ground of metaphysical "production" (*poiesis*): whether the human individual be posited as the producer of Appearing, or Appearing be posited as the producer of the individual (or as the locus in which production of the individual is realized). Even the Aristotelian distinction between *praxis* and *poiesis* (*Nicomachean Ethics*, 1140a 6) falls within *poiesis*, understood as the cause that leads contingent beings, of whatever kind, from not-Being to Being (*Symposium*, 205b–c). In praxis such beings are immanent in the individual's activity—as is the case with thought, which is realized in the selfsame activity that produces it—while in *poiesis* (as opposed to *praxis*) they are external to it.

For Plato, the human individual is the ungenerated and immortal soul, to which Being eternally appears—even though, in a cyclical process, Being shows it differing contents, as the soul contemplates and lives either in the world of immutable beings, or in the world of beings-that-become. But while for Plato the soul does not produce Appearing, in the sense that it does not pre-exist it and thus does not make it pass from not-Being to Being, in another sense the soul does eternally produce Appearing—it is the cause that makes Appearing eternally stand outside not-Being. For metaphysical nihilism Appearing is not eternal because it is being, but because it is an act that is "performed" (*prattomen*, *Republic*, 436a) in virtue of the "faculty" or "power" (*dynamis*) of a being—called "soul"—which, for various

---

17   Martin Heidegger, *Einführung in die Metaphysik*, Tübingen: Niemeyer, 1953, 134. Heidegger translates *logos* as "being, as emergence and gathering" [*Editors' note*].

reasons, is held to be ungenerated and incorruptible and eternally exercising such a "faculty." Thus nihilism thinks that being, as such, is a Nothing, and that the intervention of a "power"—a "production"—is needed to draw it out of nothingness. Such an intervention can either be realized timelessly—as in the Platonic concept of the relation between soul and Appearing, or as in creation *ab aeterno*—or at a certain moment of the cosmic process. In the latter case, "power" is the cause on account of which things, which earlier were not, afterwards are (*aitia tois me proteron ousin ysteron gignesthai, Sophist,* 265*b–c*).

But empiricism too—classical and logical empiricism alike— remains within metaphysical nihilism.

The empiristic critique of the causal nexus is, at the same time, a critique of that type of causal nexus which is seen in the relation between the human individual and consciousness. Since there is no necessary connection between cause and effect, there is none between the human individual and consciousness either, but only a *de facto* concomitance. The individual is not the protagonist or agent of consciousness—or, in empiristic language, of "experience"—but only a particular content of it, which is included in consciousness in fact, but might also not be so. In Section 484 of *Der Wille zur Macht*, Nietzsche, in agreement with the Humian critique of the principle of causality, writes: "Positing that when there is thought there has to be something 'that thinks' is simply a formulation of our grammatical custom that adds a doer to every deed" (*Dass, wenn gedacht wir, es etwas geben muss, das denkt, ist einfach eine Formulierung unserer grammatischen Gewöhnung, welche zu einem Tun einen Täter setz).*[18] And in the first chapter (paragraph XII) of his *Analyse der Empfindungen*, Mach cites Lichtenberg's polemical observation concerning the Cartesian *cogito*— later to be repeated by Russell and by all the logical positivists—that just as one says "it thunders," so one ought to say "it thinks" (and not "I think"). That experience should include the human individual and the complex of facts and mental processes proper to it, is therefore simply a matter of fact, which allows that a possible experience, no longer containing any human phenomenon, may be projected. This

---

18 Friedrich Nietzsche, *The Will to Power*, ed. and trans. Walter Kaufmann, New York: Vintage Books, 1968, 268.

"world without minds" (most sharply delineated, from the logical positivist standpoint, by Schlick, in *Meaning and Verification* [*Gesammelte Aufsätze*], 338 ff., cf. paragraph V) is not the world realistically understood as independent of mind, but is Appearing ("actual experience"), understood as existing independently of the individual and the human species. For Marx the appearing of Being is a social product, which exists only insofar as human individuals exist; for the logical positivist Appearing is not itself human, but contains the human fact and so can exist even if this fact exists no longer ("the existence of living beings is no necessary condition for the existence of the rest of the world," ibid., 366—where this "rest of the world" is the total horizon of experience). The verifiability, and so—for the logical positivist—the meaning, of this statement demands the possibility of testing what is stated; and since the connection between experience and the human is merely a fact, testing the content of the statement is in fact possible (i.e., an experience containing no type of human event is possible: "verification without a 'mind' is logically possible on account of the 'neutral,' impersonal character of experience," ibid.).

The logical positivist interpretation of Appearing is similar, then, to the idealist one, criticized by Marx, for the logical positivist "man" corresponds to the idealist "empirical I" which, in turn, is not the form, but a particular content of consciousness (i.e., of Appearing, idealistically constituted as "consciousness"). While it is true that, for idealism, the existence of the content of consciousness does not depend on the empirical "I," Fichte, Schelling, and Hegel nonetheless attempted to "deduce" the categorical determinations of this content, showing that the openness of consciousness would not be possible if it did not include such categories and thus the category of the empirical "I" as well. While the content of consciousness does not depend on this or that empirical "I," the existence of a plurality of empirical "I"s is a necessary condition for the existence of consciousness—that is, of the transcendental "I." The crisis of this "deduction"—the crisis of the "System"—brings neo-idealism all the closer to logical positivism, since the contents of consciousness can no longer be posited as necessary categories (the only such category being consciousness as form), but have to be posited as facts, which can thus be replaced by other facts—even though, in neo-idealist circles, there is a tendency to avoid the ultimate consequences of this possibility by continuing to posit the factors of man's physiological structure as "means constitutive of the very nature of the 'I'" (*mezzi costitutivi della natura stessa dell'io*).[19]

In affirming that consciousness exists, *only if* the human exists, one posits a necessary implication between the terms. In non-empiristic metaphysics, action is understood as a necessary implication of this sort. "Man thinks" (i.e., performs the action of thinking) means "Thought exists, only if man exists" (i.e., only if the body, the sense organs, the brain, the spiritual soul, the individual as substantial unity of soul and body, etc.—exist). Empiricism demanded of "metaphysics" the grounding of the "necessity" of this implication; having obtained no such grounding, it legitimately highlighted the implication's gratuitousness. The idealistic "systems" have been the only attempt to ground the necessity of the implication (which for idealism is reciprocal) between thought and the human individual. Through its very attempt to deduce the empirical "I" as the indispensable condition for the openness of thought, Romantic (and above all Hegelian) idealism undertook—in spite of what is constantly asserted to the contrary— the profoundest defense of the single individual, of the empirical "I," of concrete man. And yet, for Hegel, the single individual is eternal *qua* category of singleness, while individuations of the categories of the Idea are the accidental, which issues from, and returns to, nothingness. "Spirit," as self-possession of the Idea, is the principle of the *production* of the individual; just as Aristotle's active intellect—which always thinks and "not sometimes thinks and at other times not" (*all' ouk ote men noei ote d'ou noei*, De Anima, 430a 22)—is the principle of the *production* (in fact it is *poietikos*) of conceptual determinations. Existentialism, too, thinks of the single individual as that which issues from and returns to nothingness; but since existentialism has renounced idealism's dialectic, not only the single individual, but the very category of singleness remains in Appearing as that pure *fact* of which logical positivism speaks. Phenomenological method will not allow the Heideggerian *physis* to contain (*echon*) "man" other than as this pure fact.

---

19 Giovanni Gentile, *Sommario di pedagogia come scienza filosofica*. Bari: Laterza, 1913, Part 1, Ch. XV, paragraph XI.

But also the empiristic position of Appearing as existing independently of the individual and of the human species remains within the horizon of metaphysical thought. Here too, it is thought that beings—in this case, human facts—can not-exist, and can thus be nothing. Once again, the empiristic critique of "metaphysical" causality and production remains within the horizon of *poiesis*, since *poiesis* is the process in which being was, or could have been, a Nothing, and will return, or could return, to being a Nothing. And such a process constitutes itself whether the production and annihilation of being have a cause, or not; whether the demiurge is a being distinct from poiesis, or is identical to it.

20. THE WILL TO POWER

The continuation of the earth is Being's assent to the trust man places in that continuation. Within this trust, man trusts in the transformation and in the correlative permanence of the contents of the earth. He has learned to trust above all in the occurrence of certain movements of his own body and in the occurrence of movements and transformations of other bodies that come into contact with his own. This trusting is the will to stand up, to sit down, to pick something up, to move it; as the trust that our body will continue with the continuation of the earth, it is the will to live.

But, in isolation, the earth stands before man as a Nothing, and thus the trust in its continuing is inevitably accompanied by diffidence. What trust can man have in the earth's continuation when, in the very act in which the earth is posited as the surest of beings, he recognizes its nothingness? When man succeeds in overcoming this diffidence, his confidence in the continuation of the earth becomes "power"—i.e., the "will" to which metaphysics testifies. It becomes the trust in the earth's capacity to break away from its nothingness, to receive and to shelter—thus making them *be*—the pleasure and the joy that are still Nothing, while abandoning to nothingness anguish and pain. At first, man attributed this capacity to the gods—he "willed" the earth through the power of the gods; later, he will attribute it to himself, increasingly seeing himself not only as one of the powers of the earth, but as the supreme power. In pre-metaphysical solitude, Prometheus marks the transition from the power of the gods to the power of the mortals. Aeschylus considers him the source for mortals, of all *technai* (*pasai technai brotoisin ek Prometheos, Prometheus Bound,* v. 166). Prometheus is condemned because Zeus wills to be the sole depositary of *techne*; but the time is already looming when he will rival Zeus in power (*meden meion ischusein Dios,* v. 510).

Technai were a gift to mortals—i.e., to man who came into the solitude of the earth and whose trust in the earth's continuation and completion became the will to power. But the nihilism of solitude and of the will to power, which dominates the thought of every mortal, will be testified to only with the advent of metaphysics; until then, the truth of Being, and solitude—equally unexpressed—contend for Appearing. The truth of Being and the earth's nothingness stood before the mortal, but he did not yet name Being and Nothing. In him, the receiving of the earth in the truth of Being was, at the same time, the will to power, but his works bore mysterious traces of the non-testimony to the contenders. (If *techne* expresses the common essence of Zeus and Prometheus, what abysmal meaning is expressed by immutable necessity [*anangke*], even more powerful than the power of Zeus? —"*Techne* is weaker by far than necessity," *techne d'anangkes asthenestera makro, Prometheus Bound,* v. 514.) But with the metaphysical testimony to solitude, the traces of the contenders were stamped upon the works of mortals with unequal force. The earth is no longer only a work of untruth, but becomes a work of metaphysics. Being responds in different ways to different calls; and the call of the non-testimony is different from that of the testimony. Plato's *techne* testifies to what Aeschylus's *techne* already is, but it is from Plato onwards that mortals began to construct the project of a life on the earth that is coherent with the "world," i.e., with the structure of the earth's isolation as disclosed by the testimony of metaphysics; and therefore it is from Plato onwards that *techne,* as the will to power, produces the works of metaphysics. Yet the truth of Being does not set with the coming of the "world," nor do its traces in the works of metaphysics; the West's metaphysical coherence with solitude unconsciously receives the traces of truth, and thus becomes the encroaching call to which Being responds. It is this very coherence that leads the West to technological civilization. The "world" (and "heaven," too, as the counterpart of "world") is the *ethos* of the West—the *ethos* of mortals, insofar as they testify to their mortal essence.

Also in the history of the "world" the will began by willing the earth through the power of "God" (whence Plato places divine [*theia*] *techne* above human [*anthropine*] *techne*), and ended up seeing itself as the supreme power on earth, able to undertake the domination of man's future and the recovery of his past. Modern science and technology are the way in which the metaphysical coherence of the West came to will the earth. In them, the will sees itself as the supreme power of the earth of that which has now become, *in toto*, Being's response to the encroaching call of the "world."

The thought that guards the truth of Being does not ask itself whether Appearing continues to exist when the human body exists no longer. Rather, it poses the problem of the meaning of the earth's union with the eternal appearing of the truth of Being: the offering of the earth, the earth's isolation, and the body may be part either of the destiny of the appearing of Being, or of its freedom. Within this dominant problem, the question arises of whether and to what extent the appearing of the earth requires the appearing of our body or of other determinations of the earth (such as our thoughts, feelings, desires)—outside of metaphysical nihilism the nexus between the appearing of the earth and the appearing of its particular contents once more becomes a problem. Our body—which belongs to the solitude of the earth—maintains itself in a sort of proximity to Appearing; its absences from Appearing are always followed by a return, and this return to Appearing occurs every time we trust in its occurrence. (In technological civilization even this trust has become a will to power, and both man's body and his soul have become a "machine": the continuation of their occurring has been inscribed in the project of technological control of the occurrence of the earth.) But *that* the appearing of my body be the necessary condition for the appearing of the earth, such that the earth could not appear if my body should definitively disappear—this remains a problem.

21. THE INTERPRETING WILL AND THE POSSIBILITY OF SALVATION

Philosophy cannot yet treasure the confines of the truth of Being (it does not know the system of the determinations of the background); hence it cannot yet measure the confines of the earth. The whole truth of Being eternally appears, but it is a totality open to occurrence: such a totality, therefore, as can constitute itself within the finite appearing of Being. This is to say that philosophy does not know whether its problems—i.e., the problems that present themselves in the testimony to truth—are the problems by which the eternal appearing of the truth of Being is structured, or whether they are due to the limits of the testimony. But if this testimony has limits, it is because the earth's isolation has not set. Not only the earth, but also that of the truth of Being to which philosophy has been able to testify can be isolated from the totality of truth and posited as the sure ground, with respect to which the dimension of truth that is not testified to becomes a problem. The very problems of philosophy can arise from isolation.

Yet one cannot avoid taking a position concerning them. The problem of all problems is the possibility that the history of salvation be linked to the way in which philosophy, as guardian of the truth of Being, receives Being's offering of the earth, and so, taking a position with respect to the problems that envelop it (the realms of possibility), wills the continuation of the earth.

That man be an assembly of peoples, where Being appears in a differentiated plurality of viewpoints, is only a possibility. It is, then, also possible that I—this actual eternal appearing of the truth of Being—am the essence of man, where "others" appear as particular determinations of the earth, as my objects and not as my equals. And the possibility that I am the essence of man is the possibility that my alienation is the essence of alienation. Everything that, in the structure of truth, is given—the body, behavior, and the language of others—is not a problem insofar as it is given (i.e., insofar as it appears), but is so insofar as it is given as *interpretable*. The given, as such, allows *any* interpretation, for interpretation is a unification of givens by means of nexuses not given. The earth may be interpreted as Being's response to my call—the only call—but also as laden with calls and with responses to the calls of peoples. In the latter case too, the earth is the response to my call, but the response also contains the responses Being grants to all the calls of the peoples of the earth.

Interpretation itself is part of the call: it determines the way in which philosophy—willing the completion of the earth—evokes Being. It is through this will that certain givens become the language and the work of peoples; and it is through this will that the history of the West becomes a history of the testimony to the solitude in which peoples have enveloped the earth.

I decide to light the lamp. The decision is the certainty that, with the movement of my hand, the lamp will come on. (And this certainty is the appearing of a problematic content: that the lamp will come on is a possibility.) The appearing of the decision (the appearing of that Appearing which is the decision) is accompanied by the appearing of the arm that reaches out, of the hand that touches the switch, and of the lamp that comes on. But it is also accompanied by the passing of cars in the street, by the playing of children in the garden, by the stillness of the furnishings of my study, and by the entire occurrence of the earth, with which Being responds to the call in which the decision to light the lamp consists. I am, however, *convinced* that this response also contains the response to countless other calls, such as the intention of motorists to go from one place to another, the will of children to play, and the belief in the continuation of the stillness of this room's furnishings. This conviction is the *interpretation* of the occurrence—it is the way in which the ocurrence is *willed*. It is suggested by the difference between the occurrence of that which was decided by me (the lighting of the lamp) and the occurrence of that which was not decided by me (the passing of cars, the playing of children, etc.), or which was not decided by me in a certain moment (in deciding to light the lamp, I did not decide the continuation of the stillness of the furnishings): what was not decided by me, was so decided by others, be they mortals or gods. But truth, testified to in philosophy, is unable to prohibit that the occurrence of the earth be differently willed, and that one come to believe—despite the difference between the occurrence of what is decided and what is not—that the passing of cars, the playing of children, and the occurrence *in toto* belong to Being's response to *my decision* to light the lamp, in the same way as the arm that reaches out and the lamp that comes on do: as the response to a single request—my request; or to the single process of requests that forms my history. Nor can the testimony to truth prohibit *indecision* between these opposing interpretations, and so it cannot prohibit an interpretation that consists in willing the occurrence in the form of indecision regarding such interpretations.

Some black marks on paper become a word when they are understood as the sign of a meaning, or as the invitation to select a certain meaning. A language is an invitation to select certain meanings and to conjoin them in a certain way. Despite all other reasons for understanding something as language, the ultimate reason is the understanding itself—the *conviction*—that something *is* language and is a certain language rather than another. The given is transformed into language—and into a certain language—by the interpreting will; and, here again, the testimony to truth cannot prohibit different interpretations. The West appears as the history of the testimony to the solitude of the earth when the given is transformed into language according to one of the possible interpretations: according, that is, to the one in which I find myself *in fact*, and in which I *believe* (which is to say, I *will*) that others find themselves as well—the interpretation according to which "*on*" is a sign of the meaning "being," "*me on*" is a sign of the meaning "not-being," and "*e gar toi ek tou me ontos eis to on ionti otooun aitia pasa esti poiesis*" (*Symposium*, 205*b–c*) is an invitation to conjoin certain meanings in such a way that they form the statement "Any cause, which makes a thing pass from nothingness to Being, is production."

The Greek language may be interpreted differently from the way that is willed in fact: truth does not prohibit it. Likewise the ensemble of shapes, volumes, colors, sounds, and movements that we call "Milan" may be interpreted as something other than a great industrial city. In coordinating the sign "house" with the meaning *house*, in historical languages (i.e., in the events that the interpreting will transforms into a certain language) it is nearly always possible to coordinate the sign with the meaning initially assigned to it without language's proposing self-contradictory nexuses between meanings. But works, too, are a form of language (and language, in turn, is a work). A house is a place that shelters mortals from the elements. When we say, "Here is a house," we coordinate an ensemble of volumes, shapes, and colors (i.e., that ensemble of events which we call "rooms," "windows," and "furnishings") with the meaning "place that shelters from the elements"; and, here too, as we live in the house it is nearly always possible to coordinate that ensemble with the meaning initially assigned to it without the coordination's positing itself as self-contradictory (as could be the case if a place exposed to all sorts of inclement weather should be understood as "place that shelters from the elements"). The interpreting will is the coordination of signs and of events with meanings. Just as it is the interpreting will that unifies in a single interpretation the treatises of Western theoretical physics, the manuals of construction technique, the directives and designs of architects, the movements of workers and machines in building sites, and the erection and multiplication of new districts of the city. Within this unifying interpretation, even the gestures and movements of the bricklayer and the carpenter appear as part of the logos that today guides the civilization of all peoples on the earth.

The existence of alienation is a problem insofar as it is understood as the alienation of peoples (for the existence of peoples, as a concerted manifestation of being, is itself in the first place a problem). But it is not a problem insofar as it is the alienation of the actual Appearing. All the determinations of alienation belong to the actual Appearing. The position of this belonging is part of the truth of Being. In the actual Appearing the testimony to the truth of Being occurs, but it is continually crossed and enclosed by the time of untruth. But in the *truth* of the earth it appears that the actual Appearing has isolated the earth and testified to the nihilism of solitude. The earth, as it stands before me in this actual Appearing, is *in any case* Being's response to the isolation in which I have enclosed the earth. The description of the earth, as it actually appears, is a description of solitude. The way in which human beings are body and behavior and relate to my body and my behavior is led into Appearing by the way in which I received the offering of the earth. And so too the course of the stars, the sun, and the seasons; so the spreading of the space around my eyes and the gathering of colors and sounds. So the vertiginous growth of cities, of machines, and of goods, and the rhythm of the history of the world. The earth, as it lies in the actual Appearing, does not possess an innocence that would only be compromised by the intervention of the interpretation that wills the earth as the work *of* mortals: this interpretation shows me to be co-responsible—i.e., not the sole protagonist—but co-responsible for a guilt that is *in any case* the earth's.

But in the actual Appearing we also encounter the testimony to truth which carries isolation towards its setting. This testimony has before it the problem of all problems: the possibility that the salvation of truth be granted as the response to the way in which philosophy, repeating the receiving of the earth, wills Being. It is within this will that we find—via the interpretation of languages and of works—the interpretation of the meaning of man. Philosophy wills that I not be the essence of man and that my alienation not be the essence of alienation; so it wills, because it believes (i.e., wills) that salvation and the advent of Day can come forth only if the occurrence of the earth is interpreted (i.e., willed) as the alienation of peoples and as Being's response to their calls. It is through the interpreting will that my alienation extends until it becomes the alienation of peoples and the earth shows itself as a work of the peoples of the West; but it is through the very occurrence of this will that philosophy trusts in the granting of the occurrence of salvation.

CHAPTER III

On the Meaning of the "Death of God"

1. PRE-ONTOLOGICAL AND ONTOLOGICAL LANGUAGE

With the advent of metaphysics, historical languages were confronted for the first time with the testimony to the meaning of *Being* and of *Nothing*. In this confrontation the meaning of every pre-metaphysical word underwent an *essential* transformation. In the light of Being and Nothing life, birth and death, yes and no, pain, love, heaven and earth are divorced from their primitive meaning and given to another, unheard-of meaning. That which came on the scene with the advent of metaphysics was not simply a new world, but rather the *world* itself. The "world" is not an original *physis*, nor is it the gift of a god. It is the *ethos* of the West. Greek metaphysics brought to light the dwelling-place of Western civilization, and this dwelling-place gave its own meaning to everything accomplished within it. The world became the West's dominant thought and force; all aspects, both fundamental and derived, of existence and civilization gradually came to be thought and experienced in the world. By its force, the *ethos* of the world thus became *physis*, the indubitable and evident place where *beings* gather.

In Greek metaphysical thinking, "Being" is any determination, insofar as it is thought in its *Being*. And the "Being" of being is "not-being-a-Nothing": "being is" means "being is not a Nothing." (Heidegger, by contrast, interprets the "Being" of Greek metaphysics as "being present." But *what* is present can be so only insofar as it is not a Nothing—and presence itself can make present only insofar as it, in turn, is not a Nothing. Thus Heidegger's interpretations too, cannot but tacitly posit—in the depths of "Being" understood as presence— the original meaning of *Being*: being as negation of Nothing.) As they gather in the world, beings *become*: they die, are born, are transformed.

From the viewpoint of metaphysics, this means that the beings of the world (wholly or in part, all or some aspect of them) issue from and return to Nothing—passing from their nothingness to being a not-Nothing and vice versa—and that, insofar as they are, they are essentially exposed to the risk of annihilation. If there were nothing, in beings, that became a Nothing—if everything were to remain what it is—how would the becoming of the world be possible? The nothingness of being has become the West's supreme *evidence*, the source from which—even when unknown to us—its *ethos* draws its strength. Before acquiring Being, being is a Nothing; and so it is again when Being has been lost. The supreme evidence of Western civilization consists in the purest and most abysmal alienation—the conviction that being is nothing. It is the meaning that is lived and breathed by every thing and every work in the dwelling-place where our civilization grows. Essential alienation has become the most solid and unquestionable of realities. Have we a firmer conviction than that of our "being in the world"? Yet man began to be exposed to the world—to being in, and coming into, the world—only at a certain point in his history, that is, when the *world* came to man.

Brought into the world for the first time by metaphysics, the meaning of every word loses the intrinsic ambiguity (and mystery) it possessed before measuring itself against the testimony to the meaning of Being and Nothing. What ontological meaning does a language possess when—like every pre-metaphysical language—it does not *testify to* (does not speak explicitly about) the meaning of Being and Nothing? Certain things can be said only insofar as Being is understood in a certain way; but if the saying does not make the meaning of Being *explicit*, we lack the key that would permit us—on the basis of the things said—to discover the meaning of Being illuminating them from the depths. We see the things illuminated, but not the sun that illuminates; we see traces of a sun that remains unknown. Is there—beyond the sun testified to in the *ethos* where Western history grows—another sun? With the advent of metaphysical thought, "God" too comes out of ambiguity and into the world: not in the sense that he is necessarily understood as a "worldly" being (a sensible being, a being that becomes), but rather insofar as he is thought as the very *ground* of the *world*—as that by virtue of which the world is world.

2. THEOS

The Greek word *theos* is constructed upon the root *da*. Primarily, *Da* indicates standing-before, manifest and luminous; thus *Zeus*, the "splendent," is *delos*. But manifestation lets appear and so dispenses differences (as colors are dispensed in light). Thus *da* also indicates dispensing, an allotting which distributes differences; and God, accordingly, is the *daimon* who divides and distributes (*daiomai*) the parts of the whole. But the dispensing of differences demands skill and ability in the dispenser; it demands not only knowledge, but also mastery of the differents, so that *da* also conveys that "technical" capability indicated in such words as "destructive" (*daios*) and "knowledgeable" (*daemon*). All these threads of the root *da* are gathered up in the Word "creator" (*demiourgos*). The *demiourgos* is he who makes his work manifest, and thus public. He is the artificer capable of mastering the differences he makes manifest; differences which, so mastered, become action, deed, work (*ergon*). The *ergon* is the difference mastered and dispensed in the act in which it is made manifest (*demion*). But, then, the demiurge who assigns and distributes the different portions is at the same time the root of all misfortune, both because he may allot what is not wished by the receiver, and because, as the apportionment proceeds, he may destroy the lots already assigned. Thus the destructive sense of the root *da* is already present in *daiomai* (as it is in *daizo* and, less overtly, in *dainumi*), where a sense of distributing and dividing coexists with one of a violent cleavage, i.e., of a laceration of the parts. *Daimon* is the light where the differences allotted manifest themselves, but it is also death and misfortune. In *daios* the link between technical capability and destructiveness is equally close. The technical mastery that mediates between manifestation—light that reveals—and destruction, disappears in other words where sharply contrasting meanings emerge and coexist: *dais* is at once a torch and battle (and *daio*—which also indicates disappearing—includes both the fire's glow and its destructiveness); *dalos* is a firebrand and a flash, but it is also a burnt-out torch and fireless old age. (And, along these lines, the analogy between *deloo*—to show, to manifest—and *deleomai*—to destroy, to damage—may well be more than mere assonance.) If the root *than* is taken as an immediate (in the sense that further back than this one cannot go), one can give short shrift to any question about the etymology of the word "death" (*thanatos*). Yet in all the forms of *thnesko* (to die) we find the root *nek*, as in *nekus* (corpse; cf. *nekros*). And in *nekus*—as in the Latin *nex*, *neco*—we find negation, the *not* (*ne*, *nec*). *Necessitas* is a *ne-cedere*, and the Latins spoke of death as *necessitas* precisely in the sense of ultimate and supreme inflexibility. In light of this, the existence of a root *than* becomes unlikely. It is strange, however, that the word *danos* signifies not only that which is given, assigned, presented, but is also synonymous with *thanatos*. The root *da*, which in *danos* (*daiomai*) indicates the gift divided and dispensed, in *thanatos* is a manifestation of the danger and extreme damage that can be brought about by the dispenser of fate. The dispenser is Zeus, and another name for Zeus is *Dan*. *Dan* is the shower of gold that fecundates Danae (*Danae* is the link between the coming of the golden light of God and the dryness—*danos*—of the parched earth awaiting fecundation) and *Dan* is the slaughter perpetrated by the Danaans. The place where Zeus and *thanatos* are united is the apparition of the God who, dispenser of fate, both renders what is barren fertile and living, and bestows death on life. Thus *thanatos* is essentially a "divine" word—as is its opposite: life, *zoe* (*zao*). *Za* is the earth (*ga*), and the earth, invoked, is *da*; it is the whole which is dispensed and allotted by the God. In this whole, that which is awaited from the earth—life—opposes death.

These traits, which form the pre-metaphysical meaning of the word *theos*, unquestionably contain traces of a way of understanding the meaning of Being. But the traces remain indecipherable. One ought first to establish whether the traits evolve from one to another, on the basis of a substantial solidarity, or whether they are the traces of an abysmal and unexplored discordance in the original appearing of Being.[1] Metaphysical thought, however, does not concern itself with such questions. It brings into the "world" the languages that surround it, in the conviction that, by authentically interpreting them, their hidden ontological meaning will be made explicit. In point of fact, any possible hermeneutics of primitive (i.e., pre-metaphysical) language—including that operated by Western culture, the sole hermeneutics of which we in fact have

---

1 On the meaning of this discordance cf. "The Earth and the Essence of Man."

experience—is a violence in which one *wills* that pre-metaphysical language should speak the tongue of the *ethos* of the West. Thus it must be said that Christianity underwent the violence of this will, not only because it was offered to us in a Greek tongue which had already been captured by the "world," but also because subsequent metaphysical-theological reflection explicitly interpreted—i.e., *willed*—the Message in the light of the world.

3. THEOS IN THE NONAMBIGUITY OF ONTOLOGICAL-METAPHYSICAL LANGUAGE

What occurs when *theos* is brought into the world?

From the viewpoint of metaphysics, being can be—i.e., can exist—only if its existence is ensured by a *ground*. Otherwise, being, as being, cannot exist: it is a Nothing. "A creature receives being from outside" (*Esse non habet creatura nisi ab alio*). "Left to itself" (*sibi relicta*)—taken, that is, apart from its relation to the ground—the creature "in itself is nothing" (*in se considerata nihil est*). "Hence, in it, nothingness precedes being" (*Unde prius naturaliter inest sibi nihil quam esse*, Thomas Aquinas, *De aeternitate mundi*, 7). Yet, even "*sibi relicta*," the *creature* is not a Nothing. In positing that *the creature*, "*sibi relicta*," is a Nothing, metaphysical thought intends to differentiate this affirmation from the affirmation that *the Nothing* is nothing. It intends to posit *being* as the subject of the affirmation, and as the predicate *of being* it posits Nothing. The "Being that subsists in itself" (*ipsum Esse subsistens*) is the Being [*Ente*] that has its Being [*Essere*] in itself, the Being [*Ente*] that, "*sibi relicta*," is not a Nothing. But the existence of the Being has to be *demonstrated*, and metaphysics attempted to develop such a proof in various ways. Metaphysics is the essential belief that being, as being, is nothing. But at the same time, and no less essentially, it conceals this faith by proclaiming the opposition of Being and Nothing. The "principle of noncontradiction" is the position of the nothingness of being, expressed (and concealed) as not-nothingness of being. The "world" is the place where one *believes* that the issuing from, and returning to, nothingness of beings (their having been, and returning to being, a Nothing) is tangibly evident. If one posits that, in

Becoming, being has been and returns to being a Nothing, one thinks that being is nothing.

The essence of nihilism most radically manifests itself in this thought. For Nietzsche, nihilism is the fundamental process and the very law of Western history. In its original meaning, it is the unfaithfulness to the earth which confers all value on what lies beyond the earth, i.e., on Nothing. In approaching the question of the essence of nihilism, Heidegger credits Nietzsche with having grasped some traits of nihilism, but faults him for having interpreted them nihilistically. For Heidegger, in fact, the essence of nihilism is the interest in being, i.e., the appearing of the totality of being, as forgetfulness of the "truth of Being." The "truth of Being" is, for Heidegger, the presence itself of being. The interest in being, in which metaphysics consists, culminates with Nietzsche in the identification of Being with the will to power. In forgetfulness of Being, Being is not allowed to be that which it is *qua* Being—namely, the arising and disclosing of presence. Here, as Heidegger puts it, lies the ultimate "killing" of Being. On the basis of its forgetfulness of Being metaphysics identifies Being [*Essere*] with being [*ente*], and the totality of being becomes the object of technological production and destruction.

Heidegger too, like Nietzsche, unquestionably grasps some of the essential traits of nihilism; but, like Nietzsche, he also understands them nihilistically. And so, once again, he misses that which is missing throughout the course of Western thought: the authentic essence of nihilism. For Nietzsche's thought too, like Heidegger's, moves within the "world," which is to say, within the horizon of the faith of being's nothingness. The history of metaphysics as science is the dialectical development of the attempt to think the world without contradiction, which is to say, of the attempt to bring about in a noncontradictory and incontrovertible manner the concealing and the masking of nihilism.

In Greek and medieval metaphysics, the possibility of the world's becoming demands the affirmation of the existence of an immutable Being (*Ente*). Thus, for metaphysics, God (*theos*) comes to signify the Immutable. But *theos*, as we have seen, represents an interweaving of meanings of the pre-metaphysical root *da*. Confronted with the thought of Being and Nothing, the strands of signification divide and the capacity to dispense fates and so to master things, assigning them birth, form, and death, comes to the fore. *Theos* is less and less thought as the light and the manifestation of the offering and more and more as the Almighty who masters the Being of beings. In the world beings pass from not-Being to Being. But for Greek metaphysics beings cannot come to be from Nothing: they pre-exist in the Immutable, which dispenses them in the sense that it makes them pass from not-Being to Being and from Being to not-Being. In this sense *theos* is the demiurge, the producer and destroyer *of beings*. The element that transfigures the pre-metaphysical meaning of *theos* consists precisely in this: that dispensing, mastering, and dividing produces, destroys, and transforms *in the world* the Being of beings. As immutable being, *theos* becomes the most radical expression of nihilism: for he is thought as the supreme ground of *the nothingness* of being. The ambiguous and mysterious character of the pre-metaphysical word *theos* is altogether superseded in the rational clarity of nihilism, where *theos* is the "technical" power that dominates the Being and not-Being of beings. The "world" is the place where being displays its own nothingness and where God and man are able to make being identical to Nothing. The evidence of the world, which becomes the dominant thought of Western civilization, is in fact also the basis of immanentistic metaphysics, where divine technique (*theia techne*) is made immanent in the world. If for classical metaphysics this is held to be unthinkable without immutable being, modern metaphysics realizes that the evidence of Becoming makes any pre-existing immutable reality impossible. The creation and destruction of beings is itself the immanent process of their becoming. Thus Nietzsche's proclaiming that "God is dead" means that the world has realized not only that it has no need of a transcendent immutable being, but that such being would make man's creativity impossible. It must then be said that, from the standpoint of thinking that remains within the metaphysical essence of *techne*, the principle of the nihilation and nothingness of being is no longer a God, but the *Übermensch*. For there remains in the *Übermensch* the fundamental trait by which nihilism thinks *theos*—a trait which cannot but remain in the Heideggerean reflection on the essence of nihilism too, since for Heidegger the existence of the world is indisputably evident. Indeed it is precisely because the "world" exists—precisely because the totality of beings-*that-become* appears—that, for Heidegger, Being withdraws and, concealing itself, perishes. Moreover, it is part of the very essence of Being that, at a certain point in Western history, *techne* should realize itself as effective production and destruction of beings. Here too then, the nothingness and nihilation of being is understood as incontrovertible and manifest fact and reality. And technological civilization is understood as the way in which this *reality* is experienced today.

But when grasped in its authentic essence, nihilism is the belief that what has never been and will never be *is*. The basis of Western civilization is the conviction that being, as such, is nothing. Yet being is not a Nothing, which means that divine and human *techne* is not the effective capacity to identify being with Nothing, but rather is that way of entering into relation with the Being of being, where every aspect of the relationship is determined by the faith that the nothingness of being (namely, that which cannot be) is. For Heidegger an ineluctable development leads from Greek *techne*, understood as disclosure, to modern technology as productive-destructive violence. What Heidegger fails to discern is that, in Greek *techne*, disclosure is the disclosing of the world, *which is to say* of being understood as nothing (and this because *poiesis* does not bring to light that which is immutable and eternal, but rather being that issues from and returns to nothingness). Greek *techne*, as disclosure, is the very evidence of the world, namely, of that horizon within whose circle all the productive-destructive violence of modern technology is made possible. Precisely because Greek metaphysics posits the disclosure of the nothingness of being, modern technology can undertake to scientifically control the creation and nihilation of being—that is, to control and promote that which in traditional metaphysics was the work of God. In the history of the West production-destruction of the Being of beings is fundamentally understood as "God" and as "technology," which are thus the two fundamental forms of nihilism. The essential meaning of modern technology is already contained in the metaphysical meaning of *theos*. Any project of techno-scientific transformation and domination of the world tacitly posits an openness of the horizon within which being can issue from and return to nothingness. *Theos* was the original way in which metaphysics thought the condition for the possibility of this horizon.

4. THE ETHOS OF THE WEST AND THE CRITIQUE OF WESTERN CULTURE

Today, nihilism interprets the development of Western civilization as a development of "nihilism" (known in its inauthentic essence). This means that the authentic essence of nihilism (namely, the openness of the world as nothingness of being) continues to remain concealed and nihilism's essential traits continue to be interpreted nihilistically. Nihilism, as the meaning of Western history (from its root in Greek metaphysics), comes to fruition in Western science and technology. But this sequence must be understood altogether differently from the way nihilism understands the relationship of metaphysics-science-technology. As long as one remains within the world, even the affirmation that this relationship reflects the "history of nihilism" cannot be understood other than nihilistically. Nihilism today is so dominant that it presents itself by denouncing the inauthentic ways of understanding the essence of nihilism. Words of alienation sound just like words of truth.

The "global challenge" [*contestazione globale*] to consumer (or "affluent") society was proclaimed during the 1968 upheavals. This aimed at the refusal not of this or that aspect of society, but rather of its basic structure, i.e., of the dominant thought that sustains it. But here the problem arises. Are those who "challenge" the Affluent Society capable of identifying its basic structure? Moreover, is *anyone* in our culture capable of such a diagnosis? These are the questions which must be answered before considering the reasons which underlie the refusal of our society.

It is evident today that technological development has been bringing about a crisis in great traditional ideologies such as Christianity and Marxism. But the authentic meaning of the dissolution of traditional civilization brought about by technology is by no means clear. From a renewed Enlightenment standpoint, it is believed that science and technology have instituted a way of living that definitively and radically supersedes the fundamental traits of Western tradition. Or, from the standpoint of the beautiful souls who intend to defend this tradition, technological civilization is condemned precisely because it breaks down traditional values. Or—and this point of view is as widespread as it is banal—one does not wish to give up the advantages of technological progress, but rather to "spiritualize" and harmonize them with the values of past cultures which at various times have been considered sacrosanct. In all cases, even when one endeavors to reconcile technological with traditional culture, their heterogeneity, or at least their mutual indifference, is taken for granted. And even if one does succeed in discerning that one implies the other, one still remains within the dominant *ethos* of the West, which means that it is still impossible to discern in the dissolution of traditional civilization the inevitable development of the authentic essence of nihilism. Technological culture, in the openness of the world and as dominated by that openness, is the natural and legitimate offspring of humanistic culture. Christianity and traditional theology naturally and legitimately engender the atheism, immoralism, and anti-Christianity of our time. The myth of force is the inevitable product of the myth of culture. Technology is the natural and legitimate heir of God. Underlying the great oppositions of Western history (force-culture, Christianity-anti-Christianity, lord-bondsman, absolutism-democracy, humanism-technicism, metaphysics-antimetaphysics, capitalism-communism) is a single dominant thought which constitutes the spirit of our time—the one and only spirit of a time that goes all the way from Greek philosophy to the Affluent Society. Thus the dissolution of the old civilization in the new is in fact the celebration of the essence of the old civilization—it is the growing dominance of the West's fundamental thought.

Christianity, heretical movements of the Middle Ages, modern Utopianism, Rousseauian return to nature, Marxist revolution, the *Übermensch*, Husserl's and Heidegger's critique of technological society, the dissolution of traditional culture brought about by technological progress—all represent "global challenges" to the society of their day. Yet all of them operate within the dominant thought of Western civilization, and therefore fall short of that which they set out to be: namely, an essentially radical refusal. Such challenges neither go beyond nor change the horizon within which they move; and the history of Western revolutions therefore has been nothing but the progressive realization and coherency of an original manner of thinking and experiencing Being. Until the West really understands the fundamental trait that dominates it, no authentic alternative to technological civilization will be possible. But there are no signs that the moment of such supreme self-criticism is near. Quite the contrary, it is clear to us all that the signs portend the greatest glories of technological civilization, which is the most rigorous and powerful expression of the essence of the West. In this situation, global challenges can only be the effort—often successful—to make the technological organization of society more efficient, and Marcuse's "Great Refusal" of advanced industrial society is merely the refusal of those obstacles which, in his view, hinder such efficiency.

"Production" and "destruction" are the fundamental categories of that technological civilization which today projects the production-destruction of the whole world. The goals technology undertakes to produce through a system of scientifically controlled procedures are no longer only everyday objects, but include the great myths of pretechnological civilization—liberation from pain and death, the *Übermensch* and deification of the human essence, and paradise itself. This productive-destructive outlook presupposes that the very essence of "things" is that they let themselves be produced and destroyed. It presupposes, that is, the "world," as the scene of things which before being born were nothing and which after their death return to nothingness once more; things which therefore—precisely because of their availability and docility in the face of birth and death—can become objects of calculated production and destruction. Only if one *thinks* Being and Nothing—only then do birth and death take on that lucidity and intransigent ineluctability of meaning characteristic of our culture and our way of living. The meaning of Western civilization was established by Greek metaphysics, not because it is the "oblivion of Being" of which Heideggerean nihilism speaks, but because it established the nothingness of being which makes every sort of technological violation of the earth possible. If metaphysics has not simply remained an abstract mode of thought, cultivated by a narrow circle of people, but has become the cities and machines, the industrial and ideological organization of our civilization, this is due to the fact that only if one thinks that being issues from and returns to nothingness can one then project the total construction and destruction of being. The history of the West is the process in which metaphysical thought attains rigor and coherency. Once metaphysics has brought the world to light, it is both inevitable and legitimate that God should die and find his truth in technology, as religion does in atheism and as pre-technological civilization does in technological civilization. In this way, in fact, the "world" is coherently realized.

The history of Christianity reflects this process of the rigorous development and progressive dominance of nihilism. The history of Christianity is in fact the history of the alliance of Christianity with the emergent forms of nihilistic domination (and as such it is the history of the capture of Christianity by nihilism): with Greek metaphysics, with modern science, and, now, with technological civilization. The most significant episode of this third alliance is the Catholic Church's opening to the world, an opening which essentially goes together with the effort to "demythologize" Christianity. Any form of "demythologization" in fact remains wholly within the fundamental and dominant Western myth: namely, the *world* itself. It serves, indeed, to strengthen that myth, because it propagates the conviction that we are now moving towards a point where the Christian message can at last be liberated from any superstructure.

Critiques of advanced industrial society are in turn nothing but attempts to make the basic structures of technological civilization more coherent and radical. They belong, that is, to the movement by which nihilism makes itself increasingly rational and powerful. It is a fact that modern technology is today capable of liberating man from hunger, depersonalized labor, and much of the pain and anguish that still oppresses him. Yet we see the productive apparatus diverted towards the ever greater production of means of destruction and defense. The reason for this is to be found in the will to defend a certain ideological structure of society (be it democratic or communist, capitalist or proletarian, Christian or secular) in the conviction that, in a society so structured, man, or a privileged group of men, can find a way to happiness. But ideological liberation from pain (whether Christian, secular, or Marxist) still moves within the world; and within the world the most radical liberation from pain today increasingly means technological liberation. The defense of ideologies (and the offensive-defensive mobilization it entails) thus delays the realization of that happiness which man can attain within the world (within, that is, the essential alienation of the West).

Western culture can offer no alternative to its own dominant thought. Nor can the alternative come from those forms of civilization—such as primitive ones—which developed without rising to the level of metaphysical thought. Does not the authentic alternative—the essential and supreme revolution—now in fact demand that the world be brought to setting, and thus that heaven too, as counterpart of the world, should set? With the setting of the world the meaning of pre-metaphysical language opens itself anew to a hitherto unattempted interpretation. In such an interpretation, what would *theos*—a word belonging to the tongue in which we first received the Christian message—become? The unattempted interpretation is not a return to pre-metaphysical language, but is the will that can will that this language not speak the tongue of the world. If the setting of the West implies the setting of the world, to wait for the setting is the decisive step: for it is here, in the waiting, that one begins to pay attention to the authentic meaning of the truth of Being, and so to recognize the abysmal impotence of the civilization of power. One begins to discover the sickness unto death. But who pays any heed? The West is a sinking ship, but instead of looking for the leak in the hull everyone is busy trying to make the sailing smoother. Therefore only immediate problems are the order of the day, and one recognizes that problems have a meaning only if the specific techniques for resolving them are already in sight. But how will true health come, unless we can discover the true sickness?

CHAPTER IV

Alienation and the Salvation of Truth

1. THE INTERPRETING WILL AND THE "WORD OF GOD"

It is often said that historical documents and remains have to be interpreted. Interpretation consists in inserting their immediate meaning into a broader semantic area. Thus the meaning of a Greek temple comes to include the history of the Greek people, and the meaning of the Bible extends so far that it coincides with a complete theological elaboration of the "revealed Word." Yet interpretation begins to work at a far deeper and more original level. This is the case, not so much because the philological reconstruction of a text or the liberation of a Greek temple from subsequent superstructures are themselves based upon criteria which are in turn forms of interpretation; nor is it because we interpret not only the documents and remains of the past, but also the languages and works of the present. Interpretation begins to work on a far more original level, because the very existence of languages and works does not begin to manifest itself—that is, does not supervene in the horizon of the appearing of being—independently of interpretation. Without the intervention of interpretation, not only do languages and works not reveal the pregnancy and complexity of their meaning, but they do not appear as—indeed, are not—languages and works at all. Inscriptions on stone and the flight of birds first begin to appear as *word*, only when one looks beyond their immediate appearance and understands them as visible signs or aspects of a meaning (of a different meaning, that is, from the meaning in which they themselves consist). The meaning of which they are the sign and aspect also appears—in the vaticination there appear the favorable and adverse fortunes, which are read in the flight of birds—but interpretation adds a *nexus* to what appears, which posits a certain meaning, i.e., a certain being (the cut stone, the flight of the birds) as the sign and aspect of another meaning (the sentence cut in stone, the fortune).

Interpretation brings language into Appearing, in the same way as it does works and "things." Even the simplest and most common "things" of the world in which we live—a table, a glass, a stone, a tree—are not simply something given, but are the result of an interpretation of what is given. A glass, even when I have finished drinking and put it back on the table, is still, for me, a glass; that is, something which still has its capacity to be used in a certain way. Even if, as autumn turns into winter, the tree outside my window has become a mere trunk, it still, for me, remains a tree; namely, a living thing which in spring will put forth new shoots. But the glass appears as a glass and the tree as a tree, when the brilliant transparency of crystal is understood as the sign and visible aspect of a lasting capability of containing wine or water, and when the stark figure of a trunk is understood as the sign and visible aspect of a life that, despite being dormant, continues. Just as certain sounds from a man's mouth or certain strokes cut in stone or drawn on paper begin to appear as "word," and as determinate "word," when interpretation posits them as the aspect and sign of a certain meaning, so something begins to appear as a tree when interpretation assumes a dark, oblong, and rugose figure as the sign and aspect of vegetal life. The way in which the dark figure of a trunk is the sign and aspect of vegetal life is not identical to the way in which *physis* is an aspect and sign of such life (it may be said, for example, that in the first case the sign and aspect are correlative with an "individual," and in the second case with an "essence"; that in the former the sign is the sign of a thing, and in the latter is the sign of a sign). But in both cases the meaning of something is made to assume a meaning which is broader and more complex, the immediate meaning being posited as the sign and visible aspect of the further one. The aspect is the original sign of a thing; indeed, so original that it is part of the thing itself. A sign is an aspect that may be so inessential to a thing that it is not even considered a property of that thing. And yet we possess no absolute criterion capable of convincing us that language is itself an inessential aspect of the things of which it speaks.

Yet neither do we have an absolute criterion permitting us to incontrovertibly posit something as the sign and aspect of something else.

Interpretation brings into Appearing languages, works, "things"—the very history of man as an immense interweaving of the totality of references from signs to that which they designate; but interpretation is an interpreting *will*, which does not manifest the *necessity* of the nexus joining the sign to the designated. Rather, it imposes this nexus, which is to say that it *wills* it as such. As long as the necessity of the nexus remains unknown—and so remains a mere possibility—history is the interpreting will itself which, in the horizon of the appearing of being, *decides* that certain beings shall be the aspect and sign of others. Where there is no Necessity—*Anangke* is the dwelling-place of truth— any sort of grounding of the nexus between signs and the designated is in its essence the decision to establish such a nexus.

Any empirical verification of this nexus consolidates the decision but does not change its essence. Every time one encounters *anthropos* traced on paper, one interprets this optical fact as a Word—that is, as the way in which the Greek language designates man. On the basis of this interpretation, the diverse contexts in which *anthropos* appears are wont to acquire a meaning held to be acceptable. But this empirical verification of the use of the word *anthropos* does not rule out the possibility that the optical fact *anthropos* (and its context) is not a word (sign, aspect) at all, or that it speaks of something other than that of which it has been thought to speak for millennia (where, once again, it is interpretation itself that wills the existence of this time-honored faith). That which from a hermeneutical, historical, glottological, and scientific standpoint is an impossibility (that *anthropos* signify "man" is an axiom of the "human sciences"— *Geisteswissenschaften*—and the denial of such an axiom is, here, an impossibility), is, on the contrary, a genuine possibility if measured against the *Anangke* of truth. Each time wine is poured into a glass, it is held by the bottom and the sides: interpretation, which wills that the empty space enclosed by the brilliant transparency of crystal be capable of holding the wine poured into it, is thus empirically verified; but, once again, such verification does not discover a necessary nexus between the empty space enclosed by crystal and the capability of holding wine, and therefore does not rule out the possibility of a different interpretation, which establishes different nexuses and gives rise to new worlds.

A stone, fire, rain, one's neighbor, a house, peoples and their customs and histories, their words and the words of the gods are, unquestionably, beings that appear. But these beings are the nexuses willed by the interpreting will. This does not mean eliminating the difference between the given and the interpreted, but rather that the given meaning of the world manifests itself enveloped by the meaning that is willed (and not only is the meaning of the present and of the future willed, but that of the past as well). This will is not something merely arbitrary and conventional (as is the case in the logical positivist reassertion of Hermogenes' thesis advanced in Plato's *Cratylus*), but is the situation in which we find ourselves and from which at present we have no way out, even if we know that other situations—and so another meaning of the world—are possible. (And yet, that *we*—myself and others—find ourselves in this situation is itself a result of interpretation; the world is interpreted in such a way that, within certain limits, my neighbor is posited as interpreting the world in the same way in which I myself interpret it.)

The interpreting will also brings to light the "Word of God." Even before having faith in this Word and its infallibility, one must have faith in its existence—one must will that certain facts be the sign and aspect of a Message of salvation. In the beginning, there is no hearing of the Word, but rather the will that the Word shall be. The appearing of the Word is the appearing of this interpreting will—which is the basis of religious faith and of the lack of faith alike. Hearing the Word therefore means, primarily, hearing the *will*, which is itself the original faith in which the Word is evoked. If the peoples of the earth are engaged in hearing the Word, this, in turn, is willed by the interpretation that brings them into the appearing of being and interprets them as a waiting for God. Even if it is possible to speak of an infallibility of the "people of God" which cannot let itself be crushed by the will and the intelligence of the individual *qua* individual, it is, at the same time, the interpreting will itself that wills the real existence of the people of God and their infallibility, and so brings into Appearing that which, independently of the interpreting will, would appear as a merely possible essence.

2. THE PRINCIPLE OF NONCONTRADICTION AND EXPERIENCE

Once the interpreting will has brought the history of human existence into Appearing, the history of the West inevitably shows itself to be the development of the deepest and most essential alienation of man. Yet the meaning that Western history inevitably acquires on the basis of the interpreting will is also the most deeply hidden and unknown part of this history. Every historical denunciation of the alienation of man—be it religious denunciation of the *status deviationis* or Marxian denunciation of economic alienation, psychoanalytic denunciation of psychological alienation or the philosophic denunciation voiced by Plato and Hegel, by Nietzsche and Heidegger—in fact grows within a common, invisible horizon which encloses and guides the history of the West and, now, of all the peoples of earth. The openness of this horizon is the essential alienation in which our history unfolds. Greek metaphysics opened the horizon of essential alienation: the hidden ground of metaphysical thought is the abysmal conviction that *being, as being, is nothing*.

As long as one remains within the horizon of alienation, such a statement cannot but seem utterly irresponsible. Everything we know of Greek thought most explicitly contradicts it. It is certain that the opposition of beings to Nothing is the basis of Platonic and Aristotelian thought, which, with respect to Eleaticism, introduces a new meaning of Being, positing Being no longer as mere indeterminate Being, but rather as the concrete totality of beings. And it is certain that the principle of noncontradiction is itself the most explicit and radical expression of the opposition of being to Nothing. In what way, then, can it be said that the ground of metaphysics—and so the ground of the entire history of the West—is the persuasion that being, as being, is nothing?

And yet, in the principle of noncontradiction the nothingness of being is essentially affirmed in the very act in which one intends to most peremptorily exclude it. It manifests itself in the form of its opposite. The recovery of the hidden essence of the principle of noncontradiction has nothing to do with the interminable series of critiques that the principle has undergone in Western thought. And this is not only because—as Book IV of Aristotle's *Metaphysics* shows—any such critique is grounded on the very principle it seeks to deny, but because the sphere in which critiques move is essentially dominated and determined by that abysmal conviction of the nothingness of being whose strictest—and most masked—formulation is the principle of noncontradiction itself. In one of its fundamental formulations, the principle of noncontradiction denies that *the same (to auto) can be and not be at the same time (kata ton auton chronon einai kai me einai, Metaph., 1061b 36).* This means, on the one hand, that *the different* can be and not be at the same time; which is to say that, at a given time, some beings are and others—those not yet generated or already destroyed—are not. And, on the other hand, it means that, at different times, the same thing is and is not: before it is born and after it has perished it is not, while between its birth and its death it is. The principle of noncontradiction essentially includes the belief that beings may not be. And it does so even when, in it, no mention is made of time at all, since the being whose noncontradictoriness is posited is thought as that which, as such, can not-be. The principle of noncontradiction establishes the opposition of being to Nothing, but it is *being insofar as it is* that is opposed to Nothing, and not being insofar as it is not—where this "insofar as it is not" expresses an essential aspect of being *qua* being.

Metaphysical thought surpasses Eleaticism because it sets against Nothing not only pure indeterminate Being, but *any* determinate being: "non-Being is not a something, but is nothing" (*me on ouch en ti, alla meden, Plato, Republic, 478b–c*): *any* something (*ti*), i.e., *any* being is not-nothing. And yet metaphysics is the faith that being, *qua* being, may not-be (insofar as it is not yet born, or has already perished, or insofar as, being, it could not-have-been or not-be). The gods of metaphysics are eternal, ingenerable, and incorruptible not *qua* beings, but insofar as they are beings privileged with respect to beings that can not-be. Independently of such privileges, being *qua* being may not-be. In affirming that being is not (when it is not, or insofar as it might not-be), metaphysics thinks that not-Nothing is nothing.

In opening the horizon of the nothingness of being, where being issues from and returns to Nothing and endures as that which might have been, or might be, a Nothing, metaphysics prepares the dimension in which the techno-scientific project of the production-destruction of being as such can operate. One can undertake to produce and destroy the totality of being, only insofar as being was initially thought as a Nothing. The greatest and inevitable blindness of present-day empirical-positive-scientific-operative-antimetaphysical thought lies in its inability to discern its own essential alienation, and so its own metaphysical essence. From Greek metaphysics to techno-logical civilization, alienation has forgotten the Being of being, sepa-rating being from its Being. The Being of being is the *not-being-a-Nothing* of being: saying that being *is*, means saying that being is not a Nothing. Alienation thinks that being may not-be (when it is not, or insofar as it might have not-been or could not-be)—and in this very separation of being from its Being, alienation thinks that not-Nothing is nothing. The history of the West is the rigorously consistent devel-opment of the attitude that thinks and experiences being as a Nothing; and so, in the strictest sense possible, it is the history of nihilism.

In this history, the mammoth attempt to construct an incontro-vertible and infallible knowing is, in its hidden essence, the very attempt to posit, incontrovertibly and infallibly, the nothingness of being. In Western culture any incontrovertible and infallible knowing is *ybris*. But this affirmation has nothing to do with any form of scepti-cism, problematicism, or historicism, for the essential alienation of the West may be uncovered only by a thinking that has in some way freed itself from that alienation and testified to the truth of Being. Even today the principle of noncontradiction and experience remain the ground of any attempt to construct an incontrovertible and infallible knowing. If in the principle of noncontradiction the opposition of being to Nothing is dominated and sustained by the conviction of the nothingness of being, from Aristotle to Husserl the position of experi-ence as first principle, indemonstrable and *per se* evident, is not a letting beings be just as they appear, but rather is a receiving that which appears within the conviction of the nothingness of being. This faith thus becomes the certainty that the nothingness of being is not a mere concept of reason, but is the supreme and concrete *evidence* men have constantly before their eyes. Is experience not in fact the indisputable attestation that beings are born, undergo transformation, and die—in short, that they issue from and return to nothingness? Beings have been and return to being a Nothing—is not this the supreme and supremely evident law of the "world"? But thought that testifies to the truth of Being has the task of bringing the "world" to its setting. The things of the "world," which (from the viewpoint of alienation) are still a Nothing or have already become a Nothing, *cannot appear*, that is, cannot be present in experience just as they are when it befalls them to be. But, then, how can we affirm of what is absent from experience—of what, insofar as it is not, must also be absent from experience—that experience *attests* its nullity and annulment in the process of Becoming? Thought that brings the "world" to setting does not seek to deny what appears, but rather truly *hears* the beings that appear, and in the truth of its hearing Becoming and history present themselves as the process of the manifestation of the immutable totality of being. As in the orbit of the sun, Becoming is the manifestation of the immutable.

As the horizon of the alienation of the meaning of Being, the "world" has nothing to do with any form of worldly outlook: spiritualism, mysticism, and transcendentalism are just as much part of the "world" as materialism, secularism, and immanentism; the heavenly city just as much as the earthly city. The nothingness of being is just as essential to the concept of a divine creator as it is to that of a human creator. Alienation is much discussed, but to know what true alienation is one must know how to testify to the truth of Being. Without this reference to truth, as the locus in which the original meaning of *Anangke* opens (and so as the locus of incontrovertibility and infallibility itself), that which for some is alienation is for others salvation; and conflicts between opposing conceptions of the world are collisions between opposing wills to power. Each of these wills to power wills to impose its own way of dominating beings—to impose, that is, its own way of organizing in the "world" the nothingness and nihilation of beings in view of happiness on earth and the soul's salvation. In the absence of truth, the clash of cultures and of conceptions of the world is a clash of forces, where opposed motives and reasons serve only to mask the essential untruth of the forces. Here, "truth" inevitably comes to be impersonated by the force that predominates, and the very refusal of the will to power becomes a form of that selfsame will. As long as one is in the "world," any condemnation of the will to power is destined to remain groundless, since the original expression of the will to power is the very openness of the "world" as the horizon in which unlimited dominion over the totality of being is made possible.

3. "WORLD" AND "WORD OF GOD"

In our history, the "world," as the horizon opened up by metaphysics, has become the only hearing. Every event in Western history arises within this sick hearing, which makes dissonant even the "Word of God." For a long time and in a variety of ways, modern humanism has accused Greek thought of stifling the spirit of Christianity. The Catholic Church, having increasingly adopted this view, is today thought to be at a decisive turning point. Critiques of traditional theology and of the traditional forms of the political organization of the Church are directed against a culture that is directly dominated by Greek thought. The Church today is in the process of replacing a cultural structure animated by Greek metaphysics with a structure that is increasingly determined by the most typical forms of modern culture. It believes less and less in philosophy, and more and more in science and technology. The task of determining what "nature" is, and so of determining what is in agreement with it and what is not, has now fallen to scientific knowledge. When theology will have to confront the question of the transplant of a human brain, it will be up to science to verify the permanence of the "person"; and such a methodological verification must inevitably be accompanied by a scientific determination of the meaning of man.

While the alliance of Christianity and the Church with modern culture is profoundly coherent, this coherence remains unknown. Indeed, it is interpreted as a revolution. One fails to see the fact that modern culture and technological civilization are the way in which the horizon opened up by Greek metaphysics—the horizon of the West's essential alienation—manifests itself and dominates today. The opening of Christianity and of the Church to the "modern world" is thus an opening to the strictest and most powerful form of alienation; and the opening we are witnessing today is totally consistent with the initial opening to Greek thought, insofar as that thought constitutes the original and fundamental form of the alienation of the meaning of Being. In accusing Greek thought of stifling the spirit of Christianity, one fails to realize that even the new land to which one seeks to lead the "people of God" lies within the "world"—within, that is, the dimension in which beings are thought and experienced as a Nothing and where both God and the absence of God are invoked as conditions for the possibility of being's nothingness. After having embraced first classical philosophy and then modern science, Christianity is now faced with the problems brought about by its acquiescence in a technological civilization that is capable of absorbing and harmonizing the fundamental ideals of modern humanism. All the forces and innovatory ferment of the Catholic and Protestant world, all desired openings to the world, and all demythologizations operate within this acquiescence. Christianity has overcome its initial attitude of rejection or distrust both towards Greek thought, modern science, and the technological organization of existence. In so doing, it has progressively freed itself from that which has proved extraneous to its essence, thus gaining consciousness of its autonomy with respect to any cosmological, scientific, political, economic, or ideological conception. In philosophy too, the Church today allows pluralism, and thus strips Thomism of the privileged position it has held hitherto. Yet this progressive liberation of the essence of Christianity—this constant ability of Christianity to keep pace with the development of Western culture—only serves to further conceal the persistence of that alienation within which the liberation of the essence of Christianity is being achieved.[1] For thought that testifies to the truth of Being, neither a further, more decisive change in the relation between Christianity and culture nor the most radical demythologization of the *kerygma* can lead to the liberation of the essence of the "Word." Such liberation only begins with the setting of the sick hearing that both renders the Word dissonant and guides the historical process of the liberation of its essence.

The advent of the Word did not cure the hearing's sickness; on the contrary, the Word itself became sick. Ever since the Word was first expressed in the Greek tongue, the nothingness of being has been becoming, through language, the Word's horizon of expression. The

---

1 Corresponding to this liberation (in Catholic theology above all) is the concept of a historical development of the formulation of dogma. Such development is possible only insofar as there is a contradiction between the dogma's form and its content. Otherwise, leaving the old form for the new means relinquishing a part of the content. It is often said that the old form is merely inadequate to the content: but the contradiction lies in the very fact that the content is expressed by that which does not express it—precisely because it expresses it inadequately.

meaning of creature and creator, father and son, good and evil, guilt, expiation, incarnation, and redemption has been determined and measured by that horizon. The Word, infected by the sickness of the hearing, cannot save, and the problem of its truth and infallibility cannot be posed: the Word itself is part of the process in which the essence of man and of truth has been lost. But, despite its sickness, does the Word survive? Or, as an event freed from alienation, is it already dead, or was it never born? If what is said by the Word cannot be thought other than in terms of alienation—if, for example, "creation" necessarily means that the creature might have been, and might again become, a nothing—then any encounter between the truth of Being and Christianity is definitively precluded. But if the Word continues to speak even when it is freed from the alienated meaning of Being—if a Message survives the setting of the "world"—then receiving the Word in the hearing of the truth of Being becomes possible. The possibility of distinguishing the "world," as such, from that which, human or divine, appears in the "world" (and which, appearing there, is determined by it), is the possibility—and so, at the same time, the possibility of the impossibility—of rehearing things outside the "world." What transfiguration will things undergo outside the "world"? Or does the setting of the "world" inevitably involve their setting as well? Thought that testifies to the truth of Being sets out toward a rehearing of things and of words. In beginning to go out of the "world," the Word begins to appear, in the rehearing, as a *problem*—that is, as a saying which to truth does not yet appear as linked to truth, nor as negation of truth.

4. ORIGINAL NECESSITY, THE MORTAL, THE "WORLD"

The place with respect to which the problem is truly problem and the error truly error is the truth of Being. There, the meaning of the original (and the originality [*originarietà*] of) meaning opens. The original is original *Necessity*: it is the link that joins the appearing of the Being of beings to the self-negation of any saying that posits itself as negation of such Appearing. This self-negation—which is such only insofar as it is not merely enunciated as self-negation, but actually shows itself in its concrete determinateness—is the *incontrovertibility* of the truth of Being:[2] truth is incontrovertible, since any negation of truth consists in the negation of its own existence. This self-negation of the negation belongs to the negation not insofar as it is this or that negation, but insofar as the negation is negation. This means that truth cannot be denied by the supervention of any form of negation: truth is original dominion over the totality of the future, precisely insofar as the self-negation of the negation of truth belongs to the negation not *qua* particular (*qua* this or that form of negation), but rather to the negation *qua* universal, i.e., to the *essence* of the negation itself. This dominion over the future through the self-negation of the essence of the negation is the infallibility of truth. *Ybris*, by contrast, is the will to hold something fast, such that that thing's negation is not self-negation.

If the truth of Being is the appearing of the inseparability of being and its Being, and so is the appearing of the eternity of every being (from the most shadowy and indistinct to the most concrete and rich, from the most ideal to the most real—imagined or experienced, human or divine), and if the appearing of the truth of Being is the being whose essence is the openness of every being's truth, then the appearing of the truth of Being is not an activity that issues from and returns to nothingness, or that begins and ceases to appear. Rather, it is the place—always already open—where every event is made manifest and every word is announced. The millennia of history and the totality of time spreads out within this eternal locus, which is the essence of man. The eternal appearing of the truth of Being is open to the supervention of occurrence. The earth, as the totality of the occurrence that supervenes in the eternal circle of the truth of Being, is not only the totality of historical occurrence, but includes every possible heaven: the earth is that portion of the eternal totality of being which is given to the appearing of truth. If the truth of Being is that which it is Necessity to say of every being—if truth is the Predicate of every being—the appearing of truth is the background without which no being and no occurrence can appear. A being that appears without the appearing of the Predicate is not a being, for the Predicate belongs to the essence of

---

2 Cf. "Returning to Parmenides," secs. 6–7.

being *as such*; a being is a being only insofar as the Predicate belongs to its essence, which means that the concept of a being that appears without the appearing of the truth of Being is the concept of a being that appears without itself.

Insofar as it is open to the occurrence of the earth, the truth of Being is exposed to the irruption of error. Not in the sense that truth can become erroneous, but in the sense that the truth of Being and of the earth no longer appears by itself, but does so together with error—together, that is, with the belief that has as its content the negation of truth. The original error, which is the ground of every possible erring, is the conviction that the earth is the whole with which we deal. This conviction—which has nothing to do with any "immanentistic conception" of reality—is the basis of man's historical existence. The ground of all erring is not a philosophical conception, but is the event by which man becomes a mortal. The faith that the earth is the sure whole *isolates* the earth from the truth of Being; that is, it wills the earth as the whole that appears. The truth of being and of the earth continues to appear, but it is countered by the will that wills the earth as the sure whole. Since without the appearing of the truth of Being nothing can appear, the earth isolated from that truth—the earth as the content of the conviction that the earth is the sure whole—is a Nothing. When the earth is willed as the sure whole, what is effectively willed is the earth's *nothingness*; and the *sureness* of the earth is the appearance that both expresses and conceals that nothingness. Isolated from truth, the occurrence of the beings of the earth comes to be their issuing from and returning to nothingness. And man—taken as a being of the isolated earth—comes to be a mortal.

The beings of the earth—the surest region—are experienced as a Nothing that issues from and returns to nothingness. This experience precedes and grounds metaphysical thought. Philosophy, which was born in Greece as metaphysics, is the thought that testifies to and protects the nothingness of being. Greek metaphysics and Western history are the testimony to the event by which man becomes a mortal; the "world" is the testimony to the earth's isolation. The history of the West, as the history of nihilism, is thus not a simple erring that can be ascribed to the intellectual inexperience of man. On the contrary, it is the authentic expression of the mortal essence in which man's original essence is alienated. In Western history, the attempt to construct an incontrovertible and infallible knowing is the will to assure oneself of the sureness of the isolated earth. *Episteme* is *ybris*, the encroachment on the truth of Being that attributes the incontrovertibility of truth to the isolated earth. The principle of noncontradiction is the "unshakable principle" (*bebaiotate arche*), in which the opposition of being to Nothing is grounded on the nothingness of being; and *ta phainomena* (experience) are the beings of the isolated earth which are posited, in *episteme*, as absolute evidence. The isolated earth is the surest; but, since the surest of beings reveals its nothingness, the surest must be continually secured. The pre-metaphysical gods, the incontrovertibility of metaphysical thought, science and technological transformation of the "world" are the ways in which mortals secure the isolated earth and protect beings from the peril of their nothingness. The crisis of metaphysics as contemplation coincides with the consciousness that man can secure the earth only by becoming master of the production and destruction of beings.

Truth is infallible, because it dominates the history of the future through the self-negation of the essence of any negation of truth. But truth is not infallible insofar as the appearing of truth (this genitive is both objective and subjective) is open to the irruption of the will that wills the earth's isolation. The failure of truth does not mean that truth becomes error, but rather that it falls into a conflict where error contends with truth for the appearing of beings. The truth of Being—incontrovertible and never-setting—is also present in error and in the most abysmal alienation; indeed, it is the ground of the appearing of any error and alienation. The existence of mortals is not the setting—i.e., the disappearing—of the truth of Being, but rather the conflict between the eternal appearing of the truth of Being and the isolation of the earth. Mortals are immortals, countered by isolation. This conflict between truth and error stands—ignored—before the eyes of mortals, who name only the beings of the isolated earth and, in so doing, become their witnesses. In everyday life—which is the way in which technological civilization bears witness to our mortal essence—we take no interest in the truth of Being, even though it stands before us as the ground of any manifestation of beings. It is the very effectiveness of this distraction from never-setting truth that grounds the affirmation that the appearing of truth is countered by the appearing of the earth's isolation. It is, in other words, truth itself that (incontrovertibly) posits its own being-countered by the earth's isolation (while it is the interpreting will that grounds the affirmation of the effective existence of Western history and alienation).

5. THE CONFLICT OF THE "WORD OF GOD"

The "Word of God" too belongs to the earth. The Word, growing in the solitude of the earth and in the "world," became a way for mortals to secure the earth itself and their own salvation. Sureness and salvation are thought and experienced as the sureness and salvation of being that, *qua* being, is nothing. Thought that testifies to the truth of Being invokes the setting of the earth's isolation and of the mortal essence of man. This setting contains the ground of any possible salvation, and any word that announces itself to be the way of salvation must lead to it. In invoking the setting of the isolated earth, the testimony to the truth of Being draws toward a rehearing of the Word. It is not a question, then, of hearing the Word anew, but rather of letting it speak, just as it has spoken to us—insofar as we are the eternal appearing of the truth of Being—ever since it became part of Being's offering of the earth. The rehearing of the Word is the setting of the sick hearing, where truth continues to be the hearing that it has already been, ever since the Word first spoke to it. As the invocation of the setting of solitude, thought that testifies to the truth of Being is already the beginning of that setting. But no more than the beginning—and it can also be the end of the testimony. Thought begins to testify to the truth of Being, but the works of isolation continue to dominate the earth. The earth itself has become a work of technological civilization, which is the most powerful and consistent testimony to the Being of the beings of solitude. Invoking the setting of solitude means invoking the setting of the "world," that is, of the earth as a work of alienation. But, as the invocation of this setting, thought that testifies to the truth of Being can begin to draw near to a rehearing of the earth and of every earthly word. It is not a question of inventing new things, but of letting the words of the earth say just what they have always said since they were offered to the truth of Being.

The "Word of God," in beginning to emerge from the sick hearing, begins to appear as a problem, and so as the possibility of the Word's showing the way to the setting of the earth's solitude. This is the possibility that a Word captured by solitude may itself be able to free the earth from solitude. But this possibility is grounded on the possibility of the Word's belonging to truth, for although truth is in fact countered by error, it is truth alone that can bring error to its setting. Once the Word begins to make itself heard outside the "world," it is this very possibility of its belonging to the truth of Being that makes it appear as a problem. This possible belonging is the possibility of the Word's infallibility. The eternal appearing of the truth of Being, insofar as it is open to the occurrence of the earth, is not the manifestation of the concrete richness of the whole, but is the finite horizon in which this richness manifests itself in its abstract form; it is, in other words, the original structure of truth, which is open to the possible disclosure of its completeness. The earth's isolation and the West's alienation are an erring outside of this originality [originarietà]; but original truth does not see the face of its own completeness. The eternal appearing of the truth of Being is not the whole of truth, precisely because it is not the appearing of the concrete richness of the whole. It is therefore possible that every word, which for the original structure of truth is posited as a problem, is an announcement of the traits or ultimate meaning of truth's hidden completeness. It is possible that such words announce something that is linked to original truth in a way that is still unknown. The possibility that the "Word of God" belongs to the truth of Being— the possibility of this Word's infallibility—is the possibility of its indicating the face of truth's hidden completeness. Insofar as the Word makes itself heard outside of the "world," it is not an explicitation of the meaning of Being (i.e., it is not an ontology); but it is possible that a hidden link unites the Word to truth, and that what the Word announces indicates the complete face of that meaning of Being which shows itself explicitly in the original structure of truth. But the possibility of the Word's being linked to the truth of Being opens up together with the possibility that the Word (and every Word that is posited as a problem) is linked to the earth's solitude, and that the receiving of the

Word is the perdition in which the setting of solitude is definitively precluded. The decision that chooses to accept or to reject the Word cannot not belong to truth. Indecision is a way of deciding to choose nonacceptance.

The Word explicitly announces itself to be the "Word of God" and therefore absolute. To the eyes of truth, this absoluteness and infallibility of the Word mean the possibility of its belonging to the truth of Being. (The possibility of the Word's showing the way to the setting of the earth's solitude is grounded on this possible belonging.) But in the Word it is also said that the "people of God" are linked to and destined for the hearing of the Word. To the eyes of truth, this destination is the possibility that the Word—once it has supervened as an offering belonging to the offering of the earth—be received in the eternal circle of the appearing of the truth of Being and that, so received, it remain there forever. This possible destination is the possible infallibility of the people of God. But the possibility of this destination does not protect it from the irruption of the earth's isolation. It is possible that the receiving of the Word is guaranteed to the people of God, but this receiving is countered by the will that confines the Word on the isolated earth and hears it speak in the earth's solitude. Insofar as the eternal appearing of the truth of Being is countered by the earth's isolation, the Word's possible truth and the possible destination for the hearing of the Word are caught up in this conflict. Ever since the offering of the earth offered the Word to truth, the Word has been a conflict between its possible belonging to the truth of Being (which indicates the face of truth's completeness) and its being both the expression and prey of the earth's isolation and the West's alienation; between, that is, its possible infallibility and the historical forms of the erring that, increasingly powerful and consistent, grow up outside the truth of Being. And the hearing of the Word is a conflict between the possible infallibility of the people of God—that is, between their possible destination for the definitive receiving of the Word—and their erring in the earth's solitude and in the "world."

The contention between truth and the earth's isolation demands that both contenders remain in Appearing. But the advent of metaphysics upset the equilibrium of the conflict. Metaphysics is the first and only testimony in man's history to the meaning of Being; but metaphysics does not testify to the meaning of Being that is kept in Being's truth, but rather to the meaning that the Being of beings assumes in the earth's isolation. The history of the West is this testimony's progressive domination, where mortals, in projecting the control of the production and destruction of being as such, oppose being to Nothing within the fundamental conviction of the nothingness of being—"two-headed" (*dikranoi*) mortals, for whom "Being and not-Being are and are not the same" (*ois to pelein te kai ouk einai tauton genomistai kou tauton*, Parmenides, Fr. 6, 8–9). The testimony to the nothingness of being (which comes about in the form of the opposition of being to Nothing) upset the equilibrium of the conflict between truth and the earth's isolation, because truth—even though it remains in its eternal Appearing—is not testified to in the conflict, while the works and languages of the West, as the increasingly coherent explicitation of the alienated meaning of Being, spread over the earth. The disequilibrium of the conflict does not extinguish truth, and so does not extinguish the possible truth of the Word and of the destination for its hearing, but it does aggravate the Word's sickness, namely, its inability to bring the solitude of the earth to its setting. And yet, in the history of man, the advent that can bring the earth's solitude to its setting can only be truth, especially insofar as the completeness of its face is disclosed. Can the Word—reheard outside the "world"—be this advent?

6. THE INTERPRETING WILL AS THE POSSIBLE GROUND OF SALVATION

But thought that testifies to the truth of Being rehears outside the "world" also the interpreting will, which, thus reheard, is the ground of the affirmation that the history of the West is the history of nihilism. Interpretation of the earth belongs to the earth (it is one of the beings that begins to appear with the offering of the earth to truth), and so it becomes involved in the conflict in which truth and the earth's isolation contend for the earth. In the lives of mortals, interpretation of the earth is a conflict between the will that interprets the earth in the light of Being's truth, and the will that interprets it within the earth's isolation. With the advent of metaphysical thought, which testified to the meaning of Being that is revealed in isolation, the equilibrium of the conflict was upset, and the earth came to be interpreted under the increasingly overpowering dominion and direction of the West's alienation. Sounds, colors, and shapes are interpreted as signs and aspects of meanings which are organized within the "world," and the signs and aspects themselves are understood as parts of the "world." Sounds, colors, and shapes are beings, understood as Nothing, which are posited as signs and aspects of the various ways of protecting being's nothingness within the "world." Interpretation thus becomes the fundamental condition for controlling the production and destruction of beings. Science and technology do not dominate beings in their simply being manifest, but rather insofar as they are signs and expression of the "world."

Invoking the setting of the earth's solitude marks the advent of a different interpretation of the earth. Not in the sense that *phyton* is no longer interpreted as the sign and aspect of the meaning "plant," the bright transparency of crystal as the sign and aspect of a glass, and the stark figure of a trunk as the sign and aspect of a tree; but rather in the sense that the signs, aspects, and beings of which the aforementioned are the sign and aspect are left in the *truth* of Being—that is, as *eternal* beings, which neither nature nor human technology can allow to issue from and return to nothingness. (The nexus that joins, in interpretation, a sign to that which it designates, is itself an eternal being; and the possibility of a sign's being joined, in a different interpretation, to something other than that which it has hitherto designated, is the possibilty that the eternity of that nexus is accompanied by other eternal connections between the sign and other things which it designates.) But the invocation of the setting of the earth's solitude is enclosed by the increasingly vertinginous growth of the works of solitude testified to by the "world." Technological civilization is the way in which this testimony is offered today. A glass placed on the table, a tree that is allowed to grow, Greek words, conceived through the categories of a grammar that is based on Greek metaphysics—all are part of technological civilization. The will, which interprets the earth in the light of the invocation of the setting of solitude, interprets the transparency of crystal as that which was brought into appearing by the intention of manufacturing, within the "world," a glass (that is, a "consumer good"—something which has been made to issue from nothingness, and which is destined to be consumed in nothingness once more). "Things" are interpreted as the sign and aspect (and so as the work) of the West's alienation, precisely insofar as the eternity of the whole—and so also the eternity of alienation, and the eternity of its signs, aspects, and works—is testified to.

Independently of the interpreting will, the alienation of Western civilization is not absent from Appearing, but rather remains there as a system of essences, i.e., as a possible history. The interpreting will wills the "reality" of this possible history: it carries with it, in Appearing—indeed, it *wills*—the nexus that posits certain colors, sounds, and shapes as the aspect and sign of the lives of peoples on the earth. The possibility remains open (and perhaps there is remembrance) of a different—even radically different—interpretation of what appears: the possibility of an interpretation that does not allow us to affirm the nihilistic meaning of Western history (nor even to speak of a life of peoples on the earth). But what we find before us is the way in which, both in alienation and in the invocation of its setting, we interpret the earth in fact; the determinate mode by which interpretation wills that men and peoples, their languages and works, the "things" with which they deal and the words of the gods, are "real" beings and so have in what appears their expression and their aspect. While it is true that, independently of the interpreting will, the history of peoples on the earth remains a possible history, it is also true that the events of this history do not enter Appearing independently of the interpreting will. Interpretation, in fact, constitutes itself as a horizon of original laws—a horizon of original nexuses between signs and that which they designate—where everything that comes to be posited as sign and aspect gathers. It is in this gathering (in, that is, the application of original nexuses to events that are progressively assumed as signs) that the meaning of history in which in fact we find ourselves is first brought to light in Appearing. The vocabulary of the Greek tongue belongs to that horizon of original nexuses: as they gather in the horizon of this vocabulary, papyri, parchments, inscriptions (everything that is assumed as a determinate type of sign) become a language, and the Homeric poems, the dialogues of Plato, and the Gospels come into Appearing for the first time. That other type of vocabulary, which interprets certain colors, sounds, and shapes as glasses, trees, human bodies, houses, peoples, pain, joy, war, peace, labor, and exchange, belongs to that horizon of original nexuses; as they gather in the horizon of this vocabulary, the events that manifest themselves become the meaning of our lives as mortals, and technological civilization enters and dominates Appearing. In the light of the testimony to the truth of Being, a civilization that—after thinking beings separated from their Being—presents itself as the technology of their production and destruction, appears in so doing as the civilization of essential alienation.

In the testimony to the truth of Being, interpretation of the earth is reheard outside the "world," but it remains a fact which can be replaced by other facts. Outside the "world" the nexuses that constitute the way in which the will interprets the earth in fact, become a possibility: something that may be linked to truth, or to the earth's isolation. Nevertheless it is this *de facto* interpretation of the earth which brings to light, in Appearing, that which we call the "Word of God." If the Word of God has the possibility of being the advent that, in the history of man, brings the earth's solitude to its setting, the interpreting will is that which leads to the coming of the Word. The question, then, is this: can the interpreting will be the advent that brings the earth's solitude to its setting and makes possible the salvation of truth?

PART THREE

Aletheia

Western civilization grows within the horizon opened up by the meaning Greek thought assigned to the thingness of things. This meaning progressively—and now entirely—unifies the boundless multiplicity of events that we call "Western history." Today, in fact, it rules the whole earth: even the entire history of the East has now become the pre-history of the West.

In my writings I have indicated the Western—and now planetary—meaning of the thing: the thing (a thing, any thing) is, *qua* thing, nothing; the not-Nothing (a, any not-Nothing) is, *qua* not-Nothing, nothing. The belief that being is nothing is nihilism.[1] In a sense abysmally different from Nietzsche's or Heidegger's, nihilism is the essence of the West.

Nihilism, however, exists as a *phenomenon* and as a *thing in itself.* As a phenomenon, nihilism (i.e., the West) is that which it appears to itself; that meaning with which it manifests itself to itself; that which it sees, and thinks it knows, of itself. And nihilism does *not* see itself as nihilism, i.e., as the conviction that being is nothing.

It primarily sees of itself all those determinations which the inhabitants of the West think that they see.

But all such determinations appear *within* the meaning that the thingness of things shows *to the eyes of nihilism.* Before *these* eyes, the thing does *not* appear as a nothingness. It appears, rather, according to those traits which Greek thought assigned to it once and for all.

It appears, that is, as that of which it is to be said that it *is*, but *was not* and *will not be*. It appears, in other words, as that which, wholly or

---

1 That *ente* is *niente*: while this play on words is lost in English, it can clearly be found in saying that the *thing* is no*thing* [*Translator's note*].

in part, issues from and returns to nothingness; it oscillates between Being and Nothing—an *epamphoterizein* (*ep-amphot-erizein*, Plato, *Republic*, 479c), where "the two" (*amphotera*) "with respect" (*epi*) to which the thing "struggles with itself" (*epizei*) are Being (*to on*) and Nothing (*to me on*, understood as *to pantos me on*, *nihil absolutum*, ibid., 478*d*). Insofar as it "partakes" of both (*to amphoteron metechon*, ibid., 478*d–e*), the thing (*ti*) has both as its predicates: it is something that "at once" (*ama*) is and is not: *ti . . . ama on te kai me on* (ibid., 478*d*). But the adverb *ama*, here at the end of Book V of the *Republic*, does not have the temporal sense that it probably intends to express in the celebrated passage of Book IV of the *Metaphysics* (1005*b* 19–20), where Aristotle formulates the *principium omnium firmissimum*; in Plato's text, *ama* indicates the *inseparability* of the two (i.e., Being and Nothing), between which the thing wavers in its oscillation between the one and the other.

That which oscillates, in fact, not only cannot be thought as simply linked to Being (*out' einai*), or to not-Being (*oute me einai*), or to neither of the two (*oute oudeteron*), but neither can it be thought as being *both*—(*out' amphotera*, 479c). The *epamphoteristes* (that which oscillates) is a struggling (*erizein*) between Being and Nothing (*epi ta amphotera*) precisely because it is *not* both the one and the other *at the same time*: *out' amphotera*. This struggling is the *becoming* of the thing. Where the thing, *at once* (*ama*), is and is not, in the sense that Being and not-Being are inseparable in Becoming—and not in the sense that, in Becoming, the thing is and is not *at the same time*.

But precisely because in the phrase *ti . . . ama on te kai me on* the adverb *ama* indicates not the contemporaneity, but rather the inseparability of the two that contend for the thing (that inseparability and unity which is explicitly revealed in the Greek words *eis*, *mia* which, like *ama*, go back, through the conjecturals *sems*, *smía* respectively, to the Indoeuropean root *sem/som*, from which is derived the Latin *semol*, *simul*)—for this very reason what we have here is the very definition of Becoming, i.e., of time.

Contrary to common credence, the fact that the thing—*qua* thing—is Becoming, time, history, is not the characteristic trait of modern thought, but rather the fundamental meaning of the Greek thought of the thing (from the moment, however, when Greek thought recognized the thing's right to exist—given that, in beginning to testify to the meaning of Being and Nothing, Parmenides had denied the very existence of the thing, i.e., of that of which Being can be predicated). For Plato (and throughout the history of the West) a thing is immutable and eternal not insofar as it is a thing, but rather insofar as it possesses a privileged structure with respect to other things. *Qua* thing, a thing is an oscillation (*epamphoterizein*) between Being and Nothing.

"Being" (*to on*) is the way in which Greek thought thinks the meaning of the thing (i.e., of the *ti* of which *einai* is predicated): a being is the thing (the *ti*) in its being involved in *epamphoterizein* between Being and Nothing. From the Greeks onward, the West no longer allows the *ti* to be separated from its being "being" (as it was in pre-ontological thought): "it is impossible," Plato said, "to speak of the thing in its being alone, as if naked and isolated from everything that is being" (*monon gar auto legein, osper chumnon kai aperemomenon apo ton onton apanton, adynaton, Sophist, 237d*).

The *epamphoterizein* of the thing is the horizon within which the West, looking at itself, sees all the determinations it thinks it has. This means that nihilism, *qua* phenomenon, is a double stratification composed of a "surface" layer and a hidden one which, however, stays close to the surface and glimmers through it. This hidden layer—which may be called the "preconscious" of the West—is the Greek meaning of the thing, now present and dominant in every event and in every work of which the West has consciousness. For example, the concrete determinations of modern science and technology operate entirely within the Greek meaning of the thing.[2] Yet epistemological-scientific-technological culture is still unaware of this, its essential condition: that is, of its *essential* proximity to that meaning which therefore constitutes the "preconscious" of this culture; while that which the culture thinks it knows and does is the "surface" layer of nihilism *qua* phenomenon.

This "surface" thus contains the enormous wealth of contents of Western civilization. Its "preconscious" is the unity of the boundless multiplicity that constitutes it: a unity, such as may be constituted

---

2   Cf. E. Severino, *Legge e caso*, Milan: Adelphi, 1979.

within the phenomenon of nihilism. That such unity be "preconscious" is due to the tendency of the current forms of Western civilization to claim that Greek philosophy no longer concerns them. Yet this is only a tendency. For if the West is moving towards the complete forgotten-ness of that which nevertheless remains essentially near and dominant, there is at the same time a counter-movement, towards a deepening of the ties that link the current form of Western civilization to its Greek past. In the phenomenon of nihilism, the "preconscious" is the implicit (the implicitly seen) that *can* become explicit before the eyes of the West—that implicit, moreover, which is the horizon within which the multiplicity of determinations of the explicit is unified (that multiplic-ity which we call "history of the West" and "history of the earth").

In this sense, that which here is called "preconscious"—the thing as oscillation, *epamphoterizein*—is the essence of the phenomenon of nihilism. In its glimmering through the "surface" of this phenomenon, *epamphoterizein* is the original and fundamental "evidence" of the West. This "evidence" tends to remain in the margins of that space where the inhabitants of the West focus their attention. Western man tends to leave in a shadow-realm of the implicit and unexpressed that which, as evidence, stands before his eyes as the absolutely and origi-nally visible. To be sure, Western culture continues to speak of "Becoming," "history," "time," "production," "destruction"—that is, of the historicity and temporality of things. Yet what is left in shadow is the essential structure of these categories: the *epamphoterizein* of the thing (the thing as *epamphoterizein*) evoked by Greek ontology.

On the other hand, nihilism, as *thing in itself*, is the conviction that the thing is nothing. That nihilism is this faith is a claim by no means unusual or unacceptable. Rather, what is absolutely unheard-of for the West is that nihilism is the *thing in itself*, the phenomenon of which is the *epamphoterizein* of the thing; i.e., that nihilism is the *in-itself* of that which for the West is original and fundamental evidence. The belief that the thing is Becoming (history, time, oscillation between Being and Nothing) is linked *with Necessity* to the faith that the thing, as such, is nothing. Only insofar as the meaning of Necessity opens (it is always already open) can the Necessity of that link appear. Indeed, it is the *meaning of Necessity* that the language of my philosophy constantly addresses, indicating its traits.

But it is only insofar as the meaning of Necessity is always already open that nihilism can appear in its being *thing in itself*, i.e., as nihilism. Nihilism appears to Western eyes—to its *own* eyes—as original evidence; and this Appearing is the phenomenon (the essence of the phenomenon) of nihilism. But it is to the eyes of *Necessity* that nihilism appears as the *in-itself* of the original evidence of the West, i.e., as the conviction that the thing as such is nothing, this faith being linked with Necessity to the belief that the thing is an *epamphoterizein* between Being and Nothing. With respect to what the West, *qua* West, sees, the conviction that the thing, as such, is nothing is therefore the essential "unconscious" of the West. Nihilism, as thing in itself, is the "unconscious" of that which appears in the phenomenon of nihilism.

In *epamphoterizein*, the indecision of the thing means that it is not definitively linked either to its Being or to its not-Being, but is provisionally sheltered by each; keeping to one, it already hears the other's call. Accordingly, the thing is, "at once" (*ama*), a being [*essente*] and a non-being [*non essente*] (*ti . . . ama on te kai me on, Republic*, 478*d*). Keeping to one, it does not irrevocably separate itself from the other.

But, for this very reason, the thing is never a guest of both Being and Nothing *at the same time*. As we have seen, the same page of Plato's text which states that the thing is at the same time (*ama*) a Being and a not-Being also states that in oscillation (*epamphoterizein*) the thing is not *both the one and the other* (*out' amphotera*). Which means that it is not both *at the same time*. (In this very synthesis of *ama* and *out' amphotera* lies the essence of the Hegelian dialectic.) The strife (*eris*) of *epamphoterizein* is *Becoming* (and *eris* itself may be considered a metathesis of 'rein, which quite clearly expresses Becoming), where the thing oscillates between Being and not-Being, and where, when it is, it is, and when it is not, it is not. *Epamphoterizein* requires that, when the thing is at one of its two extremes, it be "so" (*outo*); and when it is at the other, it be "not so" (*me outo*). "So," in the sense of being [*essente*] when it is; "not so," in the sense of not being [*non essente*] when it is not. In the *Theaetetus* (183*a*–*b*) Plato rejects the Protagorean conception of Becoming, precisely because it inevitably leads to the affirmation that every thing is "so and not so" (*outo . . . kai me outos*, 183*a*) at the same time.

The Aristotelian "principle of noncontradiction" (the *bebaiotate arche pason, principium fimissimum omnium*) is essentially an expression of this structure of *epamphoterizein*. Not in the sense that it is a principle only of being-that-becomes and not of being *qua* being, but rather in the sense that, *as being* (i.e., *not* insofar as it is one specific *privileged* being), being is for Greek thought—and for all Western thought thereafter—an *epamphoterizein* between Being and Nothing. Accordingly, the *principium firmissimum* expresses the structure of the *epamphoterizein* of being, precisely because it is a principle of being *qua* being (cf. *Met.*, 1005a 19–1005b 2). In *Met.*, 1061b 36–1062a 1, Aristotle formulates it by saying that "it is impossible that the same thing be and not be [*einai kai me einai*] in the same respect and at the same time [*kao ena kai ton auton chronon*]."

The thing, here, is considered precisely as the provisional prey of each of the two antagonists (Being and Nothing) that contend for it. This contending—the *eris* of *epamphoterizein*—is the very flux ('*rein*) of time, where the thing moves between the contenders and is and is not at different times (*kata ton diaphoron chronon*). The impossibility that the same thing be and not be at the same time is the very structure of time, i.e., of *epamphoterizein*. The formula used by Plato in the *Theaetetus* in reproaching Protagoras with understanding Becoming as a being "so and not so" (*outo . . . kai me outos*), reappears in Book IV of the *Metaphysics* when Aristotle refutes the denier of the *principium firmissimum*, who "never says that it is so and not not-so (*outos out ouk outos*), but that it is so and not so (*outos te kai ouk outos*, 1008a 31–2).

The precursors of the Aristotelian *principium firmissimum*, contained in the *Theaetetus* or in the *Sophist*—or the initial formulation itself in Book IV of the *Metaphysics*—only seem to prescind from time.

It can in fact be objected that whereas the impossibility that something be and not be at the same time is equivalent to the possibility (and indeed, in certain cases, to the necessity) that it be and not be at different times, the impossibility that something be at the same time man and trireme (*Met.*, 1007b 20–1) is not equivalent to the possibility (and still less to the necessity) that it be man and trireme at different times. This second impossibility prescinds from time.

It is unquestionable that, for Aristotle, whereas a thing that to being [*essente*] can become not being [*non essente*], or a thing that is black can become white, on the other hand a thing that is man cannot become trireme. Analogously, that which is immovable substance is not not-immovable substance; nor, in this case either, may it be affirmed that it is impossible for something to be and not be immovable substance at the same time—precisely because immovable substance cannot cease to be such at different times. It *is not* in time. And neither is the opposition of man and trireme. And neither is the Platonic archetype of this opposition, i.e., the opposition (cf. *Theaetetus*, Ch. XXXII) between any two beings whatsoever—say, that between "ox" and "horse." "Not even when dreaming" (*oud' en ypno*), not even "when raving mad" (*mainomenon*), says Plato, "can one go so far" (*tolmesai*) as to affirm *simpliciter* (*pantos, pantapasin*) "that a thing is its other," "that one of the two is the other" (*to eteron eteron estin*), i.e., that "the beautiful is ugly" or "the just is unjust," "an ox is a horse" or "two is one" (*Theaetetus*, 190*b–c*).

But the impossibility of certain types of Becoming (such as from man to trireme, or from ox to horse) and the affirmation of the existence of immutable substances is due to the specific configuration of Platonic and Aristotelian *episteme*. (Aristotle's rejection of any "evolutionistic" thesis—such as a fish becoming a man, or a man becoming a machine—is grounded on the elevation of certain types of empirically observed Becoming to the status of metempirical rules.) For *episteme*, being *as being* (*on e on*)—the beingness of being—is the structure that is present in *every* being: in beings-that-become as in immutable beings. But, *as being* (considered, that is, for its being *being* and not for its being a certain being), being is that which can not-be. *Qua* being, it is not the immediate exclusion of its potentiality for not-being. Indeed, it is an *epamphoterizein* between Being and not-Being. For *episteme* to posit a certain being as immutable and therefore as that which cannot not-be, it is forced to introduce a *middle* between the beingness of that being (i.e., between that being considered *qua* being) and its immutability. This middle attempts the impossible; it mediates that which cannot be mediated, uniting the potentiality for not-being which is proper to being *qua* being—i.e., to the beingness that is present even in immutable being—to the impossibility of not-being which is proper to immutable being insofar as it is immutable. Thus the concept of immutable being is self-contradictory from the viewpoint of *episteme* itself. Being *qua* being, which ought to be the trait common to both being-that-becomes and immutable being and therefore indifferent with respect to them, is in effect itself being-that-becomes; which means that, in *episteme* (i.e., in Western thought *qua* episteme), immutable being constitutes itself as an immutable coming-to-be.

In the same way, the metatemporality of a man's not being trireme is the immutability of a being—i.e., of that being which is the opposition of man and trireme—which, nonetheless, *qua* being, is a potentiality for not-being. "Eternal truths" (such as the opposition of man and trireme) *are* eternal only as long as the dimension of Being remains open: where everything has ceased to exist, the possible-ideal world of "eternal truths" does not exist either.

All this means that, in the formulations of the "principle of noncontradiction" that seem to prescind from time, there is the conviction, albeit hidden, that being (of which noncontradictoriness is posited) is time, i.e., *epamphoterizein* between Being and Nothing. The metatemporal formulations of the "principle of noncontradiction" are *contradictory* formulations: contradictory, moreover, from the viewpoint of nihilism itself—of nihilism as the essence underlying the phenomenon of nihilism. As nihilism grows progressively more coherent, *epamphoterizein*, in freeing itself from *episteme* (and thus from every immutable evoked by *episteme*), frees itself from every metatemporal formulation of the "principle of noncontradiction."

The Kantian formulation of this principle—"no thing can have a predicate that contradicts it"—also explicitly intends to eliminate any reference to the "condition of time." But for Kant too the thing is *epamphoterizein* between Being and not-Being ("It is not time that flows, but the existence of the changeable flows in it"—and time itself can not-be: at the beginning of the "General Observations on the Transcendental Aesthetic" the hypothesis of the "suppression of the subject" is considered to be legitimate) and therefore, in the metatemporal formulation of the noncontradictory, the noncontradictory is time, i.e., *epamphoterizein* of the thing between Being and not-Being. The analytic proposition "no ignorant man is learned," "stems immediately from the principle of noncontradiction," writes Kant, "without having to add: *at the same time*." But for Kant, too, an ignorant man may cease to be so; and therefore he is ignorant *when* he is ignorant; and *when* he is ignorant he cannot be learned. And this latter proposition means quite simply that a man cannot be ignorant and learned at the same time. The metatemporal formulation of the "principle of noncontradiction" simply masks, but does not suppress, the reference to time which determines the structure of the subject of that analytic proposition.

Thus in that which Western thought calls the "principle of noncontradiction" the reference to time testifies to the fact that this principle is the very expression of the *epamphoterizein* of being.

But, as an exclusion of the thing's being and not being at the same time, the concept of *epamphoterizein* is also the exclusion of being's being nothing. As a guest (or prey) of Being, the thing is being (=that which is); and being is not Nothing, i.e., is not the thing insofar as it is not (insofar as it is a guest of not-Being). The opposition of being and nothing belongs to the essential structure of the *principium firmissimum*. In the *Sophist*, Plato expresses this opposition by saying that "Nothing cannot be applied to any being" (*ton onton epi ti to me on ouk oisteon*, 237c). The explicit affirmation that being, *as* being (to the extent that it is being; when it is being; in the act in which it is being), is *not* Nothing, is a constant that is present and dominant throughout the entire history of nihilism. This means that whereas, as thing in itself, nihilism is the conviction that *being is Nothing*—as phenomenon, it is the belief that *being is not Nothing*. Nihilism appears to itself in inverted form, i.e., as an affirmation of the noncontradictoriness of being. In short, as "principle of non-contradiction."

The Hegelian identity of *Sein* and *Nichts* is simply the identity of the indeterminate (pure Being) with the indeterminate (the pure *not*); it is not the identity of being and nothing, identity with Nothing on the part of a "concrete something" (a *Konkretes Etwas, bestimmtes Dasein, bestimmter Inhalt*; cf., in the *Science of Logic*, Remark I, immediately after the exposition of the first triad). For something—i.e., for being— "it is not indifferent whether it is or is not" (*nicht gleichgültig ob es sei oder nicht sei*, ibid.); "the being or the absence of a content is not a matter of indifference to it" (*das Sein oder die Abwesenheit eines Inhalts . . . nicht gleichgültig ist*, ibid.—where *Ab-wesen-heit* is the very *ap-ousia*, or "absence," of which Plato speaks in the *Parmenides*, pointing out that "when we affirm that something is not we intend to indicate the absence of Being [*ousia apousian*] from that of which we are saying that it is not," 163c–d). Hegel's negation of the principle of noncontradiction denies the principle only insofar as it is the content of the intellect. Indeed, the dialectical method is the most rigorously consistent *affirmation* of this principle that can be formulated by *episteme*.[3] It is by no means fortuitous that Hegel, in the celebrated passage of the *Logic*'s "Introduction," where he explains the essence of the dialectical method (of the "scientific procedure," that is, where that which contradicts itself is resolved in a determined negation), says that such essence "strictly speaking is a tautology" (*was eigentlich eine Tautologie ist*). A tautology—that is, the affirmation of the identity of the identical. Hegel does not reject the content of traditional "logical forms" ("identity," "noncontradiction," "excluded middle"); what he rejects is their being taken as devoid of that genuine content which is not their empirical content, but rather "their substantial, absolutely concrete unity" (*ihre gediegene, absolut-konkrete Einheit*), their "organic unity," without which they are "dead forms" (*tote Formen*), i.e., false (ibid.).

Even in those dimensions within the phenomenon of nihilism which have themselves been denounced as "nihilism," being is not identified with Nothing. Both the condemnation of "nihilism" proclaimed by Western thought and this "nihilism" itself belong to the phenomenon of nihilism. Both, in themselves, in their essential unconscious, are nihilism, i.e., the conviction that being, as such, is nothing. But the "nihilism" denounced by Western thought is *not* the affirmation that being, as such, is nothing; rather, it consists in not recognizing the existence (or the autonomy of the existence) of something that is held to be existent (or autonomously existent) by someone who claims to stand outside "nihilism." For the "Platonist" Jacobi, idealism is "nihilistic" since it identifies all reality external to and independent of thought with Nothing; for the "Non-Platonist" Nietzsche, a "nihilist" is one who does not recognize the autonomy of the existence of the earth and places the ground and the value of all existence in the beyond; while for Heidegger "nihilism" is the "forgottenness" of

---

3   Cf. E. Severino, *La struttura originaria*, Ch. XII, 1st ed. Brescia: La Scuola, 1958; 2nd ed. Milan: Adelphi, 1981; and E. Severino, *Gli abitatori del tempo*, 1st ed., Rome: Armando, 1978, 2.

the "Being of beings." But none of these nihilists claims that being *qua* being is nothing (in none of them is that nothingness of being affirmed, of which both the nihilists and those who deny them are, *in themselves*, the affirmation); rather, what is affirmed is the nothingness of that which others hold to be existent. And this even if the deniers of "nihilism" have believed they could discern in Western thought the identification of being with Nothing and the negation of the "principle of noncontradiction."

The faith that being *is not* Nothing, as the *phenomenon* of nihilism, can imply with Necessity the belief that being *is* Nothing (the essential conviction of the *in itself* of nihilism), since, in the phenomenon, "Being" is the way in which Western thought, from the Greeks onward, thinks the meaning of the thing (i.e., of the something, the *ti*); namely, as *epamphoterizein* between Being and Nothing. But that nihilism appear to itself in inverted form, i.e., in the form of the "principle of noncontradiction" and the denial that being is nothing, is not a mere fact—it is *Necessity*. Not only is it Necessity that the becoming of being imply the nothingness of being—it is *Necessity* that the conviction that being is nothing (nihilism as thing in itself) remain the "unconscious" of nihilism, and that the nothingness of being enter in inverted form the consciousness in which nihilism as phenomenon consists.

A decisive presentiment of the *formal* traits of this second Necessity—set out in its concrete meaning in the present work and in *Destino della necessità: Katà tò chreón*[4]—can be discerned in the very way in which Aristotle, in Book IV of the *Metaphysics*, formulates "the definition" (*o dioriomos*, *Met.*, 1005*b* 23) of the *principium firmissimum omnium*.

In *Met.*, 1061*b* 34–5, Aristotle states that "there is in beings one principle concerning which [*peri en*] it is not possible to be in error (*ouk esti diepseusthai*), but rather it is necessary always (*anangkaion aiei*) to be persuaded (*poiein*) of the contrary of error, i.e., to be in truth (*aletheuein*)." The principle concerning which "it is necessary to be always in truth" is, indeed, the *principium firmissimum omnium* (*pason bebaiotate arche*). But this principle (*arche*) is the firmest

---

4   Cf. E. Severino, *Destino della necessità: Katà tò chreón*, Milan: Adelphi, 1980.

(*bebaiotate*) because it is the firm base from which all knowing proceeds (*Met.*, 1005*b* 15–17)—(*bebaios* derives from *baino*, which conveys motion), and therefore it is truth itself (it is *aletheuein* itself in its originality). Saying, accordingly, that it is necessary to be always in truth about this principle means saying that it is necessary to be always *within* it. And this is by no means a vicious circle since, if this principle is the basis of all knowing, then the truth in which it is necessary to be with regard to it can be nothing other than the principle itself (or, in any case, something that includes it).

But Aristotle's text shows the meaning of this self-belonging of the *principium firmissimum* concretely. In Book IV of the *Metaphysics*, the text 1005*b* 11–1005*b* 31 takes *three steps*: 1) it defines the meaning of "being the firmest of all principles" (1005*b* 11–18); 2) it indicates "what principle this is" (1005*b* 18–22); 3) it shows that this principle satisfies the conditions required by the definition of "being the firmest of all principles" (1005*b* 22–31). The force of this text has not yet been gauged (although Aquinas, in his commentary on the *Metaphysics*, came closer to doing so than anyone else). Indeed, some have thought that Aristotle himself was unable to control the multiplicity of the relations between formulations of the principle that are set out in the text.

The first step consists, as we have seen, in defining the "firmest of all principles" as that "concerning which it is impossible to be in error," or (as it is expressed in *Met.*, 1061*b* 35), about which "it is necessary to be always in truth." (Such a principle, therefore, is not a hypothesis and, as the principle of being *qua* being, is presupposed by the knowledge of any being whatsoever, 1005*b* 14–17). The second step is the celebrated formulation of the principle in terms of the impossibility for the same thing to belong and simultaneously not to belong to the same thing and in the same respect. The third step shows that such a principle is the firmest of all by showing that it fits the definition of "firmest of all principles" formulated in the first step; by showing, that is, that it is indeed impossible to be in error about it. But being in error with regard to such a principle is *self-contradiction* (just as the "truth" in which it is necessary always to be with regard to the principle is the principle itself, i.e., is the negation of the contradictoriness of being); and therefore showing the impossibility of being in error concerning it means showing the *impossibility of self-contradiction*—that is, the impossibility of being convinced of what this principle denies.

The ascertainment of this impossibility is not to be confused with the *elenchos*, i.e., with the "refutation" of the negation of the principle. The *elenchos* shows that such negation, insofar as it has a determinate meaning (i.e., is a *ti . . . orismenon*, 1006a 24–5) submits to that which it intends to deny: "wishing to destroy logos it submits to logos" (*anairon gar logon ypomenei logon*, 1006a 26). The *elenchos* refers to *the semantic content of the negation* of the principle, while the ascertainment of the impossibility of the existence of self-contradiction shows that *the denier* of the principle *does not exist*—does not exist as the conviction that being is contradictory. The denier of the principle, since he too must necessarily "be always in truth," is quite clearly he who cannot express his own being in truth in his own language and cannot refer his own language back to his own being in truth. Which is to say, the denier of the principle is he who *believes* he is the denier of the principle. Indeed, shortly after the beginning of the third of the passages under consideration Aristotle remarks, "it is not necessary that the things one says should also be the things of which one is convinced (*ypolambanein*)" (1005b 24).

Now, the third passage begins by affirming "the impossibility for anyone to be convinced that the same thing is and is not" (*adunaton gar ontinoun tauton ypolambanein einai kai me einai*; *gar* refers to the preceding statement, 1005b 23, which affirms that the principle formulated in the second passage satisfies the condition required in the first). The affirmation of the *impossibility* of this conviction is not, therefore, simply a variant of the formulation of the principle given in the second passage: the affirmation of this impossibility is an affirmation of the impossibility of the *existence* of such a conviction. But *impossibility* is the very contradictoriness of being (just as necessity, and thus the necessity of being always in truth, is the negation of contradictoriness; i.e., is the principle itself). Showing the impossibility of the existence of the conviction that the same thing is and is not means, therefore, showing the contradictoriness of this existence. And this is what is explicitly done in the third passage (1005b 26–31): "Hence, if it is not possible for contraries to belong to the same thing simultaneously . . . and if the opinion contrary to an opinion is that of the contradictory, then it is evidently impossible for the same [man] to be convinced simultaneously that the same thing exist and not exist; for anyone who made that error would be holding contrary opinions simultaneously."[5] Let it be noted:

a) Here we have the third of the three ways in which the principle is formulated in the second and in the third of the passages under consideration. The first mode of formulation is in 1005*b* 19–20: "For the same thing to belong and not to belong simultaneously to the same thing and in the same respect is impossible" (*to gar auto ama uparchein te kai me uparchein adunaton to auto kai kata to auto*); the second is in 1005*b* 23–4: "It is impossible for anyone to be convinced that the same thing is and is not" (*adunaton gar ontinoun tauton ypolambanein einai kai me einai*); and the third is in 1005*b* 26–7: "It is impossible for contraries to belong to the same thing simultaneously (*me endechetai ama uparchein to auto tanantia*). In 1005*b* 29–30 the second of these modes is repeated nearly word for word.

The difference between them lies not only in the fact that the second, unlike the first and the third, makes reference to *upalamba-nein* (i.e., to "conviction"). It also lies in the fact that the first is expressed in terms of the impossibility for the same thing to belong and not to belong to the same thing, the second in terms of the impossibility for the same thing to be and not be, and the third in terms of the impossibility for contraries to belong to the same thing.

But, in the second mode of formulation, the value of "being and not being" (*einai kai me einai*, 1005*b* 24, 30) is as existential as it is copulative (with the predicate nominative understood). With copulative value *einai kai me einai* corresponds to the "to belong and not to belong" (*uparchein te kai me uparchein*) of the first mode, and the understood predicate nominative corresponds to the "same thing" (*to auto*, 1005*b* 19) that is the subject of *uparchein te kai me uparchein*. Saying, that is, that *y* belongs (*uparchei*) to *x* means saying that *x* is *y*. With existential value, the *einai*, present in the *einai kai me einai* of 1005*b* 24, joins itself with the subject (*tauton*, 1005*b* 24)—it is copula and verbal predicate simultaneously—and thus corresponds to the *to*

---

auto uparchein (1005*b* 19) of the first mode in its entirety. The third mode of formulation is a specification of the first—and thus of the second—since (as Aristotle states explicitly at the end of Ch. 6 of Book IV, 1011*b* 15–22) one of a pair of contraries is the privation, the absence (*steresis*) of the other, and a privation is a denial (*apophasis*) of that of which it is privation (1011*b* 19). Saying, therefore, that contraries inhere in the same thing implies saying that the same thing belongs and does not belong to the same thing.

b) While the second mode of formulation is equivalent to the first, in the second mode the impossibility for the same thing to be and not be is presented in the form of the impossibility for anyone *to be convinced* (*ypolambanein*) that the same thing is and, simultaneously, *to be convinced* that it is not. The impossible opposition, here, is the opposition between two convictions whose content is, respectively, the being of a thing and the not being of that same thing. As becomes explicit in 1005*b* 28–31, the impossible "simultaneity" (*ama*) refers to the two *ypolambanein* constituted by the two contrary "opinions."

In this configuration, the second mode of formulation is not equivalent to the first, but is an instance of the third mode; i.e., it is an instance of that specification of the first, which is the third mode of formulation. The relation between being convinced that a thing is and being convinced that this same thing is not is in fact a relation between contraries, just as the relation between black and white is. These two convictions constitute the "greatest difference" (*megiste diaphora*) within the same genus: in this case, the genus "to hold a conviction concerning a certain thing." It is this very relation of contrariety that is expressed, in the third of the three passages under consideration, by the phrase *enantia d'esti doxa doxe e tes antiphaseos*, which we translated as "the opinion contrary to an opinion is that of the contradictory." Strictly speaking, "contradiction" (*antiphasis*) is the opposition of contradictoriness (i.e., the not being of a thing, with respect to the being of that same thing) that subsists between the content of two contrary opinions—which are contrary precisely because their content is in this form of opposition (cf. *De Interpretatione*, Ch. 14).

c) The "same thing," to which it is impossible for contrary opinions to belong in the same respect, is man, the thinking individual: *o ypolabon, o doxazon*. Accordingly, just as the impossibility for the same surface to be black and white is an instance of the impossibility for contraries to belong to the same thing, so is the impossibility for the same thinking individual to be convinced of something and of its negation. That is, this impossibility too is an instance of that specification of the first mode of formulation of the principle, which is the impossibility for contraries to inhere in the same thing.

But the two contrary opinions (*doxai*) are contraries that inhere in the same *ypolabon*, only if the thesis and the antithesis constituting their respective contents *appear*, in the *ypolambanein*, as negations of one another. Indeed, that the "errant" (*o diepseusmenos*, 1005b 31) "hold (*echoi*) contrary opinions" means that, in *doxazein* (=*ypolamba-nein*), the thesis and antithesis *dokousin*, i.e., *appear* in their being such. If they do not so appear in the thought of the errant, while remaining negations of one another they are no longer contraries that inhere in the same *ypolambanein*.

d) Sequence 1005b 26–31 of the third of the three passages under consideration shows, accordingly, that being convinced that the same thing is and is not is an instance of that specification of the belonging of the same to the same which is the belonging of contraries to the same. *Precisely because* it is impossible for the same thing to be and not be, the existence of the errant is impossible—the existence, that is, of the conviction that the same thing is and is not. It is necessary to be always in truth (*anankaion aiei . . . aletheuein*) concerning the *principium firmissimum*, since affirming that one may be in error regarding it means affirming that the same thing is and is not (i.e., means affirming that certain contraries inhere in the same—affirming, that is, an instance of a specification of the belonging of the same to the same). It is the *principium firmissimum* itself, therefore, that grounds the ascertainment of the necessity of being always in truth concerning it.

Always: even when—as Plato tells us in the *Theaetetus*—one is "dreaming" (*en ypno*) or "raving mad" (*mainomenon*). This characteristic of original truth—namely, that it can constitute itself independently of the thinking individual's state of madness or of dream—reappears in the way in which Descartes, in the *Meditations*, understands the truth (*necessario esse verum*) of the *Ego sum*. And even in this original *sum* the oscillation (*epamphoterizein*) of being continues to be present: to the necessity that being be *when* (*otan*) it is—for it also has the possibility of not being (Aristotle, *De Interpretatione*, 19*a* 22 ff.)—there corresponds, in the second of the *Meditations*, the necessity that I be *for as long as* I think (*quandiu cogito*); for it cannot be excluded (*fieri posset*) that, ceasing to think, in that moment I altogether cease to be *(illico totus esse desinerem)*.

Let us sum up what has been said so far.

In the phenomenon, the in-itself of nihilism is presented in inverted form, i.e., as the conviction that being is *not* Nothing. The content of this belief constitutes itself as the "principle of noncontradiction," *principium firmissimum* (and the "firmness" of the principle is the very "firmness" of the oscillation, *epamphoterizein*, of being). This principle is linked with Necessity to the latent conviction that being *is* nothing.

But in one of the decisive texts (Book IV of the *Metaphysics*) in which nihilism is presented in the form of its opposite, Aristotle also shows the impossibility of the *existence* of the faith that the same belong and not belong to the same.

Yet, thinking that being is nothing means positing being as being [*ente*] and as non-being/no-thing [*ni-ente*] (i.e., positing and not positing being as being).

The "evidence" (*phaneron*) of the impossibility of being persuaded of the contradictoriness of being, affirmed in Aristotle's text, is compromised by the shadow that envelops the whole of Western thought. And yet the *formal* structure of the content of such "evidence" always already belongs to the structure of Necessity—belongs, that is, to the region that always and forever opens outside the confines of nihilism.[6] It is in relation to this region alone that the essence of the West (*epamphoterizein*) appears as nihilism.

Indeed, in a context that could not have been foreseen by Aristotelian thought, the present work (cf. "The Earth and the Essence of Man," VI) and *Destino della necessità: Katà tò chreón* (cf. Chapters XII, XIII, XIV) indicate, in relation to the original and fundamental

---

6   As I stressed in my brief commentary on Book IV of the *Metaphysics* (Aristotle, *Il principio di non contraddizione*, trans., introd., and commentary E. Severino, Brescia: La Scuola, 1959), and in E. Severino, *Studi di filosofia della prassi*, II, Ch. III, paragraph I, footnote 2.

form of contradiction, the impossibility for contradiction to appear as not negated (i.e., as the content of a conviction); they indicate, that is, the Necessity of "being always in truth" (the Necessity of being always in Necessity)—in the meaning displayed by truth and by Necessity outside the confines of nihilism.

It is in fact impossible for contradiction to appear as not negated, since otherwise the appearing of the thesis (the *ypolambanein*, the conviction that has as its content the thesis) would then be—insofar as it is also the appearing of the antithesis—not the appearing of the thesis; and the appearing of the antithesis would be—insofar as it is also the appearing of the thesis—not the appearing of the antithesis. Outside of nihilism, the structure of Necessity, as the impossibility for Being to be not-Being, is therewith the impossibility that certainty (appearing) of the thesis (or of the antithesis) not be certainty of the thesis (or of the antithesis).[7]

On the other hand, the impossibility of the existence of the conviction that has as its content the contradictoriness of being implies the impossibility of the existence of the belief that being is nothing. And yet it is the very structure of Necessity that shows the Necessity of the link that joins the conviction (the *existence* of the conviction) that being is an *epamphoterizein* between Being and Nothing, with the conviction (with the *existence* of the conviction) that being is nothing.

However, the outcome which at this point may seem an aporia is instead the condition for the Necessity both of the distinction between nihilism as thing in itself and nihilism as phenomenon which underlies this essay, and of the way in which the in-itself is displayed in the phenomenon. Precisely because it is impossible for the identity of being and Nothing (and for any contradiction) to appear in its simple being let-be—i.e., in its being simply affirmed, in its being the content of a conviction—for this very reason it is not a simple fact, but *Necessity* that the belief that being is nothing remain in the latency and in the unconscious of nihilism's in-itself, while appearing in indirect and inverted form in the phenomenon of nihilism (i.e., in the consciousness that nihilism can have of itself). The latency—*latére, lethe,*

---

7   Cf. "The Earth and the Essence of Man," paragraph VI.

lanthanein—of the conviction that being is nothing is the condition for the possibility that the nothingness of being be accepted within the dimension that Western thought calls "truth": *a-letheia*, i.e., non-latency, phenomenon. In *aletheia* the nothingness of being is accepted (i.e., is the content of a *ypolambanein*) not in its direct form, but in the (indirect) form of the *epamphoterizein* of being, which is linked with Necessity (with the bonds of Necessity—which are not the bonds of *aletheia*) to the direct form. (At the end of Book V of the *Republic*, where the word *epamphoterizein* appears in its essential meaning, the verb *phaino* is used repeatedly [478–9] to indicate the *phainomenon*, the appearing—the *aletheia* of *epamphoterizein*.)

But the conviction that being is nothing can exist, not only because it remains latent, but also because in nihilism the route that leads from the *aletheia* of *epamphoterizein* to *lethe*, i.e., to the latent belief of the nothingness of being, is cut off. And thus this conviction is isolated from its own phenomenon, to which it is nonetheless necessarily linked. Isolated from its own in itself, the *epamphoterizein* of being no longer appears as the identification of being and nothing, and thus the appearing of *epamphoterizein* is no longer an appearing of the thesis that is not an appearing of the thesis and an appearing of the antithesis that is not an appearing of the antithesis—is no longer the belonging of contraries to that "same" which is the appearing of being. In nihilism, the isolation of nihilism's in-itself from its phenomenon separates that which is linked with Necessity, but it is due to this very separation that the West can be, in its essence, the conviction that being is nothing.

The distinction between nihilism's in-itself and its phenomenon does not precede this separation. On the contrary, it is precisely because the belief that being is nothing is separated from the *epamphoterizein* of being that the conviction remains something "latent" and "unconscious." Despite this separation, the *epamphoterizein* of being is still linked with Necessity to the nothingness of being—which is to say, this link continues to appear in the gaze of Necessity. But the separation, in removing its own gaze from that link and assigning the direct form of the conviction of the nothingness of being to the in-itself of the unconscious, and the indirect form of the persuasion to the phenomenon, belongs to the ground that makes the existence of this persuasion possible. The in-itself—the unconscious—the latency of nihilism is the result of this separation—this isolation—that hides from language the route that links with Necessity that which has been separated.

In Western thought, *aletheia* is not the non-latency (the uncon-cealment) of *lethe*, i.e., of its own in-itself, but rather the unconceal-ment of that which (as the phenomenon of nihilism) conceals its own in-itself, presenting it in inverted form. In its essence, *a-letheia* is *lethe*: it conceals its own essential alienation. Aristotle shows "the necessity of being always in truth" (*anankaion aiei aletheuein*).

On the other hand, this "necessity" is the Necessity that stands outside the confines of alienation—and yet the *formal* structure of this alienated "necessity" is a trait of the Necessity of being always in Necessity. The in-itself—the unconscious—of nihilism, isolated even from its own phenomenon, is nonetheless a *belief*: the belief is the appearing in which the belief itself consists. But this means that the existence of nihilism—i.e., of ultimate alienation—is not possible as something isolated from the Necessity that sees the alienation of nihil-ism. The latent conviction that being is nothing—the conviction whose phenomenon (whose *aletheia*) today rules the whole earth—can exist *only* in its being always already negated by the Necessity that always already *stands*, open beyond the dominions of nihilism. *Beyond*: and thus in the region that is the *unconscious of the unconscious* in which nihilism's in-itself consists. To this conflict between the *standing*—the *de-stiny*—of Necessity and the will that being be nothing—to this supremely dominant contradiction—*The Essence of Nihilism* and *Destino della necessità: Katà tò chreón* are addressed.

The impossibility of the contradictoriness of being is not the impossibility of self-contradiction. The content of error *is not* (=is nothing); erring *is*. In *Gli abitatori del tempo* (cf. "Tramonto del marx-ismo") I showed how the aporetic situation, ascribed by some Italian Marxists to Marx's thought for having affirmed the existence of the contradiction in which capitalism consists, is merely apparent. All this "critical revision" of Marx is based, quite simply, on a confusion between the impossibility of the contradictoriness of being and the impossibility of self-contradiction. And the essential alienation in which Marx's thought too is enveloped resides in a substratum that cannot be reached by any "critical revision" of Marxian thought or by any form of criticism that operates within nihilism.

But the text of Aristotle's *Metaphysics* which has been examined here reveals something essential in this regard: it shows that self-contradiction itself is impossible, if it is the content of a conviction; i.e., if it appears in its pure being let-be, in its pure being affirmed. As the Aristotelian text shows, the existence of self-contradiction so understood implies the contradictoriness of being. Believing in contradiction implies that contrary determinations—i.e., the two mutually contradictory *doxai*—belong to the "same." To the extent that they *appear* as mutually contradictory they cannot belong to the same conviction (*ypolambanein*), since they are the content of a believing in contradiction, i.e., of an appearing in which affirmed contradiction is posited as such.

If they *are* mutually contradictory but their being so *does not appear*, they are not the content of a believing in contradiction, nor are they contrary determinations that inhere in the same determination. Here, "inhering" (*yparchein*) requires the appearing of their being contraries.

The condition for the possibility of the existence of self-contradiction is then, primarily, that self-contradiction not appear as such, i.e., that the route which joins the direct with the indirect form of contradiction be cut off and the direct form remain an in-itself, isolated from its own phenomenon. Aristotle cannot know that the *principium firmissimum omnium* belongs to the phenomenon of nihilism. And yet it is the *formal* structure of lines 1005*b* 11–31 of the *Metaphysics* that demands with Necessity that the condition for the possibility of the dominant self-contradiction in which nihilism consists be, on the one hand, that nihilism appear in inverted form, as phenomenon, i.e., as the affirmation of the not-nothingness of being in the *epamphoterizein* of being; and, on the other hand, that the route which links with Necessity this affirmation to the affirmation that being is nothing be cut off—with the result that this second affirmation is entrusted to the in-itself of the unconscious of nihilism.

Contradiction, however, can present itself in another way as well: namely, as that which, even as it appears *as contradiction*, is at the same time something of which *it is not known* how it can be resolved, or it is known that it cannot be resolved. The principal sense assumed by this mode of presenting contradiction (besides that of the *finite appearing of the Whole*) is constituted by the conflict between the destiny of Necessity and the will that being be nothing—the will to isolate the earth from destiny; the will that finds its most radical expression in the nihilism of the West.

But, here too, it is the *formal* structure indicated by Aristotle's text (i.e., it is the *form* that nihilistic structure shares with a trait of Necessity) that requires that contradiction, which appears in its not being resolved or in its irresolvability, not be something believed, but rather appear *as denied*, i.e., as a negation of Necessity. Even if contradiction appears as that which does not let itself be resolved, this appearing of contradiction can exist only if contradiction appears as *rejected*, i.e., only if its being as denied is the form within which it appears. Even though it is an impotent negation (powerless to bring contradiction to setting), it is this form that prevents self-contradiction from constituting itself as the contradictory and therefore impossible belonging of contradictory determinations to the same.

In *The Essence of Nihilism* and in *Destino della necessità: Katà tò chreón*, the condition for the possibility of the existence of contradiction is considered in relation to the theme of the conflict (i.e., of the contradiction) between the destiny of Necessity and the isolation of the earth. In this concluding chapter, that condition has been considered in relation to the contradiction constituting the second of those two contrasting terms: the isolation of the earth from the destiny of Necessity (the isolation that is the very occurrence in which the mortal occurs): the isolation that is expressed in the will that being be nothing and that the route from the in-itself to the phenomenon of nihilism be cut off.

Concluding Remark (1982)

La struttura originaria (1958) takes the form of a "preliminary series of investigations" into the original structure itself. The themes of the work, broadened and further developed, led to *Studi di filosofia della prassi* (1962) and *The Essence of Nihilism*, which consists of essays published between 1964 and 1971. *Studi di filosofia della prassi* introduces two themes not found in the earlier work: namely, the problematic character of freedom, and the link that necessarily unites truth and praxis. Truth, not the individual, is the fundamental subject of praxis, since it is in the bond with praxis that truth is determined as the decision—the decisive action—upon which the salvation of truth itself may depend. This theme recurs in *The Essence of Nihilism*—for example in sections 16 to 18 of the "Path of Day," where the reference to *Studi di filosofia della prassi* is explicit—as well as in the last section of "The Earth and the Essence of Man" (and the last paragraph of "Alienation and the Salvation of Truth"): the decisive action of truth, which leads to truth's salvation, may be the interpreting will. It is through this will that the Sacred, too (like the totality of that which is interpreted), enters Appearing. In "The Path of Day," as in *Studi di filosofia della prassi,* one looks to the Sacred as that which, accepted by truth, might be the key to the salvation (or perdition) of truth; but, in those works, the link between truth and *interpretation* is presented as the ground of the link between truth and the acceptance of the Sacred.

To say that truth is the fundamental subject of praxis and is determined as decision and decisive action—as was the case in *Studi di filosofia della prassi*—means that truth cannot remain indifferent to the way in which praxis (i.e., decision, faith, will, action) is determined. When the content of praxis constitutes itself as a problem, truth is unable to exclude that the occurrence of such a content (i.e., of the alternatives according to which it is constituted) be the condition for the occurrence of truth's salvation. Truth is the subject of praxis and is determined as decisive action not because truth, as such, is action and decision (in fact, insofar as the content of praxis is a problem, the conviction that belongs to the structure of acting and deciding is faith, i.e., untruth—and thus truth, as such, cannot be untruth), but because it is possible that truth's fate depend upon that—namely, action—from which truth cannot isolate itself (since even if it should do so, the possibility would persist). Due to the persistence of this possibility that the fate of truth depend upon action and decision, in *Studi di filosofia della prassi* and in *The Essence of Nihilism* it is said that truth acts and decides. For this very reason, in "The Path of Day" (XVII, last paragraph) it is said that "truth cannot not compromise itself": since it "inevitably goes along with untruth" (ibid.). The meaning of its "being forced to decide" is its "being forced to go along with a decision" (ibid., paragraph XVIII, last sentence of the third paragraph). Truth decides because it is united—bound—to decision. It is in this sense that the following statements from *The Essence of Nihilism* should be construed: "truth *accepts* the Sacred" (ibid., 181), "truth *wills* that the Sacred speak the tongue of Day" (ibid., 176), "philosophy *wills* that I not be the essence of man . . . so it wills, because it believes (i.e., *wills*) that . . ." ("The Earth and the Essence of Man," 277). And this is the fundamental meaning of the "pragmatic implications of truth," set forth in *Studi di filosofia della prassi* (I, part 2).

Saying that "truth decides" is not improper, since the inevitability of the tie binding truth to decision and to faith does not mean that truth is a taking note of a situation where alternative courses of action are presented simply as different ways that may be taken: action always already acts, certain contents are chosen and others rejected, certain actions occur and therefore others do not. Saying that truth decides means that the determinate decision which in fact occurs (and whose occurring excludes the occurrence of other decisions) occurs within the gaze where truth sees it as that upon which the salvation of truth might depend. It means that, in the decision that occurs, truth sees the possibility of its own salvation. In this situation, the decision that occurs does not occur because it is seen in this way by truth. In fact, since—in this situation—the decision that occurs is a problem, truth sees that its own salvation may depend not only upon the decision that occurs, but also upon the opposite decision; not only upon acceptance of the Sacred, but also upon its rejection; not only upon the way in which the earth is in fact interpreted, but also upon other interpretations.

Studi di filosofia della prassi and *The Essence of Nihilism* come together on these themes. But it is in *The Essence of Nihilism* that the language that begins to testify to the truth of Being and thus to the authentic essence of nihilism reaches its full maturity—so that the "action" to which, in the latter work, truth shows itself to be linked no longer has the Greek meaning of "*praxis*" which is still dominant in *Studi di filosofia della prassi*.

On the other hand, in *The Essence of Nihilism* freedom of decision continues to be a problem (cf. for example "Returning to Parmenides"; the "Postscript," VIII; "The Path of Day," XV; "The Earth and the Essence of Man," V, last paragraph). Yet it is a problem in an essentially different way (albeit analogous in its formal structure—cf. the footnote at the end of paragraph XV of "The Path of Day") from how it presents itself in the earlier work, where freedom was still determined according to the explicit ontological categories of nihilism. In *The Essence of Nihilism*, the decision to which truth is linked, and upon whose occurrence the salvation of truth may depend, is presented as something that might be either an inevitable occurrence or a free act; that is, either a decision destined to appear, or a decision that appears, but might not have appeared—and vice versa.

The problem of freedom is resolved in *Destino della necessità: Katà tò chreón* (1980/1999) (cf. chapters III–IV). There, the meaning of the "supersession of the problem of freedom" is given—the supersession of the problematicity that persists despite the "practical resolution" formulated in *Studi di filosofia della prassi* (which asserted that "it is precisely because the theoretical solution remains open that the practical resolution necessarily comes about"). The language of *Destino della necessità: Katà tò chreón* is the occurrence (the supervening in the circle of Appearing) of the resolution of this problem. The solution is the appearing of the language that testifies to freedom's belonging to the essence of nihilism. It is Necessity that the earth occur, as well as the determinate way in which it occurs (and in which, therefore, all things of the earth and all decisions occur). The earth is destined to appear.

With regard to the question of freedom there is a consistent progression from *Studi di filosofia della prassi* to *Destino della necessità: Katà tò chreón*. In the *Studi* it is shown that the existence of freedom is a problem, i.e., that freedom does not, and cannot, belong to the content that appears. In *The Essence of Nihilism* freedom continues to be a problem only insofar as it is thought outside the categories of nihilism (within which it is instead an absurdity); that is, only insofar as it is understood not as the possibility that a decision that has been made might not have been (or the possibility that a decision that has not been made might have been), but rather as the possibility that (eternal) decisions not have appeared, and that decisions that did not appear appeared. *Destino della necessità: Katà tò chreón* shows the nihilistic character of freedom's formal structure itself, i.e., the impossibility of freedom's being a problem even in the reduced sense set out in *The Essence of Nihilism*. (Just as freedom can be posited as an impossibility because it is not something that appears, so the becoming of being, its transition from not-Being to Being and vice versa, can be posited as an impossibility because Becoming is not something that appears.)

But in *Destino della necessità: Katà tò chreón* we also find the testimony that action *as such* belongs to the essence of nihilism: not only action as the will to bring things from not-Being to Being and vice versa (which was already established in the previous work), and not only the formal structure of freedom, but action's formal structure itself (of which, moreover, the formal structure of freedom is a trait). The formal structure of action, "considered *as distinct* from the ontological determinations of nihilism (and thus as the structure common to the action both of the pre-history and the history of the West) implies, as such, those very ontological determinations of nihilism from which it is distinct: it implies them, even though it leaves their distinguishing features unexpressed."[1]

The absence of this testimony to the nihilistic character of freedom and action as such (i.e., as formal structures) determines the

---

1 Cf. E. Severino, *Destino della necessità: Katà tò chreón*, Milan: Adelphi, 1980; new edition 1999, 362.

configuration of *The Essence of Nihilism*, and is due to the persistence of the isolation of the earth. This situation in its abstract possibility was already envisaged in *The Essence of Nihilism*: "Not only the earth, but also that of the truth of Being to which philosophy has been able to testify [and this testimony too belongs to the earth] can be isolated from the totality of truth and posited as the sure ground, with respect to which the dimension of truth that is not testified to becomes a problem. The very problems of philosophy can arise from isolation" ("The Earth and the Essence of Man," 21, first paragraph). This, even if in *The Essence of Nihilism* the formal structure of action is not explicitly posited as a problem; its problematicity is, however, implicitly posited, given the link that necessarily unites freedom to that structure.

This dual testimony, absent in *The Essence of Nihilism* and present in *Destino della necessità: Katà tò chreón*, also leads to the resolution of a further problem that was left open in the earlier work. In paragraph VII of "The Path of Day" "the ontological ambiguity of nonmetaphysical (i.e., nonontological) language" is affirmed. (This is then further developed in sections 8, 9, 11, 12.) The ground of the affirmation is indicated in the third paragraph of section 7. In relation to the language of *The Essence of Nihilism* which stops short of testifying that the formal structure of action belongs to essential alienation, the ground is authentic and that which is said there is what in this situation needs to be said. But the occurrence of this testimony makes possible the very inference which on that occasion was held to be impossible: the inference that leads from the explicit semantics of a pre-ontological language to its implicit ontological meaning. The formal structure of action is in fact continually named in the explicit semantics of pre-ontological language (and, as we have seen, it is common to the action of both the pre-history and the history of the West). Such language, therefore, is not ambiguous, but constitutes the pre-history of the alienation of the West. This will be developed in chapters VIII–X and XIV–XV of *Destino della necessità: Katà tò chreón*. Thus also the language of the Sacred belongs to the pre-history of alienation. It is no longer presented, *qua* pre-ontological language, as a problem. Like every language that speaks within alienation, it would again become a problem only if it should still say something when heard outside the solitude of the earth.

But in "The Path of Day" (paragraph XVIII, fourth paragraph) a dual sense is described according to which the Sacred—and every problematic content—is a problem: I) the Sacred may be the *way* that leads to the salvation of truth; II) it is possible that this salvation (the greatest disclosure of Being) be constituted by the traits that form the content of the announcement of the Sacred. In this passage of *The Essence of Nihilism* these two senses can constitute an alternative (exclusive disjunction), but they can also be present together. But once the language of the Sacred has been presented as belonging to the pre-history of alienation (and therefore as only apparently ambiguous), then the second of these two senses becomes an impossibility. This, however, does not mean that the first sense too is impossible. That is, it is possible that the darkness of alienation be the way which must be travelled to reach the salvation of truth.

Indeed, this is the overall meaning of *The Essence of Nihilism* with regard to this theme. For if it is true that "The Path of Day" continues to affirm the Sacred's ontological ambiguity (and hence its being a problem for truth), it is also true that *The Essence of Nihilism* presents a trait that later will be adequately developed in *Destino della necessità: Katà tò chreón*: in the next-to-last paragraph of "Risposta alla Chiesa" (not included in this edition) it is stated that "the will to sunder the earth from destiny is the ground of the essence of faith as such." Faith as such, and thus also the faith whose content is the Sacred, coincides with the root of essential alienation: namely, the isolation of the earth from the destiny of truth. In *Studi di filosofia della prassi* faith already appears as contradiction. And therefore faith is understood as contradiction in those above-mentioned passages of *The Essence of Nihilism* as well, where it is determined as "acceptance of the Sacred" or as "interpreting will." But now, in this passage of "Risposta alla Chiesa," faith, in presenting itself as the root of essential alienation, appears as the very root of self-contradiction. Insofar as it coincides with the root of alienation, faith is precisely that, whose setting is necessarily required for the salvation of truth. Thus in *The Essence of Nihilism*, taken as a whole, it is stated, albeit implicitly, that the occurrence of certain contents that appear in the isolation of the earth (i.e., in faith) can be the way that leads to the setting of the earth's isolation.

In its formal aspect, this thesis is already present in *Studi di filosofia della prassi*, where it is demonstrated that to affirm that being in contradiction can occasion the supersession of contradiction is not itself contradictory (cf. I, part 2, Ch. III, 2). It is to this demonstration that the fourth and fifth paragraphs of section 21 of "The Path of Day" refer. Being in contradiction, as such, cannot be; that is, it is contradictory that being in contradiction be that which resolves contradiction. Truth alone can be that which supersedes and brings to setting the negation of truth. It is in this sense that the first of those two paragraphs stated, "it is absurd that living in alienation be the price to pay for the salvation of truth."

But if it is possible for a *content* that is in contradiction to distinguish itself from its own *self-contradiction*—that is, to present itself as a problem, and therefore as that which might be a trait of truth—then it is no longer contradictory to affirm that truth's acceptance of that content may lead to the salvation of truth. From the standpoint of *Studi di filosofia della prassi*, this is the condition of Christianity (i.e., of the content of Christian faith, insofar as it distinguishes itself from the self-contradiction of having faith). *The Essence of Nihilism* concludes that what can be in this condition is not Christianity—for Christianity was born and grows within nihilism—but rather the ambiguous language of the Sacred (and every pre-metaphysical language). *Destino della necessità: Katà tò chreón* shows that not even this language can be in such a condition, since, like every pre-metaphysical language, it is *not* ambiguous. The ambiguity and problematicity have moved beyond the totality of historical languages to that which they say, if they still say something when heard outside the isolation of the earth.

And yet, the above-mentioned thesis, implicitly presented in *The Essence of Nihilism*, still holds: the thesis, that is, which affirms that the occurrence of certain contents that appear in the isolation of the earth (i.e., in faith) may be the way that leads to the setting of the earth's isolation. In the first place, while it is indeed possible that languages which speak in the solitude of the earth, with the setting of this solitude no longer say anything, the isolated earth is but one of the two faces the earth presents in the conflict where the destiny of truth and the isolation of the earth from destiny contend for the earth. The setting of the earth's isolation is not, as such, the setting of the earth. The earth which stands before us possesses not only the traits of alienation, but also those of truth. In virtue of these traits, the earth is a content that distinguishes itself from the essential contradiction according to which the isolation that envelops the earth is constituted. It is possible, that is, that alienation be the way that leads to the salvation of truth, since, if salvation is destined to occur, the traits of the truth of the earth belong to the face of truth.

There is, however, yet another sense in which the thesis of *The Essence of Nihilism* still holds. Truth is the negation of error—not accidentally, but in its essence. Hence truth *is*, only insofar as error *is*. Truth appears, only insofar as error appears. The concrete appearing of truth therefore implies the *concrete* appearing of error, not simply an abstract representation of error. In its essence, error is the isolation of the earth from the destiny of truth. *If* the salvation of truth (i.e., the supersession of the concreteness of error) is destined to occur, then, for salvation to occur, the occurrence of the alienation of truth—the earth's isolation and nihilism—is Necessity.

This does not mean, however, that given the occurrence of alienation, the occurrence of the salvation of truth—the setting of the earth's isolation and of the mortal's being mortal—is Necessity. Since in the testimony to truth there is still a possibility that truth's salvation be destined to occur, there is also a possibility that the occurrence of alienation be the road that leads to the setting of alienation. It is Necessity that the concrete occurrence of the salvation of truth imply the concrete occurrence of error; but it is only a possibility that the concrete occurrence of error—and error, like everything that occurs, occurs with Necessity—be preparing the occurrence of salvation, i.e., be a stretch of the road that leads to the occurrence of salvation. (This road's very existence is a possibility—even if salvation is always already in the deepest unconscious of the mortal.) Thus it is a possibility that the path of Night and the path of Day be, respectively, the first and the second stretch of a single road—the road destined to lead to the occurrence of the salvation of truth.

If salvation is destined to enter the circle of Appearing, then the road leading to it, and thus also the first stretch of that road, belongs to the destiny of truth. This means not that the various spectacles which are disclosed and testified to along the path of Night are traits of the face of truth, but rather that it is Necessity that such spectacles be met with, *if* it is Necessity that the salvation of truth occur. And since there is still a possibility that salvation be destined to occur—salvation which, moreover, *already is*, eternal—it is also a possibility that the path of Night be that which it is Necessity to travel if salvation is to occur—that the occurrence of alienation be necessary for the setting of alienation to occur.

The isolation of the earth is the system of decisions and of actions—including that decision which is the interpreting will. In *The Essence of Nihilism* the metaphysical interpretation of ontologically ambiguous language is contrasted with truth's interpretation of such a language: a language "which is prey to metaphysics, may also become prey to truth" ("The Path of Day," XII): "truth wills that the Sacred speak the tongue of Day" (ibid., XVI). But in *Destino della necessità: Katà tò chreón* every interpretation, i.e., the interpreting will *as such*, is brought back to the isolation of the earth. The earth's isolation is at one and the same time the original ground of alienation, the occurrence of the mortal's being mortal, original faith, decision and action, and the original interpreting will.

And the system of decisions (of choices) and of actions continues to stand before truth as that whose occurrence might be (despite its being the system of alienation) that stretch of road which leads to the salvation of truth. In this sense, one can continue to say that "truth decides," i.e., sees in the alienation of effective deciding the stretch of road that can lead to salvation. The fundamental difference, with respect to *The Essence of Nihilism*, is that freedom of decision and action as such now belong to the essence of nihilism. The system of decisions that have imposed themselves on alternative decisions and in whose occurrence truth sees the stretch of road that might lead to salvation, does not arise from the play of freedom but is sent by destiny. It is therefore *destiny* that establishes and sends the decision that appears in the saying, "truth decides." And this decision is not to be confused—indeed, in the circle of Appearing, it is the ultimate contrast—with the "will of destiny" discussed in the last chapter of *Destino della necessità: Katà tò chreón*. "Truth decides," in fact, only in the sense that the occurrence of truth's salvation can depend upon the occurrence of the alienation of deciding.

The path of Night can be the first stretch of the road to salvation. But every road—every occurrence—is sent by destiny to appear. It is destiny itself that sends, in the occurrence of salvation, the fulfillment of destiny.[2]

---

2 Precisely because in *Destino della necessità: Katà tò chreón* freedom is shown to belong to the essence of nihilism, the interpreting will can no longer be understood as the possible freedom that might have interpreted the earth differently from how it is interpreted in fact. And on the other hand, precisely because in the interpreting will the nexus between the earth and its interpretation is not the nexus of Necessity, it is still possible that what it was Necessity to interpret in a certain way may later be interpreted differently—where "possibility" now signifies the lasting incapacity of the language that testifies to the destiny of Necessity to testify to that which is destined to occur.

Index

alienation: and Appearing, 189, 210, 232, 272; and being as nothing, 276, 295, 296; contents of, 187, 269, 302; of decision, 344; and demythologization, 29; denunciation of, 293; determinations of, 272; and disappearing of alienated civilization, 187; and the earth, 231–3, 246, 303, 307, 342, 343; economic alienation, 293; essential alienation, 22, 25–32, 276, 286, 293, 295, 297, 309, 332–3, 339, 340; of European civilization, 15, 17, 18, 21; and faith, 340; humanity of, 210; and human problems, 204; and language, 339; and language of the Sacred, 167–8, 340; and language of the truth of Being, 160; and man, 171, 206, 231–2, 235–6; and meaning of Becoming, 107, 112, 136; of the meaning of Being, 113, 135–8, 152, 164, 189, 203, 204, 209–10, 296; and meaning of Being, 306; and metaphysics, 235–7; and nihilism, 283, 332; and nothingness of things, 20; and Oriental civilizations, 152; and the path of Night, 180; of peoples, 272, 273; and philosophy, 273; and Platonic *poiesis*, 162–3; and production of something from nothingness, 223; of reason, 93, 107; and salvation, 243, 296; and salvation of truth, 341, 342, 343; and separation of being from Being, 295; and time, 22, 26, 27, 28, 29, 30–32; of truth, 181, 186, 342; and truth of Being, 216, 233, 296; and the West, 20, 25, 150, 162–3, 181, 182, 197, 201, 204, 211, 221, 231–3, 276, 295, 304, 305, 307–8; and will, 220, 221; and Word of

God, 299, 304; works of, 245
Appearing: and alienation, 210, 308; and background, 133–5, 137, 138, 139, 144, 145, 158, 174, 188, 212, 214, 229, 230, 243–4, 252; and Becoming, 119, 123–4n16, 189; and Being, 32, 60, 81–83, 90, 105, 106–12, 120–2, 126–7, 130–2, 138, 144–5, 158, 159, 174–5, 180, 188, 197; and bodies, 120, 129; and certainty, 221, 226; circular structure of, 258, 343; and consciousness, 264; consciousness of, 123, 132, 133, 145; and consciousness of self-consciousness, 257–9, 259n16; and contradiction, 179, 216, 217–8, 231, 232; and creation, 144, 145, 197; and determinations, 126, 134n20, 170, 174, 211, 212, 226, 235n9, 258n16; and dimensions, 257; and disappearing, 127–8, 130, 133, 171, 210; and the earth, 252–4, 305–6; empirical appearing, 124–5; and error, 219, 225–7; and the eternal, 32, 90, 126, 127, 129, 133, 139, 144, 158, 188, 210, 213, 228, 269; existence of, 230; and experience, 261; and faith, 218; finite Appearing, 184–5, 186, 213–4, 218, 231, 269, 334; forgottenness of, 198; and freedom, 144–5; and generation and corruption of Being, 114; and God, 126, 127, 133, 139; and happiness, 177; and human individual, 261; and humans, 230, 233, 293; and the immutable, 126, 127–33, 138–40n21, 143, 185; as independent of humans, 264; infinite Appearing, 184–5, 186, 214, 218, 231; and interpretation, 270–1, 292, 308; and

man, 11, 160, 182, 203, 205, 213, 291, 293, 306; and metaphysics, 149–50; of nihilism, 16–18, 20, 295; and objectivity, 161, 162; and oscillation between Being and nothingness, 316; philosophy of, 3, 139; and production of man, 154, 163; and rising and setting of the whole, 18; of salvation, 243–6, 254, 255, 261, 269; and science, 198, 199; and setting of the West, 251; and Western civilization, 149–50, 152, 154, 155, 237, 284–7; of Western philosophy, 13, 17, 35–6; of the world, 161, 162, 212, 268, 272. *See also* Western history

Justice of Being (*Dike*), 169, 181

Kierkegaard, Søren, 161, 162, 261

language: and ambiguity of nonmetaphysical language, 160, 339; and Appearing, 166–7, 290–1; archaic languages, 28; and Being, 85, 115, 160; and certainty, 221; conventions of, 165–6; of Day, 167–8, 172, 174, 175n10; and *doxa* , 165, 166; European languages, 13; Greek language, 13, 165, 271, 277–9, 280, 291, 298, 307, 308, 314; and important things, 213; and interpretation, 269, 289–91; and interpreting will, 271, 292; and language of the Sacred, 340, 341; and Latin, 278, 314; and logical positivists, 228; and meaning of Being, 160, 201; and metaphysics, 200–1, 275, 278; and naming of things, 219, 228, 235; and Necessity, 2; of Night, 168; and "nonexistent" things, 44; and nonmetaphysical language, 157–8, 275, 276; nonscientific languages, 200–1; ontological language, 275–6; and opposition of life and death, 278; pre-metaphysical language, 278–9, 280–1, 287, 341; pre-ontological language, 339; and region of Becoming, 236; and the Sacred, 167–8, 172, 174, 343; of science, 198–9, 249; and structure of Western history, 1; and truth of Being, 160, 165, 167, 200,

204, 228, 337; and untruth, 219–20, 228; and will to meaning, 174

La struttura originaria (Severino), 229, 230, 230n8, 335

liberation: from contradiction, 214, 243; from death, 251, 285; of the essence of Christianity, 298; from hunger, 203, 286; and modernity, 27; from pain, 203, 205, 285, 286; and power, 29–30; and technology, 203, 286; and unmodifiable, 192

logos: and Appearing, 109, 126; and Being, 80, 109, 112, 169n7; and differences, 96; and *elenchos*, 325; immediacy of, 81; as opposed to the senses, 116; and opposition of positive and negative, 80; and original logos, 102; and Parmenides, 96; and Plato, 96; self-revelation of, 111n14; and truth, 81

Marcuse, Herbert, 27, 30

Marx, Karl, 12, 24; and Being, 52, 264; and contradiction of capitalism, 332; and essential alienation, 332–3; and production of consciousness, 261

Marxism: and alienation, 162–3, 293; and domination, 29; and history, 1, 9, 284, 293; and industry and technology, 6–7; and labor as purposive activity, 9–10; and techno-scientific ideology, 31; and traditional civilization, 283; and the world, 203, 286

Melissus: and Being, 52, 54, 57, 136, 156; as father of Western metaphysics, 52, 92n4; and generation of Being from Nothing, 156–7; and immutability of Being, 53, 92n4; and the manifold, 117–8

metaphysics: and alienated meaning of Being, 159–60, 301; and alienation, 201, 232–3, 235–7; and Appearing, 171, 261, 262, 266; Aristotelian metaphysics, 42, 53, 194–5; and Becoming, 83, 113, 232; and Being, 50, 207, 208, 234, 248, 275; and being (ente), 280; and Being (*Essere*), 280; and Being as generated from Nothing, 92n4; and Being as overcoming of Nothing, 104; classical